CCNA®

Routing and Switching Complete

Review Guide

WITHDRAWN

Second Edition

Todd Lammle

S0-BCS-408

SYBEX®

A Wiley Brand

Senior Acquisitions Editor: Kenyon Brown
Development Editor: Kim Wimpsett
Technical Editor: Todd Montgomery
Production Editor: Christine O'Connor
Copy Editor: Judy Flynn
Editorial Manager: Mary Beth Wakefield
Production Manager: Kathleen Wisor
Executive Editor: Jim Minatel
Book Designers: Maureen Forys, Happenstance Type-O-Rama, and Bill Gibson
Proofreader: Nancy Carrasco
Indexer: Ted Laux
Project Coordinator, Cover: Brent Savage
Cover Designer: Wiley
Cover Image: Getty Images, Inc./Jeremy Woodhouse

Copyright © 2017 by John Wiley & Sons, Inc., Indianapolis, Indiana

Published simultaneously in Canada

ISBN: 978-1-119-28836-7
ISBN: 978-1-119-28838-1 (ebk.)
ISBN: 978-1-119-28837-4 (ebk.)

Manufactured in the United States of America

Acknowledgments

First, a loud callout to Troy McMillan, who was instrumental in putting this book together. He spent countless hours combining and summarizing my work from the CCENT and CCNA ICND2 study guides into what is a really nice review guide for the CCNA Routing and Switching certification. Thank you, Troy!

Thanks to Ken Brown, who always keeps me working hard and makes sure I am headed in the right direction. This is no easy task for Ken!

And thanks to my production editor, Christine O'Connor, for keeping the book on track, and Amy Breguet, for keeping all the edits in order and on time. And I can't forget Judy Flynn, the backbone of all my books, who reads every word over and over until the chapters are nearly flawless!

Thank you all!

About the Author

Todd Lammle   Cisco certified in almost every category, is *the* authority on Cisco networking and certification. His three decades of real-world experience is prevalent in his writing. He is an experienced networking engineer with very practical experience working on the largest bounded and unbounded networks in the world at such companies as Xerox, Hughes Aircraft, Texaco, AAA, Cisco, and Toshiba, among many others. Todd has published over 60 books, including the very popular and bestselling *CCNA: Cisco Certified Network Associate Study Guide* and *Cisco Firepower NGIPS*. Todd runs an international training company from Texas and a large-scale consulting business out of Colorado. You can reach Todd through his forum and blog at www.lammle.com/ccna.

Contents at a Glance

Contents

Introduction

Welcome to the exciting world of Cisco certification! If you've picked up this book because you want to improve yourself and your life with a better, more satisfying, and secure job, you've done the right thing. Whether you're striving to enter the thriving, dynamic IT sector or seeking to enhance your skill set and advance your position within it, being Cisco certified can seriously stack the odds in your favor to help you attain your goals!

Cisco certifications are powerful instruments of success that also markedly improve your grasp of all things internetworking. As you progress through this book, you'll gain a complete understanding of networking that reaches far beyond Cisco devices. By the end of this book, you'll comprehensively know how disparate network topologies and technologies work together to form the fully operational networks that are vital to today's very way of life in the developed world. The knowledge and expertise you'll gain here is essential for and relevant to every networking job and is why Cisco certifications are in such high demand—even at companies with few Cisco devices!

Although it's now common knowledge that Cisco rules routing and switching, the fact that it also rocks the voice, data center, and service provider worlds is also well recognized. And Cisco certifications reach way beyond the popular but less extensive certifications like those offered by CompTIA and Microsoft to equip you with indispensable insight into today's vastly complex networking realm. Essentially, by deciding to become Cisco certified, you're proudly announcing that you want to become an unrivaled networking expert—a goal that this book will get you well on your way to achieving. Congratulations in advance on the beginning of your brilliant future!

For up-to-the-minute updates covering additions or modifications to the Cisco certification exams, as well as additional study tools, videos, review questions, and bonus materials, be sure to visit the Todd Lammle websites and forum at www.lammle.com/ccna.

Cisco's Network Certifications

It used to be that to secure the holy grail of Cisco certifications—the CCIE—you passed only one written test before being faced with a grueling, formidable hands-on lab. This intensely daunting, all-or-nothing approach made it nearly impossible to succeed and predictably didn't work out too well for most people. Cisco responded to this issue by creating a series of new certifications, which not only made it easier to eventually win the highly coveted CCIE prize, it gave employers a way to accurately rate and measure the skill levels of prospective and current employees. This exciting paradigm shift in Cisco's certification path truly opened doors that few were allowed through before!

Beginning in 1998, obtaining the Cisco Certified Network Associate (CCNA) certification was the first milestone in the Cisco certification climb, as well as the official prerequisite to each of the more advanced levels. But that changed in 2007, when Cisco announced the Cisco Certified Entry Network Technician (CCENT) certification. And then in May 2016, Cisco once again proclaimed updates to the CCENT and CCNA Routing and Switching (R/S) tests. Now the Cisco certification process looks like Figure I.1.

FIGURE I.1   The Cisco certification path

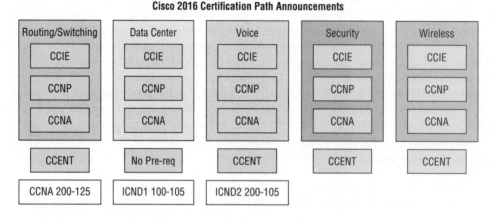

The Cisco R/S path is by far the most popular and could very well remain so, but soon you'll see the Data Center path become more and more of a focus as companies migrate to data center technologies. The Security track also actually does provide a good job opportunity as well. Still, understanding the foundation of R/S before attempting any other certification track is something I highly recommend.

Even so, and as the figure shows, you only need your CCENT certification to get underway for most of the tracks.

Cisco Certified Entry Network Technician (CCENT)

Don't be fooled by the oh-so-misleading name of this first certification because it absolutely isn't entry level! Okay—maybe entry level for Cisco's certification path, but definitely not for someone without experience trying to break into the highly lucrative yet challenging IT job market! For the uninitiated, the CompTIA A+ and Network+ certifications aren't official prerequisites, but know that Cisco does expect you to have that type and level of experience before embarking on your Cisco certification journey.

All of this gets us to 2016, when the climb to Cisco supremacy just got much harder again. The innocuous-sounding siren's call of the CCENT can lure you to some serious trouble if you're not prepared, because it's actually much harder than the old CCNA ever was. This will rapidly become apparent once you start studying, but be encouraged! The fact that the certification process is getting harder really works better for you in the long run, because that which is harder to obtain only becomes that much more valuable when you finally do, right? Yes, indeed!

Another important factor to keep in mind is that the Interconnection Cisco Network Devices Part 1 (ICND1) exam, which is the required exam for the CCENT certification, costs $150 per attempt, and it's anything but easy to pass! The good news is that this book will guide you step-by-step in building a strong foundation in routing and switching technologies. You really need to build on a strong technical foundation and stay away from exam cram type books, suspicious online material, and the like. They can help somewhat, but understand that you'll pass the Cisco certification exams only if you have a strong foundation and that you'll get that solid foundation only by reading as much as you can and practicing the review questions in this book. Additional practice exam questions, videos, and labs are offered on my website, and what seems like a million other sites offer additional material that can help you study.

However, there is one way to skip the CCENT exam and still meet the prerequisite before moving on to any other certification track, and that path is through the CCNA R/S Composite exam. First, I'll discuss the Interconnecting Cisco Network Devices Part 2 (ICND2) exam, and then I'll tell you about the CCNA Composite exam, which will provide you, when you're successful, with both the CCENT and the CCNA R/S certification.

Cisco Certified Network Associate Routing and Switching (CCNA R/S)

Once you have achieved your CCENT certification, you can take the ICND2 (200-105) exam in order to achieve your CCNA R/S certification, which is the most popular certification Cisco has by far because it's the most sought-after certification by all employers.

As with the CCENT, the ICND2 exam is also $150 per attempt—although thinking you can just skim a book and pass any of these exams would probably be a really expensive mistake! The CCENT/CCNA exams are extremely hard and cover a lot of material, so you have to really know your stuff. Taking a Cisco class or spending months with hands-on experience is definitely a requirement to succeed when faced with this monster!

And once you have your CCNA, you don't have to stop there—you can choose to continue and achieve an even higher certification, called the Cisco Certified Network Professional (CCNP). There are various ones, as shown in Figure I.1. The CCNP R/S is still the most popular, with Security certifications coming in at a close second. And I've got to tell you that the Data Center certification will be catching up fast. Also good to know is that anyone with a CCNP R/S has all the skills and knowledge needed to attempt the notoriously dreaded but coveted CCIE R/S lab. But just becoming a CCNA R/S can land you that job you've dreamed about, and that's what this book is all about: helping you to get and keep a great job!

Still, why take two exams to get your CCNA if you don't have to? Cisco still has the CCNA Composite (200-125) exam that, if passed, will land you with your CCENT and your CCNA R/S via only one test, priced accordingly at $300. Some people like the one-test approach, and some people like the two-test approach.

Why Become a CCENT and CCNA R/S?

Cisco, like Microsoft and other vendors that provide certification, has created the certification process to give administrators a set of skills and to equip prospective employers with a way to measure those skills or match certain criteria. And as you probably know, becoming a CCNA R/S is certainly the initial, key step on a successful journey toward a new, highly rewarding, and sustainable networking career.

The CCNA program was created to provide a solid introduction not only to the Cisco Internetwork Operating System (IOS) and Cisco hardware but also to internetworking in general, making it helpful to you in areas that are not exclusively Cisco's. And regarding today's certification process, it's not unrealistic that network managers—even those without Cisco equipment—require Cisco certifications for their job applicants.

Rest assured that if you make it through the CCNA and are still interested in Cisco and internetworking, you're headed down a path to certain success!

What Skills Do You Need to Become a CCNA R/S?

This ICND1 exam (100-105) tests a candidate for the knowledge and skills required to successfully install, operate, and troubleshoot a small branch office network. The exam includes questions on the operation of IP data networks, LAN switching technologies, IPv6, IP routing technologies, IP services, network device security, and basic troubleshooting. The ICND2 exam (exam 200-105) tests a candidate for the knowledge and skills required to successfully install, operate, and troubleshoot a small- to medium-size enterprise branch network. The exam includes questions on LAN switching technologies, IP routing technologies, IP services (FHRP, SNMP v2 and v3), the cloud, and ACI as well as troubleshooting and WAN technologies.

How Do You Become a CCNA R/S?

If you want to go straight for our CCNA R/S and take only one exam, all you have to do is pass the CCNA Composite exam (200-125). Oh, but don't you wish it were that easy? True, it's just one test, but it's a whopper, and to pass it you must possess enough knowledge to understand what the test writers are saying, and you need to know everything I mentioned previously, in the discussions of the ICND1 and ICND2 exams! Hey, it's hard, but it can be done!

What does the CCNA Composite exam (200-125) cover? Pretty much the same topics covered in the ICND1 and ICND2 exams. Candidates can prepare for this exam by taking the Todd Lammle authorized Cisco boot camps. Exam 200-125 tests a candidate's knowledge and skills required to install, operate, and troubleshoot a small to medium-size enterprise branch network.

While you can take the Composite exam to get your CCNA, it's good to know that Cisco offers the two-step process I discussed earlier in this introduction. And this book covers both those exams too! It may be easier than taking that one ginormous exam for you, but don't think the two-test method is easy. It takes work! However, it can be done; you just need to stick with your studies.

The two-test method involves passing the following:

- **Exam 100-105:** Interconnecting Cisco Networking Devices Part 1 (ICND1)
- **Exam 200-105:** Interconnecting Cisco Networking Devices Part 2 (ICND2)

I can't stress this point enough: It's critical that you have some hands-on experience with Cisco routers. If you can get a hold of some basic routers and switches, you're set, but if you can't, I've worked hard to provide hundreds of configuration examples throughout this book to help network administrators, or people who want to become network administrators, learn the skills they need to pass the CCENT and CCNA R/S exams.

 For Cisco certification hands-on training, which includes CCNA videos and practice test questions all from CCSI Todd Lammle, please see www.lammle.com/ccna.

What Does This Book Cover?

This book covers everything you need to know to pass the CCNA Composite exam (200-125) The composite CCNA book is available on Amazon. But regardless of which path you choose, as I've said, taking plenty of time to study and practice with routers or a router simulator is the real key to success.

You will learn the following information in this book:

Chapter 1: Network Fundamentals In Chapter 1, you will learn the basics of the Open Systems Interconnection (OSI) model the way Cisco wants you to learn it. There are plenty of review questions to help you.

Chapter 2: LAN Switching Fundamentals This chapter will provide you with the Ethernet foundation you need in order to pass the composite exam. Data encapsulation is discussed in detail in this chapter as well. And as with the other chapters, this chapter includes review questions to help you.

Chapter 3: Routing Technologies In this chapter, I will discuss routing concepts. This will include a discussion of the routing table, routing protocols, and static routing. I will also cover the configuration of RIP and single-area OSPF and the process of troubleshooting end-to-end connectivity at layer 3. Don't skip the 10 review questions.

Chapter 4: WAN Technologies In this chapter, I will cover wide area network (WAN) technologies. This will include a discussion of multilink Point-to-Point Protocol interfaces, PPP over Ethernet (PPoE), and Generic Routing Encapsulation tunnels. I will also cover the configuration of Border Gateway Protocol (BGP). And you'll find plenty of help in this chapter as long as you don't skip the review questions at the end.

Chapter 5: Infrastructure Services Here, you'll find out all about infrastructure services. These services include DNS, DHCP, HSRP, and NAT. It will cover the configuration, verification, and troubleshooting of these vital network services. As with Chapter 4, plenty of help is there for you if you don't skip the review questions.

Chapter 6: Infrastructure Security This chapter introduces you to port security and the common access layer attacks it can help prevent. It will also include the configuration, verification, and troubleshooting of access lists and the proper hardening of network devices. Be sure to complete the review questions.

Chapter 7: Infrastructure Management This chapter provides you with the management skills needed to run a Cisco IOS network. The topics will include device maintenance and the monitoring of devices. I'll also describe the tools used to troubleshoot and resolve issues, and I will close the chapter with a discussion of network programmability. As always, complete the review questions.

Appendix: Answers to Review Questions This appendix provides the answers to the end-of-chapter review questions.

Be sure to check the announcements section of my forum at www.lammle.com/ccna to find out how to download bonus material I created specifically for this book.

Interactive Online Learning Environment and Test Bank

I've worked hard to provide some really great tools to help you with your certification process. The interactive online learning environment that accompanies the *CCNA Routing and Switching Complete Review Guide, Second Edition*, provides a test bank with study tools to help you prepare for the certification exam—and increase your chances of passing it the first time! The test bank includes the following:

Sample tests All of the questions in this book are provided, including the assessment test, which you'll find at the end of this introduction, and the chapter tests that include the review questions at the end of each chapter. In addition, there are two practice exams with 50 questions each. Use these questions to test your knowledge of the study guide material. The online test bank runs on multiple devices.

Flashcards The online text bank includes 100 flashcards specifically written to hit you hard, so don't get discouraged if you don't ace your way through them at first! They're there to ensure that you're really ready for the exam. And no worries—armed with the review questions, practice exams, and flashcards, you'll be more than prepared when exam day comes! Questions are provided in digital flashcard format (a question followed by a single correct answer). You can use the flashcards to reinforce your learning and provide last-minute test prep before the exam.

Other study tools   A glossary of key terms from this book and their definitions are available as a fully searchable PDF.

 Go to www.wiley.com/go/sybextestprep to register and gain access to this interactive online learning environment and test bank with study tools.

In addition to the online test bank, I have provided additional study material that'll help you get the most out of your exam preparation:

Todd Lammle Bonus Material and Labs   Be sure to check the www.lammle.com/ccna for directions on how to download all the latest bonus material created specifically to help you study for your CCNA exam.

How to Use This Book

If you want a solid foundation for the serious effort of preparing for the CCNA Routing and Switching exam, then look no further. I've spent hundreds of hours putting together this book with the sole intention of helping you to pass the Cisco exam, as well as really learn how to correctly configure Cisco routers and switches!

This book is loaded with valuable information, and you will get the most out of your study time if you understand why the book is organized the way it is.

So to maximize your benefit from this book, I recommend the following study method:

1. Take the assessment test that's provided at the end of this introduction. (The answers are at the end of the test.) It's okay if you don't know any of the answers; that's why you bought this book! Carefully read over the explanations for any questions you get wrong and note the chapters in which the material relevant to them is covered. This information should help you plan your study strategy.

2. Study each chapter carefully, making sure you fully understand the information and the test objectives listed at the beginning of each one. Pay extra-close attention to any chapter that includes material covered in questions you missed.

3. Answer all of the review questions related to each chapter. (The answers appear in the Appendix.) Note the questions that confuse you, and study the topics they cover again until the concepts are crystal clear. And again—do not just skim these questions! Make sure you fully comprehend the reason for each correct answer. Remember that these will not be the exact questions you will find on the exam, but they're written to help you understand the chapter material and ultimately pass the exam!

4. Try your hand at the bonus practice questions that are exclusive to this book. The questions can be found only at http://sybextestbanks.wiley.com. And be sure to

check out www.lammle.com/ccna for the most up-to-date Cisco exam prep questions, videos, Todd Lammle boot camps, and more.

5. Test yourself using all the flashcards, which are also found on the download link. These are brand-new and updated flashcards to help you prepare for the CCNA and are a wonderful study tool!

To learn every bit of the material covered in this book, you'll have to apply yourself regularly, and with discipline. Try to set aside the same time period every day to study, and select a comfortable and quiet place to do so. I'm confident that if you work hard, you'll be surprised at how quickly you learn this material!

If you follow these steps and really study using the review questions, the practice exams, the Todd Lammle video sections, and the electronic flashcards,—it would actually be hard to fail the Cisco exams. But understand that studying for the Cisco exams is a lot like getting in shape—if you do not go to the gym every day, it's not going to happen!

Where Do You Take the Exams?

You may take the ICND1, ICND2, or CCNA R/S Composite or any Cisco exam at any of the Pearson VUE authorized testing centers. For information, check www.vue.com or call 877-404-EXAM (3926).

To register for a Cisco exam, follow these steps:

1. Determine the number of the exam you want to take. (The ICND1 exam number is 100-105, ICND2 is 200-105, and CCNA R/S Composite is 200-125.)

2. Register with the nearest Pearson VUE testing center. At this point, you will be asked to pay in advance for the exam. At the time of this writing, the ICND1 and ICND2 exams are $150, and the CCNA R/S Composite exam is $300. The exams must be taken within one year of payment. You can schedule exams up to six weeks in advance or as late as the day you want to take it—but if you fail a Cisco exam, you must wait five days before you will be allowed to retake it. If something comes up and you need to cancel or reschedule your exam appointment, contact Pearson VUE at least 24 hours in advance.

3. When you schedule the exam, you'll get instructions regarding all appointment and cancellation procedures, the ID requirements, and information about the testing-center location.

Tips for Taking Your Cisco Exams

The Cisco exams contain about 40 to 50 questions and must be completed in about 90 minutes or less. This information can change per exam. You must get a score of about 85 percent to pass this exam, but again, each exam can be different.

Many questions on the exam have answer choices that at first glance look identical—especially the syntax questions! So remember to read through the choices carefully because close just doesn't cut it. If you get commands in the wrong order or forget one measly character, you'll get the question wrong.

Also, never forget that the right answer is the Cisco answer. In many cases, more than one appropriate answer is presented, but the *correct* answer is the one that Cisco recommends. On the exam, you will always be told to pick one, two, or three options, never "choose all that apply." The Cisco exam may include the following test formats:

- Multiple-choice single answer
- Multiple-choice multiple answer
- Drag-and-drop
- Router simulations

Cisco proctored exams will not show the steps to follow in completing a router interface configuration, but they do allow partial command responses. For example, show run, sho running, or sh running-config would be acceptable.

Here are some general tips for exam success:

- Arrive early at the exam center so you can relax and review your study materials.

- Read the questions *carefully*. Don't jump to conclusions. Make sure you're clear about *exactly* what each question asks. "Read twice, answer once," is what I always tell my students.

- When answering multiple-choice questions that you're not sure about, use the process of elimination to get rid of the obviously incorrect answers first. Doing this greatly improves your odds if you need to make an educated guess.

- You can no longer move forward and backward through the Cisco exams, so double-check your answer before clicking Next since you can't change your mind.

After you complete an exam, you'll get immediate, online notification of your pass or fail status, a printed examination score report that indicates your pass or fail status, and your exam results by section. (The test administrator will give you the printed score report.) Test scores are automatically forwarded to Cisco within five working days after you take the test, so you don't need to send your score to them. If you pass the exam, you'll receive confirmation from Cisco, typically within two to four weeks, sometimes a bit longer.

Objective Map for CCNA Routing and Switching Certification Exam 200-125

We've provided this objective map to help you locate where the objectives for the CCNA Routing and Switching certification Exam 200-125 are covered in each chapter. Please refer to it when you want to find an objective quickly.

Exam objectives are subject to change at any time without prior notice and at Cisco's sole discretion. Please visit Cisco's certification website (www.cisco.com/web/learning) for the latest information on the CCNA Routing and Switching certification.

NETWORKING FUNDAMENTALS	Chapter(s)
Compare and contrast OSI and TCP/IP models.	1
Compare and contrast TCP and UDP protocols.	1
Describe the impact of infrastructure components in an enterprise network.	1
Describe the effects of cloud resources on enterprise network architecture.	1
Compare and contrast collapsed core and three-tier architectures.	1
Compare and contrast network topologies.	1
Select the appropriate cabling type based on implementation requirements.	1
Apply troubleshooting methodologies to resolve problems.	1
Configure, verify, and troubleshoot IPv4 addressing and subnetting.	1
Compare and contrast IPv4 address types.	1
Describe the need for private IPv4 addressing.	1
Identify the appropriate IPv6 addressing scheme to satisfy addressing requirements in a LAN/WAN environment.	1
Configure, verify, and troubleshoot IPv6 addressing.	1
Configure and verify IPv6 Stateless Address Auto Configuration.	1
Compare and contrast IPv6 address types.	1
LAN SWITCHING TECHNOLOGIES	
Describe and verify switching concepts.	2
Interpret Ethernet frame format.	2
Troubleshoot interface and cable issues (collisions, errors, duplex, speed).	2
Configure, verify, and troubleshoot VLANs (normal/extended range) spanning multiple switches.	2

NETWORKING FUNDAMENTALS	Chapter(s)
Configure, verify, and troubleshoot interswitch connectivity.	2
Configure, verify, and troubleshoot STP protocols.	2
Configure, verify and troubleshoot STP-related optional features.	2
Configure and verify layer 2 protocols.	2
Configure, verify, and troubleshoot (layer 2/layer 3) EtherChannel.	2
Describe the benefits of switch stacking and chassis aggregation.	2
ROUTING TECHNOLOGIES	
Describe the routing concepts.	3
Interpret the components of a routing table.	3
Describe how a routing table is populated by different routing information sources.	3
Configure, verify, and troubleshoot inter-VLAN routing.	3
Compare and contrast static routing and dynamic routing.	3
Compare and contrast distance-vector and link-state routing protocols.	3
Compare and contrast interior and exterior routing protocols.	3
Configure, verify, and troubleshoot IPv4 and IPv6 static routing.	3
Configure, verify, and troubleshoot single-area and multi-area OSPFv2 for IPv4 (excluding authentication, filtering, manual summarization, redistribution, stub, virtual-link, and LSAs).	3
Configure, verify, and troubleshoot single-area and multi-area OSPFv3 for IPv6 (excluding authentication, filtering, manual summarization, redistribution, stub, virtual-link, and LSAs).	3
Configure, verify, and troubleshoot EIGRP for IPv4 (excluding authentication, filtering, manual summarization, redistribution, stub).	3
Configure, verify, and troubleshoot EIGRP for IPv6 (excluding authentication, filtering, manual summarization, redistribution, stub).	3

NETWORKING FUNDAMENTALS	Chapter(s)
Configure, verify, and troubleshoot RIPv2 for IPv4 (excluding authentication, filtering, manual summarization, redistribution).	3
Troubleshoot basic layer 3 end-to-end connectivity issues.	3
WAN TECHNOLOGIES	
Configure and verify PPP and MLPPP on WAN interfaces using local authentication.	4
Configure, verify, and troubleshoot PPPoE client-side interfaces using local authentication.	4
Configure, verify, and troubleshoot GRE tunnel connectivity.	4
Describe WAN topology options.	4
Describe WAN access connectivity options.	4
Configure and verify single-homed branch connectivity using eBGP IPv4 (limited to peering and route advertisement using Network command only).	4
Describe basic QoS concepts.	4
INFRASTRUCTURE SERVICES	
Describe DNS lookup operation.	5
Troubleshoot client connectivity issues involving DNS.	5
Configure and verify DHCP on a router (excluding static reservations).	5
Troubleshoot client- and router-based DHCP connectivity issues.	5
Configure, verify, and troubleshoot basic HSRP.	5
Configure, verify, and troubleshoot inside source NAT.	5
Configure and verify NTP operating in a client/server mode.	5
INFRASTRUCTURE SECURITY	
Configure, verify, and troubleshoot port security.	6
Describe common access layer threat mitigation techniques.	6

NETWORKING FUNDAMENTALS	Chapter(s)
Configure, verify, and troubleshoot IPv4 and IPv6 access list for traffic filtering.	6
Verify ACLs using the APIC-EM Path Trace ACL Analysis tool.	6
Configure, verify, and troubleshoot basic device hardening.	6
Verify ACLs using the APIC-EM Path Trace ACL Analysis tool.	6
Describe device security using AAA with TACACS+ and RADIUS.	6
INFRASTRUCTURE MANAGEMENT	
Configure and verify device-monitoring protocols.	7
Troubleshoot network connectivity issues using ICMP echo-based IP SLA.	7
Configure and verify device management.	7
Configure and verify initial device configuration.	7
Perform device maintenance.	7
Use Cisco IOS tools to troubleshoot and resolve problems.	7
Describe network programmability in enterprise network architecture.	7

Assessment Test

1. You reload a router with a configuration register setting of 0x2101. What will the router do when it reloads?

    A. The router enters setup mode.

    B. The router enters ROM monitor mode.

    C. The router boots the mini-IOS in ROM.

    D. The router expands the first IOS in flash memory into RAM.

2. Which of the following commands provides the product ID and serial number of a router?

    A. `show license`

    B. `show license feature`

    C. `show version`

    D. `show license udi`

3. Which command allows you to view the technology options and licenses that are supported on your router along with several status variables?

    A. `show license`

    B. `show license feature`

    C. `show license udi`

    D. `show version`

4. You want to send a console message to a syslog server, but you only want to send status messages of 3 and lower. Which of the following commands will you use?

    A. `logging trap emergencies`

    B. `logging trap errors`

    C. `logging trap debugging`

    D. `logging trap notifications`

    E. `logging trap critical`

    F. `logging trap warnings`

    G. `logging trap alerts`

5. IPv6 unicast routing is running on the Corp router. Which of the following addresses would show up with the `show ipv6 int brief` command?

    ```
    Corp#sh int f0/0
    FastEthernet0/0 is up, line protocol is up
     Hardware is AmdFE, address is 000d.bd3b.0d80 (bia 000d.bd3b.0d80)
    [output cut]
    ```

    A. `FF02::3c3d:0d:bdff:fe3b:0d80`

    B. `FE80::3c3d:2d:bdff:fe3b:0d80`

   C. FE80::3c3d:0d:bdff:fe3b:0d80

   D. FE80::3c3d:2d:ffbd:3bfe:0d80

6. A host sends a type of NDP message providing the MAC address that was requested. Which type of NDP was sent?

   A. NA

   B. RS

   C. RA

   D. NS

7. Each field in an IPv6 address is how many bits long?

   A. 4

   B. 16

   C. 32

   D. 128

8. What does the command `routerA(config)#line cons 0` allow you to perform next?

   A. Set the Telnet password.

   B. Shut down the router.

   C. Set your console password.

   D. Disable console connections.

9. Which two statements describe the IP address 10.16.3.65/23? (Choose two.)

   A. The subnet address is 10.16.3.0 255.255.254.0.

   B. The lowest host address in the subnet is 10.16.2.1 255.255.254.0.

   C. The last valid host address in the subnet is 10.16.2.254 255.255.254.0.

   D. The broadcast address of the subnet is 10.16.3.255 255.255.254.0.

   E. The network is not subnetted.

10. On which interface do you configure an IP address for a switch?

   A. `int fa0/0`

   B. `int vty 0 15`

   C. `int vlan 1`

   D. `int s/0/0`

11. Which of the following is the valid host range for the subnet on which the IP address 192.168.168.188 255.255.255.192 resides?

   A. 192.168.168.129–190

   B. 192.168.168.129–191

   C. 192.168.168.128–190

   D. 192.168.168.128–192

12. Which of the following is considered to be the inside host's address after translation?

    A. Inside local

    B. Outside local

    C. Inside global

    D. Outside global

13. Your inside locals are not being translated to the inside global addresses. Which of the following commands will show you if your inside globals are allowed to use the NAT pool?

```
ip nat pool Corp 198.18.41.129 198.18.41.134 netmask 255.255.255.248
ip nat inside source list 100 int s0/0 Corp overload
```

    A. `debug ip nat`

    B. `show access-list`

    C. `show ip nat translation`

    D. `show ip nat statistics`

14. How many collision domains are created when you segment a network with a 12-port switch?

    A. 1

    B. 2

    C. 5

    D. 12

15. Which of the following commands will allow you to set your Telnet password on a Cisco router?

    A. `line telnet 0 4`

    B. `line aux 0 4`

    C. `line vty 0 4`

    D. `line con 0`

16. Which router command allows you to view the entire contents of all access lists?

    A. `show all access-lists`

    B. `show access-list`

    C. `show ip interface`

    D. `show interface`

17. What does a VLAN do?

    A. Acts as the fastest port to all servers

    B. Provides multiple collision domains on one switch port

    C. Breaks up broadcast domains in a layer 2 switch internetwork

    D. Provides multiple broadcast domains within a single collision domain

18. If you wanted to delete the configuration stored in NVRAM, choose the best answer for the Cisco objectives.

    A. `erase startup`

    B. `delete running`

    C. `erase flash`

    D. `erase running`

19. Which protocol is used to send a destination network unknown message back to originating hosts?

    A. TCP

    B. ARP

    C. ICMP

    D. BootP

20. Which class of IP address provides 15 bits for subnetting?

    A. A

    B. B

    C. C

    D. D

21. There are three possible routes for a router to reach a destination network. The first route is from OSPF with a metric of 782. The second route is from RIPv2 with a metric of 4. The third is from EIGRP with a composite metric of 20514560. Which route will be installed by the router in its routing table?

    A. RIPv2

    B. EIGRP

    C. OSPF

    D. All three

22. Which one of the following is true regarding VLANs?

    A. Two VLANs are configured by default on all Cisco switches.

    B. VLANs only work if you have a complete Cisco switched internetwork. No off-brand switches are allowed.

    C. You should not have more than 10 switches in the same VTP domain.

    D. You need to have a trunk link configured between switches in order to send information about more than one VLAN down the link.

23. How many broadcast domains are created when you segment a network with a 12-port switch?

    A. 1

    B. 2

    C. 5

    D. 12

24. What protocols are used to configure trunking on a switch? (Choose two.)

   A. VLAN Trunking Protocol

   B. VLAN

   C. 802.1q

   D. ISL

25. What is a stub network?

   A. A network with more than one exit point

   B. A network with more than one exit and entry point

   C. A network with only one entry and no exit point

   D. A network in which the one entry point is also the exit point.

26. Where is a hub specified in the OSI model?

   A. Session layer

   B. Physical layer

   C. Data Link layer

   D. Application layer

27. What are the two main types of access control lists (ACLs)? (Choose two.)

   A. Standard

   B. IEEE

   C. Extended

   D. Specialized

28. Which of the following is the best summarization of the following networks: 192.168.128.0 through 192.168.159.0?

   A. 192.168.0.0/24

   B. 192.168.128.0/16

   C. 192.168.128.0/19

   D. 192.168.128.0/20

29. What command is used to create a backup configuration?

   A. `copy running backup`

   B. `copy running-config startup-config`

   C. `config mem`

   D. `wr net`

30. 1000Base-T is which IEEE standard?

   A. 802.3f

   B. 802.3z

   C. 802.3ab

   D. 802.3ae

Answers to Assessment Test

1. **C.** 2100 boots the router into ROM monitor mode, 2101 loads the mini-IOS from ROM, and 2102 is the default and loads the IOS from flash. See Chapter 7 for more information.

2. **D.** The show license udi command displays the unique device identifier (UDI) of the router, which comprises the product ID (PID) and serial number of the router. See Chapter 7 for more information.

3. **B.** The show license feature command allows you to view the technology package licenses and feature licenses that are supported on your router along with several status variables related to software activation and licensing, both licensed and unlicensed features. See Chapter 7 for more information.

4. **B.** There are eight different trap levels. If you choose, for example, level 3, level 0 through level 3 messages will be displayed. To specify level 3 the command is logging trap errors. See Chapter 7 for more information.

5. **B.** This can be a hard question if you don't remember to invert the 7th bit of the first octet in the MAC address! Always look for the 7th bit when studying for the Cisco R/S, and when using EUI-64, invert it. The EUI-64 autoconfiguration inserts an FF:FE in the middle of the 48-bit MAC address to create a unique IPv6 address. See Chapter 1 for more information.

6. **A.** The NDP neighbor advertisement (NA) contains the MAC address. A neighbor solicitation (NS) was initially sent asking for the MAC address. See Chapter 1 for more information.

7. **B.** Each field in an IPv6 address is 16 bits long. An IPv6 address has eight fields for a total of 128 bits. See Chapter 1 for more information.

8. **C.** The command line console 0 places you at a prompt where you can then set your console user-mode password. See Chapter 6 for more information.

9. **B, D.** The mask 255.255.254.0 (/23) used with a Class A address means that there are 15 subnet bits and 9 host bits. The block size in the third octet is 2 (256 – 254). So this makes the subnets in the interesting octet 0, 2, 4, 6, etc., all the way to 254. The host 10.16.3.65 is in the 2.0 subnet. The next subnet is 4.0, so the broadcast address for the 2.0 subnet is 3.255. The valid host addresses are 2.1 through 3.254. See Chapter 1 for more information.

10. **C.** The IP address is configured under a logical interface, called a management domain or VLAN 1, by default. See Chapter 2 for more information.

11. **A.** 256 – 192 = 64, so 64 is our block size. Just count in increments of 64 to find our subnet: 64 + 64 = 128. 128 + 64 = 192. The subnet is 128, the broadcast address is 191, and the valid host range is the numbers in between, or 129–190. See Chapter 1 for more information.

12. C. An inside global address is considered to be the IP address of the host on the private network after translation. See Chapter 5 for more information.

13. B. Once you create your pool, the command `ip nat inside source` must be used to say which inside locals are allowed to use the pool. In this question, we need to see if access list 100 is configured correctly, if at all, so `show access-list` is the best answer. See Chapter 6 for more information.

14. D. Layer 2 switching creates individual collision domains per port. See Chapter 2 for more information.

15. C. The command `line vty 0 4` places you in a prompt that will allow you to set or change your Telnet password. See Chapter 6 for more information.

16. B. To see the contents of all access lists, use the `show access-list` command. See Chapter 6 for more information.

17. C. VLANs break up broadcast domains at layer 2. See Chapter 2 for more information.

18. A. The command `erase startup-config` deletes the configuration stored in NVRAM. Using `erase-startup` will also work as the IOS will complete the command for you. See Chapter 7 for more information.

19. C. ICMP is the protocol at the Network layer that is used to send messages back to an originating router. See Chapter 1 for more information.

20. A. Class A addressing provides 22 bits for host subnetting. Class B provides 16 bits, but only 14 are available for subnetting. Class C provides only 6 bits for subnetting. See Chapter 1 for more information.

21. B. Only the EIGRP route will be placed in the routing table because EIGRP has the lowest administrative distance (AD), and that is always used before metrics. See Chapter 3 for more information.

22. D. Switches send information about only one VLAN down a link unless it is configured as a trunk link. See Chapter 2 for more information.

23. A. By default, switches break up collision domains on a per-port basis but are one large broadcast domain. See Chapter 2 for more information.

24. C, D. VLAN Trunking Protocol (VTP) is not right because it has nothing to do with trunking except that it sends VLAN information across a trunk link. 802.1q and ISL encapsulations are used to configure trunking on a port. See Chapter 2 for more information.

25. D. Stub networks have only one connection to an internetwork. Default routes should be set on a stub network or network loops may occur; however, there are exceptions to this rule. See Chapter 3 for more information.

26. B. Hubs regenerate electrical signals, which are specified at the Physical layer. See Chapter 1 for more information.

27. A, C. Standard and extended access control lists (ACLs) are used to configure security on a router. See Chapter 6 for more information.

28. C. If you start at 192.168.128.0 and go through 192.168.159.0, you can see that this is a block of 32 in the third octet. Since the network address is always the first one in the range, the summary address is 192.168.128.0. What mask provides a block of 32 in the third octet? The answer is 255.255.224.0, or /19. See Chapter 1 for more information.

29. B. The command to back up the configuration on a router is
copy running-config startup-config. See Chapter 7 for more information.

30. C. IEEE 802.3ab is the standard for 1 Gbps on twisted-pair. See Chapter 1 for more information.

Chapter
1

Network Fundamentals

THE FOLLOWING CCNA ROUTING AND SWITCHING EXAM OBJECTIVES ARE COVERED IN THIS CHAPTER:

✓ Compare and contrast OSI and TCP/IP models.

✓ Compare and contrast TCP and UDP protocols.

✓ Describe the impact of infrastructure components in an enterprise network.

✓ Describe the effects of cloud resources on enterprise network architecture.

✓ Compare and contrast collapsed core and three-tier architectures.

✓ Compare and contrast network topologies.

✓ Select the appropriate cabling type based on implementation requirements.

✓ Apply troubleshooting methodologies to resolve problems.

✓ Configure, verify, and troubleshoot IPv4 addressing and subnetting.

✓ Compare and contrast IPv4 address types.

✓ Describe the need for private IPv4 addressing.

✓ Identify the appropriate IPv6 addressing scheme to satisfy addressing requirements in a LAN/WAN environment.

✓ Configure, verify, and troubleshoot IPv6 addressing.

✓ Configure and verify IPv6 Stateless Address Auto Configuration.

✓ Compare and contrast IPv6 address types.

In this chapter, I will review the basics of internetworking and what an internetwork is. I will go over some of the components that make up a network as well as some applications used in networking. I will also go over the OSI and TCP/IP models and, finally, explain how data flows across a network as well as discuss the various connectors used in a network.

Compare and contrast OSI and TCP/IP models

A *reference model* is a conceptual blueprint of how communications should take place. It addresses all the processes required for effective communication and divides them into logical groupings called layers. When a communication system is designed in this manner, it's known as a hierarchical or *layered architecture*. In this section two models covered on the exam are compared and contrasted.

The OSI Reference Model

The OSI model is hierarchical, and there are many advantages that can be applied to any layered model, but as I said, the OSI model's primary purpose is to allow different vendors' networks to interoperate.

Here's a list of some of the more important benefits of using the OSI layered model:

- It divides the network communication process into smaller and simpler components, facilitating component development, design, and troubleshooting.

- It allows multiple-vendor development through the standardization of network components.

- It encourages industry standardization by clearly defining what functions occur at each layer of the model.

- It allows various types of network hardware and software to communicate.

- It prevents changes in one layer from affecting other layers to expedite development.

The OSI has seven different layers, divided into two groups. The top three layers define how the applications within the end stations will communicate with each other as well as with users. The bottom four layers define how data is transmitted end to end.

Figure 1.1 shows the three upper layers and their functions.

FIGURE 1.1   The upper layers

Application	• Provides a user interface
Presentation	• Presents data • Handles processing such as encryption
Session	• Keeps different applications' data separate

When looking at Figure 1.1, understand that users interact with the computer at the Application layer and also that the upper layers are responsible for applications communicating between hosts. None of the upper layers knows anything about networking or network addresses because that's the responsibility of the four bottom layers.

In Figure 1.2, which shows the four lower layers and their functions, you can see that it's these four bottom layers that define how data is transferred through physical media like wire, cable, fiber optics, switches, and routers. These bottom layers also determine how to rebuild a data stream from a transmitting host to a destination host's application.

FIGURE 1.2   The lower layers

Transport	• Provides reliable or unreliable delivery • Performs error correction before retransmit
Network	• Provides logical addressing, which routers use for path determination
Data Link	• Combines packets into bytes and bytes into frames • Provides access to media using MAC address • Performs error detection not correction
Physical	• Moves bits between devices • Specifies voltage, wire speed, and pinout of cables

The following network devices operate at all seven layers of the OSI model:

- Network management stations (NMSs)
- Web and application servers
- Gateways (not default gateways)
- Servers
- Network hosts

The OSI reference model has the following seven layers:

- Application layer (layer 7)
- Presentation layer (layer 6)
- Session layer (layer 5)
- Transport layer (layer 4)

- Network layer (layer 3)
- Data Link layer (layer 2)
- Physical layer (layer 1)

Some people like to use a mnemonic to remember the seven layers, such as **All People Seem To Need Data Processing**. Figure 1.3 shows a summary of the functions defined at each layer of the OSI model.

FIGURE 1.3   OSI layer functions

Application	• File, print, message, database, and application services
Presentation	• Data encryption, compression, and translation services
Session	• Dialog control

Transport	• End-to-end connection
Network	• Routing

Data Link	• Framing
Physical	• Physical topology

I've separated the seven-layer model into three different functions: the upper layers, the middle layers, and the bottom layers. The upper layers communicate with the user interface and application, the middle layers do reliable communication and routing to a remote network, and the bottom layers communicate to the local network.

TCP/IP and the DoD Model

The DoD model is basically a condensed version of the OSI model that comprises four instead of seven layers:

- Process/Application layer
- Host-to-Host layer or Transport layer
- Internet layer
- Network Access layer or Link layer

Figure 1.4 offers a comparison of the DoD model and the OSI reference model. As you can see, the two are similar in concept, but each has a different number of layers with different names. Cisco may at times use different names for the same layer, such as both "Host-to-Host" and Transport" at the layer above the Internet layer, as well as "Network Access" and "Link" used to describe the bottom layer.

FIGURE 1.4   The DoD and OSI models

Exam Essentials

List the layers of the OSI and TCP/IP models.   List the layers in order, and describe the function of each layer.

Compare and contrast the layers of the TCP/IP and OSI models.   Identify the layers in each model that perform like functions.

Compare and contrast TCP and UDP protocols

The main purpose of the Host-to-Host layer is to shield the upper-layer applications from the complexities of the network. Coming up, I'll introduce you to the two protocols at this layer:

- Transmission Control Protocol (TCP)
- User Datagram Protocol (UDP)

Transmission Control Protocol (TCP)

Transmission Control Protocol (TCP) takes large blocks of information from an application and breaks them into segments. It numbers and sequences each segment so that the destination's TCP stack can put the segments back into the order the application intended. After these segments are sent on the transmitting host, TCP waits for an acknowledgment of the receiving end's TCP virtual circuit session, retransmitting any segments that aren't acknowledged.

Before a transmitting host starts to send segments down the model, the sender's TCP stack contacts the destination's TCP stack to establish a connection. This creates a *virtual circuit*, and this type of communication is known as *connection-oriented*. During this initial handshake, the two TCP layers also agree on the amount of information that's going to be sent before the recipient's TCP sends back an acknowledgment. With everything agreed upon in advance, the path is paved for reliable communication to take place.

TCP is a full-duplex, connection-oriented, reliable, and accurate protocol, but establishing all these terms and conditions, in addition to error checking, is no small task. TCP is very complicated, and so not surprisingly, it's costly in terms of network overhead. And since today's networks are much more reliable than those of yore, this added reliability is often unnecessary. Most programmers use TCP because it removes a lot of programming work, but for real-time video and VoIP, *User Datagram Protocol (UDP)* is often better because using it results in less overhead.

TCP Segment Format

Since the upper layers just send a data stream to the protocols in the Transport layers, I'll use Figure 1.5 to demonstrate how TCP segments a data stream and prepares it for the Internet layer. When the Internet layer receives the data stream, it routes the segments as packets through an internetwork. The segments are handed to the receiving host's Host-to-Host layer protocol, which rebuilds the data stream for the upper-layer applications or protocols.

FIGURE 1.5   TCP segment format

16-bit source port			16-bit destination port	
32-bit sequence number				
32-bit acknowledgment number				
4-bit header length	Reserved	Flags	16-bit window size	
16-bit TCP checksum			16-bit urgent pointer	
Options				
Data				

Figure 1.5 shows the TCP segment format and shows the different fields within the TCP header. This isn't important to memorize for the Cisco exam objectives, but you need to understand it well because it's really good foundational information.

The TCP header is 20 bytes long, or up to 24 bytes with options. You need to understand what each field in the TCP segment is in order to build a strong educational foundation:

Source port   This is the port number of the application on the host sending the data, which I'll talk about more thoroughly a little later in this chapter.

Destination port   This is the port number of the application requested on the destination host.

Sequence number   A number used by TCP that puts the data back in the correct order or retransmits missing or damaged data during a process called sequencing

Acknowledgment number   The value is the TCP octet that is expected next.

Header length   The number of 32-bit words in the TCP header, which indicates where the data begins. The TCP header (even one including options) is an integral number of 32 bits in length.

Reserved   Always set to zero

Code bits/flags   Controls functions used to set up and terminate a session

Window   The window size the sender is willing to accept, in octets

Checksum   The cyclic redundancy check (CRC), used because TCP doesn't trust the lower layers and checks everything. The CRC checks the header and data fields.

Urgent   A valid field only if the Urgent pointer in the code bits is set. If so, this value indicates the offset from the current sequence number, in octets, where the segment of non-urgent data begins.

Options   May be 0, meaning that no options have to be present, or a multiple of 32 bits. However, if any options are used that do not cause the option field to total a multiple of 32 bits, padding of 0s must be used to make sure the data begins on a 32-bit boundary. These boundaries are known as words.

Data   Handed down to the TCP protocol at the Transport layer, which includes the upper-layer headers

Let's take a look at a TCP segment copied from a network analyzer:

```
TCP - Transport Control Protocol
  Source Port:      5973
  Destination Port: 23
  Sequence Number:  1456389907
  Ack Number:       1242056456
  Offset:           5
  Reserved:         %000000
  Code:             %011000
        Ack is valid
        Push Request
  Window:           61320
  Checksum:         0x61a6
  Urgent Pointer:   0
  No TCP Options
  TCP Data Area:
  vL.5.+.5.+.5.+.5  76 4c 19 35 11 2b 19 35 11 2b 19 35 11
    2b 19 35 +. 11 2b 19
  Frame Check Sequence: 0x0d00000f
```

Did you notice that everything I talked about earlier is in the segment? As you can see from the number of fields in the header, TCP creates a lot of overhead. Again, this is why application developers may opt for efficiency over reliability to save overhead and go with UDP instead. It's also defined at the Transport layer as an alternative to TCP.

User Datagram Protocol (UDP)

User Datagram Protocol (UDP) is basically the scaled-down economy model of TCP, which is why UDP is sometimes referred to as a thin protocol. Like a thin person on a park bench, a thin protocol doesn't take up a lot of room—or in this case, require much bandwidth on a network.

UDP doesn't offer all the bells and whistles of TCP either, but it does do a fabulous job of transporting information that doesn't require reliable delivery, using far less network resources. (UDP is covered thoroughly in Request for Comments 768.)

So clearly, there are times that it's wise for developers to opt for UDP rather than TCP, one of them being when reliability is already taken care of at the Process/Application layer. Network File System (NFS) handles its own reliability issues, making the use of TCP both impractical and redundant. But ultimately, it's up to the application developer to opt for using UDP or TCP, not the user who wants to transfer data faster!

UDP does *not* sequence the segments and does not care about the order in which the segments arrive at the destination. UDP just sends the segments off and forgets about them. It doesn't follow through, check up on them, or even allow for an acknowledgment of safe arrival—complete abandonment. Because of this, it's referred to as an unreliable protocol. This does not mean that UDP is ineffective, only that it doesn't deal with reliability issues at all.

Furthermore, UDP doesn't create a virtual circuit, nor does it contact the destination before delivering information to it. Because of this, it's also considered a *connectionless* protocol. Since UDP assumes that the application will use its own reliability method, it doesn't use any itself. This presents an application developer with a choice when running the Internet Protocol stack: TCP for reliability or UDP for faster transfers.

It's important to know how this process works because if the segments arrive out of order, which is commonplace in IP networks, they'll simply be passed up to the next layer in whatever order they were received. This can result in some seriously garbled data! On the other hand, TCP sequences the segments so they get put back together in exactly the right order, which is something UDP just can't do.

UDP Segment Format

Figure 1.6 clearly illustrates UDP's markedly lean overhead as compared to TCP's hungry requirements. Look at the figure carefully—can you see that UDP doesn't use windowing or provide for acknowledgments in the UDP header?

FIGURE 1.6   UDP segment

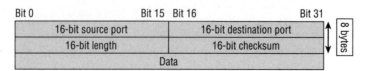

It's important for you to understand what each field in the UDP segment is:

Source port   Port number of the application on the host sending the data

Destination port   Port number of the application requested on the destination host

Length   Length of UDP header and UDP data

Checksum   Checksum of both the UDP header and UDP data fields

Data   Upper-layer data

UDP, like TCP, doesn't trust the lower layers and runs its own CRC. Remember that the Frame Check Sequence (FCS) is the field that houses the CRC, which is why you can see the FCS information.

The following shows a UDP segment caught on a network analyzer:

```
UDP - User Datagram Protocol
  Source Port:      1085
  Destination Port: 5136
  Length:           41
  Checksum:         0x7a3c
  UDP Data Area:
  ..Z......00 01 5a 96 00 01 00 00 00 00 00 11 0000 00
  ...C..2._C._C  2e 03 00 43 02 1e 32 0a 00 0a 00 80 43 00 80
Frame Check Sequence: 0x00000000
```

Notice that low overhead! Try to find the sequence number, ack number, and window size in the UDP segment. You can't because they just aren't there!

Key Concepts of Host-to-Host Protocols

Since you've now seen both a connection-oriented (TCP) and connectionless (UDP) protocol in action, it's a good time to summarize the two here. Table 1.1 highlights some of the key concepts about these two protocols for you to memorize.

TABLE 1.1   Key features of TCP and UDP

TCP	UDP
Sequenced	Unsequenced
Reliable	Unreliable
Connection-oriented	Connectionless
Virtual circuit	Low overhead
Acknowledgments	No acknowledgment
Windowing flow control	No windowing or flow control of any type

Exam Essentials

Compare and contrast UDP and TCP.   Describe the differences in purpose and capability of the two transport layer protocols, including overhead and services offered. Also describe when each is used.

Describe the impact of infrastructure components in an enterprise network

Various internetworking devices offer services that are critical to the network. In this section, I will review three important components and the role each plays in making the network function in a secure fashion.

Firewalls

Firewalls are hardware appliances or special software running on servers that control the flow of traffic between parts of the network. Routers can also be configured to perform this service.

These devices are network security systems that monitor and control the incoming and outgoing network traffic based on predetermined security rules, and they are usually intrusion protection systems (IPSs). The Cisco Adaptive Security Appliance (ASA) firewall typically establishes a barrier between a trusted, secure internal network and the Internet, which is not secure or trusted. Cisco's new acquisition of Sourcefire puts it at the top of the market with Next Generation Firewalls (NGFW) and Next Generation IPS (NGIPS), which Cisco now just calls Firepower. Cisco's new Firepower runs on dedicated appliances, Cisco ASAs, ISR routers, and even Meraki products.

Access Points

These devices allow wireless devices to connect to a wired network and extend a collision domain from a switch and are typically in their own broadcast domain, or what is referred to as a *virtual LAN* (VLAN). An AP can be a simple standalone device, but today they are usually managed by wireless controllers either in-house or through the Internet.

Wireless Controllers

These are the devices that network administrators or network operations centers use to manage access points in medium to large to extremely large quantities. The WLAN controller automatically handles the configuration of wireless access points and was typically used only in larger enterprise systems. However, with Cisco's acquisition of Meraki systems, you can easily manage a small to medium-sized wireless network via the cloud using its simple-to-configure web controller system.

Exam Essentials

Describe the features of infrastructure components in an enterprise network.   These include but are not limited to access points, WLAN controllers, and firewalls. Specific firewall solutions include the Cisco Adaptive Security Appliance (ASA), Next Generation Firewalls (NGFW), and Next Generation IPS (NGIPS), which Cisco now just calls Firepower.

Describe the effects of cloud resources on enterprise network architecture

Cloud computing is by far one of the hottest topics in today's IT world. Basically, cloud computing can provide virtualized processing, storage, and computing resources to users remotely, making the resources transparently available regardless of the user connection. To put it simply, some people just refer to the cloud as "someone else's hard drive." This is true, of course, but the cloud is much more than just storage.

   The history of the consolidation and virtualization of our servers tells us that this has become the de facto way of implementing servers because of basic resource efficiency. Two physical servers will use twice the amount of electricity as one server, but through virtualization, one physical server can host two virtual machines, hence the main thrust toward virtualization. With it, network components can simply be shared more efficiently.

   Users connecting to a cloud provider's network, whether it be for storage or applications, really don't care about the underlying infrastructure because as computing becomes a service rather than a product, it's then considered an on-demand resource, described in Figure 1.7.

FIGURE 1.7   Cloud computing is on-demand

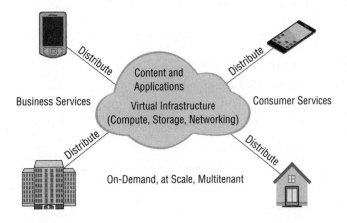

Centralization/consolidation of resources, automation of services, virtualization, and standardization are just a few of the big benefits cloud services offer. Let's take a look in Figure 1.8.

FIGURE 1.8 Advantages of cloud computing

Traffic Path to Internal and External Cloud Services

Centralization/consolidation of resources, automation of services, virtualization, and standardization are just a few of the big benefits cloud services offer as shown in Figure 1.8.

Cloud computing has several advantages over the traditional use of computer resources. Following are advantages to the provider and to the cloud user.

Here are the advantages to a cloud service builder or provider:

- Cost reduction, standardization, and automation

- High utilization through virtualized, shared resources

- Easier administration

- Fall-in-place operations model

Here are the advantages to cloud users:

- On-demand, self-service resource provisioning

- Fast deployment cycles

- Cost effective

- Centralized appearance of resources

- Highly available, horizontally scaled application architectures

- No local backups

Virtual Services

Cloud providers can offer you different available resources based on your needs and budget. You can choose just a vitalized network platform or go all in with the network, OS, and application resources.

Figure 1.9 shows the three service models available depending on the type of service you choose to get from a cloud.

FIGURE 1.9   Cloud computing service

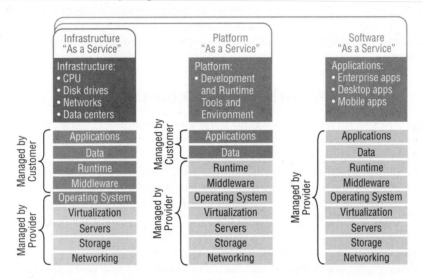

You can see that IaaS allows the customer to manage most of the network, whereas SaaS doesn't allow any management by the customer, and PaaS is somewhere in the middle of the two. Clearly, choices can be cost driven, so the most important thing is that the customer pays only for the services or infrastructure they use.

Let's take a look at each service:

Infrastructure as a Service (IaaS): Provides only the network   Delivers computer infrastructure—a platform virtualization environment—where the customer has the most control and management capability.

Platform as a Service (PaaS): Provides the operating system and the network   Delivers a computing platform and solution stack, allowing customers to develop, run, and manage applications without the complexity of building and maintaining the infrastructure typically associated with developing and launching an application. An example is Windows Azure.

Software as a Service (SaaS): Provides the required software, operating system, and network   SaaS is common application software such as databases, web servers, and email software that's hosted by the SaaS vendor. The customer accesses this software over the

Internet. Instead of having users install software on their computers or servers, the SaaS vendor owns the software and runs it on computers in its data center. Microsoft Office 365 and many Amazon Web Services (AWS) offerings are perfect examples of SaaS.

So depending on your business requirements and budget, cloud service providers market a very broad offering of cloud computing products from highly specialized offerings to a large selection of services.

What's nice here is that you're is offered a fixed price for each service that you use, which allows you to easily budget wisely for the future. It's true—at first, you'll have to spend a little cash on staff training, but with automation you can do more with less staff because administration will be easier and less complex. All of this works to free up the company resources to work on new business requirements and be more agile and innovative in the long run.

Basic Virtual Network Infrastructure

Having centralized resources is critical for today's workforce. For example, if you have your documents stored locally on your laptop and your laptop gets stolen, you're pretty much screwed unless you're doing constant local backups. That is so 2005!

After I lost my laptop and all the files for the book I was writing at the time, I swore (yes, I did that too) to never have my files stored locally again. I started using only Google Drive, OneDrive, and Dropbox for all my files, and they became my best backup friends. If I lose my laptop now, I just need to log in from any computer from anywhere to my service provider's logical drives and presto, I have all my files again. This is clearly a simple example of using cloud computing, specifically SaaS, and it's wonderful!

So cloud computing provides for the sharing of resources, lower cost operations passed to the cloud consumer, computing scaling, and the ability to dynamically add new servers without going through the procurement and deployment process.

Exam Essentials

Understand basic cloud technology.   Understand cloud services such as SaaS and others and how virtualization works.

Compare and contrast collapsed core and three-tier architectures

When arranging the infrastructure devices in the network there are a number of different models that can aid in defining these relationships. In this section we'll look at two such models.

The Cisco Three-Layer Hierarchical Model

Most of us were exposed to hierarchy early in life. Anyone with older siblings learned what it was like to be at the bottom of the hierarchy. Regardless of where you first discovered the concept of hierarchy, most of us experience it in many aspects of our lives. It's *hierarchy* that helps us understand where things belong, how things fit together, and what functions go where. It brings order to otherwise complex models. If you want a pay raise, for instance, hierarchy dictates that you ask your boss, not your subordinate, because that's the person whose role it is to grant or deny your request. So basically, understanding hierarchy helps us discern where we should go to get what we need.

Hierarchy has many of the same benefits in network design that it does in other areas of life. When used properly, it makes networks more predictable and helps us define which areas should perform certain functions. Likewise, you can use tools such as access lists at certain levels in hierarchical networks and avoid them at others.

Let's face it: Large networks can be extremely complicated, with multiple protocols, detailed configurations, and diverse technologies. Hierarchy helps us summarize a complex collection of details into an understandable model, bringing order from the chaos. Then, as specific configurations are needed, the model dictates the appropriate manner in which to apply them.

The Cisco hierarchical model can help you design, implement, and maintain a scalable, reliable, cost-effective hierarchical internetwork. Cisco defines three layers of hierarchy, as shown in Figure 1.10, each with specific functions.

FIGURE 1.10   The Cisco hierarchical model

Each layer has specific responsibilities. Keep in mind that the three layers are logical and are not necessarily physical devices. Consider the OSI model, another logical hierarchy. Its seven layers describe functions but not necessarily protocols, right? Sometimes a protocol maps to more than one layer of the OSI model, and sometimes multiple protocols communicate within a single layer. In the same way, when we build physical implementations of hierarchical networks, we may have many devices in a single layer, or there may be a single device performing functions at two layers. Just remember that the definition of the layers is logical, not physical!

So let's take a closer look at each of the layers now.

The Core Layer

The *core layer* is literally the core of the network. At the top of the hierarchy, the core layer is responsible for transporting large amounts of traffic both reliably and quickly. The only purpose of the network's core layer is to switch traffic as fast as possible. The traffic transported across the core is common to a majority of users. But remember that user data is processed at the distribution layer, which forwards the requests to the core if needed.

If there's a failure in the core, *every single user* can be affected! This is why fault tolerance at this layer is so important. The core is likely to see large volumes of traffic, so speed and latency are driving concerns here. Given the function of the core, we can now consider some design specifics. Let's start with some things we don't want to do:

- We don't want 24/7 connectivity.
- Never do anything to slow down traffic. This includes making sure you don't use access lists, perform routing between virtual local area networks, or implement packet filtering.
- Don't support workgroup access here.
- Avoid expanding the core (e.g., adding routers when the internetwork grows). If performance becomes an issue in the core, give preference to upgrades over expansion.

Here's a list of things that we want to achieve as we design the core:

- Design the core for high reliability. Consider data-link technologies that facilitate both speed and redundancy, like Gigabit Ethernet with redundant links or even 10 Gigabit Ethernet.
- Design with speed in mind. The core should have very little latency.
- Select routing protocols with lower convergence times. Fast and redundant data-link connectivity is no help if your routing tables are shot!

The Distribution Layer

The *distribution layer* is sometimes referred to as the *workgroup layer* and is the communication point between the access layer and the core. The primary functions of the distribution layer are to provide routing, filtering, and WAN access and to determine how packets can access the core, if needed. The distribution layer must determine the fastest way that network service requests are handled—for example, how a file request is forwarded to a server. After the distribution layer determines the best path, it forwards the request to the core layer if necessary. The core layer then quickly transports the request to the correct service.

The distribution layer is where we want to implement policies for the network because we are allowed a lot of flexibility in defining network operation here. There are several things that should generally be handled at the distribution layer:

- Routing
- Implementing tools (such as access lists), packet filtering, and queuing
- Implementing security and network policies, including address translation and firewalls
- Redistributing between routing protocols, including static routing
- Routing between VLANs and other workgroup support functions
- Defining broadcast and multicast domains

Key things to avoid at the distribution layer are those that are limited to functions that exclusively belong to one of the other layers!

The Access Layer

The *access layer* controls user and workgroup access to internetwork resources. The access layer is sometimes referred to as the *desktop layer*. The network resources most users need will be available locally because the distribution layer handles any traffic for remote services.

The following are some of the functions to be included at the access layer:

- Continued (from distribution layer) use of access control and policies
- Creation of separate collision domains (microsegmentation/switches)
- Workgroup connectivity into the distribution layer
- Device connectivity
- Resiliency and security services
- Advanced technology capabilities (voice/video, etc.)

Technologies like Gigabit or Fast Ethernet switching are frequently seen in the access layer.

I can't stress this enough—just because there are three separate levels does not imply three separate devices! There could be fewer or there could be more. After all, this is a *layered* approach.

Collapsed Core

In the collapsed core approach the distribution layer and the core layer are combined into a single layer, thus the name collapsed core. When using this design it is critical that the devices operating as both distribution and core devices must exhibit the following characteristics:

- High speed paths connecting to the network
- Must be a Layer-2 aggregation point
- Must enforce routing and network access policies
- Must be capable of Intelligent network services such as QoS, and network virtualization.

The benefits are reduced cost in equipment, while the drawbacks can be slower performance and reduced network availability as compared to the three tier model.

Exam Essentials

Identify the layers in the Cisco three-layer model, and describe the ideal function of each layer.   The three layers in the Cisco hierarchical model are the core (responsible for transporting large amounts of traffic both reliably and quickly), distribution (provides routing, filtering, and WAN access), and access (workgroup connectivity into the distribution layer).

Compare and contrast network topologies

Understand that every type of network has both a physical and a logical topology. The physical topology of a network refers to the physical layout of the devices, but mostly the cabling and cabling layout. The logical topology defines the logical path on which the signal will travel on the physical topology. Figure 1.11 shows the four types of topologies:

FIGURE 1.11   Physical vs. Logical Topolgies

- Physical topology is the physical layout of the devices and cabling.
- The primary physical topology categories are bus, ring, star, and mesh.

Bus Topology   Ring Topology   Star Topology   Mesh Topology

Here are the topology types, although the most common, and pretty much only network we use today is a physical star, logical bus technology, which is considered a hybrid topology (think Ethernet):

- Bus: In a bus topology, every workstation is connected to a single cable, meaning every host is directly connected to every other workstation in the network.

- Ring: In a ring topology, computers and other network devices are cabled together in a way that the last device is connected to the first to form a circle or ring.

- Star: The most common physical topology is a star topology, which is your Ethernet switching physical layout. A central cabling device (switch) connects the computers and other network devices together. This category includes star and extended star topologies. Physical connection is commonly made using twisted-pair wiring.

- Mesh: In a mesh topology, every network device is cabled together with a connection to each other. Redundant links increase reliability and self-healing. The physical connection is commonly made using fiber or twisted-pair wiring.

- Hybrid: Ethernet uses a physical star layout (cables come from all directions), and the signal travels end-to-end, like a bus route.

Exam Essentials

Describe the major physical topologies in use.   Identify the differences between a physical and logical topology. List the distinguishing features of the star, ring, bus, mesh, and hybrid topologies

Select the appropriate cabling type based on implementation requirements

The *EIA/TIA* (Electronic Industries Alliance and the newer Telecommunications Industry Association) is the standards body that creates the Physical layer specifications for Ethernet. The EIA/TIA specifies that Ethernet use a *registered jack (RJ) connector* on *unshielded twisted-pair (UTP)* cabling (RJ45). But the industry is moving toward simply calling this an 8-pin modular connector.

Every Ethernet cable type that's specified by the EIA/TIA has inherent attenuation, which is defined as the loss of signal strength as it travels the length of a cable and is measured in decibels (dB). The cabling used in corporate and home markets is measured in categories. A higher-quality cable will have a higher-rated category and lower attenuation.

For example, category 5 is better than category 3 because category 5 cables have more wire twists per foot and therefore less crosstalk. Crosstalk is the unwanted signal interference from adjacent pairs in the cable.

Here is a list of some of the most common IEEE Ethernet standards, starting with 10 Mbps Ethernet:

10Base-T (IEEE 802.3)   10 Mbps using category 3 unshielded twisted pair (UTP) wiring for runs up to 100 meters. Unlike with the 10Base-2 and 10Base-5 networks, each device must connect into a hub or switch, and you can have only one host per segment or wire. It uses an RJ45 connector (8-pin modular connector) with a physical star topology and a logical bus.

100Base-TX (IEEE 802.3u)   100Base-TX, most commonly known as Fast Ethernet, uses EIA/TIA category 5, 5E, or 6 UTP two-pair wiring. One user per segment; up to 100 meters long. It uses an RJ45 connector with a physical star topology and a logical bus.

100Base-FX (IEEE 802.3u)   Uses fiber cabling 62.5/125-micron multimode fiber. Point-to-point topology; up to 412 meters long. It uses ST and SC connectors, which are media-interface connectors.

1000Base-CX (IEEE 802.3z)   Copper twisted-pair, called twinax, is a balanced coaxial pair that can run only up to 25 meters and uses a special 9-pin connector known as the High Speed Serial Data Connector (HSSDC). This is used in Cisco's new Data Center technologies.

1000Base-T (IEEE 802.3ab)   Category 5, four-pair UTP wiring up to 100 meters long and up to 1 Gbps

1000Base-SX (IEEE 802.3z)   The implementation of 1 Gigabit Ethernet running over multimode fiber-optic cable instead of copper twisted-pair cable, using short wavelength laser. Multimode fiber (MMF) using 62.5- and 50-micron core; uses an 850 nanometer (nm) laser and can go up to 220 meters with 62.5-micron, 550 meters with 50-micron

1000Base-LX (IEEE 802.3z)   Single-mode fiber that uses a 9-micron core and 1300 nm laser and can go from 3 kilometers up to 10 kilometers

1000Base-ZX (Cisco standard)   1000BaseZX, or 1000Base-ZX, is a Cisco specified standard for Gigabit Ethernet communication. 1000BaseZX operates on ordinary single-mode fiber-optic links with spans up to 43.5 miles (70 km).

10GBase-T (802.3.an)   10GBase-T is a standard proposed by the IEEE 802.3an committee to provide 10 Gbps connections over conventional UTP cables, (category 5e, 6, or 7 cables). 10GBase-T allows the conventional RJ45 used for Ethernet LANs and can support signal transmission at the full 100-meter distance specified for LAN wiring.

A discussion about Ethernet cabling is an important one, especially if you are planning on taking the Cisco exams. You need to really understand the following three types of cables:

- Straight-through cable
- Crossover cable
- Rolled cable

We will look at each in the following sections, but first, let's take a look at the most common Ethernet cable used today, the category 5 Enhanced Unshielded Twisted Pair (UTP), shown in Figure 1.12.

FIGURE 1.12   Category 5 Enhanced UTP cable

The category 5 Enhanced UTP cable can handle speeds up to a gigabit with a distance of up to 100 meters. Typically we'd use this cable for 100 Mbps and category 6 for a gigabit, but the category 5 Enhanced is rated for gigabit speeds and category 6 is rated for 10 Gbps!

Straight-Through Cable

The *straight-through cable* is used to connect the following devices:

- Host to switch or hub
- Router to switch or hub

Four wires are used in a straight-through cable to connect Ethernet devices. It's relatively simple to create this type, and Figure 1.13 shows the four wires used in a straight-through Ethernet cable.

FIGURE 1.13   Straight-through Ethernet cable

Transmit on pins 1 & 2
Receive on pins 3 & 6

Receive on pins 1 & 2
Transmit on pins 3 & 6

Notice that only pins 1, 2, 3, and 6 are used. Just connect 1 to 1, 2 to 2, 3 to 3, and 6 to 6 and you'll be up and networking in no time. However, remember that this would be a 10/100 Mbps Ethernet-only cable and wouldn't work with gigabit, voice, or other LAN or WAN technology.

Crossover Cable

The *crossover cable* can be used to connect the following devices:

- Switch to switch
- Hub to hub
- Host to host
- Hub to switch
- Router direct to host
- Router to router

The same four wires used in the straight-through cable are used in this cable—we just connect different pins together. Figure 1.14 shows how the four wires are used in a cross-over Ethernet cable.

FIGURE 1.14   Crossover Ethernet cable

Receive on pins 1 & 2   Transmit on pins 3 & 6

Notice that instead of connecting 1 to 1, 2 to 2, and so on, here we connect pins 1 to 3 and 2 to 6 on each side of the cable. Figure 1.15 shows some typical uses of straight-through and crossover cables.

FIGURE 1.15   Typical uses for straight-through and cross-over Ethernet cables

The crossover examples in Figure 1.15 are switch port to switch port, router Ethernet port to router Ethernet port, and router Ethernet port to PC Ethernet port. For the straight-through examples I used PC Ethernet to switch port and router Ethernet port to switch port.

It's very possible to connect a straight-through cable between two switches, and it will start working because of autodetect mechanisms called auto-mdix. But be advised that the CCNA objectives do not typically consider autodetect mechanisms valid between devices!

UTP Gigabit Wiring (1000Base-T)

In the previous examples of 10Base-T and 100Base-T UTP wiring, only two wire pairs were used, but that is not good enough for Gigabit UTP transmission.

1000Base-T UTP wiring (Figure 1.16) requires four wire pairs and uses more advanced electronics so that each and every pair in the cable can transmit simultaneously. Even so, gigabit wiring is almost identical to my earlier 10/100 example, except that we'll use the other two pairs in the cable.

FIGURE 1.16   UTP Gigabit crossover Ethernet cable

For a straight-through cable it's still 1 to 1, 2 to 2, and so on up to pin 8. And in creating the gigabit crossover cable, you'd still cross 1 to 3 and 2 to 6, but you would add 4 to 7 and 5 to 8—pretty straightforward!

Rolled Cable

Although *rolled cable* isn't used to connect any Ethernet connections together, you can use a rolled Ethernet cable to connect a host EIA-TIA 232 interface to a router console serial communication (COM) port.

If you have a Cisco router or switch, you would use this cable to connect your PC, Mac, or a device like an iPad to the Cisco hardware. Eight wires are used in this cable to connect serial devices, although not all eight are used to send information, just as in Ethernet networking. Figure 1.17 shows the eight wires used in a rolled cable.

FIGURE 1.17 Rolled Ethernet cable

These are probably the easiest cables to make because you just cut the end off on one side of a straight-through cable, turn it over, and put it back on—with a new connector, of course!

Okay, once you have the correct cable connected from your PC to the Cisco router or switch console port, you can start your emulation program such as putty or SecureCRT to create a console connection and configure the device. Set the configuration as shown in Figure 1.18.

FIGURE 1.18 Configuring your console emulation program

Notice that Baud Rate is set to 9600, Data Bits to 8, Parity to None, and no Flow Control options are set. At this point, you can click Connect and press the Enter key and you should be connected to your Cisco device console port.

Figure 1.19 shows a nice new 2960 switch with two console ports.

FIGURE 1.19   A Cisco 2960 console connections

Notice there are two console connections on this new switch—a typical original RJ45 connection and the newer mini type-B USB console. Remember that the new USB port supersedes the RJ45 port if you just happen to plug into both at the same time, and the USB port can have speeds up to 115,200 Kbps, which is awesome if you have to use Xmodem to update a Cisco Internal Operating System (IOS). I've even seen some cables that work on iPhones and iPads and allow them to connect to these mini USB ports!

Now that you've seen the various RJ45 unshielded twisted-pair (UTP) cables, what type of cable is used between the switches in Figure 1.20?

FIGURE 1.20   RJ45 UTP cable question #1

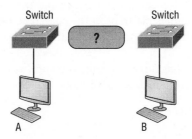

In order for host A to ping host B, you need a crossover cable to connect the two switches together. But what types of cables are used in the network shown in Figure 1.21?

In Figure 1.21, there's a whole menu of cables in use. For the connection between the switches, we'd obviously use a crossover cable like we saw in Figure 1.14. The trouble is that you must understand that we have a console connection that uses a rolled cable. Plus, the connection from the router to the switch is a straight-through cable, as is true for the hosts to the switches. Keep in mind that if we had a serial connection, which we don't, we would use a V.35 to connect us to a WAN.

FIGURE 1.21   RJ45 UTP cable question #2

Fiber Optic

Fiber-optic cabling has been around for a long time and has some solid standards. The cable allows for very fast transmission of data, is made of glass (or even plastic!), is very thin, and works as a waveguide to transmit light between two ends of the fiber. Fiber optics has been used to go very long distances, as in intercontinental connections, but it is becoming more and more popular in Ethernet LAN networks due to the fast speeds available and because, unlike UTP, it's immune to interference like crosstalk.

Some main components of this cable are the core and the cladding. The core will hold the light and the cladding confines the light in the core. The tighter the cladding, the smaller the core, and when the core is small, less light will be sent, but it can go faster and farther!

In Figure 1.22 you can see that there is a 9-micron core, which is very small and can be measured against a human hair, which is 50 microns.

FIGURE 1.22   Typical fiber cable

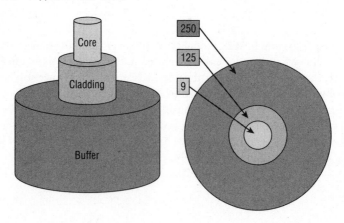

Dimensions are in um (10^{-6} meters). Not to scale.

The cladding is 125 microns, which is actually a fiber standard that allows manufacturers to make connectors for all fiber cables. The last piece of this cable is the buffer, which is there to protect the delicate glass.

There are two major types of fiber optics: single-mode and multimode. Figure 1.23 shows the differences between multimode and single-mode fibers.

FIGURE 1.23   Multimode and single-mode fibers

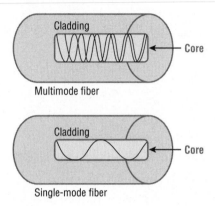

Single-mode is more expensive, has a tighter cladding, and can go much farther distances than multimode. The difference comes in the tightness of the cladding, which makes a smaller core, meaning that only one mode of light will propagate down the fiber. Multimode is looser and has a larger core so it allows multiple light particles to travel down the glass. These particles have to be put back together at the receiving end, so distance is less than that with single-mode fiber, which allows only very few light particles to travel down the fiber.

There are about 70 different connectors for fiber, and Cisco uses a few different types. Looking back at Figure 1.19, the two bottom ports are referred to as Small Form-Factor Pluggables, or SFPs.

Exam Essentials

Identify the major Ethernet cable types.   Describe Ethernet cable types, their limitations, connectors, and application.

Apply cable types to the proper scenario.   This includes straight through, crossover, and rollover cables.

Identify the major Fiber cable types.   Describe Fiber cable types, their limitations, connectors, and application.

Apply troubleshooting methodologies to resolve problems

When attempting to troubleshoot, any issue following a troubleshooting process developed over years by experienced technicians can speed the solution of the issue. The Cisco troubleshooting methodology uses the following steps:

- Define the problem.
- Gather information.
- Analyze information.
- Eliminate potential causes.
- Propose hypothesis.
- Test hypothesis.
- Solve problem and document solution.

    In the process of working this list, issues can be approached in three ways:

- **Top-down method:** Start at the top of the OSI model.
- **Bottom-up method:** Start at the bottom of the OSI model.
- **Divide and conquer:** Start in the middle of the OSI model.

    As you identify individual issues you can use the following methods to track down the source:

- Perform comparison method: Compare the configuration of the device with an issue with a like device that is functioning properly.
- Follow the path method: Trace the path of the problematic communication, checking each device in the path as you go.
- Swap components method: Replace components with like components to see if the issue follows the component.

Exam Essentials

List the steps in the Cisco troubleshooting methodology.   Know the 7 steps in this process.

Identify potential approaches to solving issues.   These include top-down, bottom-up, and divide and conquer.

Describe methods to locate communication issues.   These include follow the path, swap components, and perform comparison methods.

Configure, verify, and troubleshoot IPv4 addressing and subnetting

It is critical to be able to configure IP addresses on devices in such a way that those devices that should be in the same network are in the same network. This requires a complete understanding of IP addressing and subnetting. That will be the topic of this section.

The Hierarchical IP Addressing Scheme

An IP address consists of 32 bits of information. These bits are divided into four sections, referred to as octets or bytes, with each containing 1 byte (8 bits). You can depict an IP address using one of three methods:

- Dotted-decimal, as in 172.16.30.56

- Binary, as in 10101100.00010000.00011110.00111000

- Hexadecimal, as in AC.10.1E.38

All these examples represent the same IP address. Pertaining to IP addressing, hexadecimal isn't used as often as dotted-decimal or binary, but you still might find an IP address stored in hexadecimal in some programs.

The 32-bit IP address is a structured or hierarchical address, as opposed to a flat or nonhierarchical address. Although either type of addressing scheme could have been used, *hierarchical addressing* was chosen for a good reason. The advantage of this scheme is that it can handle a large number of addresses, namely 4.3 billion (a 32-bit address space with two possible values for each position—either 0 or 1—gives you 2^{32}, or 4,294,967,296). The disadvantage of the flat addressing scheme, and the reason it's not used for IP addressing, relates to routing. If every address were unique, all routers on the Internet would need to store the address of each and every machine on the Internet. This would make efficient routing impossible, even if only a fraction of the possible addresses were used!

The solution to this problem is to use a two- or three-level hierarchical addressing scheme that is structured by network and host or by network, subnet, and host.

This two- or three-level scheme can also be compared to a telephone number. The first section, the area code, designates a very large area. The second section, the prefix, narrows the scope to a local calling area. The final segment, the customer number, zooms in on the specific connection. IP addresses use the same type of layered structure. Rather than all 32 bits being treated as a unique identifier, as in flat addressing, a part of the address is designated as the network address and the other part is designated as either the subnet and host or just the node address.

Next, we'll cover IP network addressing and the different classes of address we can use to address our networks.

Network Addressing

The *network address* (which can also be called the network number) uniquely identifies each network. Every machine on the same network shares that network address as part of its IP address. For example, in the IP address 172.16.30.56, 172.16 is the network address.

The *node address* is assigned to, and uniquely identifies, each machine on a network. This part of the address must be unique because it identifies a particular machine—an individual—as opposed to a network, which is a group. This number can also be referred to as a *host address*. In the sample IP address 172.16.30.56, the 30.56 specifies the node address.

The designers of the Internet decided to create classes of networks based on network size. For the small number of networks possessing a very large number of nodes, they created the rank *Class A network*. At the other extreme is the *Class C network*, which is reserved for the numerous networks with a small number of nodes. The class distinction for networks between very large and very small is predictably called the *Class B network*.

Subdividing an IP address into a network and node address is determined by the class designation of one's network. Figure 1.24 summarizes the three classes of networks used to address hosts—a subject I'll explain in much greater detail throughout this chapter.

FIGURE 1.24   Summary of the three classes of networks

	8 bits	8 bits	8 bits	8 bits
Class A:	Network	Host	Host	Host
Class B:	Network	Network	Host	Host
Class C:	Network	Network	Network	Host
Class D:	Multicast			
Class E:	Research			

To ensure efficient routing, Internet designers defined a mandate for the leading-bits section of the address for each different network class. For example, since a router knows that a Class A network address always starts with a 0, the router might be able to speed a packet on its way after reading only the first bit of its address. This is where the address schemes define the difference between a Class A, a Class B, and a Class C address. Coming up, I'll discuss the differences between these three classes, followed by a discussion of the Class D and Class E addresses. Classes A, B, and C are the only ranges that are used to address hosts in our networks.

Network Address Range: Class A

The designers of the IP address scheme decided that the first bit of the first byte in a Class A network address must always be off, or 0. This means a Class A address must be between 0 and 127 in the first byte, inclusive.

Consider the following network address:

`0xxxxxxx`

If we turn the other 7 bits all off and then turn them all on, we'll find the Class A range of network addresses:

`00000000 = 0`
`01111111 = 127`

So, a Class A network is defined in the first octet between 0 and 127, and it can't be less or more. Understand that 0 and 127 are not valid in a Class A network because they're reserved addresses, which I'll explain soon.

Network Address Range: Class B

In a Class B network, the RFCs state that the first bit of the first byte must always be turned on but the second bit must always be turned off. If you turn the other 6 bits all off and then all on, you will find the range for a Class B network:

`10000000 = 128`
`10111111 = 191`

As you can see, a Class B network is defined when the first byte is configured from 128 to 191.

Network Address Range: Class C

For Class C networks, the RFCs define the first 2 bits of the first octet as always turned on, but the third bit can never be on. Following the same process as the previous classes, convert from binary to decimal to find the range. Here's the range for a Class C network:

`11000000 = 192`
`11011111 = 223`

So, if you see an IP address that starts at 192 and goes to 223, you'll know it is a Class C IP address.

Network Address Ranges: Classes D and E

The addresses between 224 to 255 are reserved for Class D and E networks. Class D (224–239) is used for multicast addresses and Class E (240–255) for scientific purposes, but I'm not going into these types of addresses because they are beyond the scope of knowledge you need to gain from this book.

Network Addresses: Special Purpose

Some IP addresses are reserved for special purposes, so network administrators can't ever assign these addresses to nodes. Table 1.2 lists the members of this exclusive little club and the reasons why they're included in it.

TABLE 1.2   Reserved IP addresses

Address	Function
Network address of all 0s	Interpreted to mean "this network or segment"
Network address of all 1s	Interpreted to mean "all networks"
Network 127.0.0.1	Reserved for loopback tests. Designates the local node and allows that node to send a test packet to itself without generating network traffic
Node address of all 0s	Interpreted to mean "network address" or any host on a specified network
Node address of all 1s	Interpreted to mean "all nodes" on the specified network; for example, 128.2.255.255 means "all nodes" on network 128.2 (Class B address)
Entire IP address set to all 0s	Used by Cisco routers to designate the default route. Could also mean "any network"
Entire IP address set to all 1s (same as 255.255.255.255)	Broadcast to all nodes on the current network; sometimes called an "all 1s broadcast" or local broadcast

Class A Addresses

In a Class A network address, the first byte is assigned to the network address and the three remaining bytes are used for the node addresses. The Class A format is as follows:

`network.node.node.node`

For example, in the IP address 49.22.102.70, the 49 is the network address and 22.102.70 is the node address. Every machine on this particular network would have the distinctive network address of 49.

Class A network addresses are 1 byte long, with the first bit of that byte reserved and the 7 remaining bits available for manipulation (addressing). As a result, the maximum number of Class A networks that can be created is 128. Why? Because each of the 7 bit positions can be either a 0 or a 1, thus 2^7, or 128.

To complicate matters further, the network address of all 0s (0000 0000) is reserved to designate the default route (see Table 1.2 in the previous section). Additionally, the address 127, which is reserved for diagnostics, can't be used either, which means that you can really only use the numbers 1 to 126 to designate Class A network addresses. This means the actual number of usable Class A network addresses is 128 minus 2, or 126.

The IP address 127.0.0.1 is used to test the IP stack on an individual node and cannot be used as a valid host address. However, the loopback address creates a shortcut method for TCP/IP applications and services that run on the same device to communicate with each other.

Each Class A address has 3 bytes (24-bit positions) for the node address of a machine. This means there are 2^{24}—or 16,777,216—unique combinations and, therefore, precisely that many possible unique node addresses for each Class A network. Because node addresses with the two patterns of all 0s and all 1s are reserved, the actual maximum usable number of nodes for a Class A network is 2^{24} minus 2, which equals 16,777,214. Either way, that's a huge number of hosts on a single network segment!

Class A Valid Host IDs

Here's an example of how to figure out the valid host IDs in a Class A network address:

- All host bits off is the network address: 10.0.0.0.
- All host bits on is the broadcast address: 10.255.255.255.

The valid hosts are the numbers in between the network address and the broadcast address: 10.0.0.1 through 10.255.255.254. Notice that 0s and 255s can be valid host IDs. All you need to remember when trying to find valid host addresses is that the host bits can't all be turned off or on at the same time.

Class B Addresses

In a Class B network address, the first 2 bytes are assigned to the network address and the remaining 2 bytes are used for node addresses. The format is as follows:

network.network.node.node

For example, in the IP address 172.16.30.56, the network address is 172.16 and the node address is 30.56.

With a network address being 2 bytes (8 bits each), you get 2^{16} unique combinations. But the Internet designers decided that all Class B network addresses should start with the binary digit 1, then 0. This leaves 14 bit positions to manipulate, therefore 16,384, or 2^{14} unique Class B network addresses.

A Class B address uses 2 bytes for node addresses. This is 2^{16} minus the two reserved patterns of all 0s and all 1s for a total of 65,534 possible node addresses for each Class B network.

Class B Valid Host IDs

Here's an example of how to find the valid hosts in a Class B network:

- All host bits turned off is the network address: 172.16.0.0.
- All host bits turned on is the broadcast address: 172.16.255.255.

The valid hosts would be the numbers in between the network address and the broadcast address: 172.16.0.1 through 172.16.255.254.

Class C Addresses

The first 3 bytes of a Class C network address are dedicated to the network portion of the address, with only 1 measly byte remaining for the node address. Here's the format:

> network.network.network.node

Using the example IP address 192.168.100.102, the network address is 192.168.100 and the node address is 102.

In a Class C network address, the first three bit positions are always the binary 110. The calculation is as follows: 3 bytes, or 24 bits, minus 3 reserved positions leaves 21 positions. Hence, there are 2^{21}, or 2,097,152, possible Class C networks.

Each unique Class C network has 1 byte to use for node addresses. This leads to 2^8, or 256, minus the two reserved patterns of all 0s and all 1s, for a total of 254 node addresses for each Class C network.

Class C Valid Host IDs

Here's an example of how to find a valid host ID in a Class C network:

- All host bits turned off is the network ID: 192.168.100.0.
- All host bits turned on is the broadcast address: 192.168.100.255.

The valid hosts would be the numbers in between the network address and the broadcast address: 192.168.100.1 through 192.168.100.254.

Troubleshooting IPv4 Addressing and Subnetting

Because running into trouble now and then in networking is a given, being able to troubleshoot IP addressing is clearly a vital skill. I'm not being negative here—just realistic. The positive side to this is that if you're the one equipped with the tools to diagnose and clear up the inevitable trouble, you get to be the hero when you save the day! Even better? You can usually fix an IP network regardless of whether you're on site or at home!

So this is where I'm going to show you the "Cisco way" of troubleshooting IP addressing. Let's use Figure 1.25 as an example of your basic IP trouble—poor Sally can't log in to the Windows server. Do you deal with this by calling the Microsoft team to tell them their server is a pile of junk and causing all your problems? Though tempting, a better approach is to first double-check and verify your network instead.

FIGURE 1.25   Basic IP troubleshooting

E0
172.16.10.1

Sally
172.16.10.2

Server
172.16.20.2

Okay, let's get started by going through the troubleshooting steps that Cisco recommends. They're pretty simple, but important nonetheless. Pretend you're at a customer host and they're complaining that they can't communicate to a server that just happens to be on a remote network. Here are the four troubleshooting steps Cisco recommends:

1. Open a Command window and ping 127.0.0.1. This is the diagnostic, or loopback, address, and if you get a successful ping, your IP stack is considered initialized. If it fails, then you have an IP stack failure and need to reinstall TCP/IP on the host.

    ```
    C:\>ping 127.0.0.1
    Pinging 127.0.0.1 with 32 bytes of data:
    Reply from 127.0.0.1: bytes=32 time<1ms TTL=128
    Reply from 127.0.0.1: bytes=32 time<1ms TTL=128
    Reply from 127.0.0.1: bytes=32 time<1ms TTL=128
    Reply from 127.0.0.1: bytes=32 time<1ms TTL=128
    Ping statistics for 127.0.0.1:
        Packets: Sent = 4, Received = 4, Lost = 0 (0% loss),
    Approximate round trip times in milli-seconds:
        Minimum = 0ms, Maximum = 0ms, Average = 0ms
    ```

2. From the Command window, ping the IP address of the local host (we'll assume correct configuration here, but always check the IP configuration too!). If that's successful, your network interface card (NIC) is functioning. If it fails, there is a problem with the NIC. Success here doesn't just mean that a cable is plugged into the NIC, only that the IP protocol stack on the host can communicate to the NIC via the LAN driver.

    ```
    C:\>ping 172.16.10.2
    Pinging 172.16.10.2 with 32 bytes of data:
    Reply from 172.16.10.2: bytes=32 time<1ms TTL=128
    Reply from 172.16.10.2: bytes=32 time<1ms TTL=128
    ```

```
Reply from 172.16.10.2: bytes=32 time<1ms TTL=128
Reply from 172.16.10.2: bytes=32 time<1ms TTL=128
Ping statistics for 172.16.10.2:
    Packets: Sent = 4, Received = 4, Lost = 0 (0% loss),
Approximate round trip times in milli-seconds:
    Minimum = 0ms, Maximum = 0ms, Average = 0ms
```

3. From the Command window, ping the default gateway (router). If the ping works, it means that the NIC is plugged into the network and can communicate on the local network. If it fails, you have a local physical network problem that could be anywhere from the NIC to the router.

```
C:\>ping 172.16.10.1
Pinging 172.16.10.1 with 32 bytes of data:
Reply from 172.16.10.1: bytes=32 time<1ms TTL=128
Reply from 172.16.10.1: bytes=32 time<1ms TTL=128
Reply from 172.16.10.1: bytes=32 time<1ms TTL=128
Reply from 172.16.10.1: bytes=32 time<1ms TTL=128
Ping statistics for 172.16.10.1:
    Packets: Sent = 4, Received = 4, Lost = 0 (0% loss),
Approximate round trip times in milli-seconds:
    Minimum = 0ms, Maximum = 0ms, Average = 0ms
```

4. If steps 1 through 3 were successful, try to ping the remote server. If that works, then you know that you have IP communication between the local host and the remote server. You also know that the remote physical network is working.

```
C:\>ping 172.16.20.2
Pinging 172.16.20.2 with 32 bytes of data:
Reply from 172.16.20.2: bytes=32 time<1ms TTL=128
Reply from 172.16.20.2: bytes=32 time<1ms TTL=128
Reply from 172.16.20.2: bytes=32 time<1ms TTL=128
Reply from 172.16.20.2: bytes=32 time<1ms TTL=128
Ping statistics for 172.16.20.2:
    Packets: Sent = 4, Received = 4, Lost = 0 (0% loss),
Approximate round trip times in milli-seconds:
    Minimum = 0ms, Maximum = 0ms, Average = 0ms
```

If the user still can't communicate with the server after steps 1 through 4 have been completed successfully, you probably have some type of name resolution problem and need to check your Domain Name System (DNS) settings. But if the ping to the remote server fails, then you know you have some type of remote physical network problem and need to go to the server and work through steps 1 through 3 until you find the snag.

Before we move on to determining IP address problems and how to fix them, I just want to mention some basic commands that you can use to help troubleshoot your network from both a PC and a Cisco router. Keep in mind that though these commands may do the same thing, they're implemented differently.

ping   Uses ICMP echo request and replies to test if a node IP stack is initialized and alive on the network

traceroute   Displays the list of routers on a path to a network destination by using TTL time-outs and ICMP error messages. This command will not work from a command prompt.

tracert   Same function as traceroute, but it's a Microsoft Windows command and will not work on a Cisco router

arp -a   Displays IP-to-MAC-address mappings on a Windows PC

show ip arp   Same function as arp -a, but displays the ARP table on a Cisco router. Like the commands traceroute and tracert, arp -a and show ip arp are not interchangeable through DOS and Cisco.

ipconfig /all   Used only from a Windows command prompt; shows you the PC network configuration

Once you've gone through all these steps and, if necessary, used the appropriate commands, what do you do when you find a problem? How do you go about fixing an IP address configuration error? Time to cover the next step—determining and fixing the issue at hand!

Determining IP Address Problems

It's common for a host, router, or other network device to be configured with the wrong IP address, subnet mask, or default gateway. Because this happens way too often, you must know how to find and fix IP address configuration errors.

A good way to start is to draw out the network and IP addressing scheme. If that's already been done, consider yourself lucky because though sensible, it's rarely done. Even if it is, it's usually outdated or inaccurate anyway. So either way, it's a good idea to bite the bullet and start from scratch.

Once you have your network accurately drawn out, including the IP addressing scheme, you need to verify each host's IP address, mask, and default gateway address to establish the problem. Of course, this is assuming that you don't have a physical layer problem, or if you did, that you've already fixed it.

Let's check out the example illustrated in Figure 1.26.

FIGURE 1.26   IP address problem 1

A user in the sales department calls and tells you that she can't get to ServerA in the marketing department. You ask her if she can get to ServerB in the marketing department, but she doesn't know because she doesn't have rights to log on to that server. What do you do?

First, guide your user through the four troubleshooting steps you learned in the preceding section. Okay—let's say steps 1 through 3 work but step 4 fails. By looking at the figure, can you determine the problem? Look for clues in the network drawing. First, the WAN link between the Lab A router and the Lab B router shows the mask as a /27. You should already know that this mask is 255.255.255.224 and determine that all networks are using this mask. The network address is 192.168.1.0. What are our valid subnets and hosts? 256 − 224 = 32, so this makes our subnets 0, 32, 64, 96, 128, etc. So, by looking at the figure, you can see that subnet 32 is being used by the sales department. The WAN link is using subnet 96, and the marketing department is using subnet 64.

Now you've got to establish what the valid host ranges are for each subnet. From what you learned at the beginning of this chapter, you should now be able to easily determine the subnet address, broadcast addresses, and valid host ranges. The valid hosts for the Sales LAN are 33 through 62, and the broadcast address is 63 because the next subnet is 64, right? For the Marketing LAN, the valid hosts are 65 through 94 (broadcast 95), and for the WAN link, 97 through 126 (broadcast 127). By closely examining the figure, you can determine that the default gateway on the Lab B router is incorrect. That address is the broadcast address for subnet 64, so there's no way it could be a valid host!

 If you tried to configure that address on the Lab B router interface, you'd receive a bad mask error. Cisco routers don't let you type in subnet and broadcast addresses as valid hosts!

Did you get all that? Let's try another one to make sure. Figure 1.27 shows a network problem.

FIGURE 1.27   IP address problem 2

A user in the Sales LAN can't get to ServerB. You have the user run through the four basic troubleshooting steps and find that the host can communicate to the local network but not to the remote network. Find and define the IP addressing problem.

If you went through the same steps used to solve the last problem, you can see that first, the WAN link again provides the subnet mask to use— /29, or 255.255.255.248. Assuming classful addressing, you need to determine what the valid subnets, broadcast addresses, and valid host ranges are to solve this problem.

The 248 mask is a block size of 8 (256 – 248 = 8, as discussed in Chapter 4), so the subnets both start and increment in multiples of 8. By looking at the figure, you see that the Sales LAN is in the 24 subnet, the WAN is in the 40 subnet, and the Marketing LAN is in the 80 subnet. Can you see the problem yet? The valid host range for the Sales LAN is 25–30, and the configuration appears correct. The valid host range for the WAN link is 41–46, and this also appears correct. The valid host range for the 80 subnet is 81–86, with a broadcast address of 87 because the next subnet is 88. ServerB has been configured with the broadcast address of the subnet.

Okay, now that you can figure out misconfigured IP addresses on hosts, what do you do if a host doesn't have an IP address and you need to assign one? What you need to do is scrutinize the other hosts on the LAN and figure out the network, mask, and default gateway. Let's take a look at a couple of examples of how to find and apply valid IP addresses to hosts.

You need to assign a server and router IP addresses on a LAN. The subnet assigned on that segment is 192.168.20.24/29. The router needs to be assigned the first usable address and the server needs the last valid host ID. What is the IP address, mask, and default gateway assigned to the server?

To answer this, you must know that a /29 is a 255.255.255.248 mask, which provides a block size of 8. The subnet is known as 24, the next subnet in a block of 8 is 32, so the broadcast address of the 24 subnet is 31 and the valid host range is 25–30.

Server IP address: 192.168.20.30

Server mask: 255.255.255.248

Default gateway: 192.168.20.25 (router's IP address)

Take a look at Figure 1.28 and solve this problem.

FIGURE 1.28   Find the valid host #1.

Router A

E0: 192.168.10.33/27

Look at the router's IP address on Ethernet0. What IP address, subnet mask, and valid host range could be assigned to the host?

The IP address of the router's Ethernet0 is 192.168.10.33/27. As you already know, a /27 is a 224 mask with a block size of 32. The router's interface is in the 32 subnet. The next subnet is 64, so that makes the broadcast address of the 32 subnet 63 and the valid host range 33–62.

Host IP address: 192.168.10.34–62 (any address in the range except for 33, which is assigned to the router)

Mask: 255.255.255.224

Default gateway: 192.168.10.33

Figure 1.29 shows two routers with Ethernet configurations already assigned. What are the host addresses and subnet masks of HostA and HostB?

FIGURE 1.29   Find the valid host #2.

Router A   Router B

E0: 192.168.10.65/26   E0: 192.168.10.33/28

HostA   HostB

Router A has an IP address of 192.168.10.65/26 and Router B has an IP address of 192.168.10.33/28. What are the host configurations? Router A Ethernet0 is in the 192.168.10.64 subnet and Router B Ethernet0 is in the 192.168.10.32 network.

Host A IP address: 192.168.10.66–126

Host A mask: 255.255.255.192

Host A default gateway: 192.168.10.65

Host B IP address: 192.168.10.34–46

Host B mask: 255.255.255.240

Host B default gateway: 192.168.10.33

Just a couple more examples before you can put this chapter behind you—hang in there!

Figure 1.30 shows two routers. You need to configure the S0/0 interface on RouterA. The network assigned to the serial link is 172.16.17.0/22. What IP address can be assigned?

FIGURE 1.30 Find the valid host address #3.

First, know that a /22 CIDR is 255.255.252.0, which makes a block size of 4 in the third octet. Since 17 is listed, the available range is 16.1 through 19.254, so in this example, the IP address S0/0 could be 172.16.18.255 since that's within the range.

Okay, last one! You need to find a classful network address that has one Class C network ID and you need to provide one usable subnet per city while allowing enough usable host addresses for each city specified in Figure 1.31. What is your mask?

FIGURE 1.31 Find the valid subnet mask.

Actually, this is probably the easiest thing you've done all day! I count 5 subnets needed, and the Wyoming office needs 16 users—always look for the network that needs the most hosts! What block size is needed for the Wyoming office? Your answer is 32. You can't use a block size of 16 because you always have to subtract 2. What mask provides you with a block size of 32? 224 is your answer because this provides 8 subnets, each with 30 hosts.

Exam Essentials

Define the Class A IP address range.   The IP range for a Class A network is 1–126. This provides 8 bits of network addressing and 24 bits of host addressing by default.

Define the Class B IP address range.   The IP range for a Class B network is 128–191. Class B addressing provides 16 bits of network addressing and 16 bits of host addressing by default.

Define the Class C IP address range.   The IP range for a Class C network is 192 through 223. Class C addressing provides 24 bits of network addressing and 8 bits of host addressing by default.

Remember the four diagnostic steps.   The four simple steps that Cisco recommends for troubleshooting are ping the loopback address, ping the NIC, ping the default gateway, and ping the remote device.

Identify and mitigate an IP addressing problem.   Once you go through the four troubleshooting steps that Cisco recommends, you must be able to determine the IP addressing problem by drawing out the network and finding the valid and invalid hosts addressed in your network.

Understand the troubleshooting tools that you can use from your host and a Cisco router.   The `ping 127.0.0.1` command tests your local IP stack, and `tracert` is a Windows command to track the path a packet takes through an internetwork to a destination. Cisco routers use the command `traceroute`, or just `trace` for short. Don't confuse the Windows and Cisco commands. Although they produce the same output, they don't work from the same prompts. The command `ipconfig /all` will display your PC network configuration from a DOS prompt, and `arp -a` (again from a DOS prompt) will display IP-to-MAC-address mapping on a Windows PC.

Compare and contrast IPv4 address types

There are a number of different IPv4 address types with which you must be familiar for the exam. Included in these are the following:

Loopback (localhost)   Used to test the IP stack on the local computer. Can be any address from 127.0.0.1 through 127.255.255.254.

Layer 2 broadcasts   These are sent to all nodes on a LAN.

Broadcasts (layer 3)   These are sent to all nodes on the network.

Unicast   This is an address for a single interface, and these are used to send packets to a single destination host.

Multicast   These are packets sent from a single source and transmitted to many devices on different networks. Referred to as "one-to-many."

Layer 2 Broadcasts

First, understand that layer 2 broadcasts are also known as hardware broadcasts—they only go out on a LAN, but they don't go past the LAN boundary (router).

The typical hardware address is 6 bytes (48 bits) and looks something like 45:AC:24:E3:60:A5. The broadcast would be all 1s in binary, which would be all *F*s in hexadecimal, as in ff:ff:ff:ff:ff:ff and shown in Figure 1.32.

FIGURE 1.32   Local layer 2 broadcasts

Every network interface card (NIC) will receive and read the frame, including the router, since this was a layer 2 broadcast, but the router would never, ever forward this!

Layer 3 Broadcasts

Then there are the plain old broadcast addresses at layer 3. Broadcast messages are meant to reach all hosts on a broadcast domain. These are the network broadcasts that have all host bits on.

Here's an example that you're already familiar with: The network address of 172.16.0.0 255.255.0.0 would have a broadcast address of 172.16.255.255—all host bits on. Broadcasts can also be "any network and all hosts," as indicated by 255.255.255.255, and shown in Figure 1.33.

FIGURE 1.33   Layer 3 broadcasts

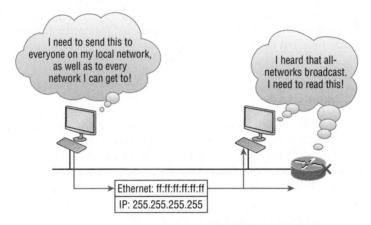

In Figure 1.33, all hosts on the LAN will get this broadcast on their NIC, including the router, but by default the router would never forward this packet.

Unicast Address

A unicast is defined as a single IP address that's assigned to a network interface card and is the destination IP address in a packet—in other words, it's used for directing packets to a specific host.

In Figure 1.34, both the MAC address and the destination IP address are for a single NIC on the network. All hosts on the broadcast domain would receive this frame and accept it. Only the destination NIC of 10.1.1.2 would accept the packet; the other NICs would discard the packet.

FIGURE 1.34   Unicast address

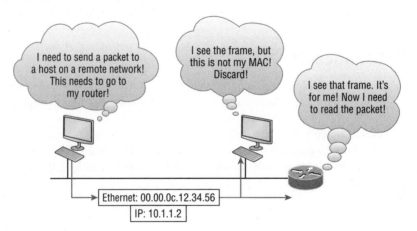

Multicast Address

Multicast is a different beast entirely. At first glance, it appears to be a hybrid of unicast and broadcast communication, but that isn't quite the case. Multicast does allow point-to-multipoint communication, which is similar to broadcasts, but it happens in a different manner. The crux of *multicast* is that it enables multiple recipients to receive messages without flooding the messages to all hosts on a broadcast domain. However, this is not the default behavior—it's what we *can* do with multicasting if it's configured correctly!

Multicast works by sending messages or data to IP *multicast group* addresses. Unlike with broadcasts, which aren't forwarded, routers then forward copies of the packet out to every interface that has hosts *subscribed* to that group address. This is where multicast differs from broadcast messages—with multicast communication, copies of packets, in theory, are sent only to subscribed hosts. For example, when I say in theory, I mean that the hosts will receive a multicast packet destined for 224.0.0.10. This is an EIGRP packet, and only a router running the EIGRP protocol will read these. All hosts on the broadcast LAN, and Ethernet is a broadcast multi-access LAN technology, will pick up the frame, read the destination address, then immediately discard the frame unless they're in the multicast group. This saves PC processing, not LAN bandwidth. Be warned though—multicasting can cause some serious LAN congestion if it's not implemented carefully! Figure 1.35 shows a Cisco router sending an EIGRP multicast packet on the local LAN and only the other Cisco router will accept and read this packet.

FIGURE 1.35   EIGRP multicast example

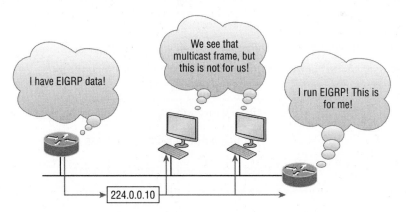

There are several different groups that users or applications can subscribe to. The range of multicast addresses starts with 224.0.0.0 and goes through 239.255.255.255. As you can see, this range of addresses falls within IP Class D address space based on classful IP assignment.

Exam Essentials

Understand the difference between a broadcast, unicast, and multicast address.   A broadcast is to all devices in a subnet, a unicast is to one device, and a multicast is to some but not all devices.

Describe the need for private IPv4 addressing

The people who created the IP addressing scheme also created private IP addresses. These addresses can be used on a private network, but they're not routable through the Internet. This is designed for the purpose of creating a measure of well-needed security, but it also conveniently saves valuable IP address space.

If every host on every network was required to have real routable IP addresses, we would have run out of IP addresses to hand out years ago. But by using private IP addresses, ISPs, corporations, and home users only need a relatively tiny group of bona fide IP addresses to connect their networks to the Internet. This is economical because they can use private IP addresses on their inside networks and get along just fine.

To accomplish this task, the ISP and the corporation—the end user, no matter who they are—need to use something called *Network Address Translation (NAT)*, which basically takes a private IP address and converts it for use on the Internet. Many people can use the same real IP address to transmit out onto the Internet. Doing things this way saves megatons of address space—good for us all!

The reserved private addresses are listed in Table 1.3.

TABLE 1.3   Reserved IP address space

Address Class	Reserved Address Space
Class A	10.0.0.0 through 10.255.255.255
Class B	172.16.0.0 through 172.31.255.255
Class C	192.168.0.0 through 192.168.255.255

Exam Essentials

Identify the private IP ranges.   The Class A private address range is 10.0.0.0 through 10.255.255.255. The Class B private address range is 172.16.0.0 through 172.31.255.255. The Class C private address range is 192.168.0.0 through 192.168.255.255.

Identify the appropriate IPv6 addressing scheme to satisfy addressing requirements in a LAN/WAN environment

There are a number of different approaches to applying an IPv6 address in the network. In this section we'll identify those methods and their characteristics.

Manual Address Assignment

In order to enable IPv6 on a router, you have to use the `ipv6 unicast-routing` global configuration command:

```
Corp(config)#ipv6 unicast-routing
```

By default, IPv6 traffic forwarding is disabled, so using this command enables it. Also, as you've probably guessed, IPv6 isn't enabled by default on any interfaces either, so we have to go to each interface individually and enable it.

There are a few different ways to do this, but a really easy way is to just add an address to the interface. You use the interface configuration command `ipv6 address <ipv6prefix>/<prefix-length>` `[eui-64]`to get this done.

Here's an example:

```
Corp(config-if)#ipv6 address 2001:db8:3c4d:1:0260:d6FF.FE73:1987/64
```

You can specify the entire 128-bit global IPv6 address as I just demonstrated with the preceding command, or you can use the EUI-64 option. Remember, the EUI-64 (extended unique identifier) format allows the device to use its MAC address and pad it to make the interface ID. Check it out:

```
Corp(config-if)#ipv6 address 2001:db8:3c4d:1::/64 eui-64
```

As an alternative to typing in an IPv6 address on a router, you can enable the interface instead to permit the application of an automatic link-local address.

To configure a router so that it uses only link-local addresses, use the `ipv6 enable` interface configuration command:

```
Corp(config-if)#ipv6 enable
```

Remember, if you have only a link-local address, you will be able to communicate only on that local subnet.

Stateless Autoconfiguration (EUI-64)

Autoconfiguration is an especially useful solution because it allows devices on a network to address themselves with a link-local unicast address as well as with a global unicast address. This process happens through first learning the prefix information from the router and then appending the device's own interface address as the interface ID. But where does it get that interface ID? Well, you know every device on an Ethernet network has a physical MAC address, which is exactly what's used for the interface ID. But since the interface ID in an IPv6 address is 64 bits in length and a MAC address is only 48 bits, where do the extra 16 bits come from? The MAC address is padded in the middle with the extra bits—it's padded with FFFE.

For example, let's say I have a device with a MAC address that looks like this: 0060:d673:1987. After it's been padded, it would look like this: 0260:d6FF:FE73:1987. Figure 1.36 illustrates what an EUI-64 address looks like.

FIGURE 1.36   EUI-64 interface ID assignment

So where did that 2 in the beginning of the address come from? Another good question. You see that part of the process of padding, called modified EUI-64 format, changes a bit to specify if the address is locally unique or globally unique. And the bit that gets changed is the 7th bit in the address.

The reason for modifying the U/L bit is that, when using manually assigned addresses on an interface, it means you can simply assign the address 2001:db8:1:9::1/64 instead of the much longer 2001:db8:1:9:0200::1/64. Also, if you are going to manually assign a link-local address, you can assign the short address fe80::1 instead of the long fe80::0200:0:0:1 or fe80:0:0:0:0200::1. So, even though at first glance it seems the IETF made this harder for you to simply understand IPv6 addressing by flipping the 7th bit, in reality this made addressing much simpler. Also, since most people don't typically override the burned-in address, the U/L bit is a 0, which means that you'll see this inverted to a 1 most of the time. But because you're studying the Cisco exam objectives, you'll need to look at inverting it both ways.

Here are a few examples:

- MAC address 0090:2716:fd0f

- IPv6 EUI-64 address: 2001:0db8:0:1:0290:27ff:fe16:fd0f

That one was easy! Too easy for the Cisco exam, so let's do another:

- MAC address aa12:bcbc:1234

- IPv6 EUI-64 address: 2001:0db8:0:1:a812:bcff:febc:1234

10101010 represents the first 8 bits of the MAC address (aa), which when inverting the 7th bit becomes 10101000. The answer becomes A8. I can't tell you how important this is for you to understand, so bear with me and work through a couple more!

- MAC address 0c0c:dede:1234

- IPv6 EUI-64 address: 2001:0db8:0:1:0e0c:deff:fede:1234

0c is 00001100 in the first 8 bits of the MAC address, which then becomes 00001110 when flipping the 7th bit. The answer is then 0e. Let's practice one more:

- MAC address 0b34:ba12:1234

- IPv6 EUI-64 address: 2001:0db8:0:1:0934:baff:fe12:1234

0b in binary is 00001011, the first 8 bits of the MAC address, which then becomes 00001001. The answer is 09.

 Pay extra-special attention to this EUI-64 address assignment and be able to convert the 7th bit based on the EUI-64 rules!

DHCPv6 (Stateful)

DHCPv6 works pretty much the same way DHCP does in v4, with the obvious difference that it supports IPv6's new addressing scheme. And it might come as a surprise, but there are a couple of other options that DHCP still provides for us that autoconfiguration doesn't. And no, I'm not kidding— in autoconfiguration, there's absolutely no mention of DNS servers, domain names, or many of the other options that DHCP has always generously provided for us via IPv4. This is a big reason that the odds favor DHCP's continued use into the future in IPv6 at least partially—maybe even most of the time!

Upon booting up in IPv4, a client sends out a DHCP Discover message looking for a server to give it the information it needs. But remember, in IPv6, the RS and RA process happens first, so if there's a DHCPv6 server on the network, the RA that comes back to the client will tell it if DHCP is available for use. If a router isn't found, the client will respond by sending out a DHCP Solicit message, which is actually a multicast message addressed with a destination of ff02::1:2 that calls out, "All DHCP agents, both servers and relays."

It's good to know that there's some support for DHCPv6 in the Cisco IOS even though it's limited. This rather miserly support is reserved for stateless DHCP servers and tells us it doesn't offer any address management of the pool or the options available for configuring that address pool other than the DNS, domain name, default gateway, and SIP servers.

This means that you're definitely going to need another server around to supply and dispense all the additional, required information—maybe to even manage the address assignment, if needed!

Exam Essentials

Describe the available methods to apply IPv6 addresses to the network. These include manual configuration, stateless autoconfiguration, and DHCPv6.

Understand and be able to read a EUI-64 address with the 7th bit inverted. Hosts can use autoconfiguration to obtain an IPv6 address, and one of the ways it can do that is through what is called EUI-64. This takes the unique MAC address of a host and inserts FF:FE in the middle of the address to change a 48-bit MAC address to a 64-bit interface ID. In addition to inserting the 16 bits into the interface ID, the 7th bit of the 1st byte is inverted, typically from a 0 to a 1.

Configure, verify, and troubleshoot IPv6 addressing

While covering the steps to confuse and troubleshoot IPv6, we'll be using the internetwork shown in Figure 1.37. This section will cover the process of both.

FIGURE 1.37 Our internetwork

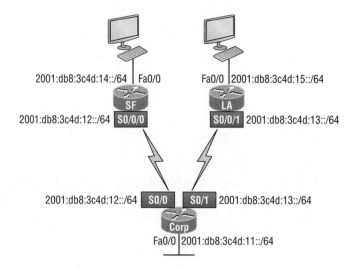

Configuring IPv6 on Our Internetwork

Well start by using a simple subnet scheme of 11, 12, 13, 14, and 15. After that, we'll add the OSPFv3 routing protocol. Notice in Figure 1.37 how the subnet numbers are the same on each end of the WAN links. Keep in mind that we'll finish this chapter by running through some verification commands.

As usual, I'll start with the Corp router:

```
Corp#config t
Corp(config)#ipv6 unicast-routing
Corp(config)#int f0/0
Corp(config-if)#ipv6 address 2001:db8:3c4d:11::/64 eui-64
Corp(config-if)#int s0/0
Corp(config-if)#ipv6 address 2001:db8:3c4d:12::/64 eui-64
Corp(config-if)#int s0/1
Corp(config-if)#ipv6 address 2001:db8:3c4d:13::/64 eui-64
Corp(config-if)#^Z
Corp#copy run start
Destination filename [startup-config]?[enter]
Building configuration...
[OK]
```

Pretty simple! In the previous configuration, I only changed the subnet address for each interface slightly. Let's take a look at the routing table now:

```
Corp(config-if)#do sho ipv6 route
C   2001:DB8:3C4D:11::/64 [0/0]
    via ::, FastEthernet0/0
L   2001:DB8:3C4D:11:20D:BDFF:FE3B:D80/128 [0/0]
    via ::, FastEthernet0/0
C   2001:DB8:3C4D:12::/64 [0/0]
    via ::, Serial0/0
L   2001:DB8:3C4D:12:20D:BDFF:FE3B:D80/128 [0/0]
    via ::, Serial0/0
C   2001:DB8:3C4D:13::/64 [0/0]
    via ::, Serial0/1
L   2001:DB8:3C4D:13:20D:BDFF:FE3B:D80/128 [0/0]
    via ::, Serial0/1
L   FE80::/10 [0/0]
    via ::, Null0
L   FF00::/8 [0/0]
    via ::, Null0
Corp(config-if)#
```

Alright, but what's up with those two addresses for each interface? One shows C for connected, one shows L. The connected address indicates the IPv6 address I configured on each interface, and the L is the link-local that's been automatically assigned. Notice in the link-local address that the FF:FE is inserted into the address to create the EUI-64 address.

Let's configure the SF router now:

```
SF#config t
SF(config)#ipv6 unicast-routing
SF(config)#int s0/0/0
SF(config-if)#ipv6 address 2001:db8:3c4d:12::/64
% 2001:DB8:3C4D:12::/64 should not be configured on Serial0/0/0, a subnet router
anycast
SF(config-if)#ipv6 address 2001:db8:3c4d:12::/64 eui-64
SF(config-if)#int fa0/0
SF(config-if)#ipv6 address 2001:db8:3c4d:14::/64 eui-64
SF(config-if)#^Z
SF#show ipv6 route
C    2001:DB8:3C4D:12::/64 [0/0]
      via ::, Serial0/0/0
L    2001:DB8:3C4D:12::/128 [0/0]
      via ::, Serial0/0/0
L    2001:DB8:3C4D:12:21A:2FFF:FEE7:4398/128 [0/0]
      via ::, Serial0/0/0
C    2001:DB8:3C4D:14::/64 [0/0]
      via ::, FastEthernet0/0
L    2001:DB8:3C4D:14:21A:2FFF:FEE7:4398/128 [0/0]
      via ::, FastEthernet0/0
L    FE80::/10 [0/0]
      via ::, Null0
L    FF00::/8 [0/0]
      via ::, Null0
```

Did you notice that I used the exact IPv6 subnet addresses on each side of the serial link? Good... but wait—what's with that anycast error I received when trying to configure the interfaces on the SF router? I didn't mean to create that error; it happened because I forgot to add the eui-64 at the end of the address. Still, what's behind that error? An anycast address is a host address of all 0s, meaning the last 64 bits are all off, but by typing in /64 without the eui-64, I was telling the interface that the unique identifier would be nothing but zeros, and that's not allowed!

Let's configure the LA router now:

```
SF#config t
SF(config)#ipv6 unicast-routing
```

```
SF(config)#int s0/0/1
SF(config-if)#ipv6 address 2001:db8:3c4d:13::/64 eui-64
SF(config-if)#int f0/0
SF(config-if)#ipv6 address 2001:db8:3c4d:15::/64 eui-64
SF(config-if)#do show ipv6 route
C    2001:DB8:3C4D:13::/64 [0/0]
       via ::, Serial0/0/1
L    2001:DB8:3C4D:13:21A:6CFF:FEA1:1F48/128 [0/0]
       via ::, Serial0/0/1
C    2001:DB8:3C4D:15::/64 [0/0]
       via ::, FastEthernet0/0
L    2001:DB8:3C4D:15:21A:6CFF:FEA1:1F48/128 [0/0]
       via ::, FastEthernet0/0
L    FE80::/10 [0/0]
       via ::, Null0
L    FF00::/8 [0/0]
       via ::, Null0
```

This looks good, but I want you to notice that I used the exact same IPv6 subnet addresses on each side of the links from the Corp router to the SF router as well as from the Corp to the LA router.

Exam Essentials

Describe the steps required to apply IPv6 addresses to a network.   These steps include selecting subnet numbers and configuring IPv6 addresses on both the router's interfaces and the host.

Configure and verify IPv6 Stateless Address Auto Configuration

To perform autoconfiguration, a host goes through a basic two-step process:

1. First, the host needs the prefix information, similar to the network portion of an IPv4 address, to configure its interface, so it sends a router solicitation (RS) request for it. This RS is then sent out as a multicast to all routers (FF02::2). The actual information being sent is a type of ICMP message, and like everything in networking, this ICMP message has a number that identifies it. The RS message is ICMP type 133.

2. The router answers back with the required prefix information via a router advertisement (RA). An RA message also happens to be a multicast packet that's sent to the

all-nodes multicast address (FF02::1) and is ICMP type 134. RA messages are sent on a periodic basis, but the host sends the RS for an immediate response so it doesn't have to wait until the next scheduled RA to get what it needs.

These two steps are shown in Figure 1.38.

FIGURE 1.38   Two steps to IPv6 autoconfiguration

Step 2: Router sends
RA message
FF02::1
ICMP type 134

Step 1: Host sends
RS message
FF02::2
ICMP type 133

Host receives the RA and included
prefix, allowing it to autoconfigure
its interface.

By the way, this type of autoconfiguration is also known as stateless autoconfiguration because it doesn't contact or connect to and receive any further information from the other device. We'll get to stateful configuration when we talk about DHCPv6 next.

But before we do that, first take a look at Figure 1.39. In this figure, the Branch router needs to be configured, but I just don't feel like typing in an IPv6 address on the interface connecting to the Corp router. I also don't feel like typing in any routing commands, but I need more than a link-local address on that interface, so I'm going to have to do something! So basically, I want to have the Branch router work with IPv6 on the internetwork with the least amount of effort from me. Let's see if I can get away with that.

FIGURE 1.39   IPv6 autoconfiguration example

Branch(config-if)#ipv6 address autoconfig default

GiO/0   GiO/1
Branch   Corp
            IPv6 address

            Default route

Internet

Aha—there is an easy way! I love IPv6 because it allows me to be relatively lazy when dealing with some parts of my network, yet it still works really well. By using the command `ipv6 address autoconfig`, the interface will listen for RAs and then, via the EUI-64 format, it will assign itself a global address—sweet!

Exam Essentials

Describe the autoconfiguration process.   List the steps a device uses to create an IPv6 address. Understand the roles played by both the router and the device.

Configure stateless autoconfiguration.   Identify the commands necessary to configure the devices and the router for stateless autoconfiguration.

Compare and contrast IPv6 address types

We're all familiar with IPv4's unicast, broadcast, and multicast addresses that basically define who or at least how many other devices we're talking to. But as I mentioned, IPv6 modifies that trio and introduces the anycast. Broadcasts, as we know them, have been eliminated in IPv6 because of their cumbersome inefficiency and basic tendency to drive us insane!

So let's find out what each of these types of IPv6 addressing and communication methods do for us:

Unicast   Packets addressed to a unicast address are delivered to a single interface. For load balancing, multiple interfaces across several devices can use the same address, but we'll call that an anycast address. There are a few different types of unicast addresses, but we don't need to get further into that here.

Global unicast addresses (2000::/3)   These are your typical publicly routable addresses and they're the same as in IPv4. Global addresses start at 2000::/3. Figure 1.40 shows how a unicast address breaks down. The ISP can provide you with a minimum /48 network ID, which in turn provides you with 16-bits to create a unique 64-bit router interface address. The last 64-bits are the unique host ID.

FIGURE 1.40   IPv6 global unicast addresses

Link-local addresses (FE80::/10)   These are like the Automatic Private IP Address (APIPA) addresses that Microsoft uses to automatically provide addresses in IPv4 in that they're not meant to be routed. In IPv6 they start with FE80::/10, as shown in Figure 1.41. Think of these addresses as handy tools that give you the ability to throw a temporary LAN together for meetings or create a small LAN that's not going to be routed but still needs to share and access files and services locally.

FIGURE 1.41   IPv6 link local FE80::/10: The first 10 bits define the address type.

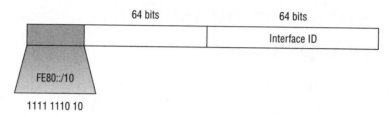

Unique local addresses (FC00::/7)   These addresses are also intended for nonrouting purposes over the Internet, but they are nearly globally unique, so it's unlikely you'll ever have one of them overlap. Unique local addresses were designed to replace site-local addresses, so they basically do almost exactly what IPv4 private addresses do: Allow communication throughout a site while being routable to multiple local networks. Site-local addresses were deprecated as of September 2004.

Multicast (FF00::/8)   Again, as in IPv4, packets addressed to a multicast address are delivered to all interfaces tuned into the multicast address. Sometimes people call them "one-to-many" addresses. It's really easy to spot a multicast address in IPv6 because they always start with *FF*.

Anycast   Like multicast addresses, an anycast address identifies multiple interfaces on multiple devices. But there's a big difference: the anycast packet is delivered to only one device—actually, to the closest one it finds defined in terms of routing distance. And again, this address is special because you can apply a single address to more than one host. These are referred to as "one-to-nearest" addresses. Anycast addresses are typically only configured on routers, never hosts, and a source address could never be an anycast address. Of note is that the IETF did reserve the top 128 addresses for each /64 for use with anycast addresses.

You're probably wondering if there are any special, reserved addresses in IPv6 because you know they're there in IPv4. Well there are—plenty of them! Let's go over those now.

Special Addresses

I'm going to list some of the addresses and address ranges (in Table 1.4) that you should definitely make sure to remember because you'll eventually use them. They're all special or reserved for a specific use, but unlike IPv4, IPv6 gives us a galaxy of addresses, so reserving a few here and there doesn't hurt at all!

TABLE 1.4   Special IPv6 addresses

Address	Meaning
0:0:0:0:0:0:0:0	Equals ::. This is the equivalent of IPv4's 0.0.0.0 and is typically the source address of a host before the host receives an IP address when you're using DHCP-driven stateful configuration.
0:0:0:0:0:0:0:1	Equals ::1. The equivalent of 127.0.0.1 in IPv4
0:0:0:0:0:0:192.168.100.1	This is how an IPv4 address would be written in a mixed IPv6/IPv4 network environment.
2000::/3	The global unicast address range
FC00::/7	The unique local unicast range
FE80::/10	The link-local unicast range
FF00::/8	The multicast range
3FFF:FFFF::/32	Reserved for examples and documentation
2001:0DB8::/32	Also reserved for examples and documentation
2002::/16	Used with 6-to-4 tunneling, which is an IPv4-to-IPv6 transition system. The structure allows IPv6 packets to be transmitted over an IPv4 network without the need to configure explicit tunnels.

When you run IPv4 and IPv6 on a router, you have what is called "dual-stack."

Exam Essentials

Understand link-local.   Link-local is like an IPv4 private IP address, but it can't be routed at all, not even in your organization.

Understand unique local.   This, like link-local, is like a private IP address in IPv4 and cannot be routed to the Internet. However, the difference between link-local and unique local is that unique local can be routed within your organization or company.

Review Questions

You can find the answers in the Appendix.

1. What cable type is shown in the following image?

   A. Fiber optic
   B. Rollover
   C. Coaxial
   D. Full-duplex

2. Which of the following statements is/are true with regard to the device shown below?

   A. It includes one collision domain and one broadcast domain.
   B. It includes no collision domain and one broadcast domains.
   C. It includes 10 collision domains and one broadcast domain.
   D. It includes one collision domain and 10 broadcast domains.
   E. It includes 10 collision domains and 10 broadcast domains.

3. Which of the following Application layer protocols sets up a secure session that's similar to Telnet?

   A. FTP

   B. SSH

   C. DNS

   D. DHCP

4. In the following diagram, identify the cable types required for connections A and B.

   A. A crossover, B crossover

   B. A crossover, B straight through

   C. A straight through, B straight through

   D. A straight through, B crossover

5. How many collision domains are present in the following diagram?

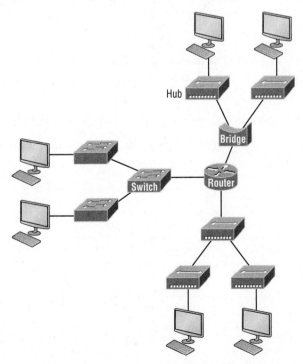

A. 8

B. 9

C. 10

D. 11

6. What type of cable is used between a host and switch?

   A. crossover

   B. rollover

   C. straight through

   D. console

7. How many octets are parts of the network portion of an IP address when the address is a Class B?

   A. one

   B. two

   C. three

   D. four

8. Which of the following layers of the OSI model was later subdivided into two layers?

   A. Presentation

   B. Transport

   C. Data Link

   D. Physical

9. What is a function of an access point (AP)?

   A. To monitor and control the incoming and outgoing network traffic

   B. To automatically handle the configuration of a wireless access point

   C. To allow wireless devices to connect to a wired network

   D. To connect networks and intelligently choose the best paths between networks

10. A _____ is an example of a device that operates only at the physical layer.

    A. Hub

    B. Switch

    C. Router

    D. Bridge

Chapter

2

LAN Switching Technologies

THE FOLLOWING CCNA ROUTING AND SWITCHING EXAM OBJECTIVES ARE COVERED IN THIS CHAPTER:

- ✓ Describe and verify switching concepts.

- ✓ Interpret Ethernet frame format.

- ✓ Troubleshoot interface and cable issues (collisions, errors, duplex, speed).

- ✓ Configure, verify, and troubleshoot VLANs (normal/extended range) spanning multiple switches.

- ✓ Configure, verify, and troubleshoot interswitch connectivity.

- ✓ Configure, verify, and troubleshoot STP protocols.

- ✓ Configure, verify, and troubleshoot STP-related optional features.

- ✓ Configure and verify layer 2 protocols.

- ✓ Configure, verify, and troubleshoot (layer 2/layer 3) EtherChannel.

- ✓ Describe the benefits of switch stacking and chassis aggregation.

In this chapter, I will discuss all things layer 2. This will include switching, Ethernet, VLANs, and other layer 2 concepts. Well also talk about switch stacking and chassis aggregation and the benefits from such an arrangement.

Describe and verify switching concepts

Layer 2 switches and bridges are faster than routers because they don't take up time looking at the Network layer header information. Instead, they look at the frame's hardware addresses before deciding to either forward, flood, or drop the frame. In the following sections, we'll look at the functions a switch preforms and the components it uses to do so.

MAC Learning and Aging

Our new, fast switches use application-specific integrated circuits (ASICs) to build and maintain their MAC filter tables. But it's still okay to think of a layer 2 switch as a multi-port bridge because their basic reason for being is the same: to break up collision domains.

When a switch is first powered on, the MAC forward/filter table (CAM) is empty, as shown in Figure 2.1.

FIGURE 2.1   Empty forward/filter table on a switch

When a device transmits and an interface receives a frame, the switch places the frame's source address in the MAC forward/filter table, allowing it to refer to the precise interface the sending device is located on. The switch then has no choice but to flood the network with this frame out of every port except the source port because it has no idea where the destination device is actually located.

If a device answers this flooded frame and sends a frame back, then the switch will take the source address from that frame and place that MAC address in its database as well, associating this address with the interface that received the frame. Because the switch now has both of the relevant MAC addresses in its filtering table, the two devices can now make a point-to-point connection. The switch doesn't need to flood the frame as it did the first time because now the frames can and will only be forwarded between these two devices. This is exactly why layer 2 switches are so superior to hubs. In a hub network, all frames are forwarded out all ports every time—no matter what. Figure 2.2 shows the processes involved in building a MAC database.

FIGURE 2.2   How switches learn hosts' locations

In this figure, you can see four hosts attached to a switch. When the switch is powered on, it has nothing in its MAC address forward/filter table, just as in Figure 2.1. But when the hosts start communicating, the switch places the source hardware address of each frame into the table along with the port that the frame's source address corresponds to.

Let me give you an example of how a forward/filter table is populated using Figure 2.2:

1. Host A sends a frame to Host B. Host A's MAC address is 0000.8c01.000A; Host B's MAC address is 0000.8c01.000B.

2. The switch receives the frame on the Fa0/0 interface and places the source address in the MAC address table.

3. Since the destination address isn't in the MAC database, the frame is forwarded out all interfaces except the source port.

4. Host B receives the frame and responds to Host A. The switch receives this frame on interface Fa0/1 and places the source hardware address in the MAC database.

5. Host A and Host B can now make a point-to-point connection and only these specific devices will receive the frames. Hosts C and D won't see the frames, nor will their MAC addresses be found in the database because they haven't sent a frame to the switch yet.

If Host A and Host B don't communicate to the switch again within a certain time period, the switch will flush their entries from the database to keep it as current as possible.

Frame Switching

When a frame arrives at a switch interface, the destination hardware address is compared to the forward/filter MAC database. If the destination hardware address is known and listed in the database, the frame is only sent out of the appropriate exit interface. The switch won't transmit the frame out any interface except for the destination interface, which preserves bandwidth on the other network segments. This process is called frame filtering.

Frame Flooding

If the destination hardware address isn't listed in the MAC database, then the frame will be flooded out all active interfaces except the interface it was received on. If a device answers the flooded frame, the MAC database is then updated with the device's location—its correct interface.

If a host or server sends a broadcast on the LAN, by default, the switch will flood the frame out all active ports except the source port. Remember, the switch creates smaller collision domains, but it's always still one large broadcast domain by default.

In Figure 2.3, Host A sends a data frame to Host D. What do you think the switch will do when it receives the frame from Host A?

FIGURE 2.3   Forward/filter table

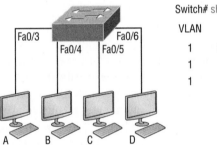

Switch# show mac address-table

VLAN	Mac Address	Ports
1	0005.dccb.d74b	Fa0/4
1	000a.f467.9e80	Fa0/5
1	000a.f467.9e8b	Fa0/6

Let's examine Figure 2.4 to find the answer.

FIGURE 2.4   Forward/filter table answer

Switch# show mac address-table

VLAN	Mac Address	Ports
1	00ca.345a.c7b9	Fa0/3
1	0005.dccb.d74b	Fa0/4
1	000a.f467.9e80	Fa0/5
1	000a.f467.9e8b	Fa0/6

Since Host A's MAC address is not in the forward/filter table, the switch will add the source address and port to the MAC address table, then forward the frame to Host D. It's really important to remember that the source MAC is always checked first to make sure it's in the CAM table. After that, if Host D's MAC address wasn't found in the forward/filter table, the switch would've flooded the frame out all ports except for port Fa0/3 because that's the specific port the frame was received on.

MAC Address Table

Now let's take a look at the output that results from using a show mac address-table command:

```
Switch#sh mac address-table
Vlan    Mac Address       Type        Ports
----    -----------       --------    -----
   1    0005.dccb.d74b    DYNAMIC     Fa0/1
   1    000a.f467.9e80    DYNAMIC     Fa0/3
   1    000a.f467.9e8b    DYNAMIC     Fa0/4
   1    000a.f467.9e8c    DYNAMIC     Fa0/3
   1    0010.7b7f.c2b0    DYNAMIC     Fa0/3
   1    0030.80dc.460b    DYNAMIC     Fa0/3
   1    0030.9492.a5dd    DYNAMIC     Fa0/1
   1    00d0.58ad.05f4    DYNAMIC     Fa0/1
```

But let's say the preceding switch received a frame with the following MAC addresses:

Source MAC: **0005.dccb.d74b**

Destination MAC: **000a.f467.9e8c**

How will the switch handle this frame? The right answer is that the destination MAC address will be found in the MAC address table and the frame will only be forwarded out Fa0/3. Never forget that if the destination MAC address isn't found in the forward/filter table, the frame will be forwarded out all of the switch's ports except for the one on which it was originally received in an attempt to locate the destination device. Now that you can see the MAC address table and how switches add host addresses to the forward filter table, how do think we can secure it from unauthorized users?

Exam Essentials

Remember the three switch functions.   Address learning, forward/filter decisions, and loop avoidance are the functions of a switch.

Remember the command show mac address-table.   The command show mac address-table will show you the forward/filter table used on the LAN switch.

Interpret Ethernet frame format

The Data Link layer is responsible for combining bits into bytes and bytes into frames. Frames are used at the Data Link layer to encapsulate packets handed down from the Network layer for transmission on a type of media access. In the following section, we'll discuss the format of these frames called Ethernet frames.

Ethernet Frames

The function of Ethernet stations is to pass data frames between each other using a group of bits known as a MAC frame format. This provides error detection from a *cyclic redundancy check (CRC)*. But remember—this is error detection, not error correction. An example of a typical Ethernet frame used today is shown in Figure 2.5.

FIGURE 2.5   Typical Ethernet frame format

Ethernet_II

Preamble 7 bytes	SFD 1 byte	Destination 6 bytes	Source 6 bytes	Type 2 bytes	Data and Pad 46 – 1500 bytes	FCS 4 bytes

Packet

    Encapsulating a frame within a different type of frame is called *tunneling*.

Following are the details of the various fields in the typical Ethernet frame type:

Preamble   An alternating 1,0 pattern provides a 5 MHz clock at the start of each packet, which allows the receiving devices to lock the incoming bit stream.

Start Frame Delimiter (SFD)/Synch   The preamble is seven octets and the SFD is one octet (synch). The SFD is 10101011, where the last pair of 1s allows the receiver to come into the alternating 1,0 pattern somewhere in the middle and still sync up to detect the beginning of the data.

Destination Address (DA)   This transmits a 48-bit value using the least significant bit (LSB) first. The DA is used by receiving stations to determine whether an incoming packet is addressed to a particular node. The destination address can be an individual address or a broadcast or multicast MAC address. Remember that a broadcast is all 1s—all *F*s in hex—and is sent to all devices. A multicast is sent only to a similar subset of nodes on a network.

Source Address (SA)   The SA is a 48-bit MAC address used to identify the transmitting device, and it uses the least significant bit first. Broadcast and multicast address formats are illegal within the SA field.

Length or Type   802.3 uses a Length field, but the Ethernet_II frame uses a Type field to identify the Network layer protocol. The old, original 802.3 cannot identify the upper-layer protocol and must be used with a proprietary LAN—IPX, for example.

Data   This is a packet sent down to the Data Link layer from the Network layer. The size can vary from 46 to 1,500 bytes.

Frame Check Sequence (FCS)   FCS is a field at the end of the frame that's used to store the cyclic redundancy check (CRC) answer. The CRC is a mathematical algorithm that's run when each frame is built based on the data in the frame. When a receiving host receives the frame and runs the CRC, the answer should be the same. If not, the frame is discarded, assuming errors have occurred.

Let's pause here for a minute and take a look at some frames caught on my trusty network analyzer. You can see that the frame below has only three fields: Destination, Source, and Type, which is shown as Protocol Type on this particular analyzer:

```
Destination:   00:60:f5:00:1f:27
Source:        00:60:f5:00:1f:2c
Protocol Type: 08-00 IP
```

This is an Ethernet_II frame. Notice that the Type field is IP, or 08-00, mostly just referred to as 0x800 in hexadecimal.

The next frame has the same fields, so it must be an Ethernet_II frame as well:

```
Destination:   ff:ff:ff:ff:ff:ff Ethernet Broadcast
Source:        02:07:01:22:de:a4
Protocol Type: 08-00 IP
```

Did you notice that this frame was a broadcast? You can tell because the destination hardware address is all 1s in binary, or all *F*s in hexadecimal.

Let's take a look at one more Ethernet_II frame. You can see that the Ethernet frame is the same Ethernet_II frame used with the IPv4 routed protocol. The Type field has 0x86dd when the frame is carrying IPv6 data, and when we have IPv4 data, the frame uses 0x0800 in the protocol field:

```
Destination: IPv6-Neighbor-Discovery_00:01:00:03 (33:33:00:01:00:03)
Source: Aopen_3e:7f:dd (00:01:80:3e:7f:dd)
Type: IPv6 (0x86dd)
```

This is the beauty of the Ethernet_II frame. Because of the Type field, we can run any Network layer routed protocol and the frame will carry the data because it can identify the Network layer protocol!

Exam Essentials

Identify the fields in the Data Link portion of an Ethernet frame.   The fields in the Data Link portion of a frame include the preamble, Start Frame Delimiter, destination MAC address, source MAC address, Length or Type, Data, and Frame Check Sequence.

Troubleshoot interface and cable issues (collisions, errors, duplex, speed)

Finding where to start when troubleshooting an interface can be the difficult part, but we can use the show interfaces command as shown below.

```
275496 packets input, 35226811 bytes, 0 no buffer
     Received 69748 broadcasts (58822 multicasts)
     0 runts, 0 giants, 0 throttles
     0 input errors, 0 CRC, 0 frame, 0 overrun, 0 ignored
     0 watchdog, 58822 multicast, 0 pause input
     0 input packets with dribble condition detected
     2392529 packets output, 337933522 bytes, 0 underruns
     0 output errors, 0 collisions, 1 interface resets
     0 babbles, 0 late collision, 0 deferred
     0 lost carrier, 0 no carrier, 0 PAUSE output
     0 output buffer failures, 0 output buffers swapped out
```

Certainly we'll look for the number of input errors and CRCs right away. Typically we'd see those statistics increase with a duplex error, but it could be another Physical layer issue such as the cable might be receiving excessive interference or the network interface cards might have a failure. Typically you can tell if it is interference when the CRC and input errors output grows but the collision counters do not.

Let's take a look at some of the output:

No buffer   This isn't a number you want to see incrementing. This means you don't have any buffer room left for incoming packets. Any packets received once the buffers are full are discarded. You can see how many packets are dropped with the ignored output.

Ignored   If the packet buffers are full, packets will be dropped. You see this increment along with the no buffer output. Typically, if the no buffer and ignored outputs are incrementing, you have some sort of broadcast storm on your LAN. This can be caused by a bad NIC or even a bad network design.

> I'll repeat this because it is so important for the exam objectives: Typically if the no buffer and ignored outputs are incrementing, you have some sort of broadcast storm on your LAN. This can be caused by a bad NIC or even a bad network design.

Runts   Frames that did not meet the minimum frame size requirement of 64 bytes. Typically caused by collisions

Giants   Frames received that are larger than 1,518 bytes

Input errors   This is the total of many counters: runts, giants, no buffer, CRC, frame, overrun, and ignored counts.

CRC   At the end of each frame is a Frame Check Sequence (FCS) field that holds the answer to a cyclic redundancy check (CRC). If the receiving host's answer to the CRC does not match the sending host's answer, then a CRC error will occur.

Frame   This output increments when frames received are of an illegal format, or not complete; the output is typically incremented when a collision occurs.

Packets output   Total number of packets (frames) forwarded out to the interface

Output errors   Total number of packets (frames) that the switch port tried to transmit but for which some problem occurred

Collisions   When transmitting a frame in half-duplex, the NIC listens on the receiving pair of the cable for another signal. If a signal is transmitted from another host, a collision has occurred. This output should not increment if you are running full-duplex.

Late collisions   If all Ethernet specifications are followed during the cable install, all collisions should occur by the 64th byte of the frame. If a collision occurs after 64 bytes, the late collisions counter increments. This counter will increment on a duplex mismatched interface, or if cable length exceeds specifications.

 A duplex mismatch causes late collision errors at the end of the connection. To avoid this situation, manually set the duplex parameters of the switch to match the attached device.

A duplex mismatch is a situation in which the switch operates at full-duplex and the connected device operates at half-duplex, or vice versa. The result of a duplex mismatch is extremely slow performance, intermittent connectivity, and loss of connection. Other possible causes of data-link errors at full-duplex are bad cables, a faulty switch port, or NIC software or hardware issues. Use the show interfaces command to verify the duplex settings.

If the mismatch occurs between two Cisco devices with Cisco Discovery Protocol enabled, you will see Cisco Discovery Protocol error messages on the console or in the logging buffer of both devices.

```
%CDP-4-DUPLEX_MISMATCH: duplex mismatch discovered on FastEthernet0/2 (not
half duplex)
```

Cisco Discovery Protocol is useful for detecting errors and for gathering port and system statistics on nearby Cisco devices.

Another issue that can cause problems is a speed mismatch. This must also match on each end of the link. To verify both the speed and the duplex of interfaces, use the show interfaces command as shown below. In the sixth line, you can see that this interface is set for full-duplex and a speed of 100 MB.

```
SW2#sh interfaces fastEthernet 6/1
FastEthernet6/1 is up, line protocol is up (connected)
   Hardware is C6k 100Mb 802.3, address is 0009.11f3.8848 (bia 0009.11f3.8848)
   MTU 1500 bytes, BW 100000 Kbit, DLY 100 usec,
       reliability 255/255, txload 1/255, rxload 1/255
   Encapsulation ARPA, loopback not set
   Full-duplex, 100Mb/s
   input flow-control is off, output flow-control is off
   ARP type: ARPA, ARP Timeout 04:00:00
   Last input 00:00:14, output 00:00:36, output hang never
   Last clearing of "show interface" counters never
   Input queue: 0/2000/0/0 (size/max/drops/flushes); Total output drops: 0
   Queueing strategy: fifo
   Output queue :0/40 (size/max)
   5 minute input rate 0 bits/sec, 0 packets/sec
   5 minute output rate 0 bits/sec, 0 packets/sec
```

To set these values, go into interface configuration mode and use the commands shown here:

```
Sw2(config)#int fastEthernet 6/1
Sw2(config-if)#speed 100
Sw2(config-if)#duplex full
```

Exam Essentials

Describe the most common interface issues.   These include disabled interfaces, speed mismatches, and duplex mismatches.

Understand how to read the output of the `show interfaces` command.   Use this output to determine the issue and define the causes of errors such as collisions or CRC errors.

Configure, verify, and troubleshoot VLANs (normal/extended range) spanning multiple switches

To configure VLANs on a Cisco Catalyst switch, use the global config vlan command. In the following example, I'm going to demonstrate how to configure VLANs on the S1 switch by creating three VLANs for three different departments—again, remember that VLAN 1 is the native and management VLAN by default:

```
S1(config)#vlan ?
  WORD        ISL VLAN IDs 1-4094
  access-map  Create vlan access-map or enter vlan access-map command mode
  dot1q       dot1q parameters
  filter      Apply a VLAN Map
  group       Create a vlan group
  internal    internal VLAN
S1(config)#vlan 2
S1(config-vlan)#name Sales
S1(config-vlan)#vlan 3
S1(config-vlan)#name Marketing
S1(config-vlan)#vlan 4
S1(config-vlan)#name Accounting
S1(config-vlan)#^Z
S1#
```

In this output, you can see that you can create VLANs from 1 to 4094. But this is only mostly true. As I said, VLANs can really only be created up to 1001, and you can't use, change, rename, or delete VLANs 1 or 1002 through 1005 because they're reserved. The VLAN with numbers above 1005 are called extended VLANs and won't be saved in the database unless your switch is set to what is called VLAN Trunking Protocol (VTP) transparent mode. You won't see these VLAN numbers used too often in production. Here's an example of me attempting to set my S1 switch to VLAN 4000 when my switch is set to VTP server mode (the default VTP mode):

```
S1#config t
S1(config)#vlan 4000
S1(config-vlan)#^Z
% Failed to create VLANs 4000
Extended VLAN(s) not allowed in current VTP mode.
%Failed to commit extended VLAN(s) changes.
```

After you create the VLANs that you want, you can use the show vlan command to check them out. But notice that, by default, all ports on the switch are in VLAN 1. To change the VLAN associated with a port, you need to go to each interface and specifically tell it which VLAN to be a part of.

NOTE   Remember that a created VLAN is unused until it is assigned to a switch port or ports and that all ports are always assigned in VLAN 1 unless set otherwise.

Once the VLANs are created, verify your configuration with the show vlan command (sh vlan for short):

S1#**sh vlan**

```
VLAN Name                           Status    Ports
---- ------------------------       --------- -------------------------------
1    default                        active    Fa0/1, Fa0/2, Fa0/3, Fa0/4
                                              Fa0/5, Fa0/6, Fa0/7, Fa0/8
                                              Fa0/9, Fa0/10, Fa0/11, Fa0/12
                                              Fa0/13, Fa0/14, Fa0/19, Fa0/20
                                              Fa0/21, Fa0/22, Fa0/23, Gi0/1
                                              Gi0/2
2    Sales                          active
3    Marketing                      active
4    Accounting                     active
[output cut]
```

In the preceding S1 output, you can see that ports Fa0/1 through Fa0/14, Fa0/19 through Fa0/23, and Gi0/1 and Gi0/2 uplinks are all in VLAN 1. But where are ports 15 through 18? First, understand that the command show vlan only displays access ports, so now that you know what you're looking at with the show vlan command, where do you think ports Fa15–18 are? That's right! They are trunked ports. Cisco switches run a proprietary protocol called *Dynamic Trunk Protocol (DTP)*, and if there is a compatible switch connected, they will start trunking automatically, which is precisely where my four ports are. You have to use the show interfaces trunk command to see your trunked ports, like this:

S1# **show interfaces trunk**
```
Port       Mode           Encapsulation  Status     Native vlan
Fa0/15     desirable      n-isl          trunking   1
Fa0/16     desirable      n-isl          trunking   1
Fa0/17     desirable      n-isl          trunking   1
Fa0/18     desirable      n-isl          trunking   1

Port       Vlans allowed on trunk
Fa0/15     1-4094
Fa0/16     1-4094
Fa0/17     1-4094
Fa0/18     1-4094

 [output cut]
```

This output reveals that the VLANs from 1 to 4094 are allowed across the trunk by default. Another helpful command, which is also part of the Cisco exam objectives, is the show interfaces *interface* switchport command:

```
S1#sh interfaces fastEthernet 0/15 switchport
Name: Fa0/15
Switchport: Enabled
Administrative Mode: dynamic desirable
Operational Mode: trunk
Administrative Trunking Encapsulation: negotiate
Operational Trunking Encapsulation: isl
Negotiation of Trunking: On
Access Mode VLAN: 1 (default)
Trunking Native Mode VLAN: 1 (default)
Administrative Native VLAN tagging: enabled
Voice VLAN: none
[output cut]
```

The highlighted output shows us the administrative mode of dynamic desirable, that the port is a trunk port, and that DTP was used to negotiate the frame-tagging method of ISL. It also predictably shows that the native VLAN is the default of 1.

Now that we can see the VLANs created, we can assign switch ports to specific ones. Each port can be part of only one VLAN, with the exception of voice access ports. Using trunking, you can make a port available to traffic from all VLANs. I'll cover that next.

Assigning Switch Ports to VLANs

You configure a port to belong to a VLAN by assigning a membership mode that specifies the kind of traffic the port carries plus the number of VLANs it can belong to. You can also configure each port on a switch to be in a specific VLAN (access port) by using the interface switchport command. You can even configure multiple ports at the same time with the interface range command.

In the next example, I'll configure interface Fa0/3 to VLAN 3. This is the connection from the S3 switch to the host device:

```
S3#config t
S3(config)#int fa0/3
S3(config-if)#switchport ?
  access       Set access mode characteristics of the interface
  autostate    Include or exclude this port from vlan link up calculation
  backup       Set backup for the interface
  block        Disable forwarding of unknown uni/multi cast addresses
  host         Set port host
```

```
mode              Set trunking mode of the interface
nonegotiate       Device will not engage in negotiation protocol on this
                  interface
port-security   Security related command
priority        Set appliance 802.1p priority
private-vlan     Set the private VLAN configuration
protected       Configure an interface to be a protected port
trunk           Set trunking characteristics of the interface
voice           Voice appliance attributes  voice
```

Well now, what do we have here? There's some new stuff showing up in our output now. We can see various commands—some that I've already covered, but no worries because I'm going to cover the access, mode, nonegotiate, and trunk commands very soon. Let's start with setting an access port on S1, which is probably the most widely used type of port you'll find on production switches that have VLANs configured:

```
S3(config-if)#switchport mode ?
   access        Set trunking mode to ACCESS unconditionally
 dot1q-tunnel  set trunking mode to TUNNEL unconditionally
 dynamic       Set trunking mode to dynamically negotiate access or trunk mode
 private-vlan  Set private-vlan mode
 trunk         Set trunking mode to TRUNK unconditionally

S3(config-if)#switchport mode access
S3(config-if)#switchport access vlan 3
```

By starting with the switchport mode access command, you're telling the switch that this is a nontrunking layer 2 port. You can then assign a VLAN to the port with the switchport access command. Remember, you can choose many ports to configure simultaneously with the interface range command.

Let's take a look at our VLANs now:

```
S3#show vlan
VLAN Name                          Status    Ports
---- ------------------------------ --------- ------------------------------
1    default                        active    Fa0/4, Fa0/5, Fa0/6, Fa0/7
                                              Fa0/8, Fa0/9, Fa0/10, Fa0/11,
                                              Fa0/12, Fa0/13, Fa0/14, Fa0/19,
                                              Fa0/20, Fa0/21, Fa0/22, Fa0/23,
                                              Gi0/1 ,Gi0/2

2    Sales                          active
3    Marketing                      active    Fa0/3
```

Notice that port Fa0/3 is now a member of VLAN 3. But, can you tell me where ports 1 and 2 are? And why aren't they showing up in the output of show vlan? That's right, because they are trunk ports!

We can also see this with the show interfaces *interface* switchport command:

```
S3#sh int fa0/3 switchport
Name: Fa0/3
Switchport: Enabled
Administrative Mode: static access
Operational Mode: static access
Administrative Trunking Encapsulation: negotiate
Negotiation of Trunking: Off
Access Mode VLAN: 3 (Marketing)
```

The highlighted output shows that Fa0/3 is an access port and a member of VLAN 3 (Marketing).

Access Ports (Data and Voice)

An *access port* belongs to and carries the traffic of only one VLAN. Traffic is both received and sent in native formats with no VLAN information (tagging) whatsoever. Anything arriving on an access port is simply assumed to belong to the VLAN assigned to the port. Because an access port doesn't look at the source address, tagged traffic—a frame with added VLAN information—can be correctly forwarded and received only on trunk ports.

With an access link, this can be referred to as the *configured VLAN* of the port. Any device attached to an *access link* is unaware of a VLAN membership—the device just assumes it's part of some broadcast domain. But it doesn't have the big picture, so it doesn't understand the physical network topology at all.

Another good bit of information to know is that switches remove any VLAN information from the frame before it's forwarded out to an access-link device. Remember that access-link devices can't communicate with devices outside their VLAN unless the packet is routed. Also, you can only create a switch port to be either an access port or a trunk port—not both. So you've got to choose one or the other and know that if you make it an access port, that port can be assigned to one VLAN only.

Voice access ports

Not to confuse you, but all that I just said about the fact that an access port can be assigned to only one VLAN is really only sort of true. Nowadays, most switches will allow you to add a second VLAN to an access port on a switch port for your voice traffic, called the voice VLAN. The voice VLAN used to be called the auxiliary VLAN, which allowed it to be overlaid on top of the data VLAN, enabling both types of traffic to travel through the same port. Even though this is technically considered to be a different type of link, it's still just an access port that can be configured for both data and voice VLANs. This allows you to connect both a phone and a PC device to one switch port but still have each device in a separate VLAN.

Default VLAN

You can't change, delete, or rename VLAN 1 because it's the default VLAN and you just can't change that—period. It's also the native VLAN of all switches by default, and Cisco recommends that you use it as your management VLAN. If you're worried about security issues, then change it! Basically, any ports that aren't specifically assigned to a different VLAN will be sent down to the native VLAN—VLAN 1.

Exam Essentials

Remember to check a switch port's VLAN assignment when plugging in a new host.   If you plug a new host into a switch, then you must verify the VLAN membership of that port. If the membership is different than what is needed for that host, the host will not be able to reach the needed network services, such as a workgroup server or printer.

Configure, verify, and troubleshoot interswitch connectivity

When traffic needs to go from one VLAN to another, even when those devices are connected to the same switch, the packets will have to be routed. In the following sections, we'll discuss how to configure inter-VLAN routing.

Trunk Ports

Trunk ports are on any link that must be able to carry the traffic of multiple VLANs. The 2960 switch only runs the IEEE 802.1q encapsulation method. To configure trunking on a FastEthernet port, use the interface command switchport mode trunk. It's a tad different on the 3560 switch.

The following switch output shows the trunk configuration on interfaces Fa0/15–18 as set to trunk:

```
S1(config)#int range f0/15-18
S1(config-if-range)#switchport trunk encapsulation dot1q
S1(config-if-range)#switchport mode trunk
```

If you have a switch that only runs the 802.1q encapsulation method, then you wouldn't use the encapsulation command as I did in the preceding output. Let's check out our trunk ports now:

```
S1(config-if-range)#do sh int f0/15 swi
Name: Fa0/15
Switchport: Enabled
Administrative Mode: trunk
Operational Mode: trunk
Administrative Trunking Encapsulation: dot1q
Operational Trunking Encapsulation: dot1q
Negotiation of Trunking: On
Access Mode VLAN: 1 (default)
Trunking Native Mode VLAN: 1 (default)
Administrative Native VLAN tagging: enabled
Voice VLAN: none
```

Notice that port Fa0/15 is a trunk and running 802.1q. Let's take another look:

```
S1(config-if-range)#do sh int trunk
Port        Mode            Encapsulation  Status      Native vlan
Fa0/15      on              802.1q         trunking    1
Fa0/16      on              802.1q         trunking    1
Fa0/17      on              802.1q         trunking    1
Fa0/18      on              802.1q         trunking    1
Port        Vlans allowed on trunk
Fa0/15      1-4094
Fa0/16      1-4094
Fa0/17      1-4094
Fa0/18      1-4094
```

Take note of the fact that ports 15–18 are now in the trunk mode of on and the encapsulation is now 802.1q instead of the negotiated ISL. Here's a description of the different options available when configuring a switch interface:

switchport mode access   I discussed this in a previous section, but this puts the interface (access port) into permanent nontrunking mode and negotiates to convert the link into a nontrunk link. The interface becomes a nontrunk interface regardless of whether the neighboring interface is a trunk interface. The port would be a dedicated layer 2 access port.

switchport mode dynamic auto   This mode makes the interface able to convert the link to a trunk link. The interface becomes a trunk interface if the neighboring interface is set to trunk or desirable mode. The default is dynamic auto on a lot of Cisco switches, but that default trunk method is changing to dynamic desirable on most new models.

`switchport mode dynamic desirable`   This one makes the interface actively attempt to convert the link to a trunk link. The interface becomes a trunk interface if the neighboring interface is set to `trunk`, `desirable`, or `auto` mode. This is now the default switch port mode for all Ethernet interfaces on all new Cisco switches.

`switchport mode trunk`   Puts the interface into permanent trunking mode and negotiates to convert the neighboring link into a trunk link. The interface becomes a trunk interface even if the neighboring interface isn't a trunk interface.

`switchport nonegotiate`   Prevents the interface from generating DTP frames. You can use this command only when the interface switchport mode is access or trunk. You must manually configure the neighboring interface as a trunk interface to establish a trunk link.

Add and Remove VLANs on a Trunk

As I've mentioned, trunk ports send and receive information from all VLANs by default, and if a frame is untagged, it's sent to the management VLAN. Understand that this applies to the extended range VLANs too.

But we can remove VLANs from the allowed list to prevent traffic from certain VLANs from traversing a trunked link. I'll show you how you'd do that, but first let me again demonstrate that all VLANs are allowed across the trunk link by default:

```
S1#sh int trunk
[output cut]
Port         Vlans allowed on trunk
Fa0/15       1-4094
Fa0/16       1-4094
Fa0/17       1-4094
Fa0/18       1-4094
S1(config)#int f0/15
S1(config-if)#switchport trunk allowed vlan 4,6,12,15
S1(config-if)#do show int trunk
[output cut]
Port         Vlans allowed on trunk
Fa0/15       4,6,12,15
Fa0/16       1-4094
Fa0/17       1-4094
Fa0/18       1-4094
```

The preceding command affected the trunk link configured on S1 port F0/15, causing it to permit all traffic sent and received for VLANs 4, 6, 12, and 15. You can try to remove VLAN 1 on a trunk link, but it will still send and receive management like CDP, DTP, and VTP, so what's the point?

To remove a range of VLANs, just use the hyphen:

```
S1(config-if)#switchport trunk allowed vlan remove 4-8
```

If by chance someone has removed some VLANs from a trunk link and you want to set the trunk back to default, just use this command:

```
S1(config-if)#switchport trunk allowed vlan all
```

DTP, VTP (v1 and v2), and 802.1q

Several protocols and services can be used in the process of configuring VLANs. While we've mentioned some of these in passing, let's look at three in detail—DTP, VTP, and 802.1q.

DTP

Dynamic Trunking Protocol (DTP) is used for negotiating trunking on a link between two devices as well as negotiating the encapsulation type of either 802.1q or ISL. It is enabled by setting the trunk port to one of the following settings that you learned about in the section on trunking.

To disable trunking on an interface, use the `switchport mode access` command, which sets the port back to a dedicated layer 2 access switch port.

VTP

The basic goals of *VLAN Trunking Protocol (VTP)* are to manage all configured VLANs across a switched internetwork and to maintain consistency throughout that network. VTP allows you to add, delete, and rename VLANs—information that is then propagated to all other switches in the VTP domain.

Here's a list of some of the cool features VTP has to offer:

- Consistent VLAN configuration across all switches in the network
- VLAN trunking over mixed networks, such as Ethernet to ATM LANE or even FDDI
- Accurate tracking and monitoring of VLANs
- Dynamic reporting of added VLANs to all switches in the VTP domain
- Adding VLANs using Plug and Play

Very nice, but before you can get VTP to manage your VLANs across the network, you have to create a VTP server (really, you don't need to even do that since all switches default to VTP server mode, but just make sure you have a server). All servers that need to share VLAN information must use the same domain name, and a switch can be in only one domain at a time. So basically, this means that a switch can share VTP domain information with other switches only if they're configured into the same VTP domain. You can use a VTP domain if you have more than one switch connected in a network, but if you've got all your switches in only one VLAN, you just don't need to use VTP. Do keep in mind that VTP information is sent between switches only via a trunk port.

Switches advertise VTP management domain information as well as a configuration revision number and all known VLANs with any specific parameters. But there's also something called *VTP transparent mode*. In it, you can configure switches to forward VTP information through trunk ports but not to accept information updates or update their VLAN databases.

If you've got sneaky users adding switches to your VTP domain behind your back, you can include passwords, but don't forget—every switch must be set up with the same password. And as you can imagine, this little snag can be a real hassle administratively!

Switches detect any added VLANs within a VTP advertisement and then prepare to send information on their trunk ports with the newly defined VLAN in tow. Updates are sent out as revision numbers that consist of summary advertisements. Anytime a switch sees a higher revision number, it knows the information it's getting is more current, so it will overwrite the existing VLAN database with the latest information.

You should know these four requirements for VTP to communicate VLAN information between switches:

- The VTP version must be set the same.
- The VTP management domain name of both switches must be set the same.
- One of the switches has to be configured as a VTP server.
- Set a VTP password if desired.

No router is necessary and is not a requirement. Now that you've got that down, we're going to delve deeper into the world of VTP with VTP modes and VTP pruning.

VTP Modes of Operation

Figure 2.6 shows you how a VTP server will update the connected VTP client's VLAN database when a change occurs in the VLAN database on the server.

FIGURE 2.6 VTP modes

Server   This is the default mode for all Catalyst switches. You need at least one server in your VTP domain to propagate VLAN information throughout that domain. Also important: The switch must be in server mode to be able to create, add, and delete VLANs in a VTP domain. VLAN information has to be changed in server mode, and any change made to VLANs on a switch in server mode will be advertised to the entire VTP domain. In VTP server mode, VLAN configurations are saved in NVRAM on the switch.

Client   In client mode, switches receive information from VTP servers, but they also receive and forward updates, so in this way, they behave like VTP servers. The difference is that they can't create, change, or delete VLANs. Plus, none of the ports on a client switch can be added to a new VLAN before the VTP server notifies the client switch of the new VLAN and the VLAN exists in the client's VLAN database. Also good to know is that VLAN information sent from a VTP server isn't stored in NVRAM, which is important because it means that if the switch is reset or reloaded, the VLAN information will be deleted. Here's a hint: If you want a switch to become a server, first make it a client so it receives all the correct VLAN information, then change it to a server—so much easier!

So basically, a switch in VTP client mode will forward VTP summary advertisements and process them. This switch will learn about but won't save the VTP configuration in the running configuration, and it won't save it in NVRAM. Switches that are in VTP client mode will only learn about and pass along VTP information—that's it!

Transparent   Switches in transparent mode don't participate in the VTP domain or share its VLAN database, but they'll still forward VTP advertisements through any configured trunk links. They can create, modify, and delete VLANs because they keep their own database—one they keep secret from the other switches. Despite being kept in NVRAM, the VLAN database in transparent mode is actually only locally significant. The whole purpose of transparent mode is to allow remote switches to receive the VLAN database from a VTP server configured switch through a switch that is not participating in the same VLAN assignments.

VTP only learns about normal-range VLANs, with VLAN IDs 1 to 1005; VLANs with IDs greater than 1005 are called extended-range VLANs and they're not stored in the VLAN database. The switch must be in VTP transparent mode when you create VLAN IDs from 1006 to 4094, so it would be pretty rare that you'd ever use these VLANs. One other thing: VLAN IDs 1 and 1002 to 1005 are automatically created on all switches and can't be removed.

VTPv2

By default, VTP operates in version 1. You can configure VTP version 2 if you want support for these features, which are not supported in version 1:

- Token Ring support—Hmmm…doesn't seem like much of a reason to go to version 2 today. Let's look at some other reasons.

- Unrecognized Type-Length-Value (TLV) support—A VTP server or client propagates configuration changes to its other trunks, even for TLVs it is not able to parse. The unrecognized TLV is saved in NVRAM when the switch is operating in VTP server mode.

- Version-dependent transparent mode—In VTP version 1, a VTP transparent switch inspects VTP messages for the domain name and version and forwards a message only if the version and domain name match. Because VTP version 2 supports only one domain, it forwards VTP messages in transparent mode without inspecting the version and domain name.

- Consistency checks—In VTP version 2, VLAN consistency checks (such as checking the consistency of VLAN names and values) are performed only when you enter new information through the CLI or SNMP. Consistency checks are not performed when new information is obtained from a VTP message or when information is read from NVRAM. If the MD5 digest on a received VTP message is correct, its information is accepted.

802.1q

Created by the IEEE as a standard method of frame tagging, IEEE 802.1q actually inserts a field into the frame to identify the VLAN. If you're trunking between a Cisco switched link and a different brand of switch, you've got to use 802.1q for the trunk to work.

Unlike ISL, which encapsulates the frame with control information, 802.1q inserts an 802.1q field along with tag control information, as shown in Figure 2.7.

FIGURE 2.7   IEEE 802.1q encapsulation with and without the 802.1q tag

For the Cisco exam objectives, it's only the 12-bit VLAN ID that matters. This field identifies the VLAN and can be 212, minus 2 for the 0 and 4,095 reserved VLANs, which means an 802.1q tagged frame can carry information for 4,094 VLANs.

It works like this: You first designate each port that's going to be a trunk with 802.1q encapsulation. The other ports must be assigned a specific VLAN ID in order for them to communicate. VLAN 1 is the default native VLAN, and when using 802.1q, all traffic for a native VLAN is untagged. The ports that populate the same trunk create a group with this native VLAN, and each port gets tagged with an identification number reflecting that. Again, the default is VLAN 1. The native VLAN allows the trunks to accept information that was received without any VLAN identification or frame tag.

Most 2960 model switches only support the IEEE 802.1q trunking protocol, but the 3560 will support both the ISL and IEEE methods, which you'll see later in this chapter.

 The basic purpose of ISL and 802.1q frame-tagging methods is to provide inter-switch VLAN communication. Remember that any ISL or 802.1q frame tagging is removed if a frame is forwarded out an access link—tagging is used internally and across trunk links only!

Native VLAN

The native VLAN is one that carries all untagged traffic or traffic from devices that still reside in the native VLAN. You can change the number of the native VLAN to mitigate certain types of attacks. In the next section, I'll show how that's done.

Changing or Modifying the Trunk Native VLAN

You can change the trunk port native VLAN from VLAN 1, which many people do for security reasons. To change the native VLAN, use the following command:

```
S1(config)#int f0/15
S1(config-if)#switchport trunk native vlan ?
  <1-4094>  VLAN ID of the native VLAN when this port is in trunking mode

S1(config-if)#switchport trunk native vlan 4
1w6d: %CDP-4-NATIVE_VLAN_MISMATCH: Native VLAN mismatch discovered on
FastEthernet0/15 (4), with S3 FastEthernet0/1 (1).
```

So we've changed our native VLAN on our trunk link to 4, and by using the show running-config command, I can see the configuration under the trunk link:

```
S1#sh run int f0/15
Building configuration . . .

Current configuration : 202 bytes
!
interface FastEthernet0/15
 description 1st connection to S3
 switchport trunk encapsulation dot1q
 switchport trunk native vlan 4
 switchport trunk allowed vlan 4,6,12,15
 switchport mode trunk
end

S1#!
```

Oops—wait a minute! You didn't think it would be this easy and would just start working, did you? Of course not! Here's the rub: If all switches don't have the same native VLAN configured on the given trunk links, then we'll start to receive this error, which happened immediately after I entered the command:

```
1w6d: %CDP-4-NATIVE_VLAN_MISMATCH: Native VLAN mismatch discovered
on FastEthernet0/15 (4), with S3 FastEthernet0/1 (1).
```

Actually, this is a good, noncryptic error, so either we can go to the other end of our trunk link(s) and change the native VLAN or we set the native VLAN back to the default to fix it. Here's how we'd do that:

```
S1(config-if)#no switchport trunk native vlan
1w6d: %SPANTREE-2-UNBLOCK_CONSIST_PORT: Unblocking FastEthernet0/15
on VLAN0004. Port consistency restored.
```

Now our trunk link is using the default VLAN 1 as the native VLAN. Just remember that all switches on a given trunk must use the same native VLAN or you'll have some serious management problems. These issues won't affect user data, just management traffic between switches.

Exam Essentials

Understand the 802.1q VLAN identification method.   This is a nonproprietary IEEE method of frame tagging. If you're trunking between a Cisco switched link and a different brand of switch, you have to use 802.1q for the trunk to work.

Remember how to set a trunk port on a 2960 switch.   To set a port to trunking on a 2960, use the switchport mode trunk command.

Remember to check a switch port's VLAN assignment when plugging in a new host.   If you plug a new host into a switch, then you must verify the VLAN membership of that port. If the membership is different than what is needed for that host, the host will not be able to reach the needed network services, such as a workgroup server or printer.

Configure, verify, and troubleshoot STP protocols

If multiple connections between switches are created for redundancy purposes, network loops can occur. Spanning Tree Protocol (STP) is used to prevent network loops while still permitting redundancy. While you don't need to configure it, you may need to verify its proper operation and troubleshoot it. In the following section, I'll cover that.

STP Mode (PVST+ and RPVST+)

There are several varieties of spanning-tree protocols in use today:

IEEE 802.1d   The original standard for bridging and STP, which is really slow but requires very little bridge resources. It's also referred to as Common Spanning Tree (CST).

PVST+ (Cisco default version)   Per-VLAN Spanning Tree+ (PVST+) is the Cisco proprietary enhancement for STP that provides a separate 802.1d spanning-tree instance for each VLAN. Know that this is just as slow as the CST protocol, but with it, we get to have multiple root bridges. This creates more efficiency of the links in the network, but it does use more bridge resources than CST does.

IEEE 802.1w   Also called Rapid Spanning Tree Protocol (RSTP), this iteration enhanced the BPDU exchange and paved the way for much faster network convergence, but it still only allows for one root bridge per network like CST. The bridge resources used with RSTP are higher than CST's but less than PVST+.

802.1s (MSTP)   IEEE standard that started out as Cisco propriety MISTP. Maps multiple VLANs into the same spanning-tree instance to save processing on the switch. It's basically a spanning-tree protocol that rides on top of another spanning-tree protocol.

Rapid PVST+   Cisco's version of RSTP that also uses PVST+ and provides a separate instance of 802.1w per VLAN. It gives us really fast convergence times and optimal traffic flow but predictably requires the most CPU and memory of all.

STP Root Bridge Selection

The bridge ID is used to elect the root bridge in the STP domain and to determine the root port for each of the remaining devices when there's more than one potential root port available because they have equal-cost paths. This key bridge ID is 8 bytes long and includes both the priority and the MAC address of the device, as illustrated in Figure 2.8. Remember—the default priority on all devices running the IEEE STP version is 32,768.

FIGURE 2.8   STP operations

So, to determine the root bridge, you combine the priority of each bridge with its MAC address. If two switches or bridges happen to have the same priority value, the MAC address becomes the tiebreaker for figuring out which one has the lowest and, therefore, best ID. This means that because the two switches in Figure 2.9 are both using the default priority of 32,768, the MAC address will be the determining factor instead. And because Switch A's MAC address is 0000.0cab.3274 and Switch B's MAC address is 0000.0cf6.9370, Switch A wins and will become the root bridge. A really easy way to figure out the lowest MAC address is to just start reading from the left toward the right until you find a lesser value. For Switch A, I only needed to get to 0000.0ca before stopping. Switch A wins since switch B is 0000.0cf. Never forget that the lower value is always the better one when it comes to electing a root bridge!

FIGURE 2.9 Our simple three-switch network

I want to point out that prior to the election of the root bridge, BPDUs are sent every 2 seconds out all active ports on a bridge/switch by default, and they're received and processed by all bridges. The root bridge is elected based on this information. You can change the bridge's ID by lowering its priority so that it will become a root bridge automatically. Being able to do that is important in a large switched network because it ensures that the best paths will actually be the ones chosen. Efficiency is always awesome in networking!

Troubleshooting

To verify spanning tree on a Cisco switch, just use the command show spanning-tree. From its output, we can determine our root bridge, priorities, root ports, and designated and blocking/discarding ports.

Let's start by taking a look at the output from S1:

```
S1#sh spanning-tree vlan 1
VLAN0001
  Spanning tree enabled protocol ieee
  Root ID    Priority    32769
             Address     0001.42A7.A603
```

```
           This bridge is the root
           Hello Time  2 sec  Max Age 20 sec  Forward Delay 15 sec

Bridge ID  Priority     32769  (priority 32768 sys-id-ext 1)
           Address      0001.42A7.A603 him
           Hello Time  2 sec  Max Age 20 sec  Forward Delay 15 sec
           Aging Time   20

Interface         Role Sts Cost      Prio.Nbr Type
---------------   ---- --- --------- -------- --------------------------------
Gi1/1             Desg FWD 4         128.25   P2p
Gi1/2             Desg FWD 4         128.26   P2p
```

First, we can see that we're running the IEEE 802.1d STP version by default, and don't forget that this is really 802.1d PVST+! Looking at the output, we can see that S1 is the root bridge for VLAN 1. When you use this command, the top information is about the root bridge, and the Bridge ID output refers to the bridge you're looking at. In this example, they are one and the same. Notice the sys-id-ext 1 (for VLAN 1). This is the 12-bit PVST+ field that is placed into the BPDU so it can carry multiple-VLAN information. You add the priority and sys-id-ext to come up with the true priority for the VLAN. We can also see from the output that both Gigabit Ethernet interfaces are designated forwarding ports. You will not see a blocked/discarding port on a root bridge. Now let's take a look at S3's output:

```
S3#sh spanning-tree
VLAN0001
  Spanning tree enabled protocol ieee
  Root ID    Priority    32769
             Address     0001.42A7.A603
             Cost        4
             Port        26(GigabitEthernet1/2)
             Hello Time  2 sec  Max Age 20 sec  Forward Delay 15 sec

  Bridge ID  Priority    32769  (priority 32768 sys-id-ext 1)
             Address     000A.41D5.7937
             Hello Time  2 sec  Max Age 20 sec  Forward Delay 15 sec
             Aging Time   20

Interface         Role Sts Cost      Prio.Nbr Type
---------------   ---- --- --------- -------- --------------------------------
Gi1/1             Desg FWD 4         128.25   P2p
Gi1/2             Root FWD 4         128.26   P2p
```

Looking at the Root ID, it's easy to see that S3 isn't the root bridge, but the output tells us it's a cost of 4 to get to the root bridge and also that it's located out port 26 of the switch (Gi1/2). This tells us that the root bridge is one Gigabit Ethernet link away, which we already know is S1, but we can confirm this with the show cdp neighbors command:

```
Switch#sh cdp nei
Capability Codes: R - Router, T - Trans Bridge, B - Source Route Bridge
                  S - Switch, H - Host, I - IGMP, r - Repeater, P - Phone
Device ID    Local Intrfce   Holdtme   Capability   Platform   Port ID
S3           Gig 1/1         135              S      2960       Gig 1/1
S1           Gig 1/2         135              S      2960       Gig 1/1
```

That's how simple it is to find your root bridge if you don't have the nice figure as we do. Use the show spanning-tree command, find your root port, and then use the show cdp neighbors command. Let's see what S2's output has to tell us now:

```
S2#sh spanning-tree
VLAN0001
  Spanning tree enabled protocol ieee
  Root ID    Priority    32769
             Address     0001.42A7.A603
             Cost        4
             Port        26(GigabitEthernet1/2)
             Hello Time  2 sec  Max Age 20 sec  Forward Delay 15 sec

  Bridge ID  Priority    32769  (priority 32768 sys-id-ext 1)
             Address     0030.F222.2794
             Hello Time  2 sec  Max Age 20 sec  Forward Delay 15 sec
             Aging Time  20

Interface         Role Sts Cost      Prio.Nbr Type
----------------- ---- --- --------- -------- --------------------------------
Gi1/1             Altn BLK 4         128.25   P2p
Gi1/2             Root FWD 4         128.26   P2p
```

We're certainly not looking at a root bridge since we're seeing a blocked port, which is S2's connection to S3!

Let's have some fun by making S2 the root bridge for VLAN 2 and for VLAN 3. Here's how easy that is to do:

```
S2#sh spanning-tree vlan 2
VLAN0002
  Spanning tree enabled protocol ieee
```

```
Root ID    Priority    32770
           Address     0001.42A7.A603
           Cost        4
           Port        26(GigabitEthernet1/2)
           Hello Time  2 sec  Max Age 20 sec  Forward Delay 15 sec

Bridge ID  Priority    32770  (priority 32768 sys-id-ext 2)
           Address     0030.F222.2794
           Hello Time  2 sec  Max Age 20 sec  Forward Delay 15 sec
           Aging Time  20

Interface        Role Sts Cost      Prio.Nbr Type
---------------- ---- --- --------- -------- --------------------------------
Gi1/1            Altn BLK 4         128.25   P2p
Gi1/2            Root FWD 4         128.26   P2p
```

We can see that the root bridge cost is 4, meaning that the root bridge is one gigabit link away. One more key factor I want to talk about before making S2 the root bridge for VLANs 2 and 3 is the sys-id-ext, which shows up as 2 in this output because this output is for VLAN 2. This sys-id-ext is added to the bridge priority, which in this case in 32768 + 2, which makes the priority 32770. Now that you understand what that output is telling us, let's make S2 the root bridge:

```
S2(config)#spanning-tree vlan 2 ?
  priority  Set the bridge priority for the spanning tree
  root      Configure switch as root
  <cr>
S2(config)#spanning-tree vlan 2 priority ?
  <0-61440>  bridge priority in increments of 4096
S2(config)#spanning-tree vlan 2 priority 16384
```

You can set the priority to any value from 0 through 61440 in increments of 4096. Setting it to zero (0) means that the switch will always be a root as long as it has a lower MAC address than another switch that also has its bridge ID set to 0. If you want to set a switch to be the root bridge for every VLAN in your network, then you have to change the priority for each VLAN, with 0 being the lowest priority you can use. But trust me—it's never a good idea to set all switches to a priority of 0!

Furthermore, you don't actually need to change priorities because there is yet another way to configure the root bridge. Take a look:

```
S2(config)#spanning-tree vlan 3 root ?
  primary    Configure this switch as primary root for this spanning tree
  secondary  Configure switch as secondary root
```

```
S2(config)#spanning-tree vlan 3 root primary
S3(config)#spanning-tree vlan 3 root secondary
```

Notice that you can set a bridge to either primary or secondary—very cool! If both the primary and secondary switches go down, then the next highest priority will take over as root.

Let's check to see if S2 is actually the root bridge for VLANs 2 and 3 now:

```
S2#sh spanning-tree vlan 2
VLAN0002
  Spanning tree enabled protocol ieee
  Root ID    Priority    16386
             Address     0030.F222.2794
             This bridge is the root
             Hello Time   2 sec  Max Age 20 sec  Forward Delay 15 sec

  Bridge ID  Priority    16386  (priority 16384 sys-id-ext 2)
             Address     0030.F222.2794
             Hello Time   2 sec  Max Age 20 sec  Forward Delay 15 sec
             Aging Time  20

Interface        Role Sts Cost      Prio.Nbr Type
---------------- ---- --- --------- -------- ------------------------------
Gi1/1            Desg FWD 4         128.25   P2p
Gi1/2            Desg FWD 4         128.26   P2p
```

Nice—S2 is the root bridge for VLAN 2, with a priority of 16386 (16384 + 2). Let's take a look to see the root bridge for VLAN 3. I'll use a different command for that this time. Check it out:

```
S2#sh spanning-tree summary
Switch is in pvst mode
Root bridge for: VLAN0002 VLAN0003
Extended system ID            is enabled
Portfast Default              is disabled
PortFast BPDU Guard Default   is disabled
Portfast BPDU Filter Default  is disabled
Loopguard Default             is disabled
EtherChannel misconfig guard  is disabled
UplinkFast                    is disabled
BackboneFast                  is disabled
```

```
Configured Pathcost method used is short

Name              Blocking Listening Learning Forwarding STP Active
---------------   -------- --------- -------- ---------- ----------
VLAN0001              1        0        0          1          2
VLAN0002              0        0        0          2          2
VLAN0003              0        0        0          2          2

---------------   -------- --------- -------- ---------- ----------
3 vlans               1        0        0          5          6
```

The preceding output tells us that S2 is the root for the two VLANs, but we can see we have a blocked port for VLAN 1 on S2, so it's not the root bridge for VLAN 1. This is because there's another bridge with a better bridge ID for VLAN 1 than S2's.

One last burning question: How do you enable RSTP on a Cisco switch? Well, doing that is actually the easiest part of this section! Take a look:

S2(config)#**spanning-tree mode rapid-pvst**

Is that really all there is to it? Yes, because it's a global command, not per VLAN. Let's verify we're running RSTP now:

```
S2#sh spanning-tree
VLAN0001
  Spanning tree enabled protocol rstp
  Root ID    Priority    32769
             Address     0001.42A7.A603
             Cost        4
             Port        26(GigabitEthernet1/2)
             Hello Time  2 sec  Max Age 20 sec  Forward Delay 15 sec
[output cut]
S2#sh spanning-tree summary
Switch is in rapid-pvst mode
Root bridge for: VLAN0002 VLAN0003
```

Looks like we're set! We're running RSTP, S1 is our root bridge for VLAN 1, and S2 is the root bridge for VLANs 2 and 3. I know this doesn't seem hard, and it really isn't, but you still need to practice what we've covered so far in this section to really get your skills solid!

Exam Essentials

Understand the main purpose of the Spanning Tree Protocol in a switched LAN.
The main purpose of STP is to prevent switching loops in a network with redundant switched paths.

Remember the command **show spanning-tree.** You must be familiar with the command show spanning-tree and how to determine the root bridge of each VLAN. Also, you can use the show spanning-tree summary command to help you get a quick glimpse of your STP network and root bridges.

Configure, verify, and troubleshoot STP-related optional features

There are several optional features you can use to enhance the security of your STP topology and to make the network more user-friendly. In the following section, we'll look at two of those.

PortFast

If you have a server or other devices connected into your switch that you're totally sure won't create a switching loop if STP is disabled, you can use a Cisco proprietary extension to the 802.1d standard called PortFast on these ports. With this tool, the port won't spend the usual 50 seconds to come up into forwarding mode while STP is converging, which is what makes it so cool.

Since ports will transition from blocking to forwarding state immediately, PortFast can prevent our hosts from being potentially unable to receive a DHCP address due to STP's slow convergence. If the host's DHCP request times out, or if every time you plug a host in you're just tired of looking at the switch port being amber for almost a minute before it transitions to forwarding state and turns green, PortFast can really help you out!

Figure 2.10 illustrates a network with three switches, each with a trunk to each of the others and a host and server off the S1 switch.

FIGURE 2.10   PortFast

We can use PortFast on the ports on S1 to help them transition to the STP forwarding state immediately upon connecting to the switch.

Here are the commands, first from global config mode—they're pretty simple:

```
S1(config)#spanning-tree portfast ?
  bpdufilter  Enable portfast bdpu filter on this switch
  bpduguard   Enable portfast bpdu guard on this switch
  default     Enable portfast by default on all access ports
```

If you were to type **spanning-tree portfast default**, you would enable all nontrunking ports with PortFast. From interface mode, you can be more specific, which is the better way to go:

```
S1(config-if)#spanning-tree portfast ?
  disable  Disable portfast for this interface
  trunk    Enable portfast on the interface even in trunk mode
  <cr>
```

From interface mode you can actually configure PortFast on a trunk port, but you would do that only if the port connects to a server or router, not to another switch, so we won't use that here. So let's take a look at the message I get when I turn on PortFast on interface Gi0/1:

```
S1#config t
S1#config)#int range gi0/1 - 2
S1(config-if)#spanning-tree portfast
%Warning: portfast should only be enabled on ports connected to a single
 host. Connecting hubs, concentrators, switches, bridges, etc . . . to this
 interface  when portfast is enabled, can cause temporary bridging loops.
 Use with CAUTION

%Portfast has been configured on GigabitEthernet0/1 but will only
 have effect when the interface is in a non-trunking mode.
Switch(config-if)#
```

PortFast is enabled on port Gi0/1 and Gi0/2, but notice that you get a pretty long message that's essentially telling you to be careful. This is because when using PortFast, you definitely don't want to create a network loop by plugging another switch or hub into a port that's also configured with PortFast! Why? Because if you let this happen, even though the network may still sort of work, data will pass super slowly, and worse, it could take you a really long time to find the source of the problem, making you very unpopular. So proceed with caution!

At this juncture, you would be happy to know that there are some safeguard commands to have handy when using PortFast just in case someone causes a loop in a port that's configured with PortFast enabled.

BPDU Guard

If you turn on PortFast for a switch port, it's a really good idea to turn on BPDU Guard as well. In fact, it's such a great idea, I personally feel that it should be enabled by default whenever a port is configured with PortFast!

This is because if a switch port that has PortFast enabled receives a BPDU on that port, it will place the port into error disabled (shutdown) state, effectively preventing anyone from accidentally connecting another switch or hub port into a switch port configured with PortFast. Basically, you're preventing (guarding) your network from being severely crippled or even brought down. So let's configure our S1 interface, which is already configured with PortFast, with BPDU Guard now—it's easy!

Here's how to set it globally:

```
S1(config)# spanning-tree portfast bpduguard default
```

And specifically on an interface:

```
S1(config-if)#spanning-tree bpduguard enable
```

Exam Essentials

Understand what PortFast and BPDU Guard provide.   PortFast allows a port to transition to the forwarding state immediately upon a connection. Because you don't want other switches connecting to this port, BPDU Guard will shut down a PortFast port if it receives a BPDU.

Configure and verify layer 2 protocols

Cisco Discovery Protocol (CDP) is a proprietary protocol designed by Cisco to help administrators collect information about locally attached devices. Armed with CDP, you can gather hardware and protocol information about neighbor devices, which is crucial information to have when troubleshooting and documenting the network. Another dynamic discovery protocol is Link Layer Discovery Protocol (LLDP), but instead of being proprietary like CDP, it is vendor independent.

Cisco Discovery Protocol

Let's start by exploring the CDP timer and CDP commands we'll need to verify our network.

Getting CDP Timers and Holdtime Information

The show cdp command (sh cdp for short) gives you information about two CDP global parameters that can be configured on Cisco devices:

- *CDP timer* delimits how often CDP packets are transmitted out all active interfaces.
- *CDP holdtime* delimits the amount of time that the device will hold packets received from neighbor devices.

Both Cisco routers and switches use the same parameters. Check out Figure 2.11 to see how CDP works within a switched network.

FIGURE 2.11   Cisco Discovery Protocol

The output on my 3560 SW-3 looks like this:

```
SW-3#sh cdp
Global CDP information:
        Sending CDP packets every 60 seconds
        Sending a holdtime value of 180 seconds
        Sending CDPv2 advertisements is enabled
```

This output tells us that the default is to transmit every 60 seconds and will hold packets from a neighbor in the CDP table for 180 seconds. I can use the global commands cdp holdtime and cdp timer to configure the CDP holdtime and timer on a router if necessary like this:

```
SW-3(config)#cdp ?
  advertise-v2  CDP sends version-2 advertisements
  holdtime      Specify the holdtime (in sec) to be sent in packets
```

```
run           Enable CDP
timer         Specify the rate at which CDP packets are sent (in sec)
tlv           Enable exchange of specific tlv information
```

```
SW-3(config)#cdp holdtime ?
 <10-255> Length of time (in sec) that receiver must keep this packet
```

```
SW-3(config)#cdp timer ?
 <5-254>  Rate at which CDP packets are sent (in  sec)
```

You can turn off CDP completely with the no cdp run command from global configuration mode of a router and enable it with the cdp run command:

```
SW-3(config)#no cdp run
SW-3(config)#cdp run
```

To turn CDP off or on for an interface, use the no cdp enable and cdp enable commands.

Gathering Neighbor Information

The show cdp neighbor command (sh cdp nei for short) delivers information about directly connected devices. It's important to remember that CDP packets aren't passed through a Cisco switch and that you only see what's directly attached. So this means that if your router is connected to a switch, you won't see any of the Cisco devices connected to that switch!

The following output shows the show cdp neighbor command I used on my SW-3:

```
SW-3#sh cdp neighbors
Capability Codes: R - Router, T - Trans Bridge, B - Source Route Bridge
                  S - Switch, H - Host, I - IGMP, r - Repeater, P - Phone,
                  D - Remote, C - CVTA, M - Two-port Mac Relay Device ID
Local Intrfce    Holdtme    Capability  Platform  Port ID
SW-1   Fas 0/1     170          S I     WS-C3560- Fas 0/15
SW-1   Fas 0/2     170          S I     WS-C3560- Fas 0/16
SW-2   Fas 0/5     162          S I     WS-C3560- Fas 0/5
SW-2   Fas 0/6     162          S I     WS-C3560- Fas 0/6
```

Okay—we can see that I'm directly connected with a console cable to the SW-3 switch and also that SW-3 is directly connected to two other switches. However, do we really need the figure to draw out our network? We don't! CDP allows me to see who my directly connected neighbors are and gather information about them. From the SW-3 switch, we can see that there are two connections to SW-1 and two connections to SW-2. SW-3 connects to SW-1 with ports Fas 0/1 and Fas 0/2, and we have connections to SW-2 with local interfaces Fas 0/5 and Fas 0/6. Both the SW-1 and SW-2 switches are 3650 switches, and SW-1 is using ports Fas 0/15 and Fas 0/16 to connect to SW-3. SW-2 is using ports Fas 0/5 and Fas 0/6.

To sum this up, the device ID shows the configured hostname of the connected device, that the local interface is our interface, and the port ID is the remote devices' directly connected interface. Remember that all you get to view are directly connected devices!

Table 2.1 summarizes the information displayed by the show cdp neighbor command for each device.

TABLE 2.1 Output of the show cdp neighbors command

Field	Description
Device ID	The hostname of the device directly connected
Local Interface	The port or interface on which you are receiving the CDP packet
Holdtime	The remaining amount of time the router will hold the information before discarding it if no more CDP packets are received
Capability	The capability of the neighbor—the router, switch, or repeater. The capability codes are listed at the top of the command output.
Platform	The type of Cisco device directly connected. In the previous output, the SW-3 shows it's directly connected to two 3560 switches.
Port ID	The neighbor device's port or interface on which the CDP packets are multicast

 It's imperative that you can look at the output of a show cdp neighbors command and decipher the information gained about the neighbor device's capability, whether it's a router or switch, the model number (platform), your port connecting to that device (local interface), and the port of the neighbor connecting to you (port ID).

Another command that will deliver the goods on neighbor information is the show cdp neighbors detail command (show cdp nei de for short). This command can be run on both routers and switches, and it displays detailed information about each device connected to the device you're running the command on. Check out the router output in Listing 2.1.

Listing 2.1: Showing CDP neighbors

```
SW-3#sh cdp neighbors detail
-------------------------
Device ID: SW-1
```

continues

Listing 2.1: Showing CDP neighbors (*continued*)

```
Entry address(es):
  IP address: 10.100.128.10
Platform: cisco WS-C3560-24TS,  Capabilities: Switch IGMP
Interface: FastEthernet0/1,  Port ID (outgoing port): FastEthernet0/15
Holdtime : 137 sec

Version :
Cisco IOS Software, C3560 Software (C3560-IPSERVICESK9-M), Version 12.2(55)SE7, ↵
RELEASE SOFTWARE (fc1)
Technical Support: http://www.cisco.com/techsupport
Copyright (c) 1986-2013 by Cisco Systems, Inc.
Compiled Mon 28-Jan-13 10:10 by prod_rel_team

advertisement version: 2
Protocol Hello:  OUI=0x00000C, Protocol ID=0x0112; payload len=27, ↵
value=00000000FFFFFFFF010221FF000000000000001C575EC880Fc00f000
VTP Management Domain: 'NULL'
Native VLAN: 1
Duplex: full
Power Available TLV:

    Power request id: 0, Power management id: 1, Power available: 0, Power ↵
management level: -1
Management address(es):
  IP address: 10.100.128.10
-------------------------

[ouput cut]

-------------------------
Device ID: SW-2
Entry address(es):
  IP address: 10.100.128.9
Platform: cisco WS-C3560-8PC,  Capabilities: Switch IGMP
Interface: FastEthernet0/5,  Port ID (outgoing port): FastEthernet0/5
Holdtime : 129 sec

Version :
Cisco IOS Software, C3560 Software (C3560-IPBASE-M), Version 12.2(35)SE5, RELEASE ↵
SOFTWARE (fc1)
Copyright (c) 1986-2007 by Cisco Systems, Inc.
Compiled Thu 19-Jul-07 18:15 by nachen
```

```
advertisement version: 2
Protocol Hello:  OUI=0x00000C, Protocol ID=0x0112; payload len=27,
value=00000000FFFFFFFF010221FF000000000000B41489D91880Fc00f000
VTP Management Domain: 'NULL'
Native VLAN: 1
Duplex: full
Power Available TLV:

    Power request id: 0, Power management id: 1, Power available: 0, Power ↵
management level: -1
Management address(es):
  IP address: 10.100.128.9
[output cut]
```

So what's revealed here? First, we've been given the hostname and IP address of all directly connected devices. And in addition to the same information displayed by the show cdp neighbors command (see Table 2.1), the show cdp neighbors detail command tells us about the IOS version and IP address of the neighbor device—that's quite a bit!

The show cdp entry * command displays the same information as the show cdp neighbors detail command. There isn't any difference between these commands.

Documenting a Network Topology Using CDP

I'm now going to show you how to document a sample network by using CDP. You'll learn to determine the appropriate router types, interface types, and IP addresses of various interfaces using only CDP commands and the show running-config command. And you can only console into the Lab_A router to document the network. You'll have to assign any remote routers the next IP address in each range. We'll use a different figure for this example—Figure 2.12—to help us to complete the necessary documentation.

FIGURE 2.12   Documenting a network topology using CDP

In this output, you can see that you have a router with four interfaces: two Fast Ethernet and two serial. First, determine the IP addresses of each interface by using the show running-config command like this:

```
Lab_A#sh running-config
Building configuration . . .

Current configuration : 960 bytes
!
version 12.2
service timestamps debug uptime
service timestamps log uptime
no service password-encryption
!
hostname Lab_A
!
ip subnet-zero
!
!
interface FastEthernet0/0
 ip address 192.168.21.1 255.255.255.0
 duplex auto
!
interface FastEthernet0/1
 ip address 192.168.18.1 255.255.255.0
 duplex auto
!
interface Serial0/0
ip address 192.168.23.1 255.255.255.0
!
interface Serial0/1
ip address 192.168.28.1 255.255.255.0
!
ip classless
!
line con 0
line aux 0
line vty 0 4
!
end
```

With this step completed, you can now write down the IP addresses of the Lab_A router's four interfaces. Next, you must determine the type of device on the other end of each of these interfaces. It's easy—just use the show cdp neighbors command:

```
Lab_A#sh cdp neighbors
Capability Codes: R - Router, T - Trans Bridge, B - Source Route Bridge
S - Switch, H - Host, I - IGMP, r - Repeater
Device ID   Local Intrfce     Holdtme    Capability Platform  Port ID
Lab_B         Fas 0/0           178          R        2501     E0
Lab_C         Fas 0/1           137          R        2621     Fa0/0
Lab_D         Ser 0/0           178          R        2514     S1
Lab_E         Ser 0/1           137          R        2620     S0/1
```

Wow—looks like we're connected to some old routers! But it's not our job to judge. Our mission is to draw out our network, so it's good that we've got some nice information to meet the challenge with now. By using both the show running-config and show cdp neighbors commands, we know about all the IP addresses of the Lab_A router, the types of routers connected to each of the Lab_A router's links, and all the interfaces of the remote routers.

Now that we're equipped with all the information gathered via show running-config and show cdp neighbors, we can accurately create the topology in Figure 2.13.

FIGURE 2.13   Network topology documented

If we needed to, we could've also used the show cdp neighbors detail command to view the neighbor's IP addresses. But since we know the IP addresses of each link on the Lab_A router, we already know what the next available IP address is going to be.

LLDP

Before moving on from CDP, I want to tell you about a nonproprietary discovery protocol that provides pretty much the same information as CDP but works in multivendor networks.

The IEEE created a new standardized discovery protocol called 802.1AB for Station and Media Access Control Connectivity Discovery. We'll just call it *Link Layer Discovery Protocol (LLDP)*.

LLDP defines basic discovery capabilities, but it was also enhanced to specifically address the voice application, and this version is called LLDP-MED (Media Endpoint Discovery). It's good to remember that LLDP and LLDP-MED are not compatible.

LLDP has the following configuration guidelines and limitations:

- LLDP must be enabled on the device before you can enable or disable it on any interface.

- LLDP is supported only on physical interfaces.

- LLDP can discover up to one device per port.

- LLDP can discover Linux servers.

You can turn off LLDP completely with the no lldp run command from global configuration mode of a device and enable it with the lldp run command, which enables it on all interfaces as well:

```
SW-3(config)#no lldp run
SW-3(config)#lldp run
```

To turn LLDP off or on for an interface, use the lldp transmit and lldp receive commands.

```
SW-3(config-if)#no lldp transmit
SW-3(config-if)#no lldp receive

SW-3(config-if)#lldp transmit
SW-3(config-if)#lldp receive
```

Exam Essentials

Describe the value of CDP and LLDP.   Cisco Discovery Protocol can be used to help you document as well as troubleshoot your network; also, LLDP is a nonproprietary protocol that can provide the same information as CDP.

Configure, verify, and troubleshoot (layer 2/layer 3) EtherChannel

Know that almost all Ethernet networks today will typically have multiple links between switches because this kind of design provides redundancy and resiliency. On a physical design that includes multiple links between switches, STP will do its job and put a port or ports into blocking mode. In addition to that, routing protocols like OSPF and EIGRP could see all these redundant links as individual ones, depending on the configuration, which can mean an increase in routing overhead.

We can gain the benefits from multiple links between switches by using port channeling. EtherChannel is a port channel technology that was originally developed by Cisco as a switch-to-switch technique for grouping several Fast Ethernet or Gigabit Ethernet ports into one logical channel.

Also important to note is that once your port channel (EtherChannel) is up and working, layer 2 STP and layer 3 routing protocols will treat those bundled links as a single one, which would stop STP from performing blocking. An additional nice result is that because the routing protocols now only see this as a single link, a single adjacency across the link can be formed—elegant!

Figure 2.14 shows how a network would look if we had four connections between switches, before and after configuring port channels.

FIGURE 2.14   Before and after port channels

Now as usual, there's the Cisco version and the IEEE version of port channel negotiation protocols to choose from—take your pick. Cisco's version is called Port Aggregation Protocol (PAgP), and the IEEE 802.3ad standard is called Link Aggregation Control Protocol (LACP). Both versions work equally well, but the way you configure each is slightly different. Keep in mind that both PAgP and LACP are negotiation protocols and that EtherChannel can actually be statically configured without PAgP or LACP. Still, it's better to use one of these protocols to help with compatibility issues as well as to manage link additions and failures between two switches.

Cisco EtherChannel allows us to bundle up to eight active ports between switches. The links must have the same speed, duplex setting, and VLAN configuration—in other words, you can't mix interface types and configurations into the same bundle.

There are a few differences in configuring PAgP and LACP, but first, let's go over some terms so you don't get confused:

Port channeling   Refers to combining two to eight Fast Ethernet or two Gigabit Ethernet ports together between two switches into one aggregated logical link to achieve more bandwidth and resiliency

EtherChannel   Cisco's proprietary term for port channeling

PAgP   This is a Cisco proprietary port channel negotiation protocol that aids in the automatic creation for EtherChannel links. All links in the bundle must match the same parameters (speed, duplex, VLAN info), and when PAgP identifies matched links, it groups the links into an EtherChannel. This is then added to STP as a single bridge port. At this point, PAgP's job is to send packets every 30 seconds to manage the link for consistency, any link additions, and failures.

LACP (802.3ad)   This has the exact same purpose as PAgP, but it's nonproprietary so it can work between multi-vendor networks.

`channel-group`   This is a command on Ethernet interfaces used to add the specified interface to a single EtherChannel. The number following this command is the port channel ID.

`interface port-channel`   Here's a command that creates the bundled interface. Ports can be added to this interface with the `channel-group` command. Keep in mind that the interface number must match the group number.

Now let's see if you can make some sense out of all these terms by actually configuring something!

Static

Remember that both PAgP and LACP are negotiation protocols and that EtherChannel can actually be statically configured without PAgP or LACP. This example shows how to create an EtherChannel:

```
switch# configure terminal
switch (config)# interface port-channel 7
```

This example shows how to add an Ethernet interface 1/3 to channel group 1:

```
switch# configure terminal
switch (config)# interface ethernet 1/3
switch(config-if)# switchport mode trunk
switch(config-if)# channel-group 7
```

PAGP and LACP

Let's use Figure 2.15 for our simple example of how to configure port channels.

FIGURE 2.15   EtherChannel example

You can enable your `channel group` for each channel by setting the channel mode for each interface to either `active` or `passive` if using LACP. When a port is configured in passive mode, it will respond to the LACP packets it receives, but it won't initiate an LACP negotiation. When a port is configured for active mode, the port initiates negotiations with other ports by sending LACP packets.

Let me show you a simple example of configuring port channels and then verifying them. First I'll go to global configuration mode and create a port channel interface, and then I'll add this port channel to the physical interfaces.

Remember, all parameters and configurations of the ports must be the same, so I'll start by trunking the interfaces before I configure EtherChannel, like this:

```
S1(config)#int range g0/1 - 2
S1(config-if-range)#switchport trunk encapsulation dot1q
S1(config-if-range)#switchport mode trunk
S1(config-if-range)#
```

All ports in your bundles must be configured the same, so I'll configure both sides with the same trunking configuration. Now I can assign these ports to a bundle:

```
S1(config-if-range)#channel-group 1 mode ?
  active     Enable LACP unconditionally
  auto       Enable PAgP only if a PAgP device is detected
  desirable  Enable PAgP unconditionally
  on         Enable Etherchannel only
  passive    Enable LACP only if a LACP device is detected
S1(config-if-range)#channel-group 1 mode active
S1(config-if-range)#exit
```

To configure the IEEE nonproprietary LACP, I'll use the active or passive command; if I wanted to use Cisco's PAgP, I'd use the auto or desirable command. You can't mix and match these on either end of the bundle, and really, it doesn't matter which one you use in a pure Cisco environment, as long as you configure them the same on both ends (setting the mode to on would be statically configuring your EtherChannel bundle).

At this point in the configuration, I'd have to set the mode to active on the S2 interfaces if I wanted the bundle to come up with LACP because, again, all parameters must be the same on both ends of the link. Let's create our port channel interface now with the interface port-channel command:

```
S1(config)#int port-channel 1
S1(config-if)#switchport trunk encapsulation dot1q
S1(config-if)#switchport mode trunk
S1(config-if)#switchport trunk allowed vlan 1,2,3
```

Notice that I set the same trunking method under the port channel interface as I did the physical interfaces, as well as VLAN information too.

Time to configure the interfaces, channel groups, and port channel interface on the S2 switch:

```
S2(config)#int range g0/13 - 14
S2(config-if-range)#switchport trunk encapsulation dot1q
S2(config-if-range)#switchport mode trunk
S2(config-if-range)#channel-group 1 mode active
S2(config-if-range)#exit
S2(config)#int port-channel 1
S2(config-if)#switchport trunk encapsulation dot1q
S2(config-if)#switchport mode trunk
S2(config-if)#switchport trunk allowed vlan 1,2,3
```

On each switch, I configured the ports I wanted to bundle with the same configuration, then created the port channel. After that, I added the ports into the port channel with the channel-group command.

Remember, for LACP we'll use either active/active on each side of the bundle or active/passive, but you can't use passive/passive. Same goes for PAgP; you can use desirable/desirable or auto/desirable but not auto/auto.

Let's verify our EtherChannel with a few commands. We'll start with the show etherchannel port-channel command to see information about a specific port channel interface:

```
S2#sh etherchannel port-channel
              Channel-group listing:
              ----------------------

Group: 1
----------
              Port-channels in the group:
              ---------------------------

Port-channel: Po1    (Primary Aggregator)
------------

Age of the Port-channel   = 00d:00h:46m:49s
Logical slot/port   = 2/1       Number of ports = 2
GC                  = 0x00000000      HotStandBy port = null
Port state          = Port-channel
Protocol            =    LACP
Port Security       = Disabled
```

```
Ports in the Port-channel:

Index   Load   Port     EC state          No of bits
------+------+------+------------------+-----------
   0    00    Gig0/2   Active               0
   0    00    Gig0/1   Active               0
Time since last port bundled:     00d:00h:46m:47s    Gig0/1
S2#
```

Notice that we have one group and that we're running the IEEE LACP version of port channeling. We're in Active mode, and that Port-channel: Po1 interface has two physical interfaces. The heading Load is not the load over the interfaces, it's a hexadecimal value that decides which interface will be chosen to specify the flow of traffic.

The show etherchannel summary command displays one line of information per port channel:

```
S2#sh etherchannel summary
Flags:  D - down         P - in port-channel
        I - stand-alone  s - suspended
        H - Hot-standby (LACP only)
        R - Layer3       S - Layer2
        U - in use       f - failed to allocate aggregator
        u - unsuitable for bundling
        w - waiting to be aggregated
        d - default port

Number of channel-groups in use: 1
Number of aggregators:           1

Group  Port-channel  Protocol    Ports
------+-------------+-----------+-----------------------------------------------

1      Po1(SU)          LACP    Gig0/1(P) Gig0/2(P)
```

This command shows that we have one group, that we're running LACP, and Gig0/1 and Gig0/2 or (P), which means these ports are in port-channel mode. This command isn't really all that helpful unless you have multiple channel groups, but it does tell us our group is working well!

Layer 3 EtherChannel

One last item to discuss before we finish this objective and that is layer 3 EtherChannel. You'd use layer 3 EtherChannel when connecting a switch to multiple ports on a router, for example. It's important to understand that you wouldn't put IP addresses under the physical interfaces of the router; instead, you'd actually add the IP address of the bundle under the logical port channel interface.

Here is an example on how to create the logical port channel 1 and assign 20.2.2.2 as its IP address:

```
Router#config t
Router(config)#int port-channel 1
Router(config-if)#ip address 20.2.2.2 255.255.255.0
```

Now we need to add the physical ports into port channel 1:

```
Router(config-if)#int range g0/0-1
Router(config-if-range)#channel-group 1
GigabitEthernet0/0 added as member-1 to port-channel1
GigabitEthernet0/1 added as member-2 to port-channel1
```

Now let's take a look at the running-config. Notice there are no IP addresses under the physical interface of the router:

```
!
interface Port-channel1
 ip address 20.2.2.2 255.255.255.0
 load-interval 30
!
 interface GigabitEthernet0/0
 no ip address
 load-interval 30
 duplex auto
 speed auto
 channel-group 1
!
 interface GigabitEthernet0/1
 no ip address
 load-interval 30
 duplex auto
 speed auto
 channel-group 1
```

Exam Essentials

Understand what EtherChannel is and how to configure it. EtherChannel allows you to bundle links to get more bandwidth, instead of allowing STP to shut down redundant ports. You can configure Cisco's PAgP or the IEEE version, LACP, by creating a port channel interface and assigning the port channel group number to the interfaces you are bundling.

Describe the benefits of switch stacking and chassis aggregation

Switch stacking has been around since the word *cloud* meant 4/20 in my hometown of Boulder, but I digress. A typical access closet contains access switches placed next to each other in the same rack and uses high-speed redundant links with copper, or more typically fiber, to the distribution layer switches.

Here are three big drawbacks to a typical switch topology:

- Management overhead is high.
- STP will block half of the uplinks.
- There is no direct communication between switches.

Cisco StackWise technology connects switches that are mounted in the same rack together so they basically become one larger switch. By doing this, you can incrementally add more access ports for each closet while avoiding the cost of upgrading to a bigger switch. So you're adding ports as you grow your company instead of front loading the investment into a pricier, larger switch all at once. And since these stacks are managed as a single unit, it reduces the management in your network.

All switches in a stack share configuration and routing information, so you can easily add or remove switches at any time without disrupting your network or affecting its performance.

Figure 2.16 shows a typical access layer StackWise unit.

FIGURE 2.16   Switch stacking

To create a StackWise unit, you combine individual switches into a single, logical unit using special stack interconnect cables as shown in Figure 2.16. This creates a bidirectional, closed-loop path in the stack.

Here are some other features of StackWise:

- Any changes to the network topology or routing information are updated continuously through the stack interconnect.

- A master switch manages the stack as a single unit. The master switch is elected from one of the stack member switches.

- You can join up to nine separate switches in a stack.

- Each stack of switches has only a single IP address, and the stack is managed as a single object. You'll use this single IP address for managing the stack, including fault detection, VLAN database updates, security, and QoS controls. Each stack has only one configuration file, which is distributed to each switch in the StackWise unit. Using Cisco StackWise will produce some management overhead, but at the same time, multiple switches in a stack can create an EtherChannel connection, eliminating the need for STP.

These are the benefits to using StackWise technology, specifically mapped to the CCNA objectives to memorize:

- StackWise provides a method to join multiple physical switches into a single logical switching unit.

- Switches are united by special interconnect cables.

- The master switch is elected.

- The stack is managed as a single object and has a single management IP address.

- Management overhead is reduced.

- STP is no longer needed if you use EtherChannel.

- Up to nine switches can be in a StackWise unit.

One more very cool thing . . . When you add a new switch to the stack, the master switch automatically configures the unit with the currently running IOS image as well as the configuration of the stack. So you don't have to do anything to bring up the switch before its ready to operate . . . nice!

Exam Essentials

Define the benefits of switch stacking. These include but are not limited to network topology or routing information updated continuously through the stack interconnect and the use of a master switch to the stack as a single unit.

Review Questions

You can find the answers in the Appendix.

1. Which of the following statements is *not* true with regard to layer 2 switching?

    A. Layer 2 switches and bridges are faster than routers because they don't take up time looking at the Data Link layer header information.

    B. Layer 2 switches and bridges look at the frame's hardware addresses before deciding to either forward, flood, or drop the frame.

    C. Switches create private, dedicated collision domains and provide independent bandwidth on each port.

    D. Switches use application-specific integrated circuits (ASICs) to build and maintain their MAC filter tables.

2. List the command that generated the output shown.

```
Mac Address Table
-------------------------------------------

Vlan    Mac Address     Type        Ports
----    -----------     --------    -----
All     0100.0ccc.cccc  STATIC      CPU
[output cut]
  1     000e.83b2.e34b  DYNAMIC     Fa0/1
  1     0011.1191.556f  DYNAMIC     Fa0/1
  1     0011.3206.25cb  DYNAMIC     Fa0/1
  1     001a.4d55.2f7e  DYNAMIC     Fa0/1
  1     001b.d40a.0538  DYNAMIC     Fa0/1
  1     001c.575e.c891  DYNAMIC     Fa0/1
  1     aaaa.bbbb.0ccc  STATIC      Fa0/7
```

3. In the diagram shown, what will the switch do if a frame with a destination MAC address of 000a.f467.63b1 is received on Fa0/4? (Choose one answer.)

```
Switch# show mac address-table

VLAN    Mac Address      Ports
 1      0005.dccb.d74b   Fa0/4
 1      000a.f467.9e80   Fa0/5
 1      000a.f467.9e8b   Fa0/6
```

    A. Drop the frame.

    B. Send the frame to every port except the one on which it arrived

    C. Send the frame out of Fa0/4.

    D. Send the frame out of Fa0/5.

    E. Send the frame out of Fa0/6.

4.   In the list in the following graphic, which items are functions of a switch.

> Address learning
>
> Packet forwarding
>
> Layer 3 security
>
> Forward/filter decisions
>
> Loop avoidance

5.   What statement(s) is/are true about the output shown here? (Choose all that apply.)

```
S3#sh port-security int f0/3
Port Security              : Enabled
Port Status                : Secure-shutdown
Violation Mode             : Shutdown
Aging Time                 : 0 mins
Aging Type                 : Absolute
SecureStatic Address Aging : Disabled
Maximum MAC Addresses      : 1
Total MAC Addresses        : 2
Configured MAC Addresses   : 0
Sticky MAC Addresses       : 0
Last Source Address:Vlan   : 0013:0ca69:00bb3:00ba8:1
Security Violation Count   : 1
```

    A. The port light for F0/3 will be amber in color.

    B. The F0/3 port is forwarding frames.

    C. This problem will resolve itself in a few minutes.

    D. This port requires the shutdown command to function.

6.   In the accompanying graphic, what is the name for the section of the MAC address marked as unknown?

Example: 0000.0c12.3456

A. IOS

B. OSI

C. ISO

D. OUI

7. _____ on an Ethernet network is the retransmission delay that's enforced when a collision occurs.

A. Backoff

B. Carrier sense

C. Forward delay

D. Jamming

8. In the Ethernet II frame shown here, what is the function of the section labeled "FCS"?

Ethernet_II

Preamble 7 bytes	SFD 1 byte	Destination 6 bytes	Source 6 bytes	Type 2 bytes	Data and Pad 46 – 1500 bytes	FCS 4 bytes

A. Allows the receiving devices to lock the incoming bit stream

B. Error detection

C. Identifies the upper-layer protocol

D. Identifies the transmitting device

9. For what two purposes does the Ethernet protocol use physical addresses? (Choose two.)

A. To uniquely identify devices at layer 2

B. To allow communication with devices on a different network

C. To differentiate a layer 2 frame from a layer 3 packet

D. To establish a priority system to determine which device gets to transmit first

E. To allow communication between different devices on the same network

F. To allow detection of a remote device when its physical address is unknown

10. Which of the following statements is true with regard to VLANs?

A. VLANs greatly reduce network security.

B. VLANs increase the number of collision domains while decreasing their size.

C. VLANs decrease the number of broadcast domains while decreasing their size.

D. Network adds, moves, and changes are achieved with ease by just configuring a port into the appropriate VLAN.

Chapter
3

Routing Technologies

THE FOLLOWING CCNA ROUTING AND SWITCHING EXAM OBJECTIVES ARE COVERED IN THIS CHAPTER:

✓ Describe the routing concepts.

✓ Interpret the components of a routing table.

✓ Describe how a routing table is populated by different routing information sources.

✓ Configure, verify, and troubleshoot inter-VLAN routing.

✓ Compare and contrast static routing and dynamic routing.

✓ Compare and contrast distance vector and link state routing protocols.

✓ Compare and contrast interior and exterior routing protocols.

✓ Configure, verify, and troubleshoot IPv4 and IPv6 static routing.

✓ Configure, verify, and troubleshoot single area and multi-area OSPFv2 for IPv4 (excluding authentication, filtering, manual summarization, redistribution, stub, virtual link, and LSAs).

✓ Configure, verify, and troubleshoot single area and multi-area OSPFv3 for IPv6 (excluding authentication, filtering, manual summarization, redistribution, stub, virtual-link, and LSAs).

✓ Configure, verify, and troubleshoot EIGRP for IPv4 (excluding authentication, filtering, manual summarization, redistribution, stub).

✓ Configure, verify, and troubleshoot EIGRP for IPv6 (excluding authentication, filtering, manual summarization, redistribution, stub).

✓ Configure, verify, and troubleshoot RIPv2 for IPv4 (excluding authentication, filtering, manual summarization, redistribution).

✓ Troubleshoot basic layer 3 end-to-end connectivity issues.

In this chapter, I will discuss routing concepts. This will include a discussion of the routing table, routing protocols, and static routing. I will also cover the configuration of RIP and single-area OSPF and the process of troubleshooting end-to-end connectivity at layer 3.

Describe the routing concepts

The term *routing* refers to taking a packet from one device and sending it through the network to another device on a different network. Routers don't really care about hosts—they only care about networks and the best path to each one of them. The logical network address of the destination host is key to get packets through a routed network. It's the hardware address of the host that's used to deliver the packet from a router and ensure it arrives at the correct destination host. In the following sections, we'll take a close look at how routing works.

Packet Handling along the Path through a Network

The IP routing process is fairly simple and doesn't change, regardless of the size of your network. For a good example of this fact, I'll use Figure 3.1 to describe step-by-step what happens when Host A wants to communicate with Host B on a different network.

FIGURE 3.1   IP routing example using two hosts and one router

In Figure 3.1 a user on Host A pinged Host B's IP address. Routing doesn't get any simpler than this, but it still involves a lot of steps, so let's work through them now:

1. Internet Control Message Protocol (ICMP) creates an echo request payload, which is simply the alphabet in the data field.

2. ICMP hands that payload to Internet Protocol (IP), which then creates a packet. At a minimum, this packet contains an IP source address, an IP destination address,

and a Protocol field with 01h. Don't forget that Cisco likes to use *0x* in front of hex characters, so this could also look like 0x01. This tells the receiving host to whom it should hand the payload when the destination is reached—in this example, ICMP.

3. Once the packet is created, IP determines whether the destination IP address is on the local network or a remote one.

4. Since IP has determined that this is a remote request, the packet must be sent to the default gateway so it can be routed to the remote network. The Registry in Windows is parsed to find the configured default gateway.

5. The default gateway of Host A is configured to 172.16.10.1. For this packet to be sent to the default gateway, the hardware address of the router's interface Ethernet 0, which is configured with the IP address of 172.16.10.1, must be known. Why? So the packet can be handed down to the Data Link layer, framed, and sent to the router's interface that's connected to the 172.16.10.0 network. Because hosts communicate only via hardware addresses on the local LAN, it's important to recognize that for Host A to communicate to Host B, it has to send packets to the Media Access Control (MAC) address of the default gateway on the local network.

 MAC addresses are always local on the LAN and never go through and past a router.

6. Next, the Address Resolution Protocol (ARP) cache of the host is checked to see if the IP address of the default gateway has already been resolved to a hardware address.

   If it has, the packet is then free to be handed to the Data Link layer for framing. Remember that the hardware destination address is also handed down with that packet. To view the ARP cache on your host, use the following command:

```
C:\>arp -a
Interface: 172.16.10.2 --- 0x3
  Internet Address      Physical Address      Type
  172.16.10.1           00-15-05-06-31-b0     dynamic
```

   If the hardware address isn't already in the ARP cache of the host, an ARP broadcast will be sent out onto the local network to search for the 172.16.10.1 hardware address. The router then responds to the request and provides the hardware address of Ethernet 0, and the host caches this address.

7. Once the packet and destination hardware address are handed to the Data Link layer, the LAN driver is used to provide media access via the type of LAN being used, which is Ethernet in this case. A frame is then generated, encapsulating the packet with control information. Within that frame are the hardware destination and source addresses plus, in this case, an Ether-Type field, which identifies the specific Network layer protocol that handed the packet to the Data Link layer. In this instance, it's IP. At the end of the frame is something called a Frame Check Sequence (FCS) field that houses

the result of the cyclic redundancy check (CRC). A CRC calculation ensures that the contents of the frame have not changed during transmission. The frame would look something like what I've detailed in Figure 3.2. It contains Host A's hardware (MAC) address and the destination hardware address of the default gateway. It does not include the remote host's MAC address—remember that!

FIGURE 3.2   Frame used from Host A to the Lab A router when Host B is pinged

Destination MAC (router's E0 MAC address)	Source MAC (Host A's MAC address)	Ether-Type field	Packet	FCS CRC

8. Once the frame is completed, it's handed down to the Physical layer to be put on the physical medium (in this example, twisted-pair wire) one bit at a time.

9. Every device in the collision domain receives these bits and builds the frame. They each run a CRC and check the answer in the FCS field. If the answers don't match, the frame is discarded.

   ▪ If the CRC matches, then the hardware destination address is checked to see if it matches (which, in this example, is the router's interface Ethernet 0).

   ▪ If it's a match, then the Ether-Type field is checked to find the protocol used at the Network layer.

10. The packet is pulled from the frame, and what is left of the frame is discarded. The packet is handed to the protocol listed in the Ether-Type field—it's given to IP.

11. IP receives the packet and checks the IP destination address. Since the packet's destination address doesn't match any of the addresses configured on the receiving router itself, the router will look up the destination IP network address in its routing table.

12. The routing table must have an entry for the network 172.16.20.0 or the packet will be discarded immediately and an ICMP message will be sent back to the originating device with a destination network unreachable message.

13. If the router does find an entry for the destination network in its table, the packet is switched to the exit interface—in this example, interface Ethernet 1. The following output displays the Lab A router's routing table. The C means "directly connected." No routing protocols are needed in this network since all networks (all two of them) are directly connected.

```
Lab A>sh ip route
C        172.16.10.0 is directly connected,    Ethernet0
L        172.16.10.1/32 is directly connected, Ethernet0
C        172.16.20.0 is directly connected,    Ethernet1
L        172.16.20.1/32 is directly connected, Ethernet1
```

14. The router packet-switches the packet to the Ethernet 1 buffer.

15. The Ethernet 1 buffer needs to know the hardware address of the destination host and first checks the ARP cache.

- If the hardware address of Host B has already been resolved and is in the router's ARP cache, then the packet and the hardware address will be handed down to the Data Link layer to be framed. Let's take a look at the ARP cache on the Lab A router by using the show ip arp command:

```
Lab A#sh ip arp
Protocol  Address       Age(min) Hardware Addr   Type   Interface
Internet  172.16.20.1   -        00d0.58ad.05f4  ARPA   Ethernet1
Internet  172.16.20.2   3        0030.9492.a5dd  ARPA   Ethernet1
Internet  172.16.10.1   -        00d0.58ad.06aa  ARPA   Ethernet0
Internet  172.16.10.2   12       0030.9492.a4ac  ARPA   Ethernet0
```

   The dash (-) signifies that this is the physical interface on the router. This output shows us that the router knows the 172.16.10.2 (Host A) and 172.16.20.2 (Host B) hardware addresses. Cisco routers will keep an entry in the ARP table for 4 hours.

- Now if the hardware address hasn't already been resolved, the router will send an ARP request out E1 looking for the 172.16.20.2 hardware address. Host B responds with its hardware address, and the packet and destination hardware addresses are then both sent to the Data Link layer for framing.

16. The Data Link layer creates a frame with the destination and source hardware addresses, Ether-Type field, and FCS field at the end. The frame is then handed to the Physical layer to be sent out on the physical medium one bit at a time.

17. Host B receives the frame and immediately runs a CRC. If the result matches the information in the FCS field, the hardware destination address will then be checked next. If the host finds a match, the Ether-Type field is then checked to determine the protocol that the packet should be handed to at the Network layer—IP in this example.

18. At the Network layer, IP receives the packet and runs a CRC on the IP header. If that passes, IP then checks the destination address. Since a match has finally been made, the Protocol field is checked to find out to whom the payload should be given.

19. The payload is handed to ICMP, which understands that this is an echo request. ICMP responds to this by immediately discarding the packet and generating a new payload as an echo reply.

20. A packet is then created including the source and destination addresses, Protocol field, and payload. The destination device is now Host A.

21. IP then checks to see whether the destination IP address is a device on the local LAN or on a remote network. Since the destination device is on a remote network, the packet needs to be sent to the default gateway.

22. The default gateway IP address is found in the Registry of the Windows device, and the ARP cache is checked to see if the hardware address has already been resolved from an IP address.

23. Once the hardware address of the default gateway is found, the packet and destination hardware addresses are handed down to the Data Link layer for framing.

24. The Data Link layer frames the packet of information and includes the following in the header:

    ▪ The destination and source hardware addresses

    ▪ The Ether-Type field with 0x0800 (IP) in it

    ▪ The FCS field with the CRC result in tow

25. The frame is now handed down to the Physical layer to be sent out over the network medium one bit at a time.

26. The router's Ethernet 1 interface receives the bits and builds a frame. The CRC is run, and the FCS field is checked to make sure the answers match.

27. Once the CRC is found to be okay, the hardware destination address is checked. Since the router's interface is a match, the packet is pulled from the frame and the Ether-Type field is checked to determine which protocol the packet should be delivered to at the Network layer.

28. The protocol is determined to be IP, so it gets the packet. IP runs a CRC check on the IP header first and then checks the destination IP address.

> IP does not run a complete CRC as the Data Link layer does—it only checks the header for errors.

Since the IP destination address doesn't match any of the router's interfaces, the routing table is checked to see whether it has a route to 172.16.10.0. If it doesn't have a route over to the destination network, the packet will be discarded immediately. I want to take a minute to point out that this is exactly where the source of confusion begins for a lot of administrators because when a ping fails, most people think the packet never reached the destination host. But as we see here, that's not *always* the case. All it takes for this to happen is for even just one of the remote routers to lack a route back to the originating host's network and—*poof!*—the packet is dropped on the *return trip*, not on its way to the host!

> Just a quick note to mention that when (and if) the packet is lost on the way back to the originating host, you will typically see a request timed-out message because it is an unknown error. If the error occurs because of a known issue, such as if a route is not in the routing table on the way to the destination device, you will see a destination unreachable message. This should help you determine if the problem occurred on the way to the destination or on the way back.

29. In this case, the router happens to know how to get to network 172.16.10.0—the exit interface is Ethernet 0—so the packet is switched to interface Ethernet 0.

30. The router then checks the ARP cache to determine whether the hardware address for 172.16.10.2 has already been resolved.

31. Since the hardware address for 172.16.10.2 is already cached from the originating trip to Host B, the hardware address and packet are then handed to the Data Link layer.

32. The Data Link layer builds a frame with the destination hardware address and source hardware address and then puts IP in the Ether-Type field. A CRC is run on the frame and the result is placed in the FCS field.

33. The frame is then handed to the Physical layer to be sent out onto the local network one bit at a time.

34. The destination host receives the frame, runs a CRC, checks the destination hardware address, then looks into the Ether-Type field to find out to whom to hand the packet.

35. IP is the designated receiver, and after the packet is handed to IP at the Network layer, it checks the Protocol field for further direction. IP finds instructions to give the payload to ICMP, and ICMP determines the packet to be an ICMP echo reply.

36. ICMP acknowledges that it has received the reply by sending an exclamation point (!) to the user interface. ICMP then attempts to send four more echo requests to the destination host.

You've just experienced Todd's 36 easy steps to understanding IP routing. The key point here is that if you had a much larger network, the process would be the *same*. It's just that the larger the internetwork, the more hops the packet goes through before it finds the destination host.

It's super-important to remember that when Host A sends a packet to Host B, the destination hardware address used is the default gateway's Ethernet interface. Why? Because frames can't be placed on remote networks—only local networks. So packets destined for remote networks must go through the default gateway.

Let's take a look at Host A's ARP cache now:

```
C:\ >arp -a
Interface: 172.16.10.2 --- 0x3
  Internet Address      Physical Address      Type
  172.16.10.1           00-15-05-06-31-b0     dynamic
  172.16.20.1           00-15-05-06-31-b0     dynamic
```

Did you notice that the hardware (MAC) address that Host A uses to get to Host B is the Lab A E0 interface? Hardware addresses are *always* local, and they never pass through a router's interface. Understanding this process is as important as air to you, so carve this into your memory!

Forwarding Decision Based on Route Lookup

Before moving on into some of the more advanced aspects of IP routing, let's look at another issue. Take a look at the output of this router's routing table:

```
Corp#sh ip route
[output cut]
R    192.168.215.0 [120/2] via 192.168.20.2, 00:00:23, Serial0/0
R    192.168.115.0 [120/1] via 192.168.20.2, 00:00:23, Serial0/0
R    192.168.30.0 [120/1] via 192.168.20.2, 00:00:23, Serial0/0
C    192.168.20.0 is directly connected, Serial0/0
L    192.168.20.1/32 is directly connected, Serial0/0
C    192.168.214.0 is directly connected, FastEthernet0/0
L    192.168.214.1/32 is directly connected, FastEthernet0/0
```

What do we see here? If I were to tell you that the corporate router received an IP packet with a source IP address of 192.168.214.20 and a destination address of 192.168.22.3, what do you think the Corp router will do with this packet?

If you said, "The packet came in on the FastEthernet 0/0 interface, but because the routing table doesn't show a route to network 192.168.22.0 (or a default route), the router will discard the packet and send an ICMP destination unreachable message back out to interface FastEthernet 0/0," you're a genius! The reason that's the correct answer is because that's the source LAN where the packet originated from.

Frame Rewrite

Recall step 16 in the IP routing process illustrated in the section "Packet Handling along the Path through a Network":

> 16. The Data Link layer creates a frame with the destination and source hardware addresses, Ether-Type field, and FCS field at the end. The frame is then handed to the Physical layer to be sent out on the physical medium one bit at a time.

The process described in step 16 is called the *frame rewrite process*. It simply refers to the change in the layer 2 header information that occurs at each hop in the path to the destination. This occurs because at each hop, while the source and destination IP addresses will not change, the source and destination MAC addresses will change.

Exam Essentials

Describe the basic IP routing process.   You need to remember that the frame changes at each hop but that the packet is never changed or manipulated in any way until it reaches the destination device (the TTL field in the IP header is decremented for each hop, but that's it!).

Interpret the components of a routing table

Figure 3.3 shows a simple network.

FIGURE 3.3   A simple routing example

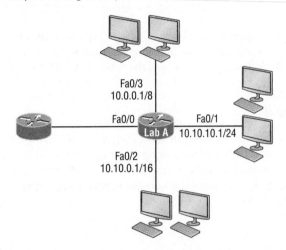

Fa0/3
10.0.0.1/8

Fa0/0   Fa0/1
Lab A   10.10.10.1/24

Fa0/2
10.10.0.1/16

Lab A has four interfaces. By using the command show ip route on a router, we can see the routing table (map of the internetwork) that Lab A has used to make its forwarding decisions:

```
Lab A#sh ip route
Codes: L - local, C - connected, S - static,
[output cut]
        10.0.0.0/8 is variably subnetted, 6 subnets, 4 masks
C       10.0.0.0/8 is directly connected, FastEthernet0/3
L       10.0.0.1/32 is directly connected, FastEthernet0/3
C       10.10.0.0/16 is directly connected, FastEthernet0/2
L       10.10.0.1/32 is directly connected, FastEthernet0/2
C       10.10.10.0/24 is directly connected, FastEthernet0/1
L       10.10.10.1/32 is directly connected, FastEthernet0/1
S*      0.0.0.0/0 is directly connected, FastEthernet0/0
```

The C in the routing table output means that the networks listed are "directly connected," and until we add a routing protocol like RIPv2, OSPF, etc. to the routers in our internetwork, or enter static routes, only directly connected networks will show up in our routing table. But wait—what about that L in the routing table—that's new, isn't it? Yes it is, because in the new Cisco IOS 15 code, Cisco defines a different route, called a local route. Each local route has a /32 prefix, defining a route just for the one address. So in this example, the router has relied upon these routes that list their own local IP addresses to more efficiently forward packets to the router itself. Let's continue our discussion by looking at the parts of the routing table.

Prefix

Recall in the previous section that each network listed in the output has a number following a forward slash. This number is the prefix and indicates the number of bits in the subnet mask. For example, a /24 prefix indicates the mask 255.255.255.0.

Network Mask

The network mask, or subnet mask, indicates the number of bits in the network portion of an IP address. Recall that this portion of two IP addresses must match for the two addresses to be in the same network. The mask is indicated in the routing table though the use of the prefix, which by indicating the number of bits in the subnet mask, also indicates the length of the network ID.

Next Hop

The next-hop field in a table entry indicates the next IP address in the path to the destination. In some cases, there is no next-hop address. Rather, the network in these entries is directly connected to the router, as indicated by an entry like the following:

```
C       10.10.0.0/16 is directly connected, FastEthernet0/2
```

Routing Protocol Code

A letter next to each entry indicates how the router learned the route. It might indicate that the network is directly connected or that the network was entered manually. In cases where the route was learned through a routing protocol, the protocol will be listed. A legend at the beginning of the output of the show ip route command indicates what each letter stands for. It appears as follows:

```
Router# show ip route

Codes: L - local, C - connected, S - static, R - RIP, M - mobile, B - BGP
       D - EIGRP, EX - EIGRP external, O - OSPF, IA - OSPF inter area
       N1 - OSPF NSSA external type 1, N2 - OSPF NSSA external type 2
       E1 - OSPF external type 1, E2 - OSPF external type 2
```

```
i - IS-IS, su - IS-IS summary, L1 - IS-IS level-1, L2 - IS-IS level-2
ia - IS-IS inter area, * - candidate default, U - per-user static route
o - ODR, P - periodic downloaded static route, H - NHRP
+ - replicated route, % - next hop override
```

Administrative Distance

The *administrative distance (AD)* is used to rate the trustworthiness of routing information received on a router from a neighbor router. An administrative distance is represented as an integer from 0 to 255, where 0 is the most trusted and 255 means no traffic will be passed via this route.

If a router receives two updates listing the same remote network, the first thing the router checks is the AD. If one of the advertised routes has a lower AD than the other, then the route with the lowest AD will be chosen and placed in the routing table.

Table 3.1 shows the default administrative distances that a Cisco router uses to decide which route to take to a remote network.

TABLE 3.1   Default administrative distances

Route Source	Default AD
Connected interface	0
Static route	1
External BGP	20
EIGRP	90
OSPF	110
RIP	120
External EIGRP	170
Internal BGP	200
Unknown	255 (This route will never be used.)

If a network is directly connected, the router will always use the interface connected to the network. If you configure a static route, the router will then believe that route over any other ones it learns about. You can change the administrative distance of static routes, but by default, they have an AD of 1.

If you have a static route, an RIP-advertised route, and an EIGRP-advertised route listing the same network, which route will the router go with? That's right—by default, the router will always use the static route unless you change its AD—which we did!

Metric

If both advertised routes to the same network have the same AD, then routing protocol metrics like *hop count* and/or the bandwidth of the lines will be used to find the best path to the remote network. The advertised route with the lowest metric will be placed in the routing table, but if both advertised routes have the same AD as well as the same metrics, then the routing protocol will load-balance to the remote network, meaning the protocol will send data down each link. In the following example, the metric is indicated by the value on the right side of the slash within the brackets (30720).

```
D        10.1.34.0/24 [90/30720] via 10.1.36.3, 00:07:32, FastEthernet0/1
```

Gateway of Last Resort

While host devices can be configured with default gateways, routers can also be configured with them. On routers, these are called gateways of last resort. They are configured by creating a *default route*. This default route is used by IP to forward any packet with a destination not found in the routing table, which is why it is also called a gateway of last resort. When a default route is present in the table, it will be indicated in two ways. First, there will be a statement at the beginning of the table, and second, there will be a route to the 0.0.0.0/0 network, as shown in the following output:

```
Gateway of last resort is 172.16.10.5 to network 0.0.0.0
172.16.0.0/30 is subnetted, 1 subnets
C        172.16.10.4 is directly connected, Serial0/0/1
L        172.16.10.6/32 is directly connected, Serial0/0/1
C     192.168.20.0/24 is directly connected, FastEthernet0/0
L     192.168.20.0/32 is directly connected, FastEthernet0/0
S*    0.0.0.0/0 [1/0] via 172.16.10.5
```

Exam Essentials

View and interpret the routing table of a router.   Use the show ip route command to view the routing table. Each route will be listed along with the source of the routing information. A C to the left of the route will indicate directly connected routes, and other letters next to the route can also indicate a particular routing protocol that provided the information, such as, for example, R for RIP.

Describe how a routing table is populated by different routing information sources

In the previous section entitled "Administrative Distance" you learned how the routing table is developed by the router. For a review of the process by which a router populates the routing table, see that section.

Admin Distance

I also introduced and explained administrative distance in detail in the section "Administrative Distance." Please refer to that section for more on the router's use of administrative distance.

Exam Essentials

Understand administrative distance and its role in the selection of the best route. Administrative distance (AD) is used to rate the trustworthiness of routing information received on a router from a neighbor router. Administrative distance is represented as an integer from 0 to 255, where 0 is the most trusted and 255 means no traffic will be passed via this route. All routing protocols are assigned a default AD, but it can be changed at the CLI.

Configure, verify, and troubleshoot inter-VLAN routing

Hosts in a VLAN live in their own broadcast domain and can communicate freely. VLANs create network partitioning and traffic separation at layer 2 of the OSI, and as I said when I told you why we still need routers, if you want hosts or any other IP-addressable device to communicate between VLANs, you must have a layer 3 device to provide routing.

For this, you can use a router that has an interface for each VLAN or a router that supports ISL or 802.1q routing. The least expensive router that supports ISL or 802.1q routing is the 2600 series router. You'd have to buy that from a used-equipment reseller because they are end-of-life, or EOL. I'd recommend at least a 2800 as a bare minimum, but even that only supports 802.1q; Cisco is really moving away from ISL, so you probably should only be using 802.1q anyway. Some 2800s may support both ISL and 802.1q; I've just never seen both supported.

Anyway, if you had two or three VLANs, you could get by with a router equipped with two or three FastEthernet connections. And 10Base-T is okay for home study purposes, and I mean only for your studies, but for anything else I'd highly recommend Gigabit interfaces for real power under the hood!

What we see in Figure 3.4 is that each router interface is plugged into an access link. This means that each of the routers' interface IP addresses would then become the default gateway address for each host in each respective VLAN.

FIGURE 3.4 Router connecting three VLANs together for inter-VLAN communication, one router interface for each VLAN

If you have more VLANs available than router interfaces, you can configure trunking on one FastEthernet interface or buy a layer 3 switch, like the Cisco 3560 or a higher-end switch like a 3750. You could even opt for a 6500 if you've got money to burn!

Instead of using a router interface for each VLAN, you can use one FastEthernet interface and run ISL or 802.1q trunking. Figure 3.5 shows how a FastEthernet interface on a router will look when configured with ISL or 802.1q trunking. This allows all VLANs to communicate through one interface. Cisco calls this a router on a stick (ROAS).

FIGURE 3.5 Router on a stick: single router interface connecting all three VLANs together for inter-VLAN communication

I really want to point out that this creates a potential bottleneck, as well as a single point of failure, so your host/VLAN count is limited. To how many? Well, that depends on your traffic level. To really make things right, you'd be better off using a higher-end switch and routing on the backplane. But if you just happen to have a router sitting around, configuring this method is free, right?

Figure 3.6 shows how we would create a router on a stick using a router's physical interface by creating logical interfaces—one for each VLAN.

FIGURE 3.6   A router creates logical interfaces.

GigabitEthernet 0/0.1
GigabitEthernet 0/0.2
GigabitEthernet 0/0.3

GigabitEthernet 0/0

Here we see one physical interface divided into multiple subinterfaces, with one subnet assigned per VLAN, each subinterface being the default gateway address for each VLAN/subnet. An encapsulation identifier must be assigned to each subinterface to define the VLAN ID of that subinterface. In the next section, where I'll configure VLANs and inter-VLAN routing, I'll configure our switched network with a router on a stick and demonstrate this configuration for you.

But wait, there's still one more way to go about routing! Instead of using an external router interface for each VLAN, or an external router on a stick, we can configure logical interfaces on the backplane of the layer 3 switch; this is called inter-VLAN routing (IVR), and it's configured with a switched virtual interface (SVI). Figure 3.7 shows how hosts see these virtual interfaces.

FIGURE 3.7   With IVR, routing runs on the backplane of the switch, and it appears to the hosts that a router is present.

VLAN 10

I'm Virtual!
VLAN 10 VLAN 20

VLAN 20

3560

In Figure 3.7, it appears there's a router present, but there is no physical router present as there was when we used router on a stick. The IVR process takes little effort and is easy to implement, which makes it very cool! Plus, it's a lot more efficient for inter-VLAN routing than an external router is. To implement IVR on a multilayer switch, we just need to create logical interfaces in the switch configuration for each VLAN.

Router on a Stick

By default, only hosts that are members of the same VLAN can communicate. To change this and allow inter-VLAN communication, you need a router or a layer 3 switch. I'm going to start with the router approach.

To support ISL or 802.1q routing on a FastEthernet interface, the router's interface is divided into logical interfaces—one for each VLAN—as was shown in Figure 3.6. These are called *subinterfaces*. From a FastEthernet or Gigabit interface, you can set the interface to trunk with the encapsulation command:

```
ISR#config t
ISR(config)#int f0/0.1
ISR(config-subif)#encapsulation ?
  dot1Q  IEEE 802.1Q Virtual LAN
ISR(config-subif)#encapsulation dot1Q ?
  <1-4094>  IEEE 802.1Q VLAN ID
```

Notice that my 2811 router (named ISR) only supports 802.1q. We'd need an older-model router to run the ISL encapsulation, but why bother?

The subinterface number is only locally significant, so it doesn't matter which subinterface numbers are configured on the router. Most of the time, I'll configure a subinterface with the same number as the VLAN I want to route. It's easy to remember that way since the subinterface number is used only for administrative purposes.

It's really important that you understand that each VLAN is actually a separate subnet. True, I know—they don't *have* to be. But it really is a good idea to configure your VLANs as separate subnets, so just do that. Before we move on, I want to define *upstream routing*. This is a term used to define the router on a stick. This router will provide inter-VLAN routing, but it can also be used to forward traffic upstream from the switched network to other parts of the corporate network or Internet.

Now, I need to make sure you're fully prepared to configure inter-VLAN routing as well as determine the IP addresses of hosts connected in a switched VLAN environment. And as always, it's also a good idea to be able to fix any problems that may arise. To set you up for success, let me give you a few examples.

First, start by looking at Figure 3.8 and read the router and switch configuration within it. By this point in the book, you should be able to determine the IP address, masks, and default gateways of each of the hosts in the VLANs.

The next step is to figure out which subnets are being used. By looking at the router configuration in the figure, you can see that we're using 192.168.10.0/28 for VLAN1, 192.168.1.64/26 with VLAN 2, and 192.168.1.128/27 for VLAN 10.

By looking at the switch configuration, you can see that ports 2 and 3 are in VLAN 2 and port 4 is in VLAN 10. This means that Host A and Host B are in VLAN 2 and Host C is in VLAN 10.

But wait—what's that IP address doing there under the physical interface? Can we even do that? Sure we can! If we place an IP address under the physical interface, the result is that frames sent from the IP address would be untagged. So what VLAN would those frames be a member of? By default, they would belong to VLAN 1, our management VLAN. This means the address 192.168.10.1/28 is my native VLAN IP address for this switch.

FIGURE 3.8   Configuring inter-VLAN example 1

Interface fastethernet 0/1
ip address 192.168.10.1 255.255.255.240
interface fastethernet 0/1.2
encapsulation dot1q 2
ip address 192.168.1.65 255.255.255.192
interface fastethernet 0/1.10
encapsulation dot1q 10
ip address 192.168.1.129 255.255.255.224

Fa0/1

Port 1: dot1q trunk
Ports 2,3: VLAN 2
Port 4: VLAN 10

Host A   Host B   Host C

Here's what the hosts' IP addresses should be:

Host A: 192.168.1.66, 255.255.255.192, default gateway 192.168.1.65

Host B: 192.168.1.67, 255.255.255.192, default gateway 192.168.1.65

Host C: 192.168.1.130, 255.255.255.224, default gateway 192.168.1.129

The hosts could be any address in the range—I just chose the first available IP address after the default gateway address. That wasn't so hard, was it?

Now, again using Figure 3.8, let's go through the commands necessary to configure switch port 1 so it will establish a link with the router and provide inter-VLAN communication using the IEEE version for encapsulation. Keep in mind that the commands can vary slightly depending on what type of switch you're dealing with.

For a 2960 switch, use the following:

```
2960#config t
2960(config)#interface fa0/1
2960(config-if)#switchport mode trunk
```

That's it! As you already know, the 2960 switch can only run the 802.1q encapsulation, so there's no need to specify it. You can't anyway. For a 3560, it's basically the same, but because it can run ISL and 802.1q, you have to specify the trunking encapsulation protocol you're going to use.

NOTE   Remember that when you create a trunked link, all VLANs are allowed to pass data by default.

Let's take a look at Figure 3.9 and see what we can determine. This figure shows three VLANs, with two hosts in each of them. The router in Figure 3.9 is connected to the Fa0/1 switch port, and VLAN 4 is configured on port Fa0/6.

FIGURE 3.9   Inter-VLAN example 2

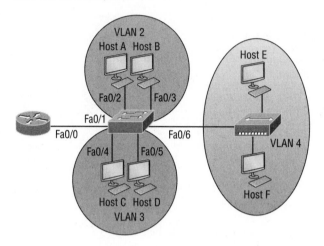

When looking at this diagram, keep in mind that these three factors are what Cisco expects you to know:

- The router is connected to the switch using subinterfaces.
- The switch port connecting to the router is a trunk port.
- The switch ports connecting to the clients and the hub are access ports, not trunk ports.

The configuration of the switch would look something like this:

```
2960#config t
2960(config)#int f0/1
2960(config-if)#switchport mode trunk
2960(config-if)#int f0/2
2960(config-if)#switchport access vlan 2
2960(config-if)#int f0/3
2960(config-if)#switchport access vlan 2
2960(config-if)#int f0/4
2960(config-if)#switchport access vlan 3
2960(config-if)#int f0/5
2960(config-if)#switchport access vlan 3
2960(config-if)#int f0/6
2960(config-if)#switchport access vlan 4
```

Before we configure the router, we need to design our logical network:

VLAN 1: 192.168.10.0/28

VLAN 2: 192.168.10.16/28

VLAN 3: 192.168.10.32/28

VLAN 4: 192.168.10.48/28

The configuration of the router would then look like this:

```
ISR#config t
ISR(config)#int fa0/0
ISR(config-if)#ip address 192.168.10.1 255.255.255.240
ISR(config-if)#no shutdown
ISR(config-if)#int f0/0.2
ISR(config-subif)#encapsulation dot1q 2
ISR(config-subif)#ip address 192.168.10.17 255.255.255.240
ISR(config-subif)#int f0/0.3
ISR(config-subif)#encapsulation dot1q 3
ISR(config-subif)#ip address 192.168.10.33 255.255.255.240
ISR(config-subif)#int f0/0.4
ISR(config-subif)#encapsulation dot1q 4
ISR(config-subif)#ip address 192.168.10.49 255.255.255.240
```

Notice I didn't tag VLAN 1. Even though I could have created a subinterface and tagged VLAN 1, it's not necessary with 802.1q because untagged frames are members of the native VLAN.

The hosts in each VLAN would be assigned an address from their subnet range, and the default gateway would be the IP address assigned to the router's subinterface in that VLAN.

Now, let's take a look at another figure and see if you can determine the switch and router configurations without looking at the answer—no cheating! Figure 3.10 shows a router connected to a 2960 switch with two VLANs. One host in each VLAN is assigned an IP address. What would your router and switch configurations be based on these IP addresses?

FIGURE 3.10   Inter-VLAN example 3

Since the hosts don't list a subnet mask, you have to look for the number of hosts used in each VLAN to figure out the block size. VLAN 2 has 85 hosts and VLAN 3 has 115 hosts. Each of these will fit in a block size of 128, which is a /25 mask, or 255.255.255.128.

You should know by now that the subnets are 0 and 128; the 0 subnet (VLAN 2) has a host range of 1–126, and the 128 subnet (VLAN 3) has a range of 129–254. You can almost be fooled since Host A has an IP address of 126, which makes it *almost* seem that Host A and Host B are in the same subnet. But they're not, and you're way too smart by now to be fooled by this one!

Here is the switch configuration:

```
2960#config t
2960(config)#int f0/1
2960(config-if)#switchport mode trunk
2960(config-if)#int f0/2
2960(config-if)#switchport access vlan 2
2960(config-if)#int f0/3
2960(config-if)#switchport access vlan 3
```

Here is the router configuration:

```
ISR#config t
ISR(config)#int f0/0
ISR(config-if)#ip address 192.168.10.1 255.255.255.0
ISR(config-if)#no shutdown
ISR(config-if)#int f0/0.2
ISR(config-subif)#encapsulation dot1q 2
ISR(config-subif)#ip address 172.16.10.1 255.255.255.128
ISR(config-subif)#int f0/0.3
ISR(config-subif)#encapsulation dot1q 3
ISR(config-subif)#ip address 172.16.10.254 255.255.255.128
```

I used the first address in the host range for VLAN 2 and the last address in the range for VLAN 3, but any address in the range would work. You would just have to configure the host's default gateway to whatever you make the router's address. Also, I used a different subnet for my physical interface, which is my management VLAN router's address.

Now, before we go on to the next example, I need to make sure you know how to set the IP address on the switch. Since VLAN 1 is typically the administrative VLAN, we'll use an IP address from out of that pool of addresses. Here's how to set the IP address of the switch (not nagging, but you really should already know this!):

```
2960#config t
2960(config)#int vlan 1
2960(config-if)#ip address 192.168.10.2 255.255.255.0
2960(config-if)#no shutdown
2960(config-if)#exit
2960(config)#ip default-gateway 192.168.10.1
```

Yes, you have to execute a no shutdown on the VLAN interface and set the ip default-gateway address to the router.

One more example, and then we'll move on to IVR using a multilayer switch—another important subject that you definitely don't want to miss! In Figure 3.11 there are two VLANs, plus the management VLAN 1. By looking at the router configuration, what's the IP address, subnet mask, and default gateway of Host A? Use the last IP address in the range for Host A's address.

FIGURE 3.11   Inter-VLAN example 4

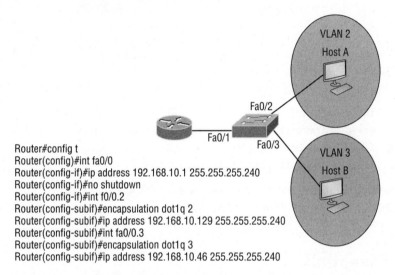

```
Router#config t
Router(config)#int fa0/0
Router(config-if)#ip address 192.168.10.1 255.255.255.240
Router(config-if)#no shutdown
Router(config-if)#int f0/0.2
Router(config-subif)#encapsulation dot1q 2
Router(config-subif)#ip address 192.168.10.129 255.255.255.240
Router(config-subif)#int fa0/0.3
Router(config-subif)#encapsulation dot1q 3
Router(config-subif)#ip address 192.168.10.46 255.255.255.240
```

If you really look carefully at the router configuration (the hostname in this configuration is just Router), there's a simple and quick answer. All subnets are using a /28, which is a 255.255.255.240 mask. This is a block size of 16. The router's address for VLAN 2 is in subnet 128. The next subnet is 144, so the broadcast address of VLAN 2 is 143 and the valid host range is 129–142. So the host configuration would be this:

IP address: 192.168.10.142

Mask: 255.255.255.240

Default gateway: 192.168.10.129

SVI

I'll use Figure 3.12 to demonstrate configuring inter-VLAN routing (IVR) with a multilayer switch, which is often referred to as a switched virtual interface (SVI). I'll use this IP address scheme: 192.168.*x*.0/24, where *x* represents the VLAN subnet. In my example this will be the same as the VLAN number.

FIGURE 3.12 Inter-VLAN routing with a multilayer switch

The hosts are already configured with the IP address, subnet mask, and default gateway address using the first address in the range. Now I just need to configure the routing on the switch, which is pretty simple actually:

```
S1(config)#ip routing
S1(config)#int vlan 10
S1(config-if)#ip address 192.168.10.1 255.255.255.0
S1(config-if)#int vlan 20
S1(config-if)#ip address 192.168.20.1 255.255.255.0
```

And that's it! Enable IP routing and create one logical interface for each VLAN using the interface vlan number command and voilà! You've now accomplished making inter-VLAN routing work on the backplane of the switch!

Exam Essentials

Remember how to create a Cisco router on a stick to provide inter-VLAN communication. You can use a Cisco FastEthernet or Gigabit Ethernet interface to provide inter-VLAN routing. The switch port connected to the router must be a trunk port; then you must create virtual interfaces (subinterfaces) on the router port for each VLAN connecting to it. The hosts in each VLAN will use this subinterface address as their default gateway address.

Remember how to provide inter-VLAN routing with a layer 3 switch. You can use a layer 3 (multilayer) switch to provide IVR just as with a router on a stick, but using a layer 3 switch is more efficient and faster. First you start the routing process with the command ip routing, then create a virtual interface for each VLAN using the command interface vlan *vlan*, and then apply the IP address for that VLAN under that logical interface.

Compare and contrast static routing and dynamic routing

There are several ways to configure the routing tables to include all the networks in our little internetwork so that packets will be properly forwarded. As usual, one size fits all rarely fits at all, and what's best for one network isn't necessarily what's best for another. That's why understanding the different types of routing will be really helpful when choosing the best solution for your specific environment and business requirements. Let's compare static and dynamic routing.

Static Routing

Static routing is the process that ensues when you manually add routes in each router's routing table. Predictably, there are pros and cons to static routing, but that's true for all routing approaches.

Here are the pros:

- There is no overhead on the router CPU, which means you could probably make do with a cheaper router than you would need for dynamic routing.
- There is no bandwidth usage between routers, saving you money on WAN links as well as minimizing overhead on the router since you're not using a routing protocol.
- It adds security because you, the administrator, can be very exclusive and choose to allow routing access to certain networks only.

And here are the cons:

- Whoever the administrator is must have a vault-tight knowledge of the internetwork and how each router is connected in order to configure routes correctly. If you don't have a good, accurate map of your internetwork, things will get very messy quickly!
- If you add a network to the internetwork, you have to tediously add a route to it on all routers by hand, which only gets increasingly insane as the network grows.
- Due to the last point, it's just not feasible to use it in most large networks because maintaining it would be a full-time job in itself.

Dynamic Routing

Dynamic routing is when protocols are used to find networks and update routing tables on routers. This is whole lot easier than using static or default routing, but it will cost you in terms of router CPU processing and bandwidth on network links. A routing protocol defines the set of rules used by a router when it communicates routing information between neighboring routers.

Exam Essentials

Compare and contrast static and dynamic routing.   Static routing creates no routing update traffic and creates less overhead on the router and network links, but it must be configured manually and does not have the ability to react to link outages. Dynamic routing creates routing update traffic and uses more overhead on the router and network links.

Compare and contrast distance vector and link state routing protocols

There are three classes of routing protocols:

Distance vector   The distance-vector protocols in use today find the best path to a remote network by judging distance. In RIP routing, each instance where a packet goes through a router is called a hop, and the route with the least number of hops to the network will be chosen as the best one. The vector indicates the direction to the remote network. RIP is a distance-vector routing protocol and periodically sends out the entire routing table to directly connected neighbors.

Link state   In link-state protocols, also called shortest path first (SPF) protocols, the routers each create three separate tables. One of these tables keeps track of directly attached neighbors, one determines the topology of the entire internetwork, and one is used as the routing table. Link-state routers know more about the internetwork than any distance-vector routing protocol ever could. OSPF is an IP routing protocol that's completely link-state. Link-state routing tables are not exchanged periodically. Instead, triggered updates containing only specific link-state information are sent. Periodic keepalives that are small and efficient, in the form of Hello messages, are exchanged between directly connected neighbors to establish and maintain neighbor relationships.

Advanced distance vector   Advanced distance-vector protocols use aspects of both distance-vector and link-state protocols, and EIGRP is a great example. EIGRP may act like a link-state routing protocol because it uses a Hello protocol to discover neighbors and form neighbor relationships and because only partial updates are sent when a change occurs. However, EIGRP is still based on the key distance-vector routing protocol principle that information about the rest of the network is learned from directly connected neighbors.

There's no set of rules to follow that dictate exactly how to broadly configure routing protocols for every situation. It's a task that really must be undertaken on a case-by-case basis, with an eye on specific requirements of each one. If you understand how the different routing protocols work, you can make good, solid decisions that will solidly meet the individual needs of any business!

Exam Essentials

Differentiate distance-vector, link-state, and hybrid routing protocols.   Distance-vector routing protocols make routing decisions based on hop count (think RIP), while link-state routing protocols are able to consider multiple factors such as bandwidth available and building a topology table. Hybrid routing protocols exhibit characteristics of both types.

Compare and contrast interior and exterior routing protocols

Two types of routing protocols are used in internetworks: *interior gateway protocols (IGPs)* and *exterior gateway protocols (EGPs)*. IGPs are used to exchange routing information with routers in the same *autonomous system (AS)*. An AS is either a single network or a collection of networks under a common administrative domain, which basically means that all routers sharing the same routing-table information are in the same AS. EGPs are used to communicate between ASs. An example of an EGP is Border Gateway Protocol (BGP), which we're not going to bother with because it's beyond the scope of this book.

Exam Essentials

Describe both interior and exterior routing protocols.   IGPs are used to exchange routing information with routers in the same *autonomous system (AS)*, while EGPs are used to route between ASs.

Configure, verify, and troubleshoot IPv4 and IPv6 static routing

Starting at the beginning, here's the command syntax you use to add a static route to a routing table from global config:

ip route [*destination_network*] [*mask*] [*next-hop_address* or
    exitinterface] [*administrative_distance*] [*permanent*]

   This list describes each command in the string:

ip route   The command used to create the static route

destination_network   The network you're placing in the routing table

mask   The subnet mask being used on the network

next-hop_address   This is the IP address of the next-hop router that will receive packets and forward them to the remote network, which must signify a router interface that's on a directly connected network. You must be able to successfully ping the router interface before you can add the route. Important note to self is that if you type in the wrong next-hop address or the interface to the correct router is down, the static route will show up in the router's configuration but not in the routing table.

exitinterface   Used in place of the next-hop address if you want, and shows up as a directly connected route

administrative_distance   By default, static routes have an administrative distance of 1 or 0 if you use an exit interface instead of a next-hop address. You can change the default value by adding an administrative weight at the end of the command.

permanent   If the interface is shut down or the router can't communicate to the next-hop router, the route will automatically be discarded from the routing table by default. Choosing the permanent option keeps the entry in the vector.

Before I guide you through configuring static routes, let's take a look at a sample static route to see what we can find out about it:

```
Router(config)#ip route 172.16.3.0 255.255.255.0 192.168.2.4
```

The ip route command tells us simply that it's a static route.

- 172.16.3.0 is the remote network we want to send packets to.
- 255.255.255.0 is the mask of the remote network.
- 192.168.2.4 is the next hop, or router, that packets will be sent to.

But what if the static route looked like this instead?

```
Router(config)#ip route 172.16.3.0 255.255.255.0 192.168.2.4 150
```

That 150 at the end changes the default administrative distance (AD) of 1 to 150. As I said, remember that the AD is the trustworthiness of a route, where 0 is best and 255 is worst.

One more example, then we'll start configuring:

```
Router(config)#ip route 172.16.3.0 255.255.255.0 s0/0/0
```

Instead of using a next-hop address, we can use an exit interface that will make the route show up as a directly connected network. Functionally, the next hop and exit interface work exactly the same.

Static Route Configuration

To help you understand how static routes work, I'll demonstrate the configuration on the internetwork shown in Figure 3.13.

Each routing table automatically includes directly connected networks. To be able to route to all indirectly connected networks within the internetwork, the routing table must include information that describes where these other networks are located and how to get to them.

Corp

The Corp router is connected to three networks. For the Corp router to be able to route to all networks, the following networks have to be configured into its routing table:

- 192.168.10.0
- 192.168.20.0

FIGURE 3.13   Our internetwork

The following router output shows the static routes on the Corp router and the routing table after the configuration. For the Corp router to find the remote networks, I had to place an entry into the routing table describing the remote network, the remote mask, and where to send the packets. I am going to add a 150 at the end of each line to raise the administrative distance. Here's the output:

```
Corp#config t
Corp(config)#ip route 192.168.10.0 255.255.255.0 172.16.10.2 150
Corp(config)#ip route 192.168.20.0 255.255.255.0 s0/1 150
Corp(config)#do show run | begin ip route
ip route 192.168.10.0 255.255.255.0 172.16.10.2 150
ip route 192.168.20.0 255.255.255.0 Serial0/1 150
```

I needed to use different paths for networks 192.168.10.0 and 192.168.20.0, so I used a next-hop address for the SF router and an exit interface for the LA router. After the router has been configured, you can just type **show ip route** to see the static routes:

```
Corp(config)#do show ip route
S     192.168.10.0/24 [150/0] via 172.16.10.2
      172.16.0.0/30 is subnetted, 2 subnets
C        172.16.10.4 is directly connected, Serial0/1
L        172.16.10.5/32 is directly connected, Serial0/1
C        172.16.10.0 is directly connected, Serial0/0
L        172.16.10.1/32 is directly connected, Serial0/0
S     192.168.20.0/24 is directly connected, Serial0/1
      10.0.0.0/24 is subnetted, 1 subnets
C        10.10.10.0 is directly connected, FastEthernet0/0
L        10.10.10.1/32 is directly connected, FastEthernet0/0
```

The Corp router is configured to route and know all routes to all networks. But can you see a difference in the routing table for the routes to SF and LA? That's right! The next-hop configuration showed up as via, and the route configured with an exit interface configuration shows up as static but also as directly connected! This demonstrates how they are functionally the same but will display differently in the routing table.

Understand that if the routes don't appear in the routing table, it's because the router can't communicate with the next-hop address you've configured. But you can still use the permanent parameter to keep the route in the routing table even if the next-hop device can't be contacted.

The S in the first routing table entry means that the route is a static entry. The [150/0] stands for the administrative distance and metric to the remote network, respectively.

Okay—we're good. The Corp router now has all the information it needs to communicate with the other remote networks. Still, keep in mind that if the SF and LA routers aren't configured with all the same information, the packets will be discarded. We can fix this by configuring static routes.

SF

The SF router is directly connected to networks 172.16.10.0/30 and 192.168.10.0/24, which means I've got to configure the following static routes on the SF router:

- 10.10.10.0/24
- 192.168.20.0/24
- 172.16.10.4/30

The configuration for the SF router is revealed in the following output. Remember that we'll never create a static route to any network we're directly connected to as well as the fact that we must use the next hop of 172.16.10.1 since that's our only router connection. Let's check out the commands:

```
SF(config)#ip route 10.10.10.0 255.255.255.0 172.16.10.1 150
SF(config)#ip route 172.16.10.4 255.255.255.252 172.16.10.1 150
SF(config)#ip route 192.168.20.0 255.255.255.0 172.16.10.1 150
SF(config)#do show run | begin ip route
ip route 10.10.10.0 255.255.255.0 172.16.10.1 150
ip route 172.16.10.4 255.255.255.252 172.16.10.1 150
ip route 192.168.20.0 255.255.255.0 172.16.10.1 150
```

By looking at the routing table, you can see that the SF router now understands how to find each network:

```
SF(config)#do show ip route
C    192.168.10.0/24 is directly connected, FastEthernet0/0
L    192.168.10.1/32 is directly connected, FastEthernet0/0
     172.16.0.0/30 is subnetted, 3 subnets
```

```
S       172.16.10.4 [150/0] via 172.16.10.1
C       172.16.10.0 is directly connected, Serial0/0/0
L       172.16.10.2/32 is directly connected, Serial0/0
S    192.168.20.0/24 [150/0] via 172.16.10.1
     10.0.0.0/24 is subnetted, 1 subnets
S       10.10.10.0 [150/0] via 172.16.10.1
```

And we now can rest assured that the SF router has a complete routing table as well. As soon as the LA router has all the networks in its routing table, SF will be able to communicate with all remote networks!

LA

The LA router is directly connected to 192.168.20.0/24 and 172.16.10.4/30, so these are the routes that must be added:

- 10.10.10.0/24
- 172.16.10.0/30
- 192.168.10.0/24

And here's the LA router's configuration:

```
LA#config t
LA(config)#ip route 10.10.10.0 255.255.255.0 172.16.10.5 150
LA(config)#ip route 172.16.10.0 255.255.255.252 172.16.10.5 150
LA(config)#ip route 192.168.10.0 255.255.255.0 172.16.10.5 150
LA(config)#do show run | begin ip route
ip route 10.10.10.0 255.255.255.0 172.16.10.5 150
ip route 172.16.10.0 255.255.255.252 172.16.10.5 150
ip route 192.168.10.0 255.255.255.0 172.16.10.5 150
```

This output displays the routing table on the LA router:

```
LA(config)#do sho ip route
S    192.168.10.0/24 [150/0] via 172.16.10.5
     172.16.0.0/30 is subnetted, 3 subnets
C       172.16.10.4 is directly connected, Serial0/0/1
L       172.16.10.6/32 is directly connected, Serial0/0/1
S       172.16.10.0 [150/0] via 172.16.10.5
C    192.168.20.0/24 is directly connected, FastEthernet0/0
L    192.168.20.1/32 is directly connected, FastEthernet0/0
     10.0.0.0/24 is subnetted, 1 subnets
S       10.10.10.0 [150/0] via 172.16.10.5
```

LA now shows all five networks in the internetwork, so it too can now communicate with all routers and networks.

Default Route

The SF and LA routers that I've connected to the Corp router are considered stub routers. A *stub* indicates that the networks in this design have only one way out to reach all other networks, which means that instead of creating multiple static routes, we can just use a single default route. This default route is used by IP to forward any packet with a destination not found in the routing table, which is why it is also called a gateway of last resort. Here's the configuration I could have done on the LA router instead of typing in the static routes due to its stub status:

```
LA#config t
LA(config)#no ip route 10.10.10.0 255.255.255.0 172.16.10.5 150
LA(config)#no ip route 172.16.10.0 255.255.255.252 172.16.10.5 150
LA(config)#no ip route 192.168.10.0 255.255.255.0 172.16.10.5 150
LA(config)#ip route 0.0.0.0 0.0.0.0 172.16.10.5
LA(config)#do sho ip route
[output cut]
Gateway of last resort is 172.16.10.5 to network 0.0.0.0
172.16.0.0/30 is subnetted, 1 subnets
C       172.16.10.4 is directly connected, Serial0/0/1
L       172.16.10.6/32 is directly connected, Serial0/0/1
C    192.168.20.0/24 is directly connected, FastEthernet0/0
L    192.168.20.0/32 is directly connected, FastEthernet0/0
S*   0.0.0.0/0 [1/0] via 172.16.10.5
```

Okay—I've removed all the initial static routes I had configured, and adding a default route is a lot easier than typing a bunch of static routes! Can you see the default route listed last in the routing table? The S* shows that as a candidate for the default route. And I really want you to notice that the gateway of last resort is now set too. Everything the router receives with a destination not found in the routing table will be forwarded to 172.16.10.5. You need to be careful where you place default routes because you can easily create a network loop!

So we're there—we've configured all our routing tables! All the routers have the correct routing table, so all routers and hosts should be able to communicate without a hitch—for now. But if you add even one more network or another router to the internetwork, you'll have to update each and every router's routing tables by hand—ugh! Not really a problem at all if you've got a small network like we do, but it would be a time-consuming monster if you're dealing with a large internetwork!

Network Route

When a route is created that points to a network (as most route entries do), it is called a network route. This simply means that the route points to a group of hosts, as does the following entry:

```
S     192.168.10.0/24 [150/0] via 172.16.10.5
```

Host Route

In most cases, we create routes to networks, but you can create a route leading to a single host. An example of a host route is shown below. Note that the mask that goes with the route is 32 bits in length, meaning it is a route to a single IP address.

```
S         10.1.1.1/32 [1/0] via 192.168.12.4 Ethernet0
```

There are dynamically created host routes called local host routes as well. One of these will be placed in the routing table for each router interface. An example is shown below. Note that is has an L next to it and is preceded by the network route for the directly connected network in which the interface resides.

```
C         10.1.1.0/30 is directly connected, Ethernet0/0
L         10.1.1.1/32 is directly connected, Ethernet0/0
```

Floating Static

A floating static route is simply one that has been created as a backup to a route learned though a routing protocol. By creating the static route with an administrative distance larger than that of the routing protocol, we can prevent the use of the static route unless the dynamic route is unavailable. The following example configures a static route with a distance of 125, which would prevent it from being placed in the routing table as long as a route to the same network with a lower distance value is present (for example, a RIP route that has a distance of 120). Router(config)#ip route 192.168.4.0 255.255.255.0 125.

Exam Essentials

Configure static routes at the CLI.   The command syntax to add a route is
ip route [*destination_network*] [*mask*] [*next-hop_
address* or *exitinterface*] [*administrative_distance*] [permanent].

Create a default route.   To add a default route, use the command syntax
ip route 0.0.0.0 0.0.0.0 *ip-address* or *exit interface type* and *number*.

Configure, verify, and troubleshoot single area and multi-area OSPFv2 for IPv4 (excluding authentication, filtering, manual summarization, redistribution, stub, virtual-link, and LSAs)

Configuring basic OSPF isn't as simple as configuring RIP and EIGRP, and it can get really complex once the many options that are allowed within OSPF are factored in. But that's okay because you really only need to focus on basic, single-area OSPF configuration at this point. Coming up, I'll show you how to configure single-area OSPF.

The two factors that are foundational to OSPF configuration are enabling OSPF and configuring OSPF areas.

Enabling Single Area OSPF

The easiest and also least scalable way to configure OSPF is to just use a single area. Doing this requires a minimum of two commands.

The first command used to activate the OSPF routing process is as follows:

```
Router(config)#router ospf ?
<1-65535> Process ID
```

A value in the range from 1 to 65,535 identifies the OSPF process ID. It's a unique number on this router that groups a series of OSPF configuration commands under a specific running process. Different OSPF routers don't have to use the same process ID to communicate. It's a purely local value that doesn't mean a lot, but you still need to remember that it cannot start at 0; it has to start at a minimum of 1.

You can have more than one OSPF process running simultaneously on the same router if you want, but this isn't the same as running multi-area OSPF. The second process will maintain an entirely separate copy of its topology table and manage its communications independently of the first one, and you use it when you want OSPF to connect multiple ASs together. Also, because the Cisco exam objectives only cover single-area OSPF with each router running a single OSPF process, that's what we'll focus on in this book.

The OSPF process ID is needed to identify a unique instance of an OSPF database and is locally significant.

Configuring OSPF Areas

After identifying the OSPF process, you need to identify the interfaces that you want to activate OSPF communications on as well as the area in which each resides. This will also configure the networks you're going to advertise to others.

Here's an example of a basic OSPF configuration for you, showing our second minimum command needed, the network command:

```
Router#config t
Router(config)#router ospf 1
Router(config-router)#network 10.0.0.0 0.255.255.255 area ?
  <0-4294967295>  OSPF area ID as a decimal value
  A.B.C.D         OSPF area ID in IP address format
Router(config-router)#network 10.0.0.0 0.255.255.255 area 0
```

The areas can be any number from 0 to 4.2 billion. Don't get these numbers confused with the process ID, which ranges from 1 to 65,535.

Remember, the OSPF process ID number is irrelevant. It can be the same on every router on the network, or it can be different—doesn't matter. It's locally significant and just enables the OSPF routing on the router.

The arguments of the network command are the network number (10.0.0.0) and the wildcard mask (0.255.255.255). The combination of these two numbers identifies the interfaces that OSPF will operate on and will also be included in its OSPF LSA advertisements. Based on my sample configuration, OSPF will use this command to find any interface on the router configured in the 10.0.0.0 network and will place any interface it finds into area 0. Notice that you can create about 4.2 billion areas! In reality, a router wouldn't let you create that many, but you can certainly name them using the numbers up to 4.2 billion. You can also label an area using an IP address format.

Let me stop here a minute to give you a quick explanation of wildcards: A 0 octet in the wildcard mask indicates that the corresponding octet in the network must match exactly. On the other hand, a 255 indicates that you don't care what the corresponding octet is in the network number. A network and wildcard mask combination of 1.1.1.1 0.0.0.0 would match an interface configured exactly with 1.1.1.1 only, and nothing else. This is really useful if you want to activate OSPF on a specific interface in a very clear and simple way. If you insist on matching a range of networks, the network and wildcard mask combination of 1.1.0.0 0.0.255.255 would match any interface in the range of 1.1.0.0 to 1.1.255.255. Because of this, it's simpler and safer to stick to using wildcard masks of 0.0.0.0 and identify each OSPF interface individually. Once configured, they'll function exactly the same— one way really isn't better than the other.

The final argument is the area number. It indicates the area to which the interfaces identified in the network and wildcard mask portion belong. Remember that OSPF routers will become neighbors only if their interfaces share a network that's configured to belong to the same area number. The format of the area number is either a decimal value from the range 0 to 4,294,967,295 or a value represented in standard dotted-decimal notation. For example, area 0.0.0.0 is a legitimate area and is identical to area 0.

Wildcard Example

Before getting down to configuring our network, let's take a quick peek at a more complex OSPF network configuration to find out what our OSPF network statements would be if we were using subnets and wildcards.

In this scenario, you have a router with these four subnets connected to four different interfaces:

- 192.168.10.64/28
- 192.168.10.80/28
- 192.168.10.96/28
- 192.168.10.8/30

All interfaces need to be in area 0, so it seems to me the easiest configuration would look like this:

```
Test#config t
Test(config)#router ospf 1
Test(config-router)#network 192.168.10.0 0.0.0.255 area 0
```

I'll admit that the preceding example is actually pretty simple, but easy isn't always best—especially when dealing with OSPF! So even though this is an easy-button way to configure OSPF, it doesn't make good use of its capabilities, and what fun is that? Worse yet, the objectives aren't very likely to present something this simple for you! So let's create a separate network statement for each interface using the subnet numbers and wildcards. Doing that would look something like this:

```
Test#config t
Test(config)#router ospf 1
Test(config-router)#network 192.168.10.64 0.0.0.15 area 0
Test(config-router)#network 192.168.10.80 0.0.0.15 area 0
Test(config-router)#network 192.168.10.96 0.0.0.15 area 0
Test(config-router)#network 192.168.10.8 0.0.0.3 area 0
```

Wow, now that's a different looking config! Truthfully, OSPF would work exactly the same way as it would with the easy configuration I showed you first—but unlike the easy configuration, this one covers the objectives!

And although this looks a bit complicated, trust me, it really isn't. All you need for clarity is to fully understand your block sizes! Just remember that when configuring wildcards, they're always one less than the block size. A /28 is a block size of 16, so we would add our network statement using the subnet number and then add a wildcard of 15 in the interesting octet. For the /30, which is a block size of 4, we would go with a wildcard of 3. Once you practice this a few times, it gets really easy. And do practice because we'll deal with them again when we get to access lists later on!

Let's use Figure 3.14 as an example and configure that network with OSPF using wildcards to make sure you have a solid grip on this. The figure shows a three-router network with the IP addresses of each interface.

FIGURE 3.14   Sample OSPF wildcard configuration

The very first thing you need to be able to do is to look at each interface and determine the subnet that the addresses are in. Hold on, I know what you're thinking: "Why don't I just use the exact IP addresses of the interface with the 0.0.0.0 wildcard?" Well, you can, but we're paying attention to Cisco exam objectives here, not just what's easiest, remember?

The IP addresses for each interface are shown in Figure 3.14. The Lab A router has two directly connected subnets: 192.168.10.64/29 and 10.255.255.80/30. Here's the OSPF configuration using wildcards:

```
Lab_A#config t
Lab_A(config)#router ospf 1
Lab_A(config-router)#network 192.168.10.64 0.0.0.7 area 0
Lab_A(config-router)#network 10.255.255.80 0.0.0.3 area 0
```

The Lab A router is using a /29, or 255.255.255.248, mask on the Fa0/0 interface. This is a block size of 8, which is a wildcard of 7. The G0/0 interface is a mask of 255.255.255.252—block size of 4, with a wildcard of 3. Notice that I typed in the network number, not the interface number. You can't configure OSPF this way if you can't look at the IP address and slash notation and then figure out the subnet, mask, and wildcard, can you? So don't take your exam until you can do this.

Here are other two configurations to help you practice:

```
Lab_B#config t
Lab_B(config)#router ospf 1
Lab_B(config-router)#network 192.168.10.48 0.0.0.7 area 0
Lab_B(config-router)#network 10.255.255.80 0.0.0.3 area 0
```

```
Lab_B(config-router)#network 10.255.255.8 0.0.0.3 area 0

Lab_C#config t
Lab_C(config)#router ospf 1
Lab_C(config-router)#network 192.168.10.16 0.0.0.7 area 0
Lab_C(config-router)#network 10.255.255.8 0.0.0.3 area 0
```

As I mentioned with the Lab A configuration, you've got to be able to determine the subnet, mask, and wildcard just by looking at the IP address and mask of an interface. If you can't do that, you won't be able to configure OSPF using wildcards as I just demonstrated. So go over this until you're really comfortable with it!

Configuring Our Network with OSPF

Now we get to have some fun! Let's configure our internetwork with OSPF using just area 0. OSPF has an administrative distance of 110, but let's remove RIP while we're at it because I don't want you to get in the habit of having RIP running on your network.

There's a bunch of different ways to configure OSPF, and as I said, the simplest and easiest is to use the wildcard mask 0.0.0.0. But I want to demonstrate that we can configure each router differently with OSPF and still come up with the exact same result. This is one reason why OSPF is more fun and challenging than other routing protocols—it gives us all a lot more ways to screw things up, which automatically provides a troubleshooting opportunity! We'll use our network as shown in Figure 3.15 to configure OSPF, and by the way, notice I added a new router!

FIGURE 3.15   Our new network layout

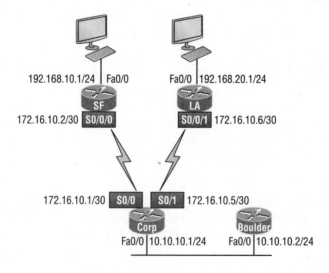

Corp

Here's the Corp router's configuration:

```
Corp#sh ip int brief
Interface        IP-Address      OK? Method Status                    Protocol

FastEthernet0/0  10.10.10.1      YES manual up                        up
Serial0/0        172.16.10.1     YES manual up                        up
FastEthernet0/1  unassigned      YES unset  administratively down down
Serial0/1        172.16.10.5     YES manual up                        up
Corp#config t
Corp(config)#no router rip
Corp(config)#router ospf 132
Corp(config-router)#network 10.10.10.1 0.0.0.0 area 0
Corp(config-router)#network 172.16.10.1 0.0.0.0 area 0
Corp(config-router)#network 172.16.10.5 0.0.0.0 area 0
```

Alright—it looks like we have a few things to talk about here. First, I removed RIP and then added OSPF. Why did I use OSPF 132? It really doesn't matter—the number is irrelevant. I guess it just felt good to use 132. But notice that I started with the show ip int brief command, just like when I was configuring RIP. I did this because it's always important to verify exactly what you are directly connected to. Doing this really helps prevent typos!

The network commands are pretty straightforward. I typed in the IP address of each interface and used the wildcard mask of 0.0.0.0, which means that the IP address must precisely match each octet. This is actually one of those times where easier is better, so just do this:

```
Corp(config)#router ospf 132
Corp(config-router)#network 172.16.10.0 0.0.0.255 area 0
```

Nice—there's only one line instead of two for the 172.16.10.0 network! I really want you to understand that OSPF will work the same here no matter which way you configure the network statement. Now, let's move on to SF. To simplify things, we're going to use our same sample configuration.

SF

The SF router has two directly connected networks. I'll use the IP addresses on each interface to configure this router.

```
SF#sh ip int brief
Interface       IP-Address     OK? Method Status                    Protocol
FastEthernet0/0 192.168.10.1   YES manual up                        up
FastEthernet0/1 unassigned     YES unset  administratively down down
Serial0/0/0     172.16.10.2    YES manual up                        up
Serial0/0/1     unassigned     YES unset  administratively down down
SF#config t
```

```
SF(config)#no router rip
SF(config)#router ospf 300
SF(config-router)#network 192.168.10.1 0.0.0.0 area 0
SF(config-router)#network 172.16.10.2 0.0.0.0 area 0
*Apr 30 00:25:43.810: %OSPF-5-ADJCHG: Process 300, Nbr 172.16.10.5 on
Serial0/0/0 from LOADING to FULL, Loading Done
```

Here, all I did was to first disable RIP, turn on OSPF routing process 300, and then I added my two directly connected networks. Now let's move on to LA!

LA

We're going to give some attention to the LA router that's directly connected to two networks:

```
LA#sh ip int brief
Interface      IP-Address     OK? Method Status                Protocol
FastEthernet0/0 192.168.20.1   YES manual up                         up
FastEthernet0/1 unassigned     YES unset  administratively down down
Serial0/0/0     unassigned     YES unset  administratively down down
Serial0/0/1     172.16.10.6    YES manual up                         up
LA#config t
LA(config)#router ospf 100
LA(config-router)#network 192.168.20.0 0.0.0.255 area 0
LA(config-router)#network 172.16.0.0 0.0.255.255 area 0
*Apr 30 00:56:37.090: %OSPF-5-ADJCHG: Process 100, Nbr 172.16.10.5 on
Serial0/0/1 from LOADING to FULL, Loading Done
```

Remember that when you're configuring dynamic routing, using the show ip int brief command first will make it all so much easier!

And don't forget, I can use any process ID I want, as long as it's a value from 1 to 65,535, because it doesn't matter if all routers use the same process ID. Also, notice that I used different wildcards in this example. Doing this works really well too.

Okay, I want you to think about something for a second before we move onto more advanced OSPF topics: What if the Fa0/1 interface of the LA router was connected to a link that we didn't need to send OSPF hellos (no other OSPF routers), as shown in Figure 3.16.

FIGURE 3.16   Adding a non-OSPF network to the LA router

We can use the `passive-interface` command under the routing process to prevent OSPF hellos from being transmitted! Take a look:

```
LA(config)#router ospf 100
LA(config-router)#passive-interface fastEthernet 0/1
```

Even though this is pretty simple, you've really got to be careful before you configure this command on your router! I added this command as an example on interface Fa0/1, which happens to be an interface we're not using in this network because I want OSPF to work on my other router's interfaces.

Now it's time to configure our Corp router to advertise a default route to the SF and LA routers because doing so will make our lives a lot easier. Instead of having to configure all our routers with a default route, we'll only configure one router and then advertise that this router is the one that holds the default route—elegant!

In Figure 3.16, keep in mind that, for now, the corporate router is connected to the Internet off of Fa0/0. We'll create a default route toward this imaginary Internet and then tell the other routers that this is the route they'll use to get to the Internet. Here is the configuration:

```
Corp#config t
Corp(config)#ip route 0.0.0.0 0.0.0.0 Fa0/0
Corp(config)#router ospf 1
Corp(config-router)#default-information originate
```

Now, let's check and see if our other routers have received this default route from the Corp router:

```
SF#show ip route
[output cut]
E1 - OSPF external type 1, E2 - OSPF external type 2
[output cut]
O*E2 0.0.0.0/0 [110/1] via 172.16.10.1, 00:01:54, Serial0/0/0
SF#
```

Sure enough—the last line in the SF router shows that it received the advertisement from the Corp router regarding the fact that the corporate router is the one holding the default route out of the AS.

But hold on a second! I need to configure our new router into my lab to create the example network we'll use from here on. Here's the configuration of the new router that I connected to the same network that the Corp router is connected to via the Fa0/0 interface:

```
Router#config t
Router(config)#hostname Boulder
Boulder(config)#int f0/0
Boulder(config-if)#ip address 10.10.10.2 255.255.255.0
Boulder(config-if)#no shut
*Apr  6 18:01:38.007: %LINEPROTO-5-UPDOWN: Line protocol on Interface
FastEthernet0/0, changed state to up
Boulder(config-if)#router ospf 2
```

```
Boulder(config-router)#network 10.0.0.0 0.255.255.255 area 0
*Apr  6 18:03:27.267: %OSPF-5-ADJCHG: Process 2, Nbr 223.255.255.254 on
FastEthernet0/0 from LOADING to FULL, Loading Done
```

This is all good, but I need to make sure that you don't follow my example to a tee because here, I just quickly brought a router up without setting my passwords first. I can get away with this only because I am in a nonproduction network, so don't do this in the real world where security is key!

Anyway, now that I have my new router nicely connected with a basic configuration, we're going to move on to cover loopback interfaces, how to set the router ID (RID) used with OSPF, and finally, how to verify OSPF.

OSPF and Loopback Interfaces

It's really vital to configure loopback interfaces when using OSPF. In fact, Cisco suggests using them whenever you configure OSPF on a router for stability purposes.

Loopback interfaces are logical interfaces, which means they're virtual, software-only interfaces, not actual, physical router interfaces. A big reason we use loopback interfaces with OSPF configurations is because they ensure that an interface is always active and available for OSPF processes.

Loopback interfaces also come in very handy for diagnostic purposes as well as for OSPF configuration. Understand that if you don't configure a loopback interface on a router, the highest active IP address on a router will become that router's RID during bootup! Figure 3.17 illustrates how routers know each other by their router ID.

FIGURE 3.17   OSPF router ID (RID)

The RID is not only used to advertise routes, it's also used to elect the designated router (DR) and the backup designated router (BDR). These designated routers create adjacencies when a new router comes up and exchanges LSAs to build topological databases.

By default, OSPF uses the highest IP address on any active interface at the moment OSPF starts up to determine the RID of the router. But this behavior can be overridden via a logical interface. Remember—the highest IP address of any logical interface will always become a router's RID!

Now it's time to show you how to configure these logical loopback interfaces and how to verify them, as well as verify RIDs.

Configuring Loopback Interfaces

Configuring loopback interfaces rocks mostly because it's the easiest part of OSPF configuration, and we all need a break about now—right? So hang on—we're in the home stretch!

First, let's see what the RID is on the Corp router with the show ip ospf command:

```
Corp#sh ip ospf
 Routing Process "ospf 1" with ID 172.16.10.5
[output cut]
```

Okay, we can see that the RID is 172.16.10.5—the Serial0/1 interface of the router. So let's configure a loopback interface using a completely different IP addressing scheme:

```
Corp(config)#int loopback 0
*Mar 22 01:23:14.206: %LINEPROTO-5-UPDOWN: Line protocol on Interface
   Loopback0, changed state to up
Corp(config-if)#ip address 172.31.1.1 255.255.255.255
```

The IP scheme really doesn't matter here, but each one being in a separate subnet does! By using the /32 mask, we can use any IP address we want as long as the addresses are never the same on any two routers.

Let's configure the other routers now:

```
SF#config t
SF(config)#int loopback 0
*Mar 22 01:25:11.206: %LINEPROTO-5-UPDOWN: Line protocol on Interface
   Loopback0, changed state to up
SF(config-if)#ip address 172.31.1.2 255.255.255.255
```

Here's the configuration of the loopback interface on LA:

```
LA#config t
LA(config)#int loopback 0
*Mar 22 02:21:59.686: %LINEPROTO-5-UPDOWN: Line protocol on Interface
   Loopback0, changed state to up
LA(config-if)#ip address 172.31.1.3 255.255.255.255
```

I'm pretty sure you're wondering what the IP address mask of 255.255.255.255 (/32) means and why we don't just use 255.255.255.0 instead. While it's true that either mask works, the /32 mask is called a host mask and works fine for loopback interfaces. It also allows us to save subnets. Notice how I was able to use 172.31.1.1, .2, and .3. If I didn't use the /32, I'd have to use a separate subnet for each and every router—not good!

One important question to answer before we move on is did we actually change the RIDs of our router by setting the loopback interfaces? Let's find out by taking a look at the Corp's RID:

```
Corp#sh ip ospf
 Routing Process "ospf 1" with ID 172.16.10.5
```

What happened here? You would think that because we set logical interfaces, the IP addresses under them would automatically become the RID of the router, right? Well, sort of, but only if you do one of two things: either reboot the router or delete OSPF and re-create the database on your router. Neither is all that great an option, so try to remember to create your logical interfaces before you start OSPF routing. That way, the loopback interface would always become your RID straight away!

With all this in mind, I'm going with rebooting the Corp router because it's the easier of the two options I have right now.

Now let's look and see what our RID is:

```
Corp#sh ip ospf
 Routing Process "ospf 1" with ID 172.31.1.1
```

That did the trick! The Corp router now has a new RID, so I guess I'll just go ahead and reboot all my routers to get their RIDs reset to our logical addresses. But should I really do that?

Maybe not because there is *one* other way. What do you think about adding a new RID for the router right under the router ospf *process-id* command instead? Sounds good, so I'd say let's give that a shot! Here's an example of doing that on the Corp router:

```
Corp#config t
Corp(config)#router ospf 1
Corp(config-router)#router-id 223.255.255.254
Reload or use "clear ip ospf process" command, for this to take effect
Corp(config-router)#do clear ip ospf process
Reset ALL OSPF processes? [no]: yes
*Jan 16 14:20:36.906: %OSPF-5-ADJCHG: Process 1, Nbr 192.168.20.1
on Serial0/1 from FULL to DOWN, Neighbor Down: Interface down
or detached
*Jan 16 14:20:36.906: %OSPF-5-ADJCHG: Process 1, Nbr 192.168.10.1
on Serial0/0 from FULL to DOWN, Neighbor Down: Interface down
or detached
*Jan 16 14:20:36.982: %OSPF-5-ADJCHG: Process 1, Nbr 192.168.20.1
on Serial0/1 from LOADING to FULL, Loading Done
*Jan 16 14:20:36.982: %OSPF-5-ADJCHG: Process 1, Nbr 192.168.10.1
on Serial0/0 from LOADING to FULL, Loading Done
Corp(config-router)#do sh ip ospf
 Routing Process "ospf 1" with ID 223.255.255.254
```

Now look at that—it worked! We changed the RID without reloading the router! But wait—remember, we set a logical loopback interface earlier. Does that mean the loopback interface will win over the `router-id` command? Well, we can see our answer. . . A loopback interface will *not* override the `router-id` command, and we don't have to reboot the router to make it take effect as the RID!

So this process follows this hierarchy:

1.   Highest active interface by default

2.   Highest logical interface overrides a physical interface.

3.   The `router-id` overrides the interface and loopback interface.

The only thing left now is to decide whether you want to advertise the loopback interfaces under OSPF. There are pros and cons to using an address that won't be advertised versus using an address that will be. Using an unadvertised address saves on real IP address space, but the address won't appear in the OSPF table, which means you can't ping it.

So basically, what you're faced with here is a choice that equals a trade-off between the ease of debugging the network and conservation of address space—what to do? A really tight strategy is to use a private IP address scheme as I did. Do this and all will be well!

Now that we've configured all the routers with OSPF, what's next? Miller time? Nope—not yet. It's that verification thing again. We still have to make sure that OSPF is really working, and that's exactly what we're going to do next.

Verifying OSPF Configuration

There are several ways to verify proper OSPF configuration and operation, so next, I'm going to demonstrate the various OSPF show commands you need to know in order to achieve this. We're going to start by taking a quick look at the routing table of the Corp router.

First, let's issue a `show ip route` command on the Corp router:

```
O    192.168.10.0/24 [110/65] via 172.16.10.2, 1d17h, Serial0/0
     172.131.0.0/32 is subnetted, 1 subnets
     172.131.0.0/32 is subnetted, 1 subnets
C        172.131.1.1 is directly connected, Loopback0
     172.16.0.0/30 is subnetted, 4 subnets
C        172.16.10.4 is directly connected, Serial0/1
L        172.16.10.5/32 is directly connected, Serial0/1
C        172.16.10.0 is directly connected, Serial0/0
L        172.16.10.1/32 is directly connected, Serial0/0
O    192.168.20.0/24 [110/65] via 172.16.10.6, 1d17h, Serial0/1
     10.0.0.0/24 is subnetted, 2 subnets
C        10.10.10.0 is directly connected, FastEthernet0/0
L        10.10.10.1/32 is directly connected, FastEthernet0/0
```

The Corp router shows only two dynamic routes for the internetwork, with the O representing OSPF internal routes. The Cs are clearly our directly connected networks, and our two remote networks are showing up too—nice! Notice the 110/65, which is our administrative distance/metric.

Now that's a really sweet-looking OSPF routing table! It's important to make it easier to troubleshoot and fix an OSPF network, which is why I always use the show ip int brief command when configuring my routing protocols. It's very easy to make little mistakes with OSPF, so keep your eyes on the details!

It's time to show you all the OSPF verification commands that you need in your toolbox for now.

The *show ip ospf* Command

The show ip ospf command is what you'll need to display OSPF information for one or all OSPF processes running on the router. Information contained therein includes the router ID, area information, SPF statistics, and LSA timer information. Let's check out the output from the Corp router:

```
Corp#sh ip ospf
 Routing Process "ospf 1" with ID 223.255.255.254
 Start time: 00:08:41.724, Time elapsed: 2d16h
 Supports only single TOS(TOS0) routes
 Supports opaque LSA
 Supports Link-local Signaling (LLS)
 Supports area transit capability
 Router is not originating router-LSAs with maximum metric
 Initial SPF schedule delay 5000 msecs
 Minimum hold time between two consecutive SPFs 10000 msecs
 Maximum wait time between two consecutive SPFs 10000 msecs
 Incremental-SPF disabled
 Minimum LSA interval 5 secs
 Minimum LSA arrival 1000 msecs
 LSA group pacing timer 240 secs
 Interface flood pacing timer 33 msecs
 Retransmission pacing timer 66 msecs
 Number of external LSA 0. Checksum Sum 0x000000
 Number of opaque AS LSA 0. Checksum Sum 0x000000
 Number of DCbitless external and opaque AS LSA 0
 Number of DoNotAge external and opaque AS LSA 0
 Number of areas in this router is 1. 1 normal 0 stub 0 nssa
 Number of areas transit capable is 0
 External flood list length 0
 IETF NSF helper support enabled
```

```
Cisco NSF helper support enabled
   Area BACKBONE(0)
       Number of interfaces in this area is 3
       Area has no authentication
       SPF algorithm last executed 00:11:08.760 ago
       SPF algorithm executed 5 times
       Area ranges are
       Number of LSA 6. Checksum Sum 0x03B054
       Number of opaque link LSA 0. Checksum Sum 0x000000
       Number of DCbitless LSA 0
       Number of indication LSA 0
       Number of DoNotAge LSA 0
       Flood list length 0
```

Notice the router ID (RID) of 223.255.255.254, which is the highest IP address configured on the router. Hopefully, you also noticed that I set the RID of the corporate router to the highest IP address available with IPv4.

The *show ip ospf database* Command

Using the show ip ospf database command will give you information about the number of routers in the internetwork (AS) plus the neighboring router's ID—the topology database I mentioned earlier. Unlike the show ip eigrp topology command, this command reveals the OSPF routers, but not each and every link in the AS like EIGRP does.

The output is broken down by area. Here's a sample output, again from Corp:

```
Corp#sh ip ospf database


                OSPF Router with ID (223.255.255.254) (Process ID 1)
Router Link States (Area 0)

Link ID         ADV Router      Age         Seq#        Checksum Link count
10.10.10.2      10.10.10.2      966         0x80000001 0x007162 1
172.31.1.4      172.31.1.4      885         0x80000002 0x00D27E 1
192.168.10.1    192.168.10.1    886         0x8000007A 0x00BC95 3
192.168.20.1    192.168.20.1    1133        0x8000007A 0x00E348 3
223.255.255.254 223.255.255.254 925         0x8000004D 0x000B90 5


           Net Link States (Area 0)

Link ID         ADV Router      Age         Seq#        Checksum
10.10.10.1      223.255.255.254 884         0x80000002 0x008CFE
```

You can see all the routers and the RID of each router—the highest IP address on each of them. For example, the link ID and ADV router of my new Boulder router shows up twice: once with the directly connected IP address (10.10.10.2) and as the RID that I set under the OSPF process (172.31.1.4).

The router output shows the link ID—remember that an interface is also a link—and the RID of the router on that link under the ADV router, or advertising router.

The *show ip ospf interface* Command

The show ip ospf interface command reveals all interface-related OSPF information. Data is displayed about OSPF information for all OSPF-enabled interfaces or for specified interfaces. I'll highlight some of the more important factors for you. Check it out:

```
Corp#sh ip ospf int f0/0
FastEthernet0/0 is up, line protocol is up
  Internet Address 10.10.10.1/24, Area 0
  Process ID 1, Router ID 223.255.255.254, Network Type BROADCAST, Cost: 1
  Transmit Delay is 1 sec, State DR, Priority 1
  Designated Router (ID) 223.255.255.254, Interface address 10.10.10.1
  Backup Designated router (ID) 172.31.1.4, Interface address 10.10.10.2
  Timer intervals configured, Hello 10, Dead 40, Wait 40, Retransmit 5
    oob-resync timeout 40
    Hello due in 00:00:08
  Supports Link-local Signaling (LLS)
  Cisco NSF helper support enabled
  IETF NSF helper support enabled
  Index 3/3, flood queue length 0
  Next 0x0(0)/0x0(0)
  Last flood scan length is 1, maximum is 1
  Last flood scan time is 0 msec, maximum is 0 msec
  Neighbor Count is 1, Adjacent neighbor count is 1
    Adjacent with neighbor 172.31.1.  Suppress hello for 0 neighbor(s)
```

So this command has given us the following information:

- Interface IP address
- Area assignment
- Process ID
- Router ID
- Network type
- Cost
- Priority

- DR/BDR election information (if applicable)
- Hello and dead timer intervals
- Adjacent neighbor information

The reason I used the show ip ospf interface f0/0 command is because I knew that there would be a designated router elected on the FastEthernet broadcast multi-access network between our Corp and Boulder routers. The information that I highlighted is all very important, so make sure you've noted it! A good question to ask you here is what are the hello and dead timers set to by default?

Type in the show ip ospf interface command and receive this response:

```
Corp#sh ip ospf int f0/0
%OSPF: OSPF not enabled on FastEthernet0/0
```

This error occurs when OSPF is enabled on the router, but not the interface. When this happens, you need to check your network statements because it means that the interface you're trying to verify is not in your OSPF process!

The *show ip ospf neighbor* Command

The show ip ospf neighbor command is super-useful because it summarizes the pertinent OSPF information regarding neighbors and the adjacency state. If a DR or BDR exists, that information will also be displayed. Here's a sample:

```
Corp#sh ip ospf neighbor

Neighbor ID     Pri   State        Dead Time    Address          Interface
172.31.1.4       1    FULL/BDR     00:00:34     10.10.10.2       FastEthernet0/0
192.168.20.1     0    FULL/  -     00:00:31     172.16.10.6      Serial0/1
192.168.10.1     0    FULL/  -     00:00:32     172.16.10.2      Serial0/0
```

 Real World Scenario

An Admin Connects Two Disparate Routers Together with OSPF and the Link between Them Never Comes Up

Quite a few years ago, an admin called me in a panic because he couldn't get OSPF working between two routers, one of which was an older router that they needed to use while they were waiting for their new router to be shipped to them.

OSPF can be used in a multi-vendor network, so he was confused as to why this wasn't working. He turned on RIP and it worked, so he was super confused with why OSPF was not creating adjacencies. I had him use the show ip ospf interface command to look at the link between the two routers and sure enough, the hello and dead timers didn't match. I had him configure the mismatched parameters so they would match, but it still wouldn't create an adjacency. Looking more closely at the show ip ospf interface command, I noticed the cost did not match! Cisco calculated the bandwidth differently than the other vendor. Once I had him configure both as the same value, the link came up! Always remember, just because OSPF can be used in a multi-vendor network does not mean it will work out of the box!

This is a critical command to understand because it's extremely useful in production networks. Let's take a look at the Boulder router output:

```
Boulder>sh ip ospf neighbor
```

```
Neighbor ID      Pri   State     Dead Time    Address      Interface
223.255.255.254   1    FULL/DR   00:00:31     10.10.10.1   FastEthernet0/0
```

Here we can see that since there's an Ethernet link (broadcast multi-access) on the link between the Boulder and the Corp router, there's going to be an election to determine who will be the designated router (DR) and who will be the backup designated router (BDR). We can see that the Corp became the designated router, and it won because it had the highest IP address on the network—the highest RID.

Now the reason that the Corp connections to SF and LA don't have a DR or BDR listed in the output is that by default, elections don't happen on point-to-point links and they show FULL/ -. But we can still determine that the Corp router is fully adjacent to all three routers from its output.

The *show ip protocols* Command

The show ip protocols command is also highly useful, whether you're running OSPF, EIGRP, RIP, BGP, IS-IS, or any other routing protocol that can be configured on your router. It provides an excellent overview of the actual operation of all currently running protocols!

Check out the output from the Corp router:

```
Corp#sh ip protocols
Routing Protocol is "ospf 1"
  Outgoing update filter list for all interfaces is not set
  Incoming update filter list for all interfaces is not set
  Router ID 223.255.255.254
  Number of areas in this router is 1. 1 normal 0 stub 0 nssa
  Maximum path: 4
  Routing for Networks:
    10.10.10.1 0.0.0.0 area 0
    172.16.10.1 0.0.0.0 area 0
    172.16.10.5 0.0.0.0 area 0
```

```
Reference bandwidth unit is 100 mbps
Routing Information Sources:
  Gateway          Distance      Last Update
  192.168.10.1          110      00:21:53
  192.168.20.1          110      00:21:53
Distance: (default is 110) Distance: (default is 110)
```

From looking at this output, you can determine the OSPF process ID, OSPF router ID, type of OSPF area, networks and areas configured for OSPF, and the OSPF router IDs of neighbors—that's a lot. It's super-efficient!

Multi-Area OSPF

Basic multi-area configuration isn't all that hard. Understanding your design, layout, and types of LSAs and DRs and configuring the elections, troubleshooting, and fully comprehending what's happening in the background are really the most complicated aspects of OSPF.

As I was saying, configuring OSPF is pretty simple, and you'll see toward the end of this chapter that configuring OSPFv3 is even easier! After I show you the basic OSPF multi-area configuration in this section, we'll work on the verification of OSPF. Let's get the ball rolling with the multi-area configuration shown in Figure 3.18.

FIGURE 3.18   Our internetwork

We're going to create three areas. I've verified that the IPv4 addresses are on the interfaces and working as well since then, so we're all set to rock the configs for this chapter! Here's the Corp configuration:

```
Corp#config t
Corp(config)#router ospf 1
Corp(config-router)#router-id 1.1.1.1
```

```
Corp(config-router)#Reload or use "clear ip ospf process" command, for this to
take effect
```

```
Corp(config-router)#network 10.10.0.0 0.0.255.255 area 0
Corp(config-router)#network 172.16.10.0 0.0.0.3 area 1
Corp(config-router)#network 172.16.10.4 0.0.0.3 area 2
```

Pretty straightforward, but let's talk about it anyway. First I started the OSPF process with the router ospf *process-id* command, using any number from 1–65,535 because they're only locally significant, so they don't need to match my neighbor routers. I set the RID of the router only to remind you that this can be configured under the router process, but with our small network it wouldn't really be necessary to mess with RIDs if this was an actual production network. The one thing that you need to keep in mind here is that in OSPF, the RID must be different on each router. With EIGRP, they can all be the same because they are not as important in that process. Still, as I'll show you in the EIGRPv6 section, we still need them!

Anyway, at this point in the configurations I needed to choose my network statements for the OSPF process to use, which allowed me to place my four interfaces on the Corp router into three different areas. In the first network statement, 10.10.0.0 0.0.255.255, I placed the g0/0 and g0/1 interfaces into area 0. The second and third statements needed to be more exact since there are /30 networks. 172.16.10.0 0.0.0.3 tells OSPF process 1 to go find an active interface that's configured with 172.16.10.1 or .2 and to place that interface into area 1. The last line tells the OSPF process to go find any active interface configured with 172.16.10.5 or .6 and place that interface into area 2. The wildcard of 0.0.0.3 means the first three octets can match any value, but the last octet is a block size of 4.

The only thing different about these configurations from those in the single-area OSPF is the different areas at the end of the command—that's it!

Here is the configuration for the SF and NY routers:

```
SF(config)#router ospf 1
SF(config-router)#network 10.10.0.0 0.0.255.255 area 1
SF(config-router)#network 172.16.0.0 0.0.255.255 area 1
```

```
NY(config)#router ospf 1
NY(config-router)#network 0.0.0.0 255.255.255.255 area 2
00:01:07: %OSPF-5-ADJCHG: Process 1, Nbr 1.1.1.1 on Serial0/0/0 from LOADING to FULL,
Loading Done
```

I configured each one slightly different from the Corp router, but since they didn't have an interface in more than area 1, I had more leeway in configuring them. For the NY router I just configured a network statement (0.0.0.0 255.255.255.255) that says "go find any active interface and place it into area 2!" I'm not recommending that you configure your routers in such a broad manner; I just wanted to show you your options.

Before we move onto verifying our network, let me show you another way that the CCNA objectives configure OSPF. For the Corp router, we had three network statements, which covered the four interfaces used. We could have configured the OSPF process like this on the Corp router (or all routers); it doesn't matter which way you choose:

```
Corp(config)#router ospf 1
Corp(config-router)#router-id 1.1.1.1
Corp(config-router)#int g0/0
Corp(config-if)#ip ospf 1 area 0
Corp(config-if)#int g0/1
Corp(config-if)#ip ospf 1 area 0
Corp(config-if)#int s0/0
Corp(config-if)#ip ospf 1 area 1
Corp(config-if)#int s0/1
Corp(config-if)#ip ospf 1 area 2
```

First I chose my process ID, then set my RID (this absolutely must be different on every router in your internetwork!), then I just went to each interface and told it what area it was in. Easy! No network commands to screw up! Nice. Again, you can configure it with the network statement or the interface statement, it doesn't matter, but you need to really remember this for the CCNA objectives!

Now that our three routers are configured, let's verify our internetwork.

Verifying and Troubleshooting Multi-Area OSPF Networks

Cisco's IOS has several show and debug commands that can help you monitor and troubleshoot OSPF networks. A sampling of these commands, which can be used to gain information about various OSPF characteristics, is included in Table 3.2.

TABLE 3.2 OSPF verification commands

Command	Provides the following
show ip ospf neighbor	Verifies your OSPF-enabled interfaces
show ip ospf interface	Displays OSPF-related information on an OSPF-enabled interface
show ip protocols	Verifies the OSPF process ID and that OSPF is enabled on the router
show ip route	Verifies the routing table, and displays any OSPF injected routes
show ip ospf database	Lists a summary of the LSAs in the database, with one line of output per LSA, organized by type

Let's go through some verification commands—the same commands we used to verify our single-area OSPF network.

Okay, once you've checked the link between your neighbors and can use the Ping program, the best command when verifying a routing protocol is to always check the status of your neighbor's connection first. The show ip ospf neighbor command is super useful because it summarizes the pertinent OSPF information regarding neighbors and their adjacency state. If a DR or BDR exists, that information will also be displayed. Here's a sample:

```
Corp#sh ip ospf neighbor
Neighbor ID     Pri   State         Dead Time   Address        Interface
172.16.10.2      0    FULL/  -      00:00:34    172.16.10.2    Serial0/0/0
172.16.10.6      0    FULL/  -      00:00:31    172.16.10.6    Serial0/0/1


SF#sh ip ospf neighbor
Neighbor ID     Pri   State         Dead Time   Address        Interface
1.1.1.1          0    FULL/  -      00:00:39    172.16.10.1    Serial0/0/0


NY#sh ip ospf neighbor
Neighbor ID     Pri   State         Dead Time   Address        Interface
1.1.1.1          0    FULL/  -      00:00:34    172.16.10.5    Serial0/0/0
```

The reason that the Corp connections to SF and NY don't have a DR or BDR listed in the output is that by default, elections don't happen on point-to-point links and they show FULL/-. But we can see that the Corp router is fully adjacent to all three routers from its output.

The output of this command shows the neighbor ID, which is the RID of the router. Notice in the output of the Corp router that the RIDs for the SF and NY routers were chosen based on the highest IP address of any active interface when I started the OSPF process on those routers. Both the SF and NY routers see the Corp router RID as 1.1.1.1 because I set that manually under the router ospf process command.

Next we see the Pri field, which is the priority field that's set to 1 by default. Don't forget that on point-to-point links, elections don't happen, so the interfaces are all set to 0 in this example because none of these routers will have elections on these interfaces with each other over this serial WAN network. The state field shows Full/-, which means all routers are synchronized with their LSDB, and the /- means there is no election on this type of interface. The dead timer is counting down, and if the router does not hear from this neighbor before this expires, the link will be considered down. The address is the actual address of the neighbor's interface connecting to the router, and the interface is the neighbor's interface—not your interface!

The *show ip ospf* Command

We use the show ip ospf command to display OSPF information for one or all OSPF processes running on the router. Information contained therein includes the router ID, area information, SPF statistics, and LSA timer information. Let's check out the output from the Corp router:

```
Corp#sh ip ospf
 Routing Process "ospf 1" with ID 1.1.1.1
 Supports only single TOS(TOS0) routes
 Supports opaque LSA
 It is an area border router
 SPF schedule delay 5 secs, Hold time between two SPFs 10 secs
 Minimum LSA interval 5 secs. Minimum LSA arrival 1 secs
 Number of external LSA 0. Checksum Sum 0x000000
 Number of opaque AS LSA 0. Checksum Sum 0x000000
 Number of DCbitless external and opaque AS LSA 0
 Number of DoNotAge external and opaque AS LSA 0
 Number of areas in this router is 3. 3 normal 0 stub 0 nssa
 External flood list length 0
    Area BACKBONE(0)
        Number of interfaces in this area is 2
        Area has no authentication
        SPF algorithm executed 19 times
        Area ranges are
        Number of LSA 7. Checksum Sum 0x0384d5
        Number of opaque link LSA 0. Checksum Sum 0x000000
        Number of DCbitless LSA 0
        Number of indication LSA 0
        Number of DoNotAge LSA 0
        Flood list length 0
    Area 1
        Number of interfaces in this area is 1
        Area has no authentication
        SPF algorithm executed 43 times
        Area ranges are
        Number of LSA 7. Checksum Sum 0x0435f8
        Number of opaque link LSA 0. Checksum Sum 0x000000
        Number of DCbitless LSA 0
        Number of indication LSA 0
        Number of DoNotAge LSA 0
        Flood list length 0
    Area 2
        Number of interfaces in this area is 1
        Area has no authentication
```

```
SPF algorithm executed 38 times
Area ranges are
Number of LSA 7. Checksum Sum 0x0319ed
Number of opaque link LSA 0. Checksum Sum 0x000000
Number of DCbitless LSA 0
Number of indication LSA 0
Number of DoNotAge LSA 0
Flood list length 0
```

You'll notice that most of the preceding information wasn't displayed with this command output in single-area OSPF. We have more displayed here because it's providing information about each area we've configured on this router.

The *show ip ospf interface* Command

The show ip ospf interface command displays all interface-related OSPF information. Data is displayed for all OSPF-enabled interfaces or for specified interfaces. I'll highlight some important portions I want you to pay special attention to.

```
Corp#sh ip ospf interface gi0/0
GigabitEthernet0/0 is up, line protocol is up
  Internet address is 10.10.10.1/24, Area 0
  Process ID 1, Router ID 1.1.1.1, Network Type BROADCAST, Cost: 1
  Transmit Delay is 1 sec, State DR, Priority 1
  Designated Router (ID) 1.1.1.1, Interface address 10.10.10.1
  No backup designated router on this network
  Timer intervals configured, Hello 10, Dead 40, Wait 40, Retransmit 5
    Hello due in 00:00:05
  Index 1/1, flood queue length 0
  Next 0x0(0)/0x0(0)
  Last flood scan length is 1, maximum is 1
  Last flood scan time is 0 msec, maximum is 0 msec
  Neighbor Count is 0, Adjacent neighbor count is 0
  Suppress hello for 0 neighbor(s)
```

Let's take a look at a serial interface so we can compare it to the Gigabit Ethernet interface just shown. The Ethernet network is a broadcast multi-access network by default, and the serial interface is a point-to-point non-broadcast multi-access network, so they will act differently with OSPF:

```
Corp#sh ip ospf interface s0/0/0
Serial0/0/0 is up, line protocol is up
  Internet address is 172.16.10.1/30, Area 1
  Process ID 1, Router ID 1.1.1.1, Network Type POINT-TO-POINT, Cost: 64
```

```
Transmit Delay is 1 sec, State POINT-TO-POINT, Priority 0
No designated router on this network
No backup designated router on this network
Timer intervals configured, Hello 10, Dead 40, Wait 40, Retransmit 5
  Hello due in 00:00:02
Index 3/3, flood queue length 0
Next 0x0(0)/0x0(0)
Last flood scan length is 1, maximum is 1
Last flood scan time is 0 msec, maximum is 0 msec
Neighbor Count is 1 , Adjacent neighbor count is 1
  Adjacent with neighbor 172.16.10.2
Suppress hello for 0 neighbor(s)
```

The following information is displayed via this command:

- Interface IP address
- Area assignment
- Process ID
- Router ID
- Network type
- Cost
- Priority
- DR/BDR election information (if applicable)
- Hello and dead timer intervals
- Adjacent neighbor information

I used the show ip ospf interface gi0/0 command first because I knew that there would be a designated router elected on the Ethernet broadcast multi-access network on the Corp router, even though it has no one to run against, which means the Corp router automatically wins. The information that I bolded is all very important! What are the hello and dead timers set to by default? Even though I haven't talked much about the cost output on an interface, it can also be very important. Two OSPF routers still could create an adjacency if the costs don't match, but it could lead to certain links not being utilized.

 Real World Scenario

Neighbor Routers Don't Form an Adjacency

I'd like to talk more about the adjacency issue and how the show ip ospf interface command can help you solve problems, especially in multi-vendor networks.

Years ago I was consulting with the folks at a large PC/laptop manufacturer and was helping them build out their large internetwork. They were using OSPF because their company was a worldwide company and used many types of routers from all manufacturers.

I received a call from a remote branch informing me that they installed a new router but it was not seeing the Cisco router off their Ethernet interface. Of course it was an emergency because this new router was holding some important WAN links to a new remote location that needed to be up yesterday!

After calming down the person on the phone, I simply had the admin use the `show ip ospf interface fa0/0` command and verify the hello and dead timers and the area configured for that interface and then had him verify that the IP addresses were correct between routers and that there was no passive interface set.

Then I had him verify that same information on the neighbor, and sure enough the neighbor's hello and dead timers didn't match. Quick and easy fix on the interface of the Cisco router with the `ip ospf dead 30` command, and they were up!

Always remember that OSPF can work with multi-vendor routers, but no one ever said it works out of the box between various vendors!

The *show ip protocols* Command

The show ip protocols command is also useful, whether you're running OSPF, EIGRP, RIP, BGP, IS-IS, or any other routing protocol that can be configured on your router. It provides an excellent overview of the actual operation of all currently running protocols.

Check the output from the Corp router:

```
Corp#sh ip protocols
Routing Protocol is "ospf 1"
  Outgoing update filter list for all interfaces is not set
  Incoming update filter list for all interfaces is not set
  Router ID 1.1.1.1
  Number of areas in this router is 3. 3 normal 0 stub 0 nssa
  Maximum path: 4
  Routing for Networks:
    10.10.0.0 0.0.255.255 area 0
    172.16.10.0 0.0.0.3 area 1
    172.16.10.4 0.0.0.3 area 2
  Routing Information Sources:
    Gateway          Distance      Last Update
    1.1.1.1               110      00:17:42
```

```
    172.16.10.2          110        00:17:42
    172.16.10.6          110        00:17:42
Distance: (default is 110)
```

Here we can determine the OSPF process ID, OSPF router ID, type of OSPF area, networks, and the three areas configured for OSPF as well as the OSPF router IDs of neighbors—that's a lot. Read efficient!

The *show ip route* Command

Now would be a great time to issue a show ip route command on the Corp router. The Corp router shows only four dynamic routes for our internetwork, with the O representing OSPF internal routes. The Cs clearly represent our directly connected networks, but our four remote networks are also showing up—nice! Notice the 110/65, which is the administrative distance/metric:

```
Corp#sh ip route
[output cut]
      10.0.0.0/8 is variably subnetted, 8 subnets, 2 masks
C        10.10.10.0/24 is directly connected, GigabitEthernet0/0
L        10.10.10.1/32 is directly connected, GigabitEthernet0/0
C        10.10.11.0/24 is directly connected, GigabitEthernet0/1
L        10.10.11.1/32 is directly connected, GigabitEthernet0/1
O        10.10.20.0/24 [110/65] via 172.16.10.2, 02:18:27, Serial0/0/0
O        10.10.30.0/24 [110/65] via 172.16.10.2, 02:18:27, Serial0/0/0
O        10.10.40.0/24 [110/65] via 172.16.10.6, 03:37:24, Serial0/0/1
O        10.10.50.0/24 [110/65] via 172.16.10.6, 03:37:24, Serial0/0/1
      172.16.0.0/16 is variably subnetted, 4 subnets, 2 masks
C        172.16.10.0/30 is directly connected, Serial0/0/0
L        172.16.10.1/32 is directly connected, Serial0/0/0
C        172.16.10.4/30 is directly connected, Serial0/0/1
L        172.16.10.5/32 is directly connected, Serial0/0/1
```

In addition, you can use the show ip route ospf command to get only OSPF-injected routes in your routing table. I can't stress enough how useful this is when dealing with large networks!

```
Corp#sh ip route ospf
      10.0.0.0/8 is variably subnetted, 8 subnets, 2 masks
O        10.10.20.0 [110/65] via 172.16.10.2, 02:18:33, Serial0/0/0
O        10.10.30.0 [110/65] via 172.16.10.2, 02:18:33, Serial0/0/0
O        10.10.40.0 [110/65] via 172.16.10.6, 03:37:30, Serial0/0/1
O        10.10.50.0 [110/65] via 172.16.10.6, 03:37:30, Serial0/0/1
```

Now that's a really nice-looking OSPF routing table! Troubleshooting and fixing an OSPF network is as vital a skill to have as it is in any other networking environment, which is why I always use the show ip int brief command when configuring my routing protocols. It's very easy to make little mistakes with OSPF, so pay very close attention to the details—especially when troubleshooting!

The *show ip ospf database* Command

Using the show ip ospf database command will give you information about the number of routers in the internetwork (AS), plus the neighboring router's ID. This is the topology database I referred to earlier.

The output is broken down by area. Here's a sample, again from Corp:

```
Corp#sh ip ospf database
            OSPF Router with ID (1.1.1.1) (Process ID 1)


                Router Link States (Area 0)

Link ID         ADV Router      Age         Seq#        Checksum Link count
1.1.1.1         1.1.1.1         196         0x8000001a 0x006d76 2

                Summary Net Link States (Area 0)
Link ID         ADV Router      Age         Seq#        Checksum
172.16.10.0     1.1.1.1         182         0x80000095 0x00be04
172.16.10.4     1.1.1.1         177         0x80000096 0x009429
10.10.40.0      1.1.1.1         1166        0x80000091 0x00222b
10.10.50.0      1.1.1.1         1166        0x80000092 0x00b190
10.10.20.0      1.1.1.1         1114        0x80000093 0x00fa64
10.10.30.0      1.1.1.1         1114        0x80000094 0x008ac9


                Router Link States (Area 1)

Link ID         ADV Router      Age         Seq#        Checksum Link count
1.1.1.1         1.1.1.1         1118        0x8000002a 0x00a59a 2
172.16.10.2     172.16.10.2     1119        0x80000031 0x00af47 4

                Summary Net Link States (Area 1)
Link ID         ADV Router      Age         Seq#        Checksum
10.10.10.0      1.1.1.1         178         0x80000076 0x0021a5
10.10.11.0      1.1.1.1         178         0x80000077 0x0014b0
172.16.10.4     1.1.1.1         173         0x80000078 0x00d00b
```

```
10.10.40.0      1.1.1.1         1164            0x80000074 0x005c0e
10.10.50.0      1.1.1.1         1164            0x80000075 0x00eb73

                Router Link States (Area 2)

Link ID         ADV Router      Age         Seq#        Checksum Link count
1.1.1.1         1.1.1.1         1119        0x8000002b 0x005cd6 2
172.16.10.6     172.16.10.6     1119        0x8000002d 0x0020a3 4

                Summary Net Link States (Area 2)
Link ID         ADV Router      Age         Seq#        Checksum
10.10.10.0      1.1.1.1         179         0x8000007a 0x0019a9
10.10.11.0      1.1.1.1         179         0x8000007b 0x000cb4
172.16.10.0     1.1.1.1         179         0x8000007c 0x00f0ea
10.10.20.0      1.1.1.1         1104        0x80000078 0x003149
10.10.30.0      1.1.1.1         1104        0x80000079 0x00c0ae
Corp#
```

Considering we only have eight networks configured in our internetwork, there's a huge amount of information in this database! You can see all the routers and the RID of each—the highest IP address related to individual routers. And each output under each area represents LSA Type 1, indicating the area they're connected to.

The router output also shows the link ID. Remember that an interface is also a link, as is the RID of the router on that link under the ADV router—the advertising router.

So far, this has been a great section, brimming with detailed OSPF information, a whole lot more than what was needed to meet past Cisco objectives, for sure!

Exam Essentials

Know how OSPF routers become neighbors and/or adjacent. OSPF routers become neighbors when each router sees the other's Hello packets.

Be able to configure single-area OSPF. A minimal single-area configuration involves only two commands: router ospf *process-id* and network *x.x.x.x y.y.y.y* area *Z*.

Be able to verify the operation of OSPF. There are many show commands that provide useful details on OSPF, and it is useful to be completely familiar with the output of each: show ip ospf, show ip ospf database, show ip ospf interface, show ip ospf neighbor, and show ip protocols.

Be able to monitor multi-area OSPF. There are a number of commands that provide information useful in a multi-area OSPF environment: show ip route ospf, show ip ospf neighbor, show ip ospf, and show ip ospf database. It's important to understand what each provides.

Configure, verify, and troubleshoot single area and multi-area OSPFv3 for IPv6 (excluding authentication, filtering, manual summarization, redistribution, stub, virtual-link, and LSAs)

The new version of OSPF continues the trend of routing protocols having a lot in common with their IPv4 versions. The foundation of OSPF remains the same—it's still a link-state routing protocol that divides an entire internetwork or autonomous system into areas, establishing a hierarchy.

In OSPF version 2, the router ID (RID) is determined by the highest IP addresses assigned to the router. And as you now know, the RID can be assigned. In version 3, nothing has really changed because you can still assign the RID, area ID, and link-state ID, which remain 32-bit values.

Adjacencies and next-hop attributes now use link-local addresses, but OSPFv3 still uses multicast traffic to send its updates and acknowledgments. It uses the addresses FF02::5 for OSPF routers and FF02::6 for OSPF-designated routers. These new addresses are the replacements for 224.0.0.5 and 224.0.0.6, respectively.

Other, less flexible IPv4 protocols don't give us the ability that OSPFv2 does to assign specific networks and interfaces into the OSPF process, but this is still configured under the router configuration process. And with OSPFv3, the interfaces and therefore the networks attached to them are configured directly on the interface in interface configuration mode.

The configuration of OSPFv3 is going to look like this: First, optionally start by assigning the RID, but if you have IPv4 addresses assigned to your interface, you can let OSPF pick the RID just as we did with OSPFv2:

```
Router(config)#ipv6 router ospf 10
Router(config-rtr)#router-id 1.1.1.1
```

You get to perform some other configurations from router configuration mode, like summarization and redistribution, but again, we don't even need to configure OSPFv3 from this prompt if we configure it from the interface!

A simple interface configuration looks like this:

```
Router(config-if)#ipv6 ospf 10 area 0.0.0.0
```

So, if we just go to each interface and assign a process ID and area—poof, we're done! See? Easy! As the configuration shows, I configured the area as 0.0.0.0, which is the same thing as just typing **area 0**. We'll use Figure 3.19.

FIGURE 3.19   Configuring OSPFv3

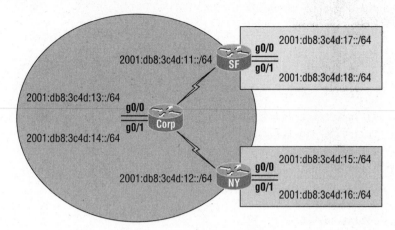

Okay, so all we have to do to enable OSPF on the internetwork is go to each interface that we want to run it on. Here's the Corp configuration:

```
Corp#config t
Corp(config)#int g0/0
Corp(config-if)#ipv6 ospf 1 area 0
Corp(config-if)#int g0/1
Corp(config-if)#ipv6 ospf 1 area 0
Corp(config-if)#int s0/0/0
Corp(config-if)#ipv6 ospf 1 area 0
Corp(config-if)#int s0/0/1
Corp(config-if)#ipv6 ospf 1 area 0
```

That wasn't so bad—much easier than it was with IPv4! To configure OSPFv3, you just need to establish the specific interfaces you'll be using! Let's configure the other two routers now:

```
SF#config t
SF(config)#int g0/0
SF(config-if)#ipv6 ospf 1 area 1
SF(config-if)#int g0/1
SF(config-if)#ipv6 ospf 1 area 1
SF(config-if)#int s0/0/0
SF(config-if)#ipv6 ospf 1 area 0
01:03:55: %OSPFv3-5-ADJCHG: Process 1, Nbr 192.168.1.5 on Serial0/0/0
from LOADING to  FULL, Loading Done
```

Sweet—the SF has become adjacent to the Corp router! One interesting output line I want to point out is that the IPv4 RID is being used in the OSPFv3 adjacent change. I didn't set the RIDs manually because I knew I had interfaces with IPv4 addresses already on them, which the OSPF process would use for a RID.

Now let's configure the NY router:

```
NY(config)#int g0/0
NY(config-if)#ipv6 ospf 1 area 2
%OSPFv3-4-NORTRID:OSPFv3 process 1 could not pick a router-id,please configure
manually
NY(config-if)#ipv6 router ospf 1
NY(config-rtr)#router-id 1.1.1.1
NY(config-if)#int g0/0
NY(config-if)#ipv6 ospf 1 area 2
NY(config-if)#int g0/1
NY(config-if)#ipv6 ospf 1 area 2
NY(config-if)#int s0/0/0
NY(config-if)#ipv6 ospf 1 area 0
00:09:00: %OSPFv3-5-ADJCHG: Process 1, Nbr 192.168.1.5 on Serial0/0/0 from
LOADING to
FULL, Loading Done
```

Our adjacency popped up—this is great. But did you notice that I had to set the RID? That's because there wasn't an IPv4 32-bit address already on an interface for the router to use as the RID, so it was mandatory to set the RID manually!

Without even verifying our network, it appears it's up and running. Even so, it's always important to verify!

Verifying OSPFv3

I'll start as usual with the show ipv6 route ospf command:

```
Corp#sh ipv6 route ospf
OI  2001:DB8:3C4D:15::/64 [110/65]
     via FE80::201:C9FF:FED2:5E01, Serial0/0/1
OI  2001:DB8:3C4D:16::/64 [110/65]
     via FE80::201:C9FF:FED2:5E01, Serial0/0/1
O   2001:DB8:C34D:11::/64 [110/128]
     via FE80::2E0:F7FF:FE13:5E01, Serial0/0/0
OI  2001:DB8:C34D:17::/64 [110/65]
     via FE80::2E0:F7FF:FE13:5E01, Serial0/0/0
OI  2001:DB8:C34D:18::/64 [110/65]
     via FE80::2E0:F7FF:FE13:5E01, Serial0/0/0
Corp#
```

Perfect. I see all six subnets. Notice the O and OI? The O is intra-area and the OI is inter-area, meaning it's a route from a different area. You can't simply distinguish the area by looking at the routing table though. Plus, don't forget that the routers communicate with their neighbor via link-local addresses: via FE80::2E0:F7FF:FE13:5E01, Serial0/0/0, for example.

Let's take a look at the show ipv6 protocols command:

```
Corp#sh ipv6 protocols
IPv6 Routing Protocol is "connected"
IPv6 Routing Protocol is "static
IPv6 Routing Protocol is "ospf 1"
  Interfaces (Area 0)
    GigabitEthernet0/0
    GigabitEthernet0/1
    Serial0/0/0
    Serial0/0/1
```

This just tells us which interfaces are part of OSPF process 1, area 0. To configure OSPFv3, you absolutely have to know which interfaces are in use. Sho ip int brief can really help you if you're having a problem finding your active interfaces.

Let's take a look at the Gigabit Ethernet OSPFv3 active interface on the Corp router:

```
Corp#sh ipv6 ospf int g0/0
GigabitEthernet0/0 is up, line protocol is up
  Link Local Address FE80::2E0:F7FF:FE0A:3301 , Interface ID 1
  Area 0, Process ID 1, Instance ID 0, Router ID 192.168.1.5
  Network Type BROADCAST, Cost: 1
  Transmit Delay is 1 sec, State DR, Priority 1
  Designated Router (ID) 192.168.1.5, local address FE80::2E0:F7FF:FE0A:3301
  No backup designated router on this network
  Timer intervals configured, Hello 10, Dead 40, Wait 40, Retransmit 5
    Hello due in 00:00:09
  Index 1/1, flood queue length 0
  Next 0x0(0)/0x0(0)
  Last flood scan length is 1, maximum is 1
  Last flood scan time is 0 msec, maximum is 0 msec
  Neighbor Count is 0, Adjacent neighbor count is 0
  Suppress hello for 0 neighbor(s)
```

Let's take a look at the neighbor table on the Corp router via
show ipv6 ospf neighbor:

```
Corp#sh ipv6 ospf neighbor
Neighbor ID    Pri   State        Dead Time   Interface ID   Interface
2.2.2.2          0   FULL/  -     00:00:36    4              Serial0/0/1
192.168.1.6      0   FULL/  -     00:00:39    4              Serial0/0/0
```

Okay, we can see our two neighbors, and there's also a slight difference in this version's command from OSPFv2. We still see the RID on the left and that we're also fully adjacent with both our neighbors—the dash is there because there are no elections on serial point-to-point links. But we don't see the neighbor's IPv6 address listed as we did with OSPFv2's IPv4 addresses, which were listed in the interface ID field.

There's one other command I want to finish with—the show `ipv6 ospf` command:

```
Corp#sh ipv6 ospf
 Routing Process "ospfv3 1" with ID 192.168.1.5
 SPF schedule delay 5 secs, Hold time between two SPFs 10 secs
 Minimum LSA interval 5 secs. Minimum LSA arrival 1 secs
 LSA group pacing timer 240 secs
 Interface flood pacing timer 33 msecs
 Retransmission pacing timer 66 msecs
 Number of external LSA 0. Checksum Sum 0x000000
 Number of areas in this router is 1. 1 normal 0 stub 0 nssa
 Reference bandwidth unit is 100 mbps
    Area BACKBONE(0)
        Number of interfaces in this area is 4
        SPF algorithm executed 10 times
        Number of LSA 10. Checksum Sum 0x05aebb
        Number of DCbitless LSA 0
        Number of indication LSA 0
        Number of DoNotAge LSA 0
        Flood list length 0
```

This shows the process ID and RID, our reference bandwidth for this interface, and how many interfaces we have in each area, which in our example is only area 0.

Exam Essentials

Understand how to configure OSPFv3.   OSPFv3 uses the same basic mechanisms that OSPFv2 uses, but OSPFv3 is more easily configured by OSPFv3 on a per-interface basis with `ipv6 ospf` *process-ID* area *area*.

Configure, verify, and troubleshoot EIGRP for IPv4 (excluding authentication, filtering, manual summarization, redistribution, stub)

We're going to start with the easy part of EIGRP, and by configuring it on our little internetwork, you'll learn a lot more this way than you would if I just continued explaining more at this point. After we've completed the initial configuration, we'll fine-tune it and have fun experimenting with it throughout the rest of this chapter!

Okay, there are two modes for entering EIGRP commands: router configuration mode and interface configuration mode. In router configuration mode, we'll enable the protocol, determine which networks will run EIGRP, and set global factors. When in interface configuration mode, we'll customize summaries and bandwidth.

To initiate an EIGRP session on a router, I'll use the `router eigrp` command followed by our network's AS number. After that, we'll enter the specific numbers of the networks that we want to connect to the router using the `network` command followed by the network number. This is pretty straightforward stuff—if you can configure RIP, then you can configure EIGRP!

I'm going to enable EIGRP for autonomous system 20 on our Corp router connected to four networks. Figure 3.20 shows the network we'll be configuring. Here's the Corp configuration:

```
Corp#config t
Corp(config)#router eigrp 20
Corp(config-router)#network 172.16.0.0
Corp(config-router)#network 10.0.0.0
```

FIGURE 3.20   Configuring our little internetwork with EIGRP

Remember, we need to use the classful network address, which is all subnet and host bits turned off. This is another thing that makes EIGRP so great: It has the complexity of a link-state protocol running in the background and the same easy configuration process used for RIP!

 Understand that the AS number is irrelevant—that is, as long as all routers use the same number! You can use any number from 1 to 65,535.

But wait, the EIGRP configuration can't be that easy, can it? A few simple EIGRP commands and my network just works? Well, it can be and usually is, but not always. Remember the wildcards you learned about in the section on OSPF? Let's say, for example, that we wanted to advertise all the directly connected networks with EIGRP off the Corp router. By using the command network 10.0.0.0, we can effectively advertise to all subnets within that classful network; however, take a look at this configuration now:

```
Corp#config t
Corp(config)#router eigrp 20
Corp(config-router)#network 10.10.11.0 0.0.0.255
Corp(config-router)#network 172.16.10.0 0.0.0.3
Corp(config-router)#network 172.16.10.4 0.0.0.3
```

This configuration should look pretty familiar to you because by now you should have a solid understanding of how wildcards are configured. This configuration will advertise the network connected to g0/1 on the Corp router as well as the two WAN links. Still, all we accomplished with this configuration was to stop the g0/0 interface from being placed into the EIGRP process, and unless you have tens of thousands of networks worldwide, then there is really no need to use wildcards because they don't provide any other administrative purpose other than what I've already described.

Now let's take a look at the simple configuration needed for the SF and NY routers in our internetwork:

```
SF(config)#router eigrp 20
SF(config-router)#network 172.16.0.0
SF(config-router)#network 10.0.0.0
000060:%DUAL-5-NBRCHANGE:IP-EIGRP(0) 20:Neighbor 172.16.10.1 (Serial0/0/0) is
up:
new adjacency

NY(config)#router eigrp 20
NY(config-router)#network 172.16.0.0
NY(config-router)#network 10.0.0.0
*Jun 26 02:41:36:%DUAL-5-NBRCHANGE:IP-EIGRP(0) 20:Neighbor 172.16.10.5
(Serial0/0/1) is up: new adjacency
```

Nice and easy—or is it? We can see that the SF and NY router created an adjacency to the Corp router, but are they actually sharing routing information? To find out, let's take a look at the number that I pointed out as the autonomous system (AS) number in the configuration.

EIGRP uses ASs to identify the group of routers that will share route information. Only routers that have the same AS share routes. The range of values we can use to create an AS with EIGRP is 1–65535:

```
Corp(config)#router eigrp ?
  <1-65535>  Autonomous System
  WORD       EIGRP Virtual-Instance Name
Corp(config)#router eigrp 20
```

Notice that I could have used any number from 1 to 65,535, but I chose to use 20 because it just felt good at the time. As long as all routers use the same number, they'll create an adjacency. Okay, now the AS makes sense, but it looks like I can type a word in the place of the AS number, and I can! Let's take a look at the configuration:

```
Corp(config)#router eigrp Todd
Corp(config-router)#address-family ipv4 autonomous-system 20
Corp(config-router-af)#network 10.0.0.0
Corp(config-router-af)#network 172.16.0.0
```

Verifying and Troubleshooting EIGRP

Even though EIGRP usually runs smoothly and is relatively low maintenance, there are several commands you need to memorize for using on a router that can be super helpful when troubleshooting EIGRP! I've already shown you a few of them, but I'm going to demonstrate all the tools you'll need to verify and troubleshoot EIGRP now. Table 3.3 contains all of the commands you need to know for verifying that EIGRP is functioning well and offers a brief description of what each command does.

TABLE 3.3   EIGRP troubleshooting commands

Command	Description/Function
show ip eigrp neighbors	Shows all EIGRP neighbors, their IP addresses, and the retransmit interval and queue counts for the adjacent routers
show ip eigrp interfaces	Lists the interfaces on which the router has actually enabled EIGRP
show ip route eigrp	Shows EIGRP entries in the routing table
show ip eigrp topology	Shows entries in the EIGRP topology table
show ip eigrp traffic	Shows the packet count for EIGRP packets sent and received
show ip protocols	Shows information about the active protocol sessions

When troubleshooting an EIGRP problem, it's always a good idea to start by getting an accurate map of the network, and the best way to do that is by using the show ip eigrp neighbors command to find out who your directly connected neighbors are. This command shows all adjacent routers that share route information within a given AS. If neighbors are missing, check the configuration, AS number, and link status on both routers to verify that the protocol has been configured correctly.

Let's execute the command on the Corp router:

```
Corp#sh ip eigrp neighbors
IP-EIGRP neighbors for process 20
H   Address              Interface       Hold Uptime     SRTT   RTO  Q   Seq
                                         (sec)           (ms)        Cnt Num
1   172.16.10.2          Se0/0            11 03:54:25      1    200  0   127
0   172.16.10.6          Se0/1            11 04:14:47      1    200  0   2010
```

Here's a breakdown of the important information we can see in the preceding output:

- H indicates the order in which the neighbor was discovered.

- Hold time in seconds is how long this router will wait for a Hello packet to arrive from a specific neighbor.

- The Uptime value indicates how long the neighbor relationship has been established.

- The SRTT field is the smooth round-trip timer and represents how long it takes to complete a round-trip from this router to its neighbor and back. This value delimits how long to wait after a multicast for a reply from this neighbor. As mentioned earlier, the router will attempt to establish communication via unicasts if it doesn't receive a reply.

- The time between multicast attempts is specified by the Retransmission Time Out (RTO) field, which is based upon the SRTT values.

- The Q value tells us if there are any outstanding messages in the queue. We can make a mental note that there's a problem if we see consistently large values here!

- Finally, the Seq field shows the sequence number of the last update from that neighbor, which is used to maintain synchronization and avoid duplicate messages or their out-of-sequence processing.

The neighbors command is a great command, but we can get the local status of our router by also using the show ip eigrp interfaces command like this:

```
Corp#sh ip eigrp interfaces
IP-EIGRP interfaces for process 20
```

Interface	Peers	Xmit Queue Un/Reliable	Mean SRTT	Pacing Time Un/Reliable	Multicast Flow Timer	Pending Routes
Gi0/0	0	0/0	0	0/1	0	0
Se0/1	1	0/0	1	0/15	50	0
Se0/0	1	0/0	1	0/15	50	0
Gi0/1	0	0/0	0	0/1	0	0

```
Corp#sh ip eigrp interface detail s0/0
IP-EIGRP interfaces for process 20
```

Interface	Peers	Xmit Queue Un/Reliable	Mean SRTT	Pacing Time Un/Reliable	Multicast Flow Timer	Pending Routes

```
Se0/0              1        0/0       1      0/15      50          0
   Hello interval is 5 sec
   Next xmit serial <none>
   Un/reliable mcasts: 0/0  Un/reliable ucasts: 21/26
   Mcast exceptions: 0  CR packets: 0  ACKs suppressed: 9
   Retransmissions sent: 0  Out-of-sequence rcvd: 0
   Authentication mode is not set
```

The first command, show ip eigrp interfaces, lists all interfaces for which EIGRP is enabled as well as those the router is currently sending Hello messages to in an attempt to find new EIGRP neighbors. The show ip eigrp interface detail *interface* command lists more details per interface, including the local router's own Hello interval. Understand that you can use these commands to verify that all your interfaces are within the AS process used by EIGRP, but also note that the passive interfaces won't show up in these outputs. So be sure to also check to see if an interface has been configured as passive if is not present in the outputs.

Okay, if all neighbors are present, then verify the routes learned. By executing the show ip route eigrp command, you're given a quick picture of the routes in the routing table. If a certain route doesn't appear in the routing table, you need to verify its source. If the source is functioning properly, then check the topology table.

The routing table according to Corp looks like this:

```
Corp#sh ip ip eigrp topology
D     192.168.10.0/24 [90/2172416] via 172.16.10.6, 02:29:09, Serial0/1
                      [90/2172416] via 172.16.10.2, 02:29:09, Serial0/0
      172.16.0.0/30 is subnetted, 2 subnets
C        172.16.10.4 is directly connected, Serial0/1
C        172.16.10.0 is directly connected, Serial0/0
      10.0.0.0/24 is subnetted, 6 subnets
C        10.10.10.0 is directly connected, Loopback0
C        10.10.11.0 is directly connected, Loopback1
D        10.10.20.0 [90/2300416] via 172.16.10.6, 02:29:09, Serial0/1
                    [90/2297856] via 172.16.10.2, 02:29:10, Serial0/0
D        10.10.30.0 [90/2300416] via 172.16.10.6, 02:29:10, Serial0/1
                    [90/2297856] via 172.16.10.2, 02:29:10, Serial0/0
D        10.10.40.0 [90/2297856] via 172.16.10.6, 02:29:10, Serial0/1
                    [90/2300416] via 172.16.10.2, 02:29:10, Serial0/0
D        10.10.50.0 [90/2297856] via 172.16.10.6, 02:29:11, Serial0/1
                    [90/2300416] via 172.16.10.2, 02:29:11, Serial0/0
```

You can see here that most EIGRP routes are referenced with a D and that their administrative distance is 90. Remember that the [90/2300416] represents AD/FD, and in the preceding output, EIGRP is performing equal- and unequal-cost load balancing between two links to our remote networks.

We can see this by looking closer at two different networks. Pay special attention to the FD of each output:

```
Corp#sh ip route | section 192.168.10.0
D    192.168.10.0/24 [90/2172416] via 172.16.10.6, 01:15:44, Serial0/1
                     [90/2172416] via 172.16.10.2, 01:15:44, Serial0/0
```

The preceding output shows equal-cost load balancing, and here's our unequal-cost load balancing in action:

```
Corp#sh ip route | section 10.10.50.0
D     10.10.50.0 [90/2297856] via 172.16.10.6, 01:16:16, Serial0/1
                 [90/2300416] via 172.16.10.2, 01:16:16, Serial0/0
```

We can get the topology table displayed for us via the show ip eigrp topology command. If the route is in the topology table but not in the routing table, it's a pretty safe assumption that there's a problem between the topology database and the routing table. After all, there must be a good reason the topology database isn't adding the route into the routing table, right? We discussed this issue in detail earlier in the chapter, and it's oh so important!

Corp's topology table looks like this:

```
Corp#sh ip ip eigrp topology
P 10.10.10.0/24, 1 successors, FD is 128256
        via Connected, GigabitEthernet0/0
P 10.10.11.0/24, 1 successors, FD is 128256
        via Connected, GigabitEthernet0/1
P 10.10.20.0/24, 1 successors, FD is 2297856
        via 172.16.10.2 (2297856/128256), Serial0/0
        via 172.16.10.6 (2300416/156160), Serial0/1
P 10.10.30.0/24, 1 successors, FD is 2297856
        via 172.16.10.2 (2297856/128256), Serial0/0
        via 172.16.10.6 (2300416/156160), Serial0/1
P 10.10.40.0/24, 1 successors, FD is 2297856
        via 172.16.10.6 (2297856/128256), Serial0/1
        via 172.16.10.2 (2300416/156160), Serial0/0
P 10.10.50.0/24, 1 successors, FD is 2297856
        via 172.16.10.6 (2297856/128256), Serial0/1
        via 172.16.10.2 (2300416/156160), Serial0/0
P 192.168.10.0/24, 2 successors, FD is 2172416
        via 172.16.10.2 (2172416/28160), Serial0/0
        via 172.16.10.6 (2172416/28160), Serial0/1
P 172.16.10.4/30, 1 successors, FD is 2169856
        via Connected, Serial0/1
P 172.16.10.0/30, 1 successors, FD is 2169856
        via Connected, Serial0/0
```

Notice that every route in this output is preceded by a P, which shows that these routes are in a *passive state*. This is good because routes in the active state indicate that the router has lost its path to this network and is searching for a replacement. Each entry also reveals the feasible distance, or FD, to each remote network as well as the next-hop neighbor through which packets will travel to this destination. Each entry also has two numbers in brackets, with the first indicating the feasible distance and the second, the advertised distance to a remote network.

Again, here's our equal- and unequal-cost load-balancing output shown in the topology table:

```
Corp#sh ip eigrp top | section 192.168.10.0
P 192.168.10.0/24, 2 successors, FD is 2172416
        via 172.16.10.2 (2172416/28160), Serial0/0
        via 172.16.10.6 (2172416/28160), Serial0/1
```

The preceding output shows equal-cost load balancing, and here is our unequal-cost load balancing in action:

```
Corp#sh ip eigrp top | section 10.10.50.0
P 10.10.50.0/24, 1 successors, FD is 2297856
        via 172.16.10.6 (2297856/128256), Serial0/1
        via 172.16.10.2 (2300416/156160), Serial0/0
```

The command show ip eigrp traffic enables us to see if updates are being sent. If the counters for EIGRP input and output packets don't increase, it means that no EIGRP information is being sent between peers. The following output indicates that the Corp router is experiencing normal traffic:

```
Corp#show ip eigrp traffic
IP-EIGRP Traffic Statistics for process 200
  Hellos sent/received: 2208/2310
  Updates sent/received: 184/183
  Queries sent/received: 17/4
  Replies sent/received: 4/18
  Acks sent/received: 62/65
  Input queue high water mark 2, 0 drops
```

All EIGRP packet types are represented in the output of this command. And we can't forget the always useful troubleshooting command show ip protocols. Here's the output the Corp router gives us after using it:

```
Routing Protocol is "eigrp 20"
  Outgoing update filter list for all interfaces is not set
  Incoming update filter list for all interfaces is not set
  Default networks flagged in outgoing updates
  Default networks accepted from incoming updates
  EIGRP metric weight K1=1, K2=0, K3=1, K4=0, K5=0
```

```
EIGRP maximum hopcount 100
EIGRP maximum metric variance 2
Redistributing: eigrp 20
EIGRP NSF-aware route hold timer is 240s
Automatic network summarization is not in effect
Maximum path: 4
Routing for Networks:
  10.0.0.0
  172.16.0.0
Routing Information Sources:
  Gateway         Distance      Last Update
  (this router)        90       04:23:51
  172.16.10.6          90       02:30:48
  172.16.10.2          90       02:30:48
Distance: internal 90 external 170
```

In this output, we can see that EIGRP is enabled for autonomous system 20 and that the K values are set to their defaults. The variance is 2, so both equal- and unequal-cost load balancing is happening here. Automatic summarization has been turned off. We can also see that EIGRP is advertising two classful networks and that it sees two neighbors.

The show ip eigrp events command displays a log of every EIGRP event: when routes are injected and removed from the routing table and when EIGRP adjacencies are reset or fail. This information is so helpful in determining if there are routing instabilities in the network! Be advised that this command can result in quite a flood of information even for really simple configurations like ours. To demonstrate, here's the output the Corp router divulged after I used it:

```
Corp#show ip eigrp events
Event information for AS 20:
1    22:24:24.258 Metric set: 172.16.10.0/30 2169856
2    22:24:24.258 FC sat rdbmet/succmet: 2169856 0
3    22:24:24.258 FC sat nh/ndbmet: 0.0.0.0 2169856
4    22:24:24.258 Find FS: 172.16.10.0/30 2169856
5    22:24:24.258 Metric set: 172.16.10.4/30 2169856
6    22:24:24.258 FC sat rdbmet/succmet: 2169856 0
7    22:24:24.258 FC sat nh/ndbmet: 0.0.0.0 2169856
8    22:24:24.258 Find FS: 172.16.10.4/30 2169856
9    22:24:24.258 Metric set: 192.168.10.0/24 2172416
10   22:24:24.258 Route install: 192.168.10.0/24 172.16.10.2
11   22:24:24.258 Route install: 192.168.10.0/24 172.16.10.6
12   22:24:24.254 FC sat rdbmet/succmet: 2172416 28160
13   22:24:24.254 FC sat nh/ndbmet: 172.16.10.6 2172416
```

```
14    22:24:24.254 Find FS: 192.168.10.0/24 2172416
15    22:24:24.254 Metric set: 10.10.50.0/24 2297856
16    22:24:24.254 Route install: 10.10.50.0/24 172.16.10.6
17    22:24:24.254 FC sat rdbmet/succmet: 2297856 128256
18    22:24:24.254 FC sat nh/ndbmet: 172.16.10.6 2297856
19    22:24:24.254 Find FS: 10.10.50.0/24 2297856
20    22:24:24.254 Metric set: 10.10.40.0/24 2297856
21    22:24:24.254 Route install: 10.10.40.0/24 172.16.10.6
22    22:24:24.250 FC sat rdbmet/succmet: 2297856 128256
 --More--
```

Exam Essentials

Know how to configure EIGRP.   Be able to configure basic EIGRP. This is configured the same as RIP with classful addresses.

Know how to verify EIGRP operation.   Know all of the EIGRP show commands and be familiar with their output and the interpretation of the main components of their output.

Be able to read an EIGRP topology table.   Understand which are successors, which are feasible successors, and which routes will become successors if the main successor fails.

You must be able to troubleshoot EIGRP.   Go through the EIGRP troubleshooting scenario and make sure you understand to look for the AS number, ACLs, passive interfaces, variance, and other factors.

Configure, verify, and troubleshoot EIGRP for IPv6 (excluding authentication, filtering, manual summarization, redistribution, stub)

EIGRPv6 works much the same way as its IPv4 predecessor does—most of the features that EIGRP provided before EIGRPv6 will still be available.

EIGRPv6 is still an advanced distance-vector protocol that has some link-state features. The neighbor discovery process using Hellos still happens, and it still provides reliable communication with Reliable Transport Protocol that gives us loop-free fast convergence using the Diffusing Update Algorithm (DUAL).

Hello packets and updates are sent using multicast transmission, and as with RIPng, EIGRPv6's multicast address stayed almost the same. In IPv4 it was 224.0.0.10; in IPv6, it's FF02::A (A = 10 in hexadecimal notation).

But clearly, there are key differences between the two versions. Most notably the use of the pesky network command is gone, so it's hard to make a mistake with EIGRPv6. Also, the network and interface to be advertised must be enabled from interface configuration mode with one simple command.

But you still have to use the router configuration mode to enable the routing protocol in EIGRPv6 because the routing process must be literally enabled like an interface with the no shutdown command—interesting! However, the 15.0 code does enable this by default, so this command actually may or may not be needed.

Here's an example of enabling EIGRPv6 on the Corp router:

```
Corp(config)#ipv6 unicast-routing
Corp(config)#ipv6 router eigrp 10
```

The 10 in this case is still the AS number. The prompt changes to (config-rtr), and from here, just initiate a no shutdown if needed:

```
Corp(config-rtr)#no shutdown
```

Other options also can be configured in this mode, like redistribution and router ID (RID). So now, let's go to the interface and enable IPv6:

```
Corp(config-if)#ipv6 eigrp 10
```

The 10 in the interface command again references the AS number that was enabled in the configuration mode.

Figure 3.21 shows the layout we've been using throughout this chapter, only with IPv6 addresses now assigned to interfaces. I used the EUI-64 option on each interface so each router assigned itself an IPv6 address after I typed in the 64-bit network/subnet address.

FIGURE 3.21   Configuring EIGRPv6 on our internetwork

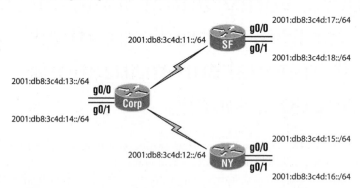

We'll start with the Corp router. Really, all we need to know in order to enable EIGRPv6 are which interfaces we're using and want to advertise our networks.

```
Corp#config t
Corp(config)#ipv6 router eigrp 10
```

```
Corp(config-rtr)#no shut
Corp(config-rtr)#router-id 1.1.1.1
Corp(config-rtr)#int s0/0/0
Corp(config-if)#ipv6 eigrp 10
Corp(config-if)#int s0/0/1
Corp(config-if)#ipv6 eigrp 10
Corp(config-if)#int g0/0
Corp(config-if)#ipv6 eigrp 10
Corp(config-if)#int g0/1
Corp(config-if)#ipv6 eigrp 10
```

I had erased and reloaded the routers before I started this EIGRPv6 section of the chapter. What this means is that there were no 32-bit addresses on the router in order to create the RID for EIGRP, so I had to set it under the IPv6 router global command, which is the same command used with EIGRP and EIGRPv6. Unlike with OSPF, the RID isn't that important, and it can actually be the same address on every router. You just can't get away with doing this with OSPF! The configuration for EIGRPv6 was pretty straightforward because unless you type the AS number wrong, it's pretty hard to screw this up!

Okay, let's configure the SF and NY routers now, and then we'll verify our networks:

```
SF#config t
SF(config)#ipv6 router eigrp 10
SF(config-rtr)#no shut
SF(config-rtr)#router-id 2.2.2.2
SF(config-rtr)#int s0/0/0
SF(config-if)#ipv6 eigrp 10
SF(config-if)#int g0/0
SF(config-if)#ipv6 eigrp 10
SF(config-if)#int g0/1
SF(config-if)#ipv6 eigrp 10

NY#config t
NY(config)#ipv6 router eigrp 10
NY(config-rtr)#no shut
NY(config-rtr)#router-id 3.3.3.3
NY(config-rtr)#int s0/0/0
NY(config-if)#ipv6 eigrp 10
NY(config-if)#int g0/0
NY(config-if)#ipv6 eigrp 10
NY(config-if)#int g0/1
```

Since we configured EIGRPv6 on a per-interface basis, no worries about having to use the passive-interface command. This is because if we don't enable the routing protocol on an interface, it's just not part of the EIGRPv6 process. We can see which interfaces are part of the EIGRPv6 process with the show ipv6 eigrp interfaces command like this:

```
Corp#sh ipv6 eigrp interfaces
IPv6-EIGRP interfaces for process 10
                     Xmit Queue    Mean    Pacing Time    Multicast    Pending
Interface    Peers   Un/Reliable   SRTT    Un/Reliable    Flow Timer   Routes
Se0/0/0        1        0/0        1236        0/10            0           0
Se0/0/1        1        0/0        1236        0/10            0           0
Gig0/1         0        0/0        1236        0/10            0           0
Gig0/0         0        0/0        1236        0/10            0           0
Corp#
```

Looks great so far—all the interfaces we want in our AS are listed, so we're looking good for our Corp's local configuration. Now it's time to check if our adjacencies came up with the show ipv6 eigrp neighbors command:

```
Corp#sh ipv6 eigrp neighbors
IPv6-EIGRP neighbors for process 10
H   Address                  Interface    Hold    Uptime    SRTT    RTO    Q    Seq
                                          (sec)             (ms)           Cnt  Num
0   Link-local address:      Se0/0/0       10     00:01:40   40     1000   0    11
    FE80::201:C9FF:FED0:3301
1   Link-local address:      Se0/0/1       14     00:01:24   40     1000   0    11
    FE80::209:7CFF:FE51:B401
```

It's great that we can see neighbors listed off of each serial interface, but do you notice something missing from the preceding output? That's right, the actual IPv6 network/subnet addresses of the links aren't listed in the neighbor table! Only the link-local addresses are used for forming EIGRP neighbor adjacencies. With IPv6, neighbor interfaces and next-hop addresses are always link-local.

We can verify our configuration with the show ip protocols command:

```
Corp#sh ipv6 protocols
IPv6 Routing Protocol is "connected"
IPv6 Routing Protocol is "static
IPv6 Routing Protocol is "eigrp 10 "
  EIGRP metric weight K1=1, K2=0, K3=1, K4=0, K5=0
  EIGRP maximum hopcount 100
  EIGRP maximum metric variance 1
  Interfaces:
    Serial0/0/0
```

```
     Serial0/0/1
     GigabitEthernet0/0
     GigabitEthernet0/1
Redistributing: eigrp 10
  Maximum path: 16
  Distance: internal 90 external 170
```

You can verify the AS number from this output, but be sure to verify your K values, variance, and interfaces too. Remember that the AS number and interfaces are the first factors to check when troubleshooting.

The topology table lists all feasible routes in the network, so this output can be rather long, but let's see what this shows us:

```
Corp#sh ipv6 eigrp topology
IPv6-EIGRP Topology Table for AS 10/ID(1.1.1.1)

Codes: P - Passive, A - Active, U - Update, Q - Query, R - Reply,
       r - Reply status

P 2001:DB8:C34D:11::/64, 1 successors, FD is 2169856
        via Connected, Serial0/0/0
P 2001:DB8:C34D:12::/64, 1 successors, FD is 2169856
        via Connected, Serial0/0/1
P 2001:DB8:C34D:14::/64, 1 successors, FD is 2816
        via Connected, GigabitEthernet0/1
P 2001:DB8:C34D:13::/64, 1 successors, FD is 2816
        via Connected, GigabitEthernet0/0
P 2001:DB8:C34D:17::/64, 1 successors, FD is 2170112
        via FE80::201:C9FF:FED0:3301 (2170112/2816), Serial0/0/0
P 2001:DB8:C34D:18::/64, 1 successors, FD is 2170112
        via FE80::201:C9FF:FED0:3301 (2170112/2816), Serial0/0/0
P 2001:DB8:C34D:15::/64, 1 successors, FD is 2170112
        via FE80::209:7CFF:FE51:B401 (2170112/2816), Serial0/0/1
P 2001:DB8:C34D:16::/64, 1 successors, FD is 2170112
        via FE80::209:7CFF:FE51:B401 (2170112/2816), Serial0/0/1
```

Since we only have eight networks in our internetwork, we can see all eight networks in the topology table, which clearly is as it should be. I've highlighted a couple of things I want to discuss, and the first is that you need to be able to read and understand a topology table. This includes understanding which routes are directly connected and which are being advertised via neighbors. The via Connected shows us our directly connected networks. The second item I want to show you is (2170112/2816), which is the FD/AD, and by the way, it's no different than if you're working with IPv4.

So let's wrap this up by taking a look at a routing table:

```
Corp#sh ipv6 route eigrp
IPv6 Routing Table - 13 entries
Codes: C - Connected, L - Local, S - Static, R - RIP, B - BGP
       U - Per-user Static route, M - MIPv6
       I1 - ISIS L1, I2 - ISIS L2, IA - ISIS interarea, IS - ISIS summary
       O - OSPF intra, OI - OSPF inter, OE1 - OSPF ext 1, OE2 - OSPF ext 2
       ON1 - OSPF NSSA ext 1, ON2 - OSPF NSSA ext 2
       D - EIGRP, EX - EIGRP external
C   2001:DB8:C34D:11::/64 [0/0]
     via ::, Serial0/0/0
L   2001:DB8:C34D:11:230:A3FF:FE36:B101/128 [0/0]
     via ::, Serial0/0/0
C   2001:DB8:C34D:12::/64 [0/0]
     via ::, Serial0/0/1
L   2001:DB8:C34D:12:230:A3FF:FE36:B102/128 [0/0]
     via ::, Serial0/0/1
C   2001:DB8:C34D:13::/64 [0/0]
     via ::, GigabitEthernet0/0
L   2001:DB8:C34D:13:2E0:F7FF:FEDA:7501/128 [0/0]
     via ::, GigabitEthernet0/0
C   2001:DB8:C34D:14::/64 [0/0]
     via ::, GigabitEthernet0/1
L   2001:DB8:C34D:14:2E0:F7FF:FEDA:7502/128 [0/0]
     via ::, GigabitEthernet0/1
D   2001:DB8:C34D:15::/64 [90/2170112]
     via FE80::209:7CFF:FE51:B401, Serial0/0/1
D   2001:DB8:C34D:16::/64 [90/2170112]
     via FE80::209:7CFF:FE51:B401, Serial0/0/1
D   2001:DB8:C34D:17::/64 [90/2170112]
     via FE80::201:C9FF:FED0:3301, Serial0/0/0
D   2001:DB8:C34D:18::/64 [90/2170112]
     via FE80::201:C9FF:FED0:3301, Serial0/0/0
L   FF00::/8 [0/0]
     via ::, Null0
```

I highlighted the EIGRPv6 injected routes that were injected into the routing table. It's important to notice that in order for IPv6 to get to a remote network, the router uses the next-hop link-local address. Do you see that in the table? For example, via FE80::209:7CFF:FE51:B401, Serial0/0/1 is the link-local address of the NY router.

Exam Essentials

Understand how to configure EIGRPv6.   To configure EIGRPv6, first create the autonomous system from global configuration mode and perform a no shutdown. Then enable EIGRPv6 on each interface individually.

Configure, verify, and troubleshoot RIPv2 for IPv4 (excluding authentication, filtering, manual summarization, redistribution)

To configure RIP routing, just turn on the protocol with the router rip command and tell the RIP routing protocol the networks to advertise. Remember that with static routing, we always configured remote networks and never typed a route to our directly connected networks? Well, dynamic routing is carried out the complete opposite way. You would never type a *remote* network under your routing protocol—only enter your directly connected networks!

Configuring RIPv2

Let's configure a three-router internetwork, shown in Figure 3.22, with RIP routing.

FIGURE 3.22   Our internetwork

Corp

RIP has an administrative distance of 120. Static routes have an administrative distance of 1 by default, and since we currently have static routes configured, the routing tables won't be populated with RIP information. We're still good though because I added the 150 to the end of each static route!

You can add the RIP routing protocol by using the `router rip` command and the `network` command. The `network` command tells the routing protocol which classful network to advertise. By doing this, you're activating the RIP routing process on the interfaces whose addressing falls within the specified classful networks configured with the `network` command under the RIP routing process.

Look at the Corp router configuration to see how easy this is. Oh wait—first, I want to verify my directly connected networks so I know what to configure RIP with:

```
Corp#sh ip int brief
Interface       IP-Address     OK? Method Status                Protocol
FastEthernet0/0 10.10.10.1     YES manual up                    up
Serial0/0       172.16.10.1    YES manual up                    up
FastEthernet0/1 unassigned     YES unset  administratively down down
Serial0/1       172.16.10.5    YES manual up                    up
Corp#config t
Corp(config)#router rip
Corp(config-router)#network 10.0.0.0
Corp(config-router)#network 172.16.0.0
Corp(config-router)#version 2
Corp(config-router)#no auto-summary
```

That's it—really! Typically just two or three commands and you're done, which sure makes your job a lot easier than dealing with static routes, doesn't it? Be sure to keep in mind the extra router CPU process and bandwidth that you're consuming.

Anyway, so what exactly did I do here? I enabled the RIP routing protocol, added my directly connected networks, made sure I was only running RIPv2, which is a classless routing protocol, and then I disabled auto-summary. We typically don't want our routing protocols summarizing for us because it's better to do that manually and both RIP and EIGRP (before 15.x code) auto-summarize by default. So a general rule of thumb is to disable auto-summary, which allows them to advertise subnets.

Notice I didn't type in subnets, only the classful network address, which is betrayed by the fact that all subnet bits and host bits are off! That's because with dynamic routing, it's not my job and it's up to the routing protocol to find the subnets and populate the routing tables. And since we have no router buddies running RIP, we won't see any RIP routes in the routing table yet.

Remember that RIP uses the classful address when configuring the network address. To clarify this, refer to the example in our network with an address of 172.16.0.0/24 using subnets 172.16.10.0 and 172.16.20.0. You would only type in the classful network address of 172.16.0.0 and let RIP find the subnets and place them in the routing table. This doesn't mean you are running a classful routing protocol; this is just the way that both RIP and EIGRP are configured.

SF

Let's configure our SF router now, which is connected to two networks. We need to configure both directly connected classful networks, not subnets:

```
SF#sh ip int brief
Interface        IP-Address      OK? Method Status                 Protocol
FastEthernet0/0  192.168.10.1    YES manual up                     up
FastEthernet0/1  unassigned      YES unset  administratively down  down
Serial0/0/0      172.16.10.2     YES manual up                     up
Serial0/0/1      unassigned      YES unset  administratively down  down
SF#config
SF(config)#router rip
SF(config-router)#network 192.168.10.0
SF(config-router)#network 172.16.0.0
SF(config-router)#version 2
SF(config-router)#no auto-summary
SF(config-router)#do show ip route
C    192.168.10.0/24 is directly connected, FastEthernet0/0
L    192.168.10.1/32 is directly connected, FastEthernet0/0
     172.16.0.0/30 is subnetted, 3 subnets
R       172.16.10.4 [120/1] via 172.16.10.1, 00:00:08, Serial0/0/0
C       172.16.10.0 is directly connected, Serial0/0/0
L       172.16.10.2/32 is directly connected, Serial0/0/0
S    192.168.20.0/24 [150/0] via 172.16.10.1
     10.0.0.0/24 is subnetted, 1 subnets
R       10.10.10.0 [120/1] via 172.16.10.1, 00:00:08, Serial0/0/0
```

That was pretty straightforward. Let's talk about this routing table. Since we have one RIP buddy out there with whom we are exchanging routing tables, we can see the RIP networks coming from the Corp router. All the other routes still show up as static and local. RIP also found both connections through the Corp router to networks 10.10.10.0 and 172.16.10.4. But we're not done yet!

LA

Let's configure our LA router with RIP, only I'm going to remove the default route first, even though I don't have to. You'll see why soon:

```
LA#config t
LA(config)#no ip route 0.0.0.0 0.0.0.0
LA(config)#router rip
LA(config-router)#network 192.168.20.0
LA(config-router)#network 172.16.0.0
LA(config-router)#no auto
LA(config-router)#vers 2
LA(config-router)#do show ip route
R    192.168.10.0/24 [120/2] via 172.16.10.5, 00:00:10, Serial0/0/1
     172.16.0.0/30 is subnetted, 3 subnets
C       172.16.10.4 is directly connected, Serial0/0/1
L       172.16.10.6/32 is directly connected, Serial0/0/1
R       172.16.10.0 [120/1] via 172.16.10.5, 00:00:10, Serial0/0/1
C    192.168.20.0/24 is directly connected, FastEthernet0/0
L    192.168.20.1/32 is directly connected, FastEthernet0/0
     10.0.0.0/24 is subnetted, 1 subnets
R       10.10.10.0 [120/1] via 172.16.10.5, 00:00:10, Serial0/0/1
```

The routing table is sprouting new Rs as we add RIP buddies! We can still see that all routes are in the routing table.

This output shows us basically the same routing table and the same entries that it had when we were using static routes—except for those Rs. An R indicates that the networks were added dynamically using the RIP routing protocol. The [120/1] is the administrative distance of the route (120) along with the metric, which for RIP is the number of hops to that remote network (1). From the Corp router, all networks are one hop away.

So, while yes, it's true that RIP has worked in our little internetwork, it's just not a great solution for most enterprises. Its maximum hop count of only 15 is a highly limiting factor. And it performs full routing-table updates every 30 seconds, which would bring a larger internetwork to a painful crawl in no time!

There's still one more thing I want to show you about RIP routing tables and the parameters used to advertise remote networks. Using a different router on a different network as an example for a second, look into the following output. Can you spot where the following routing table shows [120/15] in the 10.1.3.0 network metric? This means that the administrative distance is 120, the default for RIP, but the hop count is 15. Remember that each time a router sends out an update to a neighbor router, the hop count goes up by one incrementally for each route! Here's that output now:

```
Router#sh ip route
     10.0.0.0/24 is subnetted, 12 subnets
```

```
C        10.1.11.0 is directly connected, FastEthernet0/1
L        10.1.11.1/32 is directly connected, FastEthernet0/1
C        10.1.10.0 is directly connected, FastEthernet0/0
L        10.1.10.1/32 is directly connected, FastEthernet/0/0
R        10.1.9.0 [120/2] via 10.1.5.1, 00:00:15, Serial0/0/1
R        10.1.8.0 [120/2] via 10.1.5.1, 00:00:15, Serial0/0/1
R        10.1.12.0 [120/1] via 10.1.11.2, 00:00:00, FastEthernet0/1
R        10.1.3.0 [120/15] via 10.1.5.1, 00:00:15, Serial0/0/1
R        10.1.2.0 [120/1] via 10.1.5.1, 00:00:15, Serial0/0/1
R        10.1.1.0 [120/1] via 10.1.5.1, 00:00:15, Serial0/0/1
R        10.1.7.0 [120/2] via 10.1.5.1, 00:00:15, Serial0/0/1
R        10.1.6.0 [120/2] via 10.1.5.1, 00:00:15, Serial0/0/1
C        10.1.5.0 is directly connected, Serial0/0/1
L        10.1.5.1/32 is directly connected, Serial0/0/1
R        10.1.4.0 [120/1] via 10.1.5.1, 00:00:15, Serial0/0/1
```

So this [120/15] is really bad. We're basically doomed because the next router that receives the table from this router will just discard the route to network 10.1.3.0 since the hop count would rise to 16, which is invalid!

 If a router receives a routing update that contains a higher-cost path to a network that's already in its routing table, the update will be ignored.

Holding Down RIP Propagations

You probably don't want your RIP network advertised everywhere on your LAN and WAN. There's enough stress in networking already and not a whole lot to be gained by advertising your RIP network to the Internet!

There are a few different ways to stop unwanted RIP updates from propagating across your LANs and WANs, and the easiest one is through the passive-interface command. This command prevents RIP update broadcasts from being sent out of a specified interface but still allows that same interface to receive RIP updates.

Here's an example of how to configure a passive-interface on the Corp router's Fa0/1 interface, which we will pretend is connected to a LAN that we don't want RIP on (and the interface isn't shown in the figure):

```
Corp#config t
Corp(config)#router rip
Corp(config-router)#passive-interface FastEthernet 0/1
```

This command will stop RIP updates from being propagated out of FastEthernet interface 0/1, but it can still receive RIP updates.

Advertising a Default Route Using RIP

Now I'm going to guide you through how to advertise a way out of your autonomous system to other routers, and you'll see this is completed the same way with OSPF. Imagine that our Corp router's Fa0/0 interface is connected to some type of Metro-Ethernet as a connection to the Internet. This is a pretty common configuration today that uses a LAN interface to connect to the ISP instead of a serial interface.

If we do add an Internet connection to Corp, all routers in our AS (SF and LA) must know where to send packets destined for networks on the Internet or they'll just drop the packets when they get a remote request. One solution to this little hitch would be to place a default route on every router and funnel the information to Corp, which in turn would have a default route to the ISP. Most people do this type of configuration in small- to medium-size networks because it actually works pretty well!

But since I'm running RIPv2 on all routers, I'll just add a default route on the Corp router to our ISP, as I would normally. I'll then add another command to advertise my network to the other routers in the AS as the default route to show them where to send packets destined for the Internet.

Here's my new Corp configuration:

```
Corp(config)#ip route 0.0.0.0 0.0.0.0 fa0/0
Corp(config)#router rip
Corp(config-router)#default-information originate
```

Now, let's take a look at the last entry found in the Corp routing table:

```
S*    0.0.0.0/0 is directly connected, FastEthernet0/0
```

Let's see if the LA router can see this same entry:

```
LA#sh ip route
Gateway of last resort is 172.16.10.5 to network 0.0.0.0

R    192.168.10.0/24 [120/2] via 172.16.10.5, 00:00:04, Serial0/0/1
     172.16.0.0/30 is subnetted, 2 subnets
C       172.16.10.4 is directly connected, Serial0/0/1
L       172.16.10.5/32 is directly connected, Serial0/0/1
R       172.16.10.0 [120/1] via 172.16.10.5, 00:00:04, Serial0/0/1
C    192.168.20.0/24 is directly connected, FastEthernet0/0
L    192.168.20.1/32 is directly connected, FastEthernet0/0
     10.0.0.0/24 is subnetted, 1 subnets
R       10.10.10.0 [120/1] via 172.16.10.5, 00:00:04, Serial0/0/1
R    192.168.218.0/24 [120/3] via 172.16.10.5, 00:00:04, Serial0/0/1
R    192.168.118.0/24 [120/2] via 172.16.10.5, 00:00:05, Serial0/0/1
R*   0.0.0.0/0 [120/1] via 172.16.10.5, 00:00:05, Serial0/0/1
```

Can you see that last entry? It screams that it's an RIP injected route, but it's also a default route, so our default-information originate command is working! Last, notice that the gateway of last resort is now set as well.

Exam Essentials

Configure RIPv2 routing.   To configure RIP routing, first you must be in global configuration mode and then you type the command `router rip`. Then you add all directly connected networks, making sure to use the classful address and the `version 2` command and to disable auto-summarization with the `no auto-summary` command.

Troubleshoot basic layer 3 end-to-end connectivity issues

To be prepared for the exam, it's a great idea to get used to connecting to various routers and pinging from them. Of course, pinging from a router is not as good as pinging from the host reporting the problem, but that doesn't mean we can't isolate some problems from the routers themselves.

Let's use Figure 3.23 as a basis to run through some troubleshooting scenarios.

FIGURE 3.23   Troubleshooting scenario

In this first scenario, a manager calls you and says that he cannot log in to Server1 from PC1. Your job is to find out why and fix it. The Cisco objectives are clear on the troubleshooting steps you need to take when a problem has been reported, and here they are:

1. Check the cables to find out if there's a faulty cable or interface in the mix and verify the interface's statistics.

2. Make sure that devices are determining the correct path from the source to the destination. Manipulate the routing information if needed.

3. Verify that the default gateway is correct.

4. Verify that name resolution settings are correct.

5. Verify that there are no *access control lists (ACLs)* blocking traffic.

In order to effectively troubleshoot this problem, we'll narrow down the possibilities by the process of elimination. We'll start with PC1 and verify that it's configured correctly and also that IP is working correctly.

There are four steps for checking the PC1 configuration:

1. Test that the local IP stack is working by pinging the loopback address.

2. Test that the local IP stack is talking to the Data Link layer (LAN driver) by pinging the local IP address.

3. Test that the host is working on the LAN by pinging the default gateway.

4. Test that the host can get to remote networks by pinging remote Server1.

Let's check out the PC1 configuration by using the ipconfig command, or ifconfig on a Mac:

```
C:\Users\Todd Lammle>ipconfig


Windows IP Configuration


Ethernet adapter Local Area Connection:

    Connection-specific DNS Suffix  . : localdomain
    Link-local IPv6 Address . . . . . : fe80::64e3:76a2:541f:ebcb%11
    IPv4 Address. . . . . . . . . . . : 10.1.1.10
    Subnet Mask . . . . . . . . . . . : 255.255.255.0
    Default Gateway . . . . . . . . . : 10.1.1.1
```

We can also check the route table on the host with the route print command to see if it truly does know the default gateway:

```
C:\Users\Todd Lammle>route print
[output cut]
IPv4 Route Table
=======================================================================
Active Routes:
Network Destination        Netmask          Gateway        Interface  Metric
          0.0.0.0          0.0.0.0          10.1.1.10      10.1.1.1   10
[output cut]
```

Between the output of the ipconfig command and the route print command, we can be assured that the hosts are aware of the correct default gateway.

For the Cisco objectives, it's extremely important to be able to check and verify the default gateway on a host and also that this address matches the router's interface!

So, let's verify that the local IP stack is initialized by pinging the loopback address now:

```
C:\Users\Todd Lammle>ping 127.0.0.1

Pinging 127.0.0.1 with 32 bytes of data:
Reply from 127.0.0.1: bytes=32 time<1ms TTL=128
Reply from 127.0.0.1: bytes=32 time<1ms TTL=128
Reply from 127.0.0.1: bytes=32 time<1ms TTL=128
Reply from 127.0.0.1: bytes=32 time<1ms TTL=128

Ping statistics for 127.0.0.1:
    Packets: Sent = 4, Received = 4, Lost = 0 (0% loss),
Approximate round trip times in milli-seconds:
    Minimum = 0ms, Maximum = 0ms, Average = 0ms
```

This first output confirms the IP address and configured default gateway of the host, and then I verified the fact that the local IP stack is working. Our next move is to verify that the IP stack is talking to the LAN driver by pinging the local IP address.

```
C:\Users\Todd Lammle>ping 10.1.1.10

Pinging 10.1.1.10 with 32 bytes of data:
Reply from 10.1.1.10: bytes=32 time<1ms TTL=128
Reply from 10.1.1.10: bytes=32 time<1ms TTL=128
Reply from 10.1.1.10: bytes=32 time<1ms TTL=128
Reply from 10.1.1.10: bytes=32 time<1ms TTL=128

Ping statistics for 10.1.1.10:
    Packets: Sent = 4, Received = 4, Lost = 0 (0% loss),
Approximate round trip times in milli-seconds:
    Minimum = 0ms, Maximum = 0ms, Average = 0ms
```

And now that we know the local stack is solid and the IP stack is communicating to the LAN driver, it's time to check our local LAN connectivity by pinging the default gateway:

```
C:\Users\Todd Lammle>ping 10.1.1.1

Pinging 10.1.1.1 with 32 bytes of data:
Reply from 10.1.1.1: bytes=32 time<1ms TTL=128
Reply from 10.1.1.1: bytes=32 time<1ms TTL=128
Reply from 10.1.1.1: bytes=32 time<1ms TTL=128
Reply from 10.1.1.1: bytes=32 time<1ms TTL=128
```

```
Ping statistics for 10.1.1.1:
    Packets: Sent = 4, Received = 4, Lost = 0 (0% loss),
Approximate round trip times in milli-seconds:
    Minimum = 0ms, Maximum = 0ms, Average = 0ms
```

Looking good! I'd say our host is in good shape. Let's try to ping the remote server next to see if our host is actually getting off the local LAN to communicate remotely:

```
C:\Users\Todd Lammle>ping 172.16.20.254


Pinging 172.16.20.254 with 32 bytes of data:
Request timed out.
Request timed out.
Request timed out.
Request timed out.


Ping statistics for 172.16.20.254:
    Packets: Sent = 4, Received = 0, Lost = 4 (100% loss),
```

Well, looks like we've confirmed local connectivity but not remote connectivity, so we're going to have to dig deeper to isolate our problem. But first, and just as important, it's key to make note of what we can rule out at this point:

1. The PC is configured with the correct IP address and the local IP stack is working.

2. The default gateway is configured correctly and the PC's default gateway configuration matches the router interface IP address.

3. The local switch is working because we can ping through the switch to the router.

4. We don't have a local LAN issue, meaning our Physical layer is good because we can ping the router. If we couldn't ping the router, we would need to verify our physical cables and interfaces.

Let's see if we can narrow the problem down further using the traceroute command:

```
C:\Users\Todd Lammle>tracert 172.16.20.254


Tracing route to 172.16.20.254 over a maximum of 30 hops


  1     1 ms     1 ms    <1 ms   10.1.1.1
  2     *        *        *      Request timed out.
  3     *        *        *      Request timed out.
```

Well, we didn't get beyond our default gateway, so let's go over to R2 and see if we can talk locally to the server:

```
R2#ping 172.16.20.254
```

```
Pinging 172.16.20.254 with 32 bytes of data:
Reply from 172.16.20.254: bytes=32 time<1ms TTL=128
Reply from 172.16.20.254: bytes=32 time<1ms TTL=128
Reply from 172.16.20.254: bytes=32 time<1ms TTL=128
Reply from 172.16.20.254: bytes=32 time<1ms TTL=128

Ping statistics for 172.16.20.254:
    Packets: Sent = 4, Received = 0, Lost = 4 (100% loss),
```

Okay, we just eliminated a local LAN problem by connecting to Server1 from the R2 router, so we're good there. Let's summarize what we know so far:

1. PC1 is configured correctly.

2. The switch located on the 10.1.1.0 LAN is working.

3. PC1's default gateway is configured correctly.

4. R2 can communicate to Server1, so we don't have a remote LAN issue.

But something is still clearly wrong, so what should we check now? Now would be a great time to verify the Server1 IP configuration and make sure the default gateway is configured correctly. Let's take a look:

```
C:\Users\Server1>ipconfig

Windows IP Configuration

Ethernet adapter Local Area Connection:

    Connection-specific DNS Suffix  . : localdomain
    Link-local IPv6 Address . . . . . : fe80::7723:76a2:e73c:2acb%11
    IPv4 Address. . . . . . . . . . . : 172.16.20.254
    Subnet Mask . . . . . . . . . . . : 255.255.255.0
    Default Gateway . . . . . . . . . : 172.16.20.1
```

Okay—the Server1 configuration looks good and the R2 router can ping the server, so it seems that the server's local LAN is solid, the local switch is working, and there are no cable or interface issues. But let's zoom in on interface Fa0/0 on R2 and talk about what to expect if there were errors on this interface:

```
R2#sh int fa0/0
FastEthernet0/0 is up, line protocol is up
[output cut]
  Full-duplex, 100Mb/s, 100BaseTX/FX
  ARP type: ARPA, ARP Timeout 04:00:00
  Last input 00:00:05, output 00:00:01, output hang never
```

```
Last clearing of "show interface" counters never
Input queue: 0/75/0/0 (size/max/drops/flushes); Total output drops: 0
Queueing strategy: fifo
Output queue: 0/40 (size/max)
5 minute input rate 0 bits/sec, 0 packets/sec
5 minute output rate 0 bits/sec, 0 packets/sec
    1325 packets input, 157823 bytes
    Received 1157 broadcasts (0 IP multicasts)
    0 runts, 0 giants, 0 throttles
    0 input errors, 0 CRC, 0 frame, 0 overrun, 0 ignored
    0 watchdog
    0 input packets with dribble condition detected
    2294 packets output, 244630 bytes, 0 underruns
    0 output errors, 0 collisions, 3 interface resets
    347 unknown protocol drops
    0 babbles, 0 late collision, 0 deferred
    4 lost carrier, 0 no carrier
    0 output buffer failures, 0 output buffers swapped out
```

You've got to be able to analyze interface statistics to find problems there if they exist, so let's pick out the important factors relevant to meeting that challenge effectively now.

Speed and duplex settings   Good to know that the most common cause of interface errors is a mismatched duplex mode between two ends of an Ethernet link. This is why it's so important to make sure that the switch and its hosts (PCs, router interfaces, etc.) have the same speed setting. If not, they just won't connect. And if they have mismatched duplex settings, you'll receive a legion of errors, which cause nasty performance issues, intermittent connectivity—even total loss of communication!

Using autonegotiation for speed and duplex is a very common practice, and it's enabled by default. But if this fails for some reason, you'll have to set the configuration manually like this:

```
Switch(config)#int gi0/1
Switch(config-if)#speed ?
  10     Force 10 Mbps operation
  100    Force 100 Mbps operation
  1000   Force 1000 Mbps operation
  auto   Enable AUTO speed configuration
Switch(config-if)#speed 1000
Switch(config-if)#duplex ?
  auto   Enable AUTO duplex configuration
  full   Force full duplex operation
  half   Force half-duplex operation
Switch(config-if)#duplex  full
```

If you have a duplex mismatch, a telling sign is that the late collision counter will increment.

Input queue drops   If the input queue drops counter increments, this signifies that more traffic is being delivered to the router that it can process. If this is consistently high, try to determine exactly when these counters are increasing and how the events relate to CPU usage. You'll see the ignored and throttle counters increment as well.

Output queue drops   This counter indicates that packets were dropped due to interface congestion, leading to queuing delays. When this occurs, applications like VoIP will experience performance issues. If you observe this constantly incrementing, consider QoS.

Input errors   Input errors often indicate high errors such as CRCs. This can point to cabling problems, hardware issues, or duplex mismatches.

Output errors   This is the total number of frames that the port tried to transmit when an issue such as a collision occurred.

We're going to move on in our troubleshooting process of elimination by analyzing the routers' actual configurations. Here's R1's routing table:

```
R1>sh ip route
[output cut]
Gateway of last resort is 192.168.10.254 to network 0.0.0.0

S*     0.0.0.0/0 [1/0] via 192.168.10.254
       10.0.0.0/8 is variably subnetted, 2 subnets, 2 masks
C         10.1.1.0/24 is directly connected, FastEthernet0/0
L         10.1.1.1/32 is directly connected, FastEthernet0/0
       192.168.10.0/24 is variably subnetted, 2 subnets, 2 masks
C         192.168.10.0/24 is directly connected, FastEthernet0/1
L         192.168.10.1/32 is directly connected, FastEthernet0/1
```

This actually looks pretty good! Both of our directly connected networks are in the table and we can confirm that we have a default route going to the R2 router. So now let's verify the connectivity to R2 from R1:

```
R1>sh ip int brief
Interface          IP-Address       OK? Method Status                     Protocol
FastEthernet0/0    10.1.1.1         YES manual up                          up
FastEthernet0/1    192.168.10.1     YES manual up                          up
Serial0/0/0        unassigned       YES unset  administratively down       down
Serial0/1/0        unassigned       YES unset  administratively down       down
R1>ping 192.168.10.254
Type escape sequence to abort.
```

```
Sending 5, 100-byte ICMP Echos to 192.168.10.254, timeout is 2 seconds:
!!!!!
Success rate is 100 percent (5/5), round-trip min/avg/max = 1/2/4 ms
```

This looks great too! Our interfaces are correctly configured with the right IP address and the Physical and Data Link layers are up. By the way, I also tested layer 3 connectivity by pinging the R2 Fa0/1 interface.

Since everything looks good so far, our next step is to check into the status of R2's interfaces:

```
R2>sh ip int brief
Interface            IP-Address        OK? Method Status         Protocol
FastEthernet0/0      172.16.20.1       YES manual up                 up
FastEthernet0/1      192.168.10.254    YES manual up                 up
R2>ping 192.168.10.1
Type escape sequence to abort.
Sending 5, 100-byte ICMP Echos to 192.168.10.1, timeout is 2 seconds:
!!!!!
Success rate is 100 percent (5/5), round-trip min/avg/max = 1/2/4 ms
```

Well, everything still checks out at this point. The IP addresses are correct and the Physical and Data Link layers are up. I also tested the layer 3 connectivity with a ping to R1, so we're all good so far. We'll examine the routing table next:

```
R2>sh ip route
[output cut]
Gateway of last resort is not set

    10.0.0.0/24 is subnetted, 1 subnets
S       10.1.1.0 is directly connected, FastEthernet0/0
    172.16.0.0/16 is variably subnetted, 2 subnets, 2 masks
C       172.16.20.0/24 is directly connected, FastEthernet0/0
L       172.16.20.1/32 is directly connected, FastEthernet0/0
    192.168.10.0/24 is variably subnetted, 2 subnets, 2 masks
C       192.168.10.0/24 is directly connected, FastEthernet0/1
L       192.168.10.254/32 is directly connected, FastEthernet0/1
```

Okay—we can see that all our local interfaces are in the table, as well as a static route to the 10.1.1.0 network. But do you see the problem? Look closely at the static route. The route was entered with an exit interface of Fa0/0, and the path to the 10.1.1.0 network is out Fa0/1! Aha! We've found our problem! Let's fix R2:

```
R2#config t
R2(config)#no ip route 10.1.1.0 255.255.255.0 fa0/0
R2(config)#ip route 10.1.1.0 255.255.255.0 192.168.10.1
```

That should do it. Let's verify from PC1:

```
C:\Users\Todd Lammle>ping 172.16.20.254

Pinging 172.16.20.254 with 32 bytes of data:
Reply from 172.16.20.254: bytes=32 time<1ms TTL=128
Reply from 172.16.20.254: bytes=32 time<1ms TTL=128
Reply from 172.16.20.254: bytes=32 time<1ms TTL=128
Reply from 172.16.20.254: bytes=32 time<1ms TTL=128

Ping statistics for 172.16.20.254
    Packets: Sent = 4, Received = 4, Lost = 0 (0% loss),
Approximate round trip times in milli-seconds:
    Minimum = 0ms, Maximum = 0ms, Average = 0ms
```

Our snag appears to be solved, but just to make sure, we really need to verify with a higher-level protocol like Telnet:

```
C:\Users\Todd Lammle>telnet 172.16.20.254
Connecting To 172.16.20.254...Could not open connection to the host, on
port 23: Connect failed
```

Okay, that's not good! We can ping to Server1, but we can't telnet to it. In the past, I've verified that telnetting to this server worked, but it's still possible that we have a failure on the server side. To find out, let's verify our network first, starting at R1:

```
R1>ping 172.16.20.254
Type escape sequence to abort.
Sending 5, 100-byte ICMP Echos to 172.16.20.254, timeout is 2 seconds:
!!!!!
Success rate is 100 percent (5/5), round-trip min/avg/max = 1/1/4 ms
R1>telnet 172.16.20.254
Trying 172.16.20.254 ...
% Destination unreachable; gateway or host down
```

This is some pretty ominous output! Let's try from R2 and see what happens:

```
R2#telnet 172.16.20.254
Trying 172.16.20.254 ... Open

User Access Verification

Password:
```

Oh my—I can ping the server from a remote network, but I can't telnet to it; however, the local router R2 can! These factors eliminate the server being a problem since I can telnet to the server when I'm on the local LAN.

And we know we don't have a routing problem because we fixed that already. So what's next? Let's check to see if there's an ACL on R2:

```
R2>sh access-lists
Extended IP access list 110
    10 permit icmp any any (25 matches)
```

Seriously? What a loopy access list to have on a router! This ridiculous list permits ICMP, but that's it. It denies everything except ICMP due to the implicit deny ip any any at the end of every ACL. But before we uncork the champagne, we need to see if this foolish list has been applied to our interfaces on R2 to confirm that this is really our problem:

```
R2>sh ip int fa0/0
FastEthernet0/0 is up, line protocol is up
  Internet address is 172.16.20.1/24
  Broadcast address is 255.255.255.255
  Address determined by setup command
  MTU is 1500 bytes
  Helper address is not set
  Directed broadcast forwarding is disabled
  Outgoing access list is 110
  Inbound  access list is not set
```

There it is—that's our problem all right! In case you're wondering why R2 could telnet to Server1, it's because an ACL filters only packets trying to go through the router—not packets generated at the router. Let's get to work and fix this:

```
R2#config t
R2(config)#no access-list 110
```

I just verified that I can telnet from PC1 to Server1, but let's try telnetting from R1 again:

```
R1#telnet 172.16.20.254
Trying 172.16.20.254 ... Open

User Access Verification

Password:
```

Nice—looks like we're set, but what about using the name?

```
R1#telnet Server1
Translating "Server1"...domain server (255.255.255.255)

% Bad IP address or host name
```

Well, we're not all set just yet. Let's fix R1 so that it can provide name resolution:

```
R1(config)#ip host Server1 172.16.20.254
R1(config)#^Z
R1#telnet Server1
Trying Server1 (172.16.20.254)... Open

User Access Verification

Password:
```

Great—things are looking good from the router, but if the customer can't telnet to the remote host using the name, we've got to check the DNS server to confirm connectivity and for the correct entry to the server. Another option would be to configure the local host table manually on PC1.

The last thing to do is to check the server to see if it's responding to HTTP requests via the telnet command, believe it or not! Here's an example:

```
R1#telnet 172.16.20.254 80
Trying 172.16.20.254, 80 ... Open
```

Yes—finally! Server1 is responding to requests on port 80, so we're in the clear.

Troubleshooting IPv6 Network Connectivity

I'm going to be straight with you: There isn't a lot that's going to be much different between this section and the process you just went through with the IPv4 troubleshooting steps. Except regarding the addressing of course! So other than that key factor, we'll take the same approach, using Figure 3.24, specifically because I really want to highlight the differences associated with IPv6. So the problem scenario I'm going to use will also stay the same: PC1 cannot communicate to Server1.

FIGURE 3.24   IPv6 troubleshooting scenario

I want to point out that this is not an "introduction to IPv6," so I'm assuming you've got some IPv6 fundamentals down.

Notice that I documented both the *link-local* and *global addresses* assigned to each router interface in Figure 3.24. We need both in order to troubleshoot, so right away, you can see that things get a bit more complicated because of the longer addresses and the fact that there are multiple addresses per interface involved!

Here are the troubleshooting steps we'll progress through in our investigation:

1. Check the cables because there might be a faulty cable or interface. Verify interface statistics.

2. Make sure that devices are determining the correct path from the source to the destination. Manipulate the routing information if needed.

3. Verify that the default gateway is correct.

4. Verify that name resolution settings are correct, and especially for IPv6, make sure the DNS server is reachable via IPv4 and IPv6.

5. Verify that there are no ACLs that are blocking traffic.

In order to troubleshoot this problem, we'll use the same process of elimination, beginning with PC1. We must verify that it's configured correctly and that IP is working properly. Let's start by pinging the loopback address to verify the IPv6 stack:

```
C:\Users\Todd Lammle>ping ::1

Pinging ::1 with 32 bytes of data:
Reply from ::1: time<1ms
Reply from ::1: time<1ms
Reply from ::1: time<1ms
Reply from ::1: time<1ms
```

Well, the IPv6 stack checks out, so let's ping the Fa0/0 of R1, which PC1 is directly connected to on the same LAN, starting with the link-local address:

```
C:\Users\Todd Lammle>ping fe80::21a:6dff:fe37:a44e

Pinging fe80:21a:6dff:fe37:a44e with 32 bytes of data:
Reply from fe80::21a:6dff:fe37:a44e: time<1ms
Reply from fe80::21a:6dff:fe37:a44e: time<1ms
Reply from fe80::21a:6dff:fe37:a44e: time<1ms
Reply from fe80::21a:6dff:fe37:a44e: time<1ms
```

Next, we'll ping the global address on Fa0/0:

```
C:\Users\Todd Lammle>ping 2001:db8:3c4d:3:21a:6dff:fe37:a44e

Pinging 2001:db8:3c4d:3:21a:6dff:fe37:a44e with 32 bytes of data:
Reply from 2001:db8:3c4d:3:21a:6dff:fe37:a44e: time<1ms
```

```
Reply from 2001:db8:3c4d:3:21a:6dff:fe37:a44e: time<1ms
Reply from 2001:db8:3c4d:3:21a:6dff:fe37:a44e: time<1ms
Reply from 2001:db8:3c4d:3:21a:6dff:fe37:a44e: time<1ms
```

Okay—looks like PC1 is configured and working on the local LAN to the R1 router, so we've confirmed the Physical, Data Link, and Network layers between the PC1 and the R1 router Fa0/0 interface.

Our next move is to check the local connection on Server1 to the R2 router to verify that LAN. First we'll ping the link-local address of the router from Server1:

```
C:\Users\Server1>ping fe80::21a:6dff:fe64:9b2
```

```
Pinging fe80::21a:6dff:fe64:9b2  with 32 bytes of data:
Reply from fe80::21a:6dff:fe64:9b2: time<1ms
Reply from fe80::21a:6dff:fe64:9b2: time<1ms
Reply from fe80::21a:6dff:fe64:9b2: time<1ms
Reply from fe80::21a:6dff:fe64:9b2: time<1ms
```

And next, we'll ping the global address of Fa0/0 on R2:

```
C:\Users\Server1>ping 2001:db8:3c4d:1:21a:6dff:fe37:a443
```

```
Pinging 2001:db8:3c4d:1:21a:6dff:fe37:a443 with 32 bytes of data:
Reply from 2001:db8:3c4d:1:21a:6dff:fe37:a443: time<1ms
Reply from 2001:db8:3c4d:1:21a:6dff:fe37:a443: time<1ms
Reply from 2001:db8:3c4d:1:21a:6dff:fe37:a443: time<1ms
Reply from 2001:db8:3c4d:1:21a:6dff:fe37:a443: time<1ms
```

Let's quickly summarize what we know at this point:

1. By using the `ipconfig /all` command on PC1 and Server1, I was able to document their global and link-local IPv6 addresses.

2. We know the IPv6 link-local addresses of each router interface.

3. We know the IPv6 global address of each router interface.

4. We can ping from PC1 to router R1's Fa0/0 interface.

5. We can ping from Server1 to router R2's Fa0/0 interface.

6. We can eliminate a local problem on both LANs.

From here, we'll go to PC1 and see if we can route to Server1:

```
C:\Users\Todd Lammle>tracert 2001:db8:3c4d:1:a14c:8c33:2d1:be3d
```

```
Tracing route to 2001:db8:3c4d:1:a14c:8c33:2d1:be3d over a maximum of 30 hops

  1    Destination host unreachable.
```

Okay, now that's not good. Looks like we might have a routing problem. And on this little network, we're doing static IPv6 routing, so getting to the bottom of things will definitely take a little effort! But before we start looking into our potential routing issue, let's check the link between R1 and R2. We'll ping R2 from R1 to test the directly connected link.

The first thing you need to do before attempting to ping between routers is verify your addresses—yes, verify them again! Let's check out both routers, then try pinging from R1 to R2:

```
R1#sh ipv6 int brief
FastEthernet0/0              [up/up]
    FE80::21A:6DFF:FE37:A44E
    2001:DB8:3C4D:3:21A:6DFF:FE37:A44E
FastEthernet0/1              [up/up]
    FE80::21A:6DFF:FE37:A44F
    2001:DB8:3C4D:2:21A:6DFF:FE37:A44F


R2#sh ipv6 int brief
FastEthernet0/0              [up/up]
    FE80::21A:6DFF:FE64:9B2
    2001:DB8:3C4D:1:21A:6DFF:FE37:A443
FastEthernet0/1              [up/up]
    FE80::21A:6DFF:FE64:9B3
    2001:DB8:3C4D:2:21A:6DFF:FE64:9B3


R1#ping 2001:DB8:3C4D:2:21A:6DFF:FE64:9B3
Type escape sequence to abort.
Sending 5, 100-byte ICMP Echos to ping 2001:DB8:3C4D:2:21A:6DFF:FE64:9B3,
timeout is 2 seconds:
!!!!!
Success rate is 100 percent (5/5), round-trip min/avg/max = 0/2/8 ms
```

In the preceding output, you can see that I now have the IPv6 addresses for both the R1 and R2 directly connected interfaces. The output also shows that I used the Ping program to verify layer 3 connectivity. Just as with IPv4, we need to resolve the logical (IPv6) address to a MAC address in order to communicate on the local LAN. But unlike IPv4, IPv6 doesn't use ARP—it uses ICMPv6 neighbor solicitations instead—so after the successful ping, we can now see the neighbor resolution table on R1:

```
R1#sh ipv6 neighbors
IPv6 Address                         Age Link-layer Addr State Interface
FE80::21A:6DFF:FE64:9B3                0 001a.6c46.9b09  DELAY Fa0/1
2001:DB8:3C4D:2:21A:6DFF:FE64:9B3      0 001a.6c46.9b09  REACH Fa0/1
```

Let's take a minute to talk about the possible states that a resolved address shows us:

INCMP (incomplete)   Address resolution is being performed on the entry. A neighbor solicitation message has been sent, but the neighbor message has not yet been received.

REACH (reachable)   Positive confirmation has been received confirming that the path to the neighbor is functioning correctly. REACH is good!

STALE   The state is STALE when the interface has not communicated within the neighbor reachable time frame. The next time the neighbor communicates, the state will change back to REACH.

DELAY   Occurs after the STALE state, when no reachability confirmation has been received within what's known as the DELAY_FIRST_PROBE_TIME. This means that the path was functioning but it hasn't had communication within the neighbor reachable time frame.

PROBE   When in PROBE state, the configured interface is resending a neighbor solicitation and waiting for a reachability confirmation from a neighbor.

We can verify our default gateway with IPv6 with the `ipconfig` command like this:

```
C:\Users\Todd Lammle>ipconfig
    Connection-specific DNS Suffix  . : localdomain
    IPv6 Address. . . . . . . . . . . : 2001:db8:3c4d:3:ac3b:2ef:1823:8938
    Temporary IPv6 Address. . . . . . : 2001:db8:3c4d:3:2f33:44dd:211:1c3d
    Link-local IPv6 Address . . . . . : fe80::ac3b:2ef:1823:8938%11
    IPv4 Address. . . . . . . . . . . : 10.1.1.10
    Subnet Mask . . . . . . . . . . . : 255.255.255.0
    Default Gateway . . . . . . . . . : Fe80::21a:6dff:fe37:a44e%11
        10.1.1.1
```

It's important to understand that the default gateway will be the link-local address of the router, and in this case, we can see that the address the host learned is truly the link-local address of the Fa0/0 interface of R1. The %11 is just used to identify an interface and isn't used as part of the IPv6 address.

Temporary IPv6 Addresses

The temporary IPv6 address, listed under the unicast IPv6 address as 2001:db8:3c4d:3:2f3 3:44dd:211:1c3d, was created by Windows to provide privacy from the EUI-64 format. This creates a global address from your host without using your MAC address by generating a random number for the interface and hashing it; the result is then appended to the /64 prefix from the router. You can disable this feature with the following commands:

```
netsh interface ipv6 set global randomizeidentifiers=disabled
netsh interface ipv6 set privacy state-disabled
```

In addition to the `ipconfig` command, we can use the command
`netsh interface ipv6 show neighbor` to verify our default gateway address:

```
C:\Users\Todd Lammle>netsh interface ipv6 show neighbor
[output cut]


Interface 11: Local Area Connection


Internet Address                            Physical Address    Type
-------------------------------------       -----------------   ----------
2001:db8:3c4d:3:21a:6dff:fe37:a44e          00-1a-6d-37-a4-4e   (Router)
Fe80::21a:6dff:fe37:a44e                    00-1a-6d-37-a4-4e   (Router)
ff02::1                                     33-33-00-00-00-01   Permanent
ff02::2                                     33-33-00-00-00-02   Permanent
ff02::c                                     33-33-00-00-00-0c   Permanent
ff02::16                                    33-33-00-00-00-16   Permanent
ff02::fb                                    33-33-00-00-00-fb   Permanent
ff02::1:2                                   33-33-00-01-00-02   Permanent
ff02::1:3                                   33-33-00-01-00-03   Permanent
ff02::1:ff1f:ebcb                           33-33-ff-1f-eb-cb   Permanent
```

 I've checked the default gateway addresses on Server1 and they are correct. They should be, because this is provided directly from the router with an ICMPv6 RA (router advertisement) message. The output for that verification is not shown.

Let's establish the information we have right now:

1. Our PC1 and Server1 configurations are working and have been verified.

2. The LANs are working and verified, so there is no Physical layer issue.

3. The default gateways are correct.

4. The link between the R1 and R2 routers is working and verified.

So all this tells us is that it's now time to check our routing tables! We'll start with the R1 router:

```
R1#sh ipv6 route
C    2001:DB8:3C4D:2::/64 [0/0]
     via FastEthernet0/1, directly connected
L    2001:DB8:3C4D:2:21A:6DFF:FE37:A44F/128 [0/0]
     via FastEthernet0/1, receive
C    2001:DB8:3C4D:3::/64 [0/0]
     via FastEthernet0/0, directly connected
L    2001:DB8:3C4D:3:21A:6DFF:FE37:A44E/128 [0/0]
```

```
    via FastEthernet0/0, receive
L   FF00::/8 [0/0]
    via Null0, receive
```

All we can see in the output is the two directly connected interfaces configured on the router, and that won't help us send IPv6 packets to the 2001:db8:3c4d:1::/64 subnet off of Fa0/0 on R2. So let's find out what R2 can tell us:

```
R2#sh ipv6 route
C   2001:DB8:3C4D:1::/64 [0/0]
    via FastEthernet0/0, directly connected
L   2001:DB8:3C4D:1:21A:6DFF:FE37:A443/128 [0/0]
    via FastEthernet0/0, receive
C   2001:DB8:3C4D:2::/64 [0/0]
    via FastEthernet0/1, directly connected
L   2001:DB8:3C4D:2:21A:6DFF:FE64:9B3/128 [0/0]
    via FastEthernet0/1, receive
S   2001:DB8:3C4D:3::/64 [1/0]
    via 2001:DB8:3C4D:2:21B:D4FF:FE0A:539
L   FF00::/8 [0/0]
    via Null0, receive
```

Now we're talking—that tells us a lot more than R1's table did! We have both of our directly connected configured LANs, Fa0/0 and Fa0/1, right there in the routing table, as well as a static route to 2001:DB8:3C4D:3::/64, which is the remote LAN Fa0/0 off of R1, which is good. Now let's fix the route problem on R1 by adding a route that gives us access to the Server1 network.

```
R1(config)#ipv6 route ::/0 fastethernet 0/1 FE80::21A:6DFF:FE64:9B3
```

I want to point out that I didn't need to make the default route as difficult as I did. I entered both the exit interface and next-hop link-local address when just the exit interface or next-hop global addresses would be mandatory, but not the link-local. So it could have simply just been this:

```
R1(config)#ipv6 route ::/0 fa0/1
```

Next, we'll verify that we can now ping from PC1 to Server1:

```
C:\Users\Todd Lammle>ping 2001:db8:3c4d:1:a14c:8c33:2d1:be3d

Pinging 2001:db8:3c4d:1:a14c:8c33:2d1:be3d with 32 bytes of data:
Reply from 2001:db8:3c4d:1:a14c:8c33:2d1:be3d: time<1ms
Reply from 2001:db8:3c4d:1:a14c:8c33:2d1:be3d: time<1ms
Reply from 2001:db8:3c4d:1:a14c:8c33:2d1:be3d: time<1ms
Reply from 2001:db8:3c4d:1:a14c:8c33:2d1:be3d: time<1ms
```

Sweet—we're looking golden with this particular scenario! But know that it is still possible to have name resolution issues. If that were the case, you would just need to check your DNS server or local host table.

Moving on, it's a good time to check into your ACLs, especially if you're still having a problem after troubleshooting all your local LANs and all other potential routing issues.

Troubleshooting IPv6 Extended Access Lists

Let's create an extended IPv6 ACL on R2. First, understand that you can only create named extended IPv6 ACLs, so you don't need to specify standard or extended in your named list, and although you won't see any sequence numbers, you can still somewhat edit a named IPv6 ACL, meaning you can delete a single line but there is no way to insert a line other than at the end of the ACL.

In addition, there is an implicit deny ip any any at the bottom of every IPv4 access list; however, IPv6 access lists actually have *three* implied statements at the bottom:

- permit icmp any any nd-na
- permit icmp any any nd-ns
- deny ipv6 any any

The two permit statements are required for *neighbor discovery*, which is an important protocol in IPv6 because it's the replacement for ARP.

Using Figure 3.24 network layout and IPv6 addresses, let's create an IPv6 extended named ACL that blocks Telnet to Server1 with an IPv6 address of 2001:db8:3c4d:1:a14c:8c 33:2d1:be3d from PC1 with a destination IPv6 address of 2001:db8:3c4d:3:2ef:1823:8938. Since it's an IPv6 extended named ACL (always), we'll place it closest to the source address if possible.

Step 1: Test that you can telnet to the remote host.

```
R1#telnet 2001:db8:3c4d:1:a14c:8c33:2d1:be3d
Trying 2001:db8:3c4d:1:a14c:8c33:2d1:be3d... Open


Server1>
```

Okay, great—but that was way too much effort! Let's create an entry into the hosts table of R1 so I don't have to type an IPv6 address when trying to access that host:

```
R1(config)#ipv6 host Server1 2001:db8:3c4d:1:a14c:8c33:2d1:be3d
R1(config)#do sh host
[output cut]


Host Port Flags Age Type Address(es)
Server1 None (perm, OK) 0 IPV6 2001:DB8:3C4D:1:A14C:8C33:2D1:BE3D
```

Now I can just type this from now on (the name is case sensitive):

```
R1#telnet Server1
Trying 2001:DB8:3C4D:1:A14C:8C33:2D1:BE3D... Open

Server1>
```

Or better yet, just the name (telnet is the default):

```
R1#Server1
Trying 2001:DB8:3C4D:1:A14C:8C33:2D1:BE3D... Open

Server1>exit
```

Also, ping using the name:

```
R1#ping Server1
Type escape sequence to abort.
Sending 5, 100-byte ICMP Echos to 2001:DB8:3C4D:1:A14C:8C33:2D1:BE3D,
timeout is 2 seconds:
!!!!!
Success rate is 100 percent (5/5), round-trip min/avg/max = 0/0/1 ms
```

Step 2: Create an ACL on R2 that stops Telnet to the remote host Server1 (2001:db8 :3c4d:1:a14c:8c33:2d1:be3d). The name is absolutely case sensitive when applying to an interface.

```
R2(config)#ipv6 access-list Block_Telnet
R2(config-ipv6-acl)#
```

Step 3: Once you have created the named list, add your test parameters.

```
R2(config-ipv6-acl)#deny tcp host 2001:DB8:3C4D:2:21A:6DFF:FE37:A44F host
2001:DB8:3C4D:1:A14C:8C33:2D1:BE3D eq telnet
R2(config-ipv6-acl)#permit ipv6 any any
```

Step 4: Configure your ACP on your router interface.

Since we're adding this to the R2 router in Figure 3.24, we'll add it to interface FastEthernet 0/1, stopping traffic closest to the source, and use the ipv6 traffic-filter command.

```
R2(config)#int fa0/1
R2(config-if)#ipv6 traffic-filter Block_Telnet out
```

Step 5: Test your access list by telnetting from Server1 on the R1 router.

```
R1#Server1
Trying 2001:DB8:3C4D:1:A14C:8C33:2D1:BE3D ...Open
Server1>
```

Hmm...and I tried really hard not to make a typo! Let's take a look.

```
R2#sh access-lists
IPv6 access list Block_Telnet
        deny tcp host 2001:DB8:3C4D:2:21A:6DFF:FE37:A44F host
2001:DB8:3C4D:1:A14C:8C33:2D1:BE3D eq telnet (96 match(es))
        permit ipv6 any any (181 match(es))
```

Verifying the IPv6 addresses with the interfaces of the routers, this list looks correct. It's important to verify your addresses with a show ipv6 interface brief command. Let's take a look:

```
R1#sh ipv6 int brief
FastEthernet0/0 [up/up]
        FE80::2E0:B0FF:FED2:B701
        2001:DB8:3C4D:3:21A:6DFF:FE37:A44E
FastEthernet0/1 [up/up]
        FE80::2E0:B0FF:FED2:B702
        2001:DB8:3C4D:2:21A:6DFF:FE37:A44F
```

Since R1 Fa0/1 is my source address, we can see that this address is correct in my ACL. Let's take a look at the destination device:

```
Server1#sh ipv6 int br
FastEthernet0/0 [up/up]
        FE80::260:70FF:FED8:DD01
        2001:DB8:3C4D:1:A14C:8C33:2D1:BE3D
```

Yup, this one is correct too! My IPv6 ACL is correct, so now we need to check our interface.

Step 6: Fix and/or edit your access list and/or interfaces.

```
R2#show running-config
[output cut]
!
interface FastEthernet0/0
        no ip address
        duplex auto
        speed auto
        ipv6 address 2001:DB8:3C4D:1:21A:6DFF:FE37:A443/64
```

```
        ipv6 rip 1 enable
!
interface FastEthernet0/1
        no ip address
        ipv6 traffic-filter Block_Telnet out
        duplex auto
        speed auto
        ipv6 address 2001:DB8:3C4D:2:21A:6DFF:FE64:9B3/64
        ipv6 rip 1 enable
!
```

Unlike with IPv4, where we can use the show ip interface command to see if an ACL is set, we can only use the show running-config command to verify if an IPv6 ACL is set on an interface. In the preceding output, we can see that I certainly did set the ACL to the interface Fa0/1; however, I configured it to out instead of in on the interface. Let's fix that.

R2#**config t**
R2(config)#**int fa0/1**
R2(config-if)#**no ipv6 traffic-filter Block_Telnet out**
R2(config-if)#**ipv6 traffic-filter Block_Telnet in**

Step 7: Retest your ACL.

R1#**Server1**

Trying 2001:DB8:3C4D:1:A14C:8C33:2D1:BE3D ...% Connection timed out;
remote host not responding
R1#

Looks good! Although I don't recommend using this method to block Telnet to a router, it was a great way to test our IPv6 ACLs.

Exam Essentials

Remember the Cisco steps in troubleshooting an IPv4 and IPv6 network.

1. Check the cables to find out if there's a faulty cable or interface in the mix and verify the interface's statistics.

2. Make sure that devices are determining the correct path from the source to the destination. Manipulate the routing information if needed.

3. Verify that the default gateway is correct.

4. Verify that name resolution settings are correct.

5. Verify that there are no ACLs blocking traffic.

Remember the commands to verify and troubleshoot IPv4 and IPv6.   You need to remember and practice the commands used in this chapter, especially `ping` and `traceroute` (`tracert` on Windows). But we also used the Windows commands `ipconfig` and `route print` and Cisco's commands `show ip int brief`, `show interface`, and `show ip route`.

Remember to look at the statistics on a router and switch interface to determine problems. You've got to be able to analyze interface statistics to find problems if they exist, and this includes speed and duplex settings, input queue drops, output queue drops, and input and output errors.

Review Questions

You can find the answers in the Appendix.

1. What command was used to generate the following output?

```
Codes: L - local, C - connected, S - static,
[output cut]
         10.0.0.0/8 is variably subnetted, 6 subnets, 4 masks
C        10.0.0.0/8 is directly connected, FastEthernet0/3
L        10.0.0.1/32 is directly connected, FastEthernet0/3
C        10.10.0.0/16 is directly connected, FastEthernet0/2
L        10.10.0.1/32 is directly connected, FastEthernet0/2
C        10.10.10.0/24 is directly connected, FastEthernet0/1
L        10.10.10.1/32 is directly connected, FastEthernet0/1
S*       0.0.0.0/0 is directly connected, FastEthernet0/0
```

2. You are viewing the routing table and you see an entry 10.1.1.1/32. What legend code would you expect to see next to this route?

   A. C

   B. L

   C. S

   D. D

3. Which of the following statements are true regarding the command
   `ip route 172.16.4.0 255.255.255.0 192.168.4.2`? (Choose two.)

   A. The command is used to establish a static route.

   B. The default administrative distance is used.

   C. The command is used to configure the default route.

   D. The subnet mask for the source address is 255.255.255.0.

   E. The command is used to establish a stub network.

4. What destination addresses will be used by HostA to send data to the HTTPS server as shown in the following network? (Choose two.)

    A. The IP address of the switch

    B. The MAC address of the remote switch

    C. The IP address of the HTTPS server

    D. The MAC address of the HTTPS server

    E. The IP address of RouterA's Fa0/0 interface

    F. The MAC address of RouterA's Fa0/0 interface

5. Using the output shown, what protocol was used to learn the MAC address for 172.16.10.1?

```
Interface: 172.16.10.2 --- 0x3
  Internet Address      Physical Address      Type
  172.16.10.1           00-15-05-06-31-b0     dynamic
```

    A. ICMP

    B. ARP

    C. TCP

    D. UDP

6. Which of the following is called an advanced distance-vector routing protocol?

    A. OSPF

    B. EIGRP

    C. BGP

    D. RIP

7. When a packet is routed across a network, the _____ in the packet changes at every hop while the _____ does not.

    A. MAC address, IP address

    B. IP address, MAC address

    C. Port number, IP address

    D. IP address, port number

8. Write the command that must be present for this layer 3 switch to provide inter-VLAN routing between the two VLANs created with these commands:

```
S1(config)#int vlan 10
S1(config-if)#ip address 192.168.10.1 255.255.255.0
S1(config-if)#int vlan 20
S1(config-if)#ip address 192.168.20.1 255.255.255.0
```

9. In the configuration and diagram shown, what command is missing to enable inter-VLAN routing between VLAN 2 and VLAN 3?

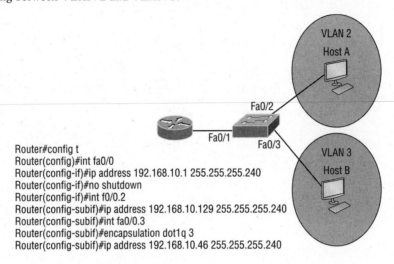

```
Router#config t
Router(config)#int fa0/0
Router(config-if)#ip address 192.168.10.1 255.255.255.240
Router(config-if)#no shutdown
Router(config-if)#int f0/0.2
Router(config-subif)#ip address 192.168.10.129 255.255.255.240
Router(config-subif)#int fa0/0.3
Router(config-subif)#encapsulation dot1q 3
Router(config-subif)#ip address 192.168.10.46 255.255.255.240
```

A. `encapsulation dot1q 3` under int f0/0.2

B. `encapsulation dot1q 2` under int f0/0.2

C. `no shutdown` under int f0/0.2

D. `no shutdown` under int f0/0.3

10. Based on the configuration shown here, what statement is true?

```
S1(config)#ip routing
S1(config)#int vlan 10
S1(config-if)#ip address 192.168.10.1 255.255.255.0
S1(config-if)#int vlan 20
S1(config-if)#ip address 192.168.20.1 255.255.255.0
```

A. This is a multilayer switch.

B. The two VLANs are in the same subnet.

C. Encapsulation must be configured.

D. VLAN 10 is the management VLAN.

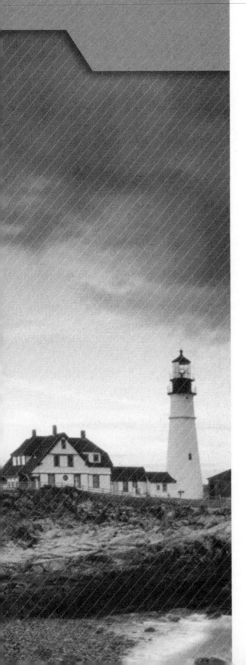

Chapter
4

WAN Technologies

THE FOLLOWING CCNA ROUTING AND SWITCHING EXAM OBJECTIVES ARE COVERED IN THIS CHAPTER:

- ✓ Configure and verify PPP and MLPPP on WAN interfaces using local authentication.

- ✓ Configure, verify, and troubleshoot PPPoE client-side interfaces using local authentication.

- ✓ Configure, verify, and troubleshoot GRE tunnel connectivity.

- ✓ Describe WAN topology options.

- ✓ Describe WAN access connectivity options.

- ✓ Configure and verify single-homed branch connectivity using eBGP IPv4 (limited to peering and route advertisement using Network command only).

- ✓ Describe basic QoS concepts.

In this chapter, I will cover wide area network (WAN) technologies. This will include a discussion of the multilink Point-to-Point protocol interfaces, PPP over Ethernet (PPoE), and Generic Routing Encapsulation tunnels. I will also cover the configuration of Border Gateway Protocol (BGP).

Configure and verify PPP and MLPPP on WAN interfaces using local authentication

Point-to-Point Protocol (PPP) is a Data Link layer protocol that can be used over either asynchronous serial (dial-up) or synchronous serial (ISDN) media. It relies on Link Control Protocol (LCP) to build and maintain data-link connections. Network Control Protocol (NCP) enables multiple Network layer protocols (routed protocols) to be used on a point-to-point connection.

Because HDLC is the default serial encapsulation on Cisco serial links and it works great, why in the world would you choose to use PPP? Well, the basic purpose of PPP is to transport layer 3 packets across a Data Link layer point-to-point link, and it's nonproprietary. So unless you have all Cisco routers, you need PPP on your serial interfaces because the HDLC encapsulation is Cisco proprietary, remember? Plus, since PPP can encapsulate several layer 3 routed protocols and provide authentication, dynamic addressing, and callback, PPP could actually be the best encapsulation solution for you over HDLC anyway.

Figure 4.1 shows the PPP protocol stack compared to the OSI reference model.

PPP contains four main components:

EIA/TIA-232-C, V.24, V.35, and ISDN   A Physical layer international standard for serial communication

HDLC   A method for encapsulating datagrams over serial links

LCP   A method of establishing, configuring, maintaining, and terminating the point-to-point connection. It also provides features such as authentication. I'll give you a complete list of these features in the next section.

NCP   NCP is a method of establishing and configuring different Network layer protocols for transport across the PPP link. NCP is designed to allow the simultaneous use of multiple Network layer protocols. Two examples of protocols here are Internet Protocol Control Protocol (IPCP) and Cisco Discovery Protocol Control Protocol (CDPCP).

FIGURE 4.1   Point-to-Point Protocol stack

Burn it into your mind that the PPP protocol stack is specified at the Physical and Data Link layers only. NCP is used to allow communication of multiple Network layer protocols by identifying and encapsulating the protocols across a PPP data link.

> Remember that if you have a Cisco router and a non-Cisco router connected with a serial connection, you must configure PPP or another encapsulation method like Frame Relay because the HDLC default just won't work!

Next, we'll cover the options for LCP and PPP session establishment.

Link Control Protocol (LCP) Configuration Options

Link Control Protocol (LCP) offers different PPP encapsulation options, including the following:

Authentication   This option tells the calling side of the link to send information that can identify the user. The two methods for this task are PAP and CHAP.

Compression   This is used to increase the throughput of PPP connections by compressing the data or payload prior to transmission. PPP decompresses the data frame on the receiving end.

Error detection   PPP uses Quality and Magic Number options to ensure a reliable, loop-free data link.

Multilink PPP (MLP)   Starting with IOS version 11.1, multilink is supported on PPP links with Cisco routers. This option makes several separate physical paths appear to be one logical path at layer 3. For example, two T1s running multilink PPP would show up as a single 3 Mbps path to a layer 3 routing protocol.

PPP callback   On a dial-up connection, PPP can be configured to call back after successful authentication. *PPP callback* can be a very good thing because it allows us to keep track of usage based upon access charges for accounting records and a bunch of other reasons. With callback enabled, a calling router (client) will contact a remote router (server) and authenticate. Predictably, both routers have to be configured for the callback feature for this to work. Once authentication is completed, the remote router will terminate the connection and then reinitiate a connection to the calling router from the remote router.

PPP Session Establishment

When PPP connections are started, the links go through three phases of session establishment, as shown in Figure 4.2:

FIGURE 4.2   PPP session establishment

PPP Session Establishment
1. Link-establishment phase
2. Authentication phase (optional)
3. Network layer protocol phase

Link-establishment phase   LCP packets are sent by each PPP device to configure and test the link. These packets contain a field called Configuration Option that allows each device to see the size of the data, the compression, and authentication. If no Configuration Option field is present, then the default configurations will be used.

Authentication phase   If required, either CHAP or PAP can be used to authenticate a link. Authentication takes place before Network layer protocol information is read, and it's also possible that link-quality determination will occur simultaneously.

Network layer protocol phase   PPP uses the *Network Control Protocol (NCP)* to allow multiple Network layer protocols to be encapsulated and sent over a PPP data link. Each Network layer protocol (e.g., IP, IPv6, which are routed protocols) establishes a service with NCP.

PPP Authentication Methods

There are two methods of authentication that can be used with PPP links:

Password Authentication Protocol (PAP)   The *Password Authentication Protocol (PAP)* is the less secure of the two methods. Passwords are sent in clear text and PAP is performed only upon the initial link establishment. When the PPP link is first established, the remote node sends the username and password back to the originating target router until authentication is acknowledged. Not exactly Fort Knox!

Challenge Handshake Authentication Protocol (CHAP)   The *Challenge Handshake Authentication Protocol (CHAP)* is used at the initial startup of a link and at periodic checkups on the link to ensure that the router is still communicating with the same host.

After PPP finishes its initial link-establishment phase, the local router sends a challenge request to the remote device. The remote device sends a value calculated using a one-way hash function called MD5. The local router checks this hash value to make sure it matches. If the values don't match their own locally calculated MD5 hash, the link is immediately terminated.

 CHAP authenticates at the beginning of the session and periodically throughout the session.

Configuring PPP on Cisco Routers

Configuring PPP encapsulation on an interface is really pretty straightforward. To configure it from the CLI, use these simple router commands:

```
Router#config t
Router(config)#int s0
Router(config-if)#encapsulation ppp
Router(config-if)#^Z
Router#
```

Of course, PPP encapsulation has to be enabled on both interfaces connected to a serial line in order to work, and there are several additional configuration options available to you via the ppp ? command.

Configuring PPP Authentication

After you configure your serial interface to support PPP encapsulation, you can then configure authentication using PPP between routers. But first, you must set the hostname of the router if it hasn't been set already. After that, you set the username and password for the remote router that will be connecting to your router, like this:

```
Router#config t
Router(config)#hostname RouterA
RouterA(config)#username RouterB password cisco
```

When using the username command, remember that the username is the hostname of the remote router that's connecting to your router. And it's case sensitive too. Also, the password on both routers must be the same. It's a plain-text password that you can see with a show run command, and you can encrypt the password by using the command service password-encryption. You must have a username and password configured for each remote system you plan to connect to. The remote routers must also be similarly configured with usernames and passwords.

Now, after you've set the hostname, usernames, and passwords, choose either CHAP or PAP as the authentication method:

```
RouterA#config t
RouterA(config)#int s0
RouterA(config-if)#ppp authentication chap pap
RouterA(config-if)#^Z
RouterA#
```

If both methods are configured on the same line as I've demonstrated here, then only the first method will be used during link negotiation. The second acts as a backup just in case the first method fails.

There is yet another command you can use if you're using PAP authentication for some reason. The ppp pap sent-username *username* password *password* command enables outbound PAP authentication. The local router uses the username and password that the ppp pap sent-username command specifies to authenticate itself to a remote device. The other router must have this same username/password configured as well.

Verifying and Troubleshooting Serial Links

Now that PPP encapsulation is enabled, you need to verify that it's up and running. First, let's take a look at a figure of a sample nonproduction network serial link. Figure 4.3 shows two routers connected with a point-to-point serial connection, with the DCE side on the Pod1R1 router.

FIGURE 4.3   PPP authentication example

Pod1R1   Pod1R2

```
hostname Pod1R1                    hostname Pod1R2
username Pod1R2 password cisco     username Pod1R1 password cisco
interface serial 0                 interface serial 0
ip address 10.0.1.1 255.255.255.0  ip address 10.0.1.2 255.255.255.0
encapsulation ppp                  encapsulation ppp
clock rate 64000                   bandwidth 512
bandwidth 512                      ppp authentication chap
ppp authentication chap
```

You can start verifying the configuration with the show interface command like this:

```
Pod1R1#sh int s0/0
Serial0/0 is up, line protocol is up
  Hardware is PowerQUICC Serial
  Internet address is 10.0.1.1/24
```

```
MTU 1500 bytes, BW 1544 Kbit, DLY 20000 usec,
    reliability 239/255, txload 1/255, rxload 1/255
Encapsulation PPP
loopback not set
Keepalive set (10 sec)
LCP Open
Open: IPCP, CDPCP
```
[output cut]

The first line of output is important because it tells us that Serial 0/0 is up/up. Notice that the interface encapsulation is PPP and that LCP is open. This means that it has negotiated the session establishment and all is well. The last line tells us that NCP is listening for the protocols IP and CDP, shown with the NCP headers IPCP and CDPCP.

But what would you see if everything isn't so perfect? I'm going to type in the configuration shown in Figure 4.4 to find out.

FIGURE 4.4   Failed PPP authentication

Pod1R1   Pod1R2

hostname Pod1R1   hostname Pod1R2
username Pod1R2 password Cisco   username Pod1R1 password cisco
interface serial 0   interface serial 0
ip address 10.0.1.1 255.255.255.0   ip address 10.0.1.2 255.255.255.0
clock rate 64000   bandwidth 512
bandwidth 512   encapsulation ppp
encapsulation ppp   ppp authentication chap
ppp authentication chap

What's wrong here? Take a look at the usernames and passwords. Do you see the problem now? That's right, the C is capitalized on the Pod1R2 username command found in the configuration of router Pod1R1. This is wrong because the usernames and passwords are case sensitive. Now let's take a look at the show interface command and see what happens:

```
Pod1R1#sh int s0/0
Serial0/0 is up, line protocol is down
  Hardware is PowerQUICC Serial
  Internet address is 10.0.1.1/24
  MTU 1500 bytes, BW 1544 Kbit, DLY 20000 usec,
    reliability 243/255, txload 1/255, rxload 1/255
  Encapsulation PPP, loopback not set
  Keepalive set (10 sec)
  LCP Closed
  Closed: IPCP, CDPCP
```

First, notice that the first line of output shows us that Serial0/0 is up and line protocol is down. This is because there are no keepalives coming from the remote router. The next thing I want you to notice is that the LCP and NCP are closed because the authentication failed.

Debugging PPP Authentication

To display the CHAP authentication process as it occurs between two routers in the network, just use the command debug ppp authentication.

If your PPP encapsulation and authentication are set up correctly on both routers and your usernames and passwords are all good, then the debug ppp authentication command will display an output that looks like the following output, which is called the three-way handshake:

```
d16h: Se0/0 PPP: Using default call direction
1d16h: Se0/0 PPP: Treating connection as a dedicated line
1d16h: Se0/0 CHAP: O CHALLENGE id 219 len 27 from "Pod1R1"
1d16h: Se0/0 CHAP: I CHALLENGE id 208 len 27 from "Pod1R2"
1d16h: Se0/0 CHAP: O RESPONSE id 208 len 27 from "Pod1R1"
1d16h: Se0/0 CHAP: I RESPONSE id 219 len 27 from "Pod1R2"
1d16h: Se0/0 CHAP: O SUCCESS id 219 len 4
1d16h: Se0/0 CHAP: I SUCCESS id 208 len 4
```

But if you have the password wrong as they were previously in the PPP authentication failure example back in Figure 4.4, the output would look something like this:

```
1d16h: Se0/0 PPP: Using default call direction
1d16h: Se0/0 PPP: Treating connection as a dedicated line
1d16h: %SYS-5-CONFIG_I: Configured from console by console
1d16h: Se0/0 CHAP: O CHALLENGE id 220 len 27 from "Pod1R1"
1d16h: Se0/0 CHAP: I CHALLENGE id 209 len 27 from "Pod1R2"
1d16h: Se0/0 CHAP: O RESPONSE id 209 len 27 from "Pod1R1"
1d16h: Se0/0 CHAP: I RESPONSE id 220 len 27 from "Pod1R2"
1d16h: Se0/0 CHAP: O FAILURE id 220 len 25 msg is "MD/DES compare failed"
```

PPP with CHAP authentication is a three-way authentication, and if the username and passwords aren't configured exactly the way they should be, then the authentication will fail and the link will go down.

Mismatched WAN Encapsulations

If you have a point-to-point link but the encapsulations aren't the same, the link will never come up. Figure 4.5 shows one link with PPP and one with HDLC.

FIGURE 4.5   Mismatched WAN encapsulations

Pod1R1   Pod1R2

hostname Pod1R1   hostname Pod1R2
username Pod1R2 password cisco   username Pod1R1 password cisco
interface serial 0   interface serial 0
ip address 10.0.1.1 255.255.255.0   ip address 10.0.1.2 255.255.255.0
clock rate 64000   bandwidth 512
bandwidth 512   encapsulation hdlc
encapsulation ppp

Look at router Pod1R1 in this output:

```
Pod1R1#sh int s0/0
Serial0/0 is up, line protocol is down
  Hardware is PowerQUICC Serial
  Internet address is 10.0.1.1/24
  MTU 1500 bytes, BW 1544 Kbit, DLY 20000 usec,
     reliability 254/255, txload 1/255, rxload 1/255
  Encapsulation PPP, loopback not set
  Keepalive set (10 sec)
  LCP REQsent
Closed: IPCP, CDPCP
```

The serial interface is up/down and LCP is sending requests but will never receive any responses because router Pod1R2 is using the HDLC encapsulation. To fix this problem, you would have to go to router Pod1R2 and configure the PPP encapsulation on the serial interface. One more thing: Even though the usernames are configured incorrectly, it doesn't matter because the command ppp authentication chap isn't used under the serial interface configuration. This means that the username command isn't relevant in this example.

You can set a Cisco serial interface back to the default of HDLC with the no encapsulation command like this:

```
Router(config)#int s0/0
Router(config-if)#no encapsulation
*Feb 7 16:00:18.678:%LINEPROTO-5-UPDOWN: Line protocol on Interface Serial0/0,
changed state to up
```

Notice the link came up because it now matches the encapsulation on the other end of the link!

Always remember that you just can't have PPP on one side and HDLC on the other—they don't get along!

Mismatched IP Addresses

A tricky problem to spot is if you have HDLC or PPP configured on your serial interface but your IP addresses are wrong. Things seem to be just fine because the interfaces will show that they are up. Take a look at Figure 4.6 and see if you can see what I mean—the two routers are connected with different subnets—router Pod1R1 with 10.0.1.1/24 and router Pod1R2 with 10.2.1.2/24.

FIGURE 4.6   Mismatched IP addresses

Pod1R1   Pod1R2

```
hostname Pod1R1                          hostname Pod1R2
username Pod1R2 password cisco           username Pod1R1 password cisco
interface serial 0                       interface serial 0
ip address 10.0.1.1  255.255.255.0       ip address 10.2.1.2  255.255.255.0
clock rate 64000                         bandwidth 512
bandwidth 512                            encapsulation ppp
encapsulation ppp                        ppp authentication chap
ppp authentication chap
```

This will never work. Let's take a look at the output:

```
Pod1R1#sh int s0/0
Serial0/0 is up, line protocol is up
  Hardware is PowerQUICC Serial
  Internet address is 10.0.1.1/24
  MTU 1500 bytes, BW 1544 Kbit, DLY 20000 usec,
     reliability 255/255, txload 1/255, rxload 1/255
  Encapsulation PPP, loopback not set
  Keepalive set (10 sec)
  LCP Open
  Open: IPCP, CDPCP
```

See that? The IP addresses between the routers are wrong but the link appears to be working just fine. This is because PPP, like HDLC and Frame Relay, is a layer 2 WAN encapsulation, so it doesn't care about IP addresses at all. So yes, the link is up, but you can't use IP across this link since it's misconfigured, or can you? Well, yes and no. If you try to ping, you'll see that this actually works! This is a feature of PPP, but not HDLC or Frame Relay. But just because you can ping to an IP address that's not in the same subnet doesn't mean your network traffic and routing protocols will work. So be careful with this issue, especially when troubleshooting PPP links!

Take a look at the routing table of Pod1R1 and see if you can find the mismatched IP address problem:

```
[output cut]
  10.0.0.0/8 is variably subnetted, 2 subnets, 2 masks
```

```
C        10.2.1.2/32 is directly connected, Serial0/0
C        10.0.1.0/24 is directly connected, Serial0/0
```

Interesting! We can see our serial interface S0/0 address of 10.0.1.0/24, but what is that other address on interface S0/0— 10.2.1.2/32? That's our remote router's interface IP address! PPP determines and places the neighbor's IP address in the routing table as a connected interface, which then allows you to ping it even though it's actually configured on a separate IP subnet.

For the Cisco exam, you need to be able to troubleshoot PPP from the routing table as I just described.

To find and fix this problem, you can also use the show running-config, show interfaces, or show ip interfaces brief command on each router, or you can use the show cdp neighbors detail command:

```
Pod1R1#sh cdp neighbors detail
-------------------------
Device ID: Pod1R2
Entry address(es):
  IP address: 10.2.1.2
```

Since the layer 1 Physical and layer 2 Data Link is up/up, you can view and verify the directly connected neighbor's IP address and then solve your problem.

Multilink PPP (MLP)

There are many load-balancing mechanisms available, but this one is free for use on serial WAN links! It provides multi-vendor support and is specified in RFC 1990, which details the fragmentation and packet sequencing specifications.

You can use MLP to connect your home network to an Internet service provider using two traditional modems or to connect a company via two leased lines.

The MLP feature provides a load-balancing functionality over multiple WAN links while allowing for multi-vendor interoperability. It offers support for packet fragmentation, proper sequencing, and load calculation on both inbound and outbound traffic.

MLP allows packets to be fragmented and then sent simultaneously over multiple point-to-point links to the same remote address. It can work over synchronous and asynchronous serial types.

MLP combines multiple physical links into a logical link called an MLP bundle, which is essentially a single, virtual interface that connects to the remote router. None of the links inside the bundle have any knowledge about the traffic on the other links.

The MLP over serial interfaces feature provides us with the following benefits:

Load balancing   MLP provides bandwidth on demand, utilizing load balancing on up to 10 links, and can even calculate the load on traffic between specific sites. You don't actually need to make all links the same bandwidth, but doing so is recommended. Another key MLP advantage is that it splits packets and fragments across all links, which reduces latency across the WAN.

Increased redundancy   This one is pretty straightforward. . . If a link fails, the others will still transmit and receive.

Link fragmentation and interleaving   The fragmentation mechanism in MLP works by fragmenting large packets, then sending the packet fragments over the multiple point-to-point links. Smaller real-time packets are not fragmented. So interleaving basically means real-time packets can be sent in between sending the fragmented, non-real-time packets, which helps reduce delay on the lines. So let's configure MLP now to get a good feel for how it actually works now.

Configuring MLP

We're going to use Figure 4.7 to demonstrate how to configure MLP between two routers.

FIGURE 4.7   MLP between the Corp and SF routers

But first, I want you to study the configuration of the two serial interfaces on the Corp router that we're going to use for making our bundle:

```
Corp# show interfaces Serial0/0
Serial0/0 is up, line protocol is up
  Hardware is M4T
  Internet address is 172.16.10.1/30
  MTU 1500 bytes, BW 1544 Kbit/sec, DLY 20000 usec,
     reliability 255/255, txload 1/255, rxload 1/255
  Encapsulation PPP, LCP Open
  Open: IPCP, CDPCP, crc 16, loopback not set

Corp# show interfaces Serial1/1
Serial1/1 is up, line protocol is up
  Hardware is M4T
  Internet address is 172.16.10.9/30
  MTU 1500 bytes, BW 1544 Kbit/sec, DLY 20000 usec,
     reliability 255/255, txload 1/255, rxload 1/255
  Encapsulation PPP, LCP Open
  Open: IPCP, CDPCP, crc 16, loopback not set
```

Did you notice that each serial connection is on a different subnet (they have to be) and that the encapsulation is PPP?

When you configure MLP, you must first remove your IP addresses off your physical interface. Then, you configure a multilink bundle by creating a multilink interface on both sides of the link. After that, you assign an IP address to this multilink interface, which effectively restricts a physical link so that it can only join the designated multilink group interface.

So first I'm going to remove the IP addresses from the physical interfaces that I'm going to include in my PPP bundle.

```
Corp# config t
Corp(config)# int Serial0/0
Corp(config-if)# no ip address
Corp(config-if)# int Serial1/1
Corp(config-if)# no ip address
Corp(config-if)# end
Corp#


SF# config t
SF(config)# int Serial0/0
SF(config-if)# no ip address
SF(config-if)# int Serial0/1
SF(config-if)# no ip address
SF(config-if)# end
SF#
```

Now we create the multilink interface on each side of the link and the MLP commands to enable the bundle.

```
Corp#config t
Corp(config)# interface Multilink1
Corp(config-if)# ip address 10.1.1.1 255.255.255.0
Corp(config-if)# ppp multilink
Corp(config-if)# ppp multilink group 1
Corp(config-if)# end

SF#config t
SF(config)# interface Multilink1
SF(config-if)# ip address 10.1.1.2 255.255.255.0
SF(config-if)# ppp multilink
SF(config-if)# ppp multilink group 1
SF(config-if)# exit
```

We can see that a link joins an MLP bundle only if it negotiates to use the bundle when a connection is established and the identification information that has been exchanged matches the info for an existing bundle.

When you configure the ppp multilink group command on a link, that link won't be allowed to join any bundle other than the indicated group interface.

Verifying MLP

To verify that your bundle is up and running, just use the show ppp multilink and show interfaces multilink1 commands:

```
Corp# show ppp multilink

Multilink1
  Bundle name: Corp
  Remote Endpoint Discriminator: [1] SF
  Local Endpoint Discriminator: [1] Corp
  Bundle up for 02:12:05, total bandwidth 4188, load 1/255
  Receive buffer limit 24000 bytes, frag timeout 1000 ms
    0/0 fragments/bytes in reassembly list
    0 lost fragments, 53 reordered
    0/0 discarded fragments/bytes, 0 lost received
    0x56E received sequence, 0x572 sent sequence
  Member links: 2 active, 0 inactive (max 255, min not set)
    Se0/1, since 01:32:05
    Se1/2, since 01:31:31
No inactive multilink interfaces
```

We can see that the physical interfaces, Se0/1 and Se1/2, are members of the logical interface bundle Multilink 1. So now we'll verify the status of the interface Multilink1 on the Corp router:

```
Corp# show int Multilink1
Multilink1 is up, line protocol is up
  Hardware is multilink group interface
  Internet address is 10.1.1.1/24
  MTU 1500 bytes, BW 1544 Kbit/sec, DLY 20000 usec,
    reliability 255/255, txload 1/255, rxload 1/255
Encapsulation PPP, LCP Open, multilink Open
Open: IPCP, CDPCP, loopback not set
 Keepalive set (10 sec)
[output cut]
```

Exam Essentials

Remember the default serial encapsulation on Cisco routers.   Cisco routers use a proprietary High-Level Data Link Control (HDLC) encapsulation on all their serial links by default.

Remember the PPP Data Link layer protocols.   The three Data Link layer protocols are Network Control Protocol (NCP), which defines the Network layer protocols; Link Control Protocol (LCP), a method of establishing, configuring, maintaining, and terminating the point-to-point connection; and High-Level Data Link Control (HDLC), the MAC layer protocol that encapsulates the packets.

Be able to troubleshoot a PPP link.   Understand that a PPP link between two routers will show up and a ping would even work between the router if the layer 3 addresses are wrong.

Configure, verify, and troubleshoot PPPoE client-side interfaces using local authentication

Used with ADSL services, PPPoE (Point-to-Point Protocol over Ethernet) encapsulates PPP frames in Ethernet frames and uses common PPP features like authentication, encryption, and compression. But as I said earlier, it can be trouble. This is especially true if you've got a badly configured firewall!

Basically, PPPoE is a tunneling protocol that layers IP and other protocols running over PPP with the attributes of a PPP link. This is done so protocols can then be used to contact other Ethernet devices and initiate a point-to-point connection to transport IP packets.

Figure 4.8 displays typical usage of PPPoE over ADSL. As you can see, a PPP session is connected from the PC of the end user to the router. Subsequently, the subscriber PC IP address is assigned by the router via IPCP.

FIGURE 4.8   PPPoE with ADSL

Your ISP will typically provide you with a DSL line and this will act as a bridge if your line doesn't provide enhanced features. This means only one host will connect using PPPoE. You can run the PPPoE client IOS feature on a Cisco router, which will connect multiple PCs on the Ethernet segment that is connected to the router.

Configuring a PPPoE Client

The PPPoE client configuration is simple and straightforward. First, you need to create a dialer interface and then tie it to a physical interface.

Here are the easy steps:

1. Create a dialer interface using the `interface dialer` *number* command.

2. Instruct the client to use an IP address provided by the PPPoE server with the `ip address negotiated` command.

3. Set the encapsulation type to PPP.

4. Configure the dialer pool and number.

5. Under the physical interface, use the `pppoe-client dial-pool number` *number* command.

On your PPPoE client router, enter the following commands:

```
R1# conf t
R1(config)# int dialer1
R1(config-if)# ip address negotiated
R1(config-if)# encapsulation ppp
R1(config-if)# dialer pool 1
R1(config-if)# interface f0/1
R1(config-if)# no ip address
R1(config-if)# pppoe-client dial-pool-number 1
*May 1 1:09:07.540: %DIALER-6-BIND: Interface Vi2 bound to profile Di1
*May 1 1:09:07.541: %LINK-3-UPDOWN: Interface Virtual-Access2, changed state to up
```

That's it! Now let's verify the interface with the `show ip interface brief` and the `show pppoe session` commands:

```
R1# show ip int brief
Interface              IP-Address       OK? Method Status        Protocol
FastEthernet0/1        unassigned       YES manual up               up
<output cut>
Dialer1                10.10.10.3       YES IPCP   up               up
Loopback0              192.168.1.1      YES NVRAM  up               up
Loopback1              172.16.1.1       YES NVRAM  up               up
Virtual-Access1        unassigned       YES unset  up               up
```

```
Virtual-Access2          unassigned    YES unset  up                up

R1#show pppoe session
    1 client session


Uniq ID  PPPoE  RemMAC         Port              VT  VA        State
         SID    LocMAC                               VA-st     Type
    N/A    4    aacb.cc00.1419 FEt0/1            Di1 Vi2       UP
                aacb.cc00.1f01                       UP
```

Exam Essentials

Be able to configure a PPPoE link. The high-level steps include creating a dialer interface and then tieing it to a physical interface.

Configure, verify, and troubleshoot GRE tunnel connectivity

Generic Routing Encapsulation (GRE) is a tunneling protocol that can encapsulate many protocols inside IP tunnels. Some examples would be routing protocols such as EIGRP and OSPF and the routed protocol IPv6. Figure 4.9 shows the different pieces of a GRE header.

FIGURE 4.9 Generic Routing Encapsulation (GRE) tunnel structure

A GRE tunnel interface supports a header for each of the following:

- A passenger protocol or encapsulated protocols like IP or IPv6, which is the protocol being encapsulated by GRE
- GRE encapsulation protocol
- A Transport delivery protocol, typically IP

GRE tunnels have the following characteristics:

- GRE uses a protocol-type field in the GRE header so any layer 3 protocol can be used through the tunnel.
- GRE is stateless and has no flow control.
- GRE offers no security.
- GRE creates additional overhead for tunneled packets—at least 24 bytes.

Configuring GRE Tunnels

Before you attempt to configure a GRE tunnel, you need to create an implementation plan. Here's a checklist for what you need to configure and implement a GRE:

1. Use IP addressing.
2. Create the logical tunnel interfaces.
3. Specify that you're using GRE tunnel mode under the tunnel interface (this is optional since this is the default tunnel mode).
4. Specify the tunnel source and destination IP addresses.
5. Configure an IP address for the tunnel interface.

Let's take a look at how to bring up a simple GRE tunnel. Figure 4.10 shows the network with two routers.

FIGURE 4.10   Example of GRE configuration

First, we need to make the logical tunnel with the `interface tunnel` *number* command. We can use any number up to 2.14 billion.

```
Corp(config)#int s0/0/0
Corp(config-if)#ip address 63.1.1.1 255.255.255.252
Corp(config)#int tunnel ?
  <0-2147483647>  Tunnel interface number
Corp(config)#int tunnel 0
*Jan 5 16:58:22.719:%LINEPROTO-5-UPDOWN: Line protocol on Interface Tunnel0,
changed state to down
```

Once we have configured our interface and created the logical tunnel, we need to configure the mode and then the transport protocol.

```
Corp(config-if)#tunnel mode ?
  aurp    AURP TunnelTalk AppleTalk encapsulation
  cayman  Cayman TunnelTalk AppleTalk encapsulation
  dvmrp   DVMRP multicast tunnel
  eon     EON compatible CLNS tunnel
  gre     generic route encapsulation protocol
  ipip    IP over IP encapsulation
  ipsec   IPSec tunnel encapsulation
  iptalk  Apple IPTalk encapsulation
  ipv6    Generic packet tunneling in IPv6
  ipv6ip  IPv6 over IP encapsulation
  nos     IP over IP encapsulation (KA9Q/NOS compatible)
  rbscp   RBSCP in IP tunnel
Corp(config-if)#tunnel mode gre ?
  ip         over IP
  ipv6       over IPv6
  multipoint over IP (multipoint)

Corp(config-if)#tunnel mode gre ip
```

Now that we've created the tunnel interface, the type, and the transport protocol, we must configure our IP addresses for use inside of the tunnel. Of course, you need to use your actual physical interface IP for the tunnel to send traffic across the Internet, but you also need to configure the tunnel source and tunnel destination addresses.

```
Corp(config-if)#ip address 192.168.10.1 255.255.255.0
Corp(config-if)#tunnel source 63.1.1.1
Corp(config-if)#tunnel destination 63.1.1.2

Corp#sho run interface tunnel 0
Building configuration...

Current configuration : 117 bytes
!
interface Tunnel0
 ip address 192.168.10.1 255.255.255.0
 tunnel source 63.1.1.1
 tunnel destination 63.1.1.2
end
```

Now let's configure the other end of the serial link and watch the tunnel pop up!

```
SF(config)#int s0/0/0
SF(config-if)#ip address 63.1.1.2 255.255.255.252
SF(config-if)#int t0
SF(config-if)#ip address 192.168.10.2 255.255.255.0
SF(config-if)#tunnel source 63.1.1.2
SF(config-if)#tun destination 63.1.1.1
*May 19 22:46:37.099: %LINEPROTO-5-UPDOWN: Line protocol on Interface Tunnel0,
changed state to up
```

Oops—did I forget to set my tunnel mode and transport to GRE and IP on the SF router? No, I didn't need to because it's the default tunnel mode on Cisco IOS. Nice! So, first I set the physical interface IP address (which used a global address even though I didn't have to), then I created the tunnel interface and set the IP address of the tunnel interface. It's really important that you remember to configure the tunnel interface with the actual source and destination IP addresses to use or the tunnel won't come up. In my example, the 63.1.1.2 was the source and 63.1.1.1 was the destination.

Verifying GRP Tunnels

As usual I'll start with my favorite troubleshooting command, show ip interface brief.

```
Corp#sh ip int brief
Interface        IP-Address     OK? Method Status                     Protocol
FastEthernet0/0  10.10.10.5     YES manual up                         up
Serial0/0        63.1.1.1       YES manual up                         up
FastEthernet0/1  unassigned     YES unset  administratively down down
Serial0/1        unassigned     YES unset  administratively down down
Tunnel0          192.168.10.1   YES manual up                         up
```

In this output, you can see that the tunnel interface is now showing as an interface on my router. You can see the IP address of the tunnel interface, and the Physical and Data Link status show as up/up. So far so good. Let's take a look at the interface with the show interfaces tunnel 0 command.

```
Corp#sh int tun 0
Tunnel0 is up, line protocol is up
  Hardware is Tunnel
  Internet address is 192.168.10.1/24
  MTU 1514 bytes, BW 9 Kbit, DLY 500000 usec,
     reliability 255/255, txload 1/255, rxload 1/255
  Encapsulation TUNNEL, loopback not set
  Keepalive not set
  Tunnel source 63.1.1.1, destination 63.1.1.2
  Tunnel protocol/transport GRE/IP
```

```
   Key disabled, sequencing disabled
   Checksumming of packets disabled
 Tunnel TTL 255
 Fast tunneling enabled
 Tunnel transmit bandwidth 8000 (kbps)
 Tunnel receive bandwidth 8000 (kbps)
```

The show interfaces command shows the configuration settings and the interface status as well as the IP address, tunnel source, and destination address. The output also shows the tunnel protocol, which is GRE/IP. Last, let's take a look at the routing table with the show ip route command.

```
Corp#sh ip route
[output cut]
     192.168.10.0/24 is subnetted, 2 subnets
C      192.168.10.0/24 is directly connected, Tunnel0
L      192.168.10.1/32 is directly connected, Tunnel0
     63.0.0.0/30 is subnetted, 2 subnets
C      63.1.1.0 is directly connected, Serial0/0
L      63.1.1.1/32 is directly connected, Serial0/0
```

The tunnel0 interface shows up as a directly connected interface, and although it's a logical interface, the router treats it as a physical interface, just like serial 0/0 in the routing table.

```
Corp#ping 192.168.10.2

Type escape sequence to abort.
Sending 5, 100-byte ICMP Echos to 192.168.10.2, timeout is 2 seconds:
!!!!!
Success rate is 100 percent (5/5)
```

Did you notice that I just pinged 192.168.10.2 across the Internet? I hope so! Anyway, there's one last thing I want to cover before we move on to EBGP, and that's troubleshooting an output, which is showing a tunnel routing error. If you configure your GRE tunnel and receive this GRE flapping message:

```
        Line protocol on Interface Tunnel0, changed state to up
07:11:55: %TUN-5-RECURDOWN:
        Tunnel0 temporarily disabled due to recursive routing
07:11:59: %LINEPROTO-5-UPDOWN:
        Line protocol on Interface Tunnel0, changed state to down
07:12:59: %LINEPROTO-5-UPDOWN:
```

it means that you've misconfigured your tunnel, which will cause your router to try and route to the tunnel destination address using the tunnel interface itself!

Exam Essentials

Understand how to configure and verify a GRE tunnel.   To configure GRE, first configure the logical tunnel with the `interface tunnel` *number* command. Configure the mode and transport, if needed, with the `tunnel mode` *mode protocol* command, then configure the IP addresses on the tunnel interfaces, the tunnel source and tunnel destination addresses, and your physical interfaces with global addresses. Verify with the `show interface tunnel` command as well as the Ping protocol.

Describe WAN topology options

A physical topology describes the physical layout of the network, in contrast to logical topologies, which describe the path a signal takes through the physical topology. There are four basic topologies for a WAN design.

Point-to-Point

A point-to-point connection is one in which there are single devices, locations, or connections at either end. Point -to-point connections can be used as building blocks for more involved topologies such as the hub and spoke and the full mesh, described in the next two sections.

Hub and Spoke

This topology features a single hub (central router) that provides access from remote networks to a core router. Figure 4.11 illustrates a hub-and-spoke topology.

FIGURE 4.11   Hub and spoke

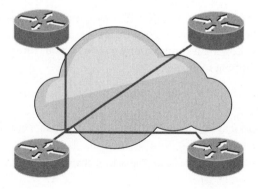

All communication among the networks travels through the core router. The advantages of a star physical topology are less cost and easier administration, but the disadvantages can be significant:

- The central router (hub) represents a single point of failure.

- The central router limits the overall performance for access to centralized resources. It is a single pipe that manages all traffic intended either for the centralized resources or for the other regional routers.

Full Mesh

In this topology, each routing node on the edge of a given packet-switching network has a direct path to every other node on the cloud. Figure 4.12 shows a fully meshed topology.

FIGURE 4.12   Fully meshed topology

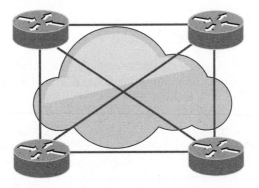

This configuration clearly provides a high level of redundancy, but the costs are the highest. So a fully meshed topology really isn't viable in large packet-switched networks. Here are some issues you'll contend with using a fully meshed topology:

- Many virtual circuits are required—one for every connection between routers, which brings up the cost.

- Configuration is more complex for routers without multicast support in non-broadcast environments.

Partially Meshed Topology

This type of topology reduces the number of routers within a network that have direct connections to all other routers in the topology. Figure 4.13 depicts a partially meshed topology.

Unlike in the full mesh network, all routers are not connected to all other routers, but it still provides more redundancy than a typical hub-and-spoke design will. This is actually considered the most balanced design because it provides more virtual circuits, plus redundancy and performance.

FIGURE 4.13   Partially meshed topology

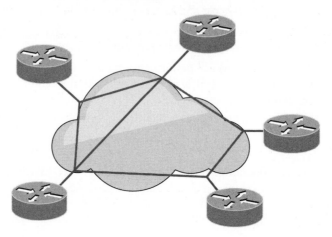

Single- vs. Dual-Homed

When a single connection is used on one end of a WAN link, using a single network interface, it is called a single-homed connection. When an additional network interface is dedicated to the same WAN link, it is called a dual-homed connection. This is typically done for purposes of redundancy.

In many cases, this concept is applied to the organization's connection to its ISP. Taking this concept a step further, both single-homed and dual-homed connections can be duplicated, with one set of connections to one ISP and another set of connections to a different ISP, providing both link redundancy and ISP redundancy. When this is done with a dual-homed connection to each ISP, they are called dual-multihomed connections. If a single-homed connection is provided for each ISP, it is called dual-single-homed connection.

Exam Essentials

Remember the various types of serial WAN topologies.   The serial WAN topologies that are most widely used are point-to-point, full mesh, and hub and spoke.

Describe WAN access connectivity options

You're probably aware that a WAN can use a number of different connection types available on the market today. Figure 4.14 shows the different WAN connection types that can be used to connect your LANs (made up of data terminal equipment, or DTE) together over the data communication equipment (DCE) network.

FIGURE 4.14 WAN connection types

Let me explain the different WAN connection types in detail now:

Dedicated (leased lines)   These are usually referred to as *point-to-point* or dedicated connections. A *leased line* is a pre-established WAN communications' path that goes from the CPE through the DCE switch, then over to the CPE of the remote site. The CPE enables DTE networks to communicate at any time with no cumbersome setup procedures to muddle through before transmitting data. When you've got plenty of cash, this is definitely the way to go because it uses synchronous serial lines up to 45 Mbps. HDLC and PPP encapsulations are frequently used on leased lines, and we went over those at the beginning of the chapter.

Circuit switching   When you hear the term *circuit switching*, think phone call. The big advantage is cost; most plain old telephone service (POTS) and ISDN dial-up connections are not flat rate, which is their advantage over dedicated lines because you pay only for what you use, and you pay only when the call is established. No data can transfer before an end-to-end connection is established. Circuit switching uses dial-up modems or ISDN and is used for low-bandwidth data transfers. Okay, I know what you're thinking, "Modems? Did he say modems? Aren't those found only in museums now?" After all, with all the wireless technologies available, who would use a modem these days? Well, some people do have ISDN; it's still viable and there are a few who still use a modem now and then. And circuit switching can be used in some of the newer WAN technologies as well.

Packet switching   This is a WAN switching method that allows you to share bandwidth with other companies to save money, just like a super old party line, where homes shared the same phone number and line to save money. *Packet switching* can be thought of as a network that's designed to look like a leased line yet it charges you less, like circuit switching does. As usual, you get what you pay for, and there's definitely a serious downside to this technology. If you need to transfer data constantly, well, just forget about this option and get a leased line instead! Packet switching will only really work for you if your data transfers are bursty, not continuous; think of a highway, where you can only go as fast as the traffic—packet switching is the same thing. Frame Relay and X.25 are packet-switching technologies with speeds that can range from 56 Kbps up to T3 (45 Mbps).

MPLS

MultiProtocol Label Switching (MPLS) is a data-carrying mechanism that emulates some properties of a circuit-switched network over a packet-switched network. MPLS is a switching mechanism that imposes labels (numbers) to packets and then uses them to forward the packets. The labels are assigned on the edge of the MPLS network, and forwarding inside the MPLS network is carried out solely based on the labels. The labels usually correspond to a path to layer 3 destination addresses, which is on par with IP destination-based routing. MPLS was designed to support the forwarding of protocols other than TCP/IP. Because of this, label switching within the network is achieved the same way irrespective of the layer 3 protocol. In larger networks, the result of MPLS labeling is that only the edge routers perform a routing lookup. All the core routers forward packets based on the labels, which makes forwarding the packets through the service provider network faster. This is a big reason most companies have replaced their Frame Relay networks with MPLS service today. Last, you can use Ethernet with MPLS to connect a WAN, and this is called Ethernet over MPLS, or EoMPLS.

> MultiProtocol Label Switching (MPLS) uses a combination of both circuit switching and packet switching.

Metro Ethernet

Metropolitan-area Ethernet is a metropolitan area network (MAN) that's based on Ethernet standards and can connect a customer to a larger network and the Internet. If available, businesses can use Metro Ethernet to connect their own offices together, which is another very cost-effective connection option. MPLS-based Metro Ethernet networks use MPLS in the ISP by providing an Ethernet or fiber cable to the customer as a connection. From the customer, it leaves the Ethernet cable, jumps onto MPLS, and then Ethernet again on the remote side. This is a smart and thrifty solution that's very popular if you can get it in your area.

Broadband PPPoE

Point-to-Point Protocol over Ethernet encapsulates PPP frames in Ethernet frames and is usually used in conjunction with xDSL services. It gives you a lot of the familiar PPP features like authentication, encryption, and compression, but there's a downside—it has a lower maximum transmission unit (MTU) than standard Ethernet does. If your firewall isn't solidly configured, this little factor can really give you some grief!

Still somewhat popular in the United States, PPPoE's main feature is that it adds a direct connection to Ethernet interfaces while also providing DSL support. It's often used by many hosts on a shared Ethernet interface for opening PPP sessions to various destinations via at least one bridging modem.

Internet VPN (DMVPN, Site-to-Site VPN, Client VPN)

I'd be pretty willing to bet you've heard the term *VPN* more than once before. Maybe you even know what one is, but just in case, a *virtual private network (VPN)* allows the creation of private networks across the Internet, enabling privacy and tunneling of non-TCP/IP protocols. VPNs are used daily to give remote users and disjointed networks connectivity over a public medium like the Internet instead of using more expensive permanent means.

No worries—VPNs aren't really that hard to understand. A VPN fits somewhere between a LAN and WAN, with the WAN often simulating a LAN link because your computer, on one LAN, connects to a different, remote LAN and uses its resources remotely. The key drawback to using VPNs is a big one—security! So the definition of connecting a LAN (or VLAN) to a WAN may sound the same as using a VPN, but a VPN is actually much more.

Here's the difference: A typical WAN connects two or more remote LANs together using a router and someone else's network, like, say, your Internet service provider's. Your local host and router see these networks as remote networks and not as local networks or local resources. This would be a WAN in its most general definition. A VPN actually makes your local host part of the remote network by using the WAN link that connects you to the remote LAN. The VPN will make your host appear as though it's actually local on the remote network. This means that we now have access to the remote LAN's resources, and that access is also very secure!

This may sound a lot like a VLAN definition, and really, the concept is the same: "Take my host and make it appear local to the remote resources." Just remember this key distinction: For networks that are physically local, using VLANs is a good solution, but for physically remote networks that span a WAN, opt for using VPNs instead.

For a simple VPN example, let's use my home office in Boulder, Colorado. Here, I have my personal host, but I want it to appear as if it's on a LAN in my corporate office in Dallas, Texas, so I can get to my remote servers. VPN is the solution I would opt for to achieve my goal.

Figure 4.15 shows this example of my host using a VPN connection from Boulder to Dallas, which allows me to access the remote network services and servers as if my host were right there on the same VLAN as my servers.

Why is this so important? If you answered, "Because your servers in Dallas are secure, and only the hosts on the same VLAN are allowed to connect to them and use the resources of these servers," you nailed it! A VPN allows me to connect to these resources by locally attaching to the VLAN through a VPN across the WAN. The other option is to open up my network and servers to everyone on the Internet or another WAN service, in which case my security goes "poof." So clearly, it's imperative I have a VPN!

FIGURE 4.15   Example of using a VPN

DMVPN (Cisco Proprietary)

The Cisco Dynamic Multipoint Virtual Private Network (DMVPN) feature enables you to easily scale large and small IPsec VPNs. The Cisco DMVPN is Cisco's answer to allow a corporate office to connect to branch offices with low cost, easy configuration, and flexibility. DMVPN has one central router, such as a corporate router, which is referred to as the hub, and the branches are called spokes. So the corporate-to-branch connection is referred to as the hub-and-spoke interconnection. Also supported is the spoke-to-spoke design used for branch-to-branch interconnections. If you're thinking this design sounds eerily similar to your old Frame Relay network, you're right! The DMVPN features enables you to configure a single GRE tunnel interface and a single IPsec profile on the hub router to manage all spoke routers, which keeps the size of the configuration on the hub router basically the same even if you add more spoke routers to the network. DMVPN also allows spoke routers to dynamically create VPN tunnels between them as network data travels from one spoke to another.

Site to Site

Site-to-site VPNs, or intranet VPNs, allow a company to connect its remote sites to the corporate backbone securely over a public medium like the Internet instead of requiring more expensive WAN connections like Frame Relay.

Client VPN (Remote Access)

Remote-access VPNs allow remote users such as telecommuters to securely access the corporate network wherever and whenever they need to.

Extranet VPN

Extranet VPNs allow an organization's suppliers, partners, and customers to be connected to the corporate network in a limited way for business-to-business (B2B) communications.

You'd use an enterprise-managed VPN if your company manages its own VPNs, which happens to be a very popular way of providing this service. To get a picture of this, check out Figure 4.16.

FIGURE 4.16   Enterprise-managed VPNs

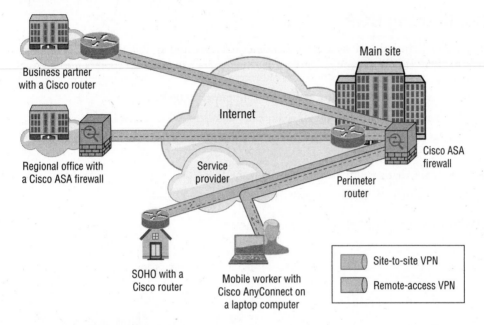

Exam Essentials

Understand the term *virtual private network*.   You need to understand why and how to use a VPN between two sites and the purpose that IPsec serves with VPNs.

Describe the VPN types.   These include site to site, client or remote access, extranet, and Cisco Dynamic Multipoint Virtual Private Network (DMVPN).

Configure and verify single-homed branch connectivity using eBGP IPv4 (limited to peering and route advertisement using Network command only)

The *Border Gateway Protocol (BGP)* is perhaps one of the most well-known routing protocols in the world of networking. This is understandable because BGP is the routing protocol that powers the Internet and makes possible what we take for granted: connecting to remote systems on the other side of the country or planet. Because of its pervasive use, it's likely that each of us will have to deal with it at some point in our careers. So it's appropriate that we spend some time learning about BGP.

Configuring BGP

If you're configuring BGP between a customer network and an ISP, this process is called external BGP (EBGP). If you're configuring BGP peers between two routers in the same AS, it's not considered EBGP.

You must have the basic information to configure EBGP:

- AS numbers (your own, and all remote AS numbers, which must be different)
- All the neighbors (peers) that are involved in BGP, and IP addressing that is used among the BGP neighbors
- Networks that need to be advertised into BGP

For an example of configuring EBGP, here's Figure 4.17.

FIGURE 4.17   Example of EBGP lay layout

There are three main steps to configure basic BGP:

1. Define the BGP process.
2. Establish one or more neighbor relationships.
3. Advertise the local networks into BGP.

Define the BGP Process

To start the BGP process on a router, use the `router bgp` *AS* command. Each process must be assigned a local AS number. There can only be one BGP process in a router, which means that each router can only be in one AS at any given time.

Here is an example:

```
ISP#config t
ISP(config)#router bgp ?
<1-65535> Autonomous system number
ISP(config)#router bgp 1
```

Notice the AS number can be from 1 to 65,535.

Establish One or More Neighbor Relationships

Since BGP does not automatically discover neighbors like other routing protocols do, you have to explicitly configure them using the `neighbor` *peer-ip-address* `remote-as` *peer-as-number* command. Here is an example of configuring the ISP router in Figure 4.17:

```
ISP(config-router)#neighbor 192.168.1.2 remote-as 100
ISP(config-router)#neighbor 192.168.2.2 remote-as 200
```

Be sure to understand that the above command is the neighbor's IP address and neighbor's AS number.

Advertise the Local Networks into BGP

To specify your local networks and advertise them into BGP, you use the `network` command with the mask keyword and then the subnet mask:

```
ISP(config-router)#network 10.0.0.0 mask 255.255.255.0
```

These network numbers must match what is found on the local router's forwarding table exactly, which can be seen with the `show ip route` or `show ip int brief` command. For other routing protocols, the network command has a different meaning. For OSPF and EIGRP, for example, the network command indicates the interfaces for which the routing protocol will send and receive route updates. In BGP, the network command indicates which routes should be injected into the BGP table on the local router.

Here's the BGP routing configuration for the R1 and R2 routers:

```
R1#config t
R1(config)#router bgp 100
R1(config-router)#neighbor 192.168.1.1 remote-as 1
```

```
R1(config-router)#network 10.0.1.0 mask 255.255.255.0

R2#config t
R2(config)#router bgp 200
R2(config-router)#neighbor 192.168.2.1 remote-as 1
R2(config-router)#network 10.0.2.0 mask 255.255.255.0
```

That's it! Pretty simple. Now let's verify our configuration.

Verifying EBGP

We'll use the following commands to verify our little EBGP network:

- show ip bgp summary
- show ip bgp
- show ip bgp neighbors

The *show ip bgp summary* Command

The show ip bgp summary command gives you an overview of the BGP status. Each configured neighbor is listed in the output of the command. The output will display the IP address and AS number of the neighbor, along with the status of the session. You can use this information to verify that BGP sessions are up and established or to verify the IP address and AS number of the configured BGP neighbor.

```
ISP#sh ip bgp summary
BGP router identifier 10.0.0.1, local AS number 1
BGP table version is 4, main routing table version 6
3 network entries using 396 bytes of memory
3 path entries using 156 bytes of memory
2/2 BGP path/bestpath attribute entries using 368 bytes of memory
3 BGP AS-PATH entries using 72 bytes of memory
0 BGP route-map cache entries using 0 bytes of memory
0 BGP filter-list cache entries using 0 bytes of memory
Bitfield cache entries: current 1 (at peak 1) using 32 bytes of memory
BGP using 1024 total bytes of memory
BGP activity 3/0 prefixes, 3/0 paths, scan interval 60 secs
```

Neighbor	V	AS	MsgRcvd	MsgSent	TblVer	InQ	OutQ	Up/Down	State/PfxRcd
192.168.1.2	4	100	56	55	4	0	0	00:53:33	4
192.168.2.2	4	200	47	46	4	0	0	00:44:53	4

The first section of the show ip bgp summary command output describes the BGP table and its content:

- The router ID of the router and local AS number
- The BGP table version is the version number of the local BGP table. This number is increased every time the table is changed.

The second section of the show ip bgp summary command output is a table in which the current neighbor statuses are shown. Here's information about what you see displayed in the output of this command:

- IP address of the neighbor

- BGP version number that is used by the router when communicating with the neighbor (v4)

- AS number of the remote neighbor

- Number of messages and updates that have been received from the neighbor since the session was established

- Number of messages and updates that have been sent to the neighbor since the session was established

- Version number of the local BGP table that has been included in the most recent update to the neighbor

- Number of messages that are waiting to be processed in the incoming queue from this neighbor

- Number of messages that are waiting in the outgoing queue for transmission to the neighbor

- How long the neighbor has been in the current state and the name of the current state. Interestingly, notice there is no state listed, which is actually what you want because that means the peers are established.

- Number of received prefixes from the neighbor

- ISP1 has two established sessions with the following neighbors:

  - 192.168.1.2, which is the IP address of R1 router and is in AS 100

  - 192.168.2.2, which is the IP address of R2 router and is in AS 200

- From each of the neighbors, ISP1 has received one prefix (one network).

Now, for the CCNA objectives, remember that if you see this type of output at the end of the show ip bgp summary command, the BGP session is not established between peers:

```
Neighbor       V    AS MsgRcvd MsgSent   TblVer  InQ OutQ Up/Down State/PfxRcd
192.168.1.2    4    64      0       0        0   0    0 never    Active
```

Notice the state of Active. Remember, seeing no state output is good! Active means we're actively trying to establish with the peer.

The *show ip bgp* Command

With the show ip bgp command, the entire BGP table is displayed. A list of information about each route is displayed, so this is a nice command to get quick information on your BGP routes.

```
ISP#sh ip bgp
BGP table version is 4, local router ID is 10.0.0.1
```

```
Status codes: s suppressed, d damped, h history, * valid, > best, i - internal,
r RIB-failure, S Stale
Origin codes: i - IGP, e - EGP, ? - incomplete

Network Next Hop Metric LocPrf Weight Path
*> 10.0.0.0/24 0.0.0.0 0 0 32768 i
*> 10.0.1.0/24 192.168.1.2 0 0 0 100 i
*> 10.0.2.0/24 192.168.2.2 0 0 0 200 i
```

The output is sorted in network number order, and if the BGP table contains more than one route to the same network, the backup routes are displayed on separate lines. We don't have multiple routes, so none are shown.

The BGP path selection process selects one of the available routes to each of the networks as the best. This route is pointed out by the > character in the left column.

ISP1 has the following networks in the BGP table:

- 10.0.0.0/24, which is locally originated via the network command in BGP on the ISP router

- 10.0.1.0/24, which has been advertised from 192.168.1.2 (R1) neighbor

- 10.0.2.0/24, which has been advertised from 192.168.2.2 (R2) neighbor

Since the command displays all routing information, note that network 10.0.0.0/24, with the next-hop attribute set to 0.0.0.0, is also displayed. The next-hop attribute is set to 0.0.0.0 when you view the BGP table on the router that originates the route in BGP. The 10.0.0.0/24 network is the network that I locally configured on ISP1 into BGP.

The *show ip bgp neighbors* Command

The show ip bgp neighbors command provides more information about BGP connections to neighbors than the show ip bgp command does. This command can be used to get information about the TCP sessions and the BGP parameters of the session, as well as showing the TCP timers and counters, and it's a long output! I'll just give you the top part of the command here:

```
ISP#sh ip bgp neighbors
BGP neighbor is 192.168.1.2, remote AS 100, external link
BGP version 4, remote router ID 10.0.1.1
BGP state = Established, up for 00:10:55
Last read 00:10:55, last write 00:10:55, hold time is 180, keepalive interval is
60 seconds
Neighbor capabilities:
Route refresh: advertised and received(new)
Address family IPv4 Unicast: advertised and received
Message statistics:
InQ depth is 0
OutQ depth is 0
[output cut]
```

Notice (and remember!) you can use the `show ip bgp neighbors` command to see the hold time on two BGP peers, and in the above example from the ISP to R1, the holdtime is 180 seconds.

Exam Essentials

Understand how to configure and verify EBGP.   There are three main steps to configure basic BGP:

1. Define the BGP process.
2. Establish one or more neighbor relationships.
3. Advertise the local networks into BGP.

Describe basic QoS concepts

Quality of service (QoS) refers to the way the resources are controlled so that the quality of services is maintained. It's basically the ability to provide a different priority to one or more types of traffic over other levels for different applications, data flows, or users so that they can be guaranteed a certain performance level. QoS is used to manage contention for network resources for better end-user experience.

QoS methods focus on problems that can affect data as it traverses network cable:

Delay   Data can run into congested lines or take a less-than-ideal route to the destination, and delays like these can make some applications, such as VoIP, fail. This is the best reason to implement QoS when real-time applications are in use in the network—to prioritize delay-sensitive traffic.

Dropped packets   Some routers will drop packets if they receive a packet while their buffers are full. If the receiving application is waiting for the packets but doesn't get them, it will usually request that the packets be retransmitted—another common cause of a service(s) delay. With QoS, when there is contention on a link, less important traffic is delayed or dropped in favor of delay-sensitive business-important traffic.

Error   Packets can be corrupted in transit and arrive at the destination in an unacceptable format, again requiring retransmission and resulting in delays such as video and voice.

Jitter   Not every packet takes the same route to the destination, so some will be more delayed than others if they travel through a slower or busier network connection. The variation in packet delay is called *jitter*, and this can have a nastily negative impact on programs that communicate in real time.

Out-of-Order Delivery   Out-of-order delivery is also a result of packets taking different paths through the network to their destinations. The application at the receiving end needs to put them back together in the right order for the message to be completed. So if there are significant delays, or the packets are reassembled out of order, users will probably notice degradation of an application's quality.

QoS can ensure that applications with a required level of predictability will receive the necessary bandwidth to work properly. Clearly, on networks with excess bandwidth, this is not a factor, but the more limited your bandwidth is, the more important a concept like this becomes!

In the following sections, we'll be covering these important mechanisms:

- Classification and marking tools
- Policing, shaping, and re-marking tools
- Congestion management (or scheduling) tools
- Link-specific tools

So let's take a deeper look at each mechanism now.

Marking

A classifier is a tool that inspects packets within a field to identify the type of traffic they are carrying. This is so that QoS can determine which traffic class they belong to and determine how they should be treated. It's important that this isn't a constant cycle for traffic because it does take up time and resources. Traffic is then directed to a policy-enforcement mechanism, referred to as policing, for its specific type.

Policy enforcement mechanisms include marking, queuing, policing, and shaping, and there are various layer 2 and layer 3 fields in a frame and packet for marking traffic. You are definitely going to have to understand these marking techniques to meet the objectives, so here we go:

Class of Service (CoS)   An Ethernet frame marking at layer 2, which contains 3 bits. This is called the Priority Code Point (PCP) within an Ethernet frame header when VLAN tagged frames as defined by IEEE 802.1q are used.

Type of Service (ToS)   ToS comprises 8 bits, 3 of which are designated as the IP precedence field in an IPv4 packet header. The IPv6 header field is called Traffic Class.

Differentiated Services Code Point (DSCP or DiffServ)   One of the methods we can use for classifying and managing network traffic and providing quality of service (QoS) on modern IP networks is DSCP. This technology uses a 6-bit differentiated services code point in the 8-bit Differentiated Services field (DS field) in the IP header for packet classification. DSCP allows for the creation of traffic classes that can be used to assign priorities. While IP precedence is the old way to mark ToS, DSCP is the new way. DSCP is backward compatible with IP precedence.

Layer 3 packet marking with IP precedence and DSCP is the most widely deployed marking option because layer 3 packet markings have end-to-end significance.

Class Selector   Class Selector uses the same 3 bits of the field as IP precedence and is used to indicate a 3-bit subset of DSCP values.

Traffic Identifier (TID)   TID, used in wireless frames, describe a 3-bit field in the QoS control field in 802.11. It's very similar to CoS, so just remember CoS is wired Ethernet and TID is wireless.

Classification Marking Tools

As discussed in the previous section, classification of traffic determines which type of traffic the packets or frames belong to, which then allows you to apply policies to it by marking, shaping, and policing. Always try to mark traffic as close to the trust boundary as possible.

To classify traffic, we generally use three ways:

Markings   This looks at the header informant on existing layer 2 or 3 settings, and classification is based on existing markings.

Addressing   This classification technique looks at header information using source and destinations of interfaces, layer 2 and 3 addresses, and layer 4 port numbers. You can group traffic with devices using IP and traffic by type using port numbers.

Application signatures   This is the way to look at the information in the payload, and this classification technique is called deep packet inspection.

Let's dive deeper into deep packet inspection by discussing something called Network Based Application Recognition (NBAR).

NBAR is a classifier that provides deep-packet inspection on layer 4 to 7 on a packet; however, know that using NBAR is the most CPU-intensive technique compared to using addresses (IP or ports) or access control lists (ACLs).

Since it's not always possible to identify applications by looking at just layers 3 and 4, NBAR looks deep into the packet payload and compares the payload content against its signature database called a Packet Description Language Model (PDLM).

There are two different modes of operation used with NBAR:

Passive mode   Using passive mode will give you real-time statistics on applications by protocol or interface as well as the bit rate, packet, and byte counts.

Active mode   Classifies applications for traffic marking so that QoS policies can be applied.

Device Trust

The trust boundary is a point in the network where packet markings (which identify traffic such as voice, video, or data) are not necessarily trusted. You can create, remove, or rewrite markings at that point. The borders of a trust domain are the network locations where packet markings are accepted and acted upon. Figure 4.18 shows some typical trust boundaries.

FIGURE 4.18   Trust boundaries

The figure shows that IP phones and router interfaces are typically trusted, but interfaces beyond those end points are not. Here are some things you need to remember for the exam objectives:

Untrusted domain   This is the part of the network that you are not managing, such as PC, printers, etc.

Trusted domain   This is part of the network with only administrator-managed devices such as switches, routers, etc.

Trust boundary   This is where packets are classified and marked. For example, the trust boundary would be IP phones and the boundary between the ISP and enterprise network. In an enterprise campus network, the trust boundary is almost always at the edge switch.

Traffic at the trust boundary is classified and marked before being forwarded to the trusted domain. Markings on traffic coming from an untrusted domain are usually ignored to prevent end-user-controlled markings from taking unfair advantage of the network QoS configuration.

Prioritization

In today's networks, you will find a mix of data, voice, and video traffic. Each traffic type has different properties.

Figure 4.19 shows the traffic characteristics found in today's networks for data, voice, and video.

FIGURE 4.19   Traffic characteristics

Voice

Voice traffic is real-time traffic with constant, predictable bandwidth and known packet arrival times.

The following are voice characteristics on a network:

- Smooth traffic
- Benign
- Drop insensitive
- Delay sensitive
- UDP priority

One-way voice traffic needs the following:

- Latency of less than or equal to 150 milliseconds
- Jitter of less than or equal to 30 milliseconds
- Loss of less than or equal to 1%
- Bandwidth of only 30–128 Kbps

Video

There are several types of video traffic, and a lot of the traffic on the Internet today is video traffic, with Netflix, Hulu, etc. Video traffic can include streaming video, real-time interactive video, and video conferences.

One-way video traffic needs the following:

- Latency of less than or equal to 200–400 milliseconds
- Jitter of less than or equal to 30–50 milliseconds
- Loss of less than or equal to 0.1%–1%
- Bandwidth of 384 Kbps to 20 Mbps or greater

Data

Data traffic is not real-time traffic and includes data packets comprising bursty (or unpredictable) traffic and widely varying packet arrival times. The following are data characteristics on a network:

- Smooth/bursty
- Benign/greedy
- Drop insensitive
- Delay insensitive
- TCP retransmits

Data traffic doesn't really require special handling in today's network, especially if TCP is used.

Shaping

Policers and shapers are two tools that identify and respond to traffic problems and are both rate limiters. Figure 4.20 shows how they differ.

FIGURE 4.20   Policing and shaping rate limiters

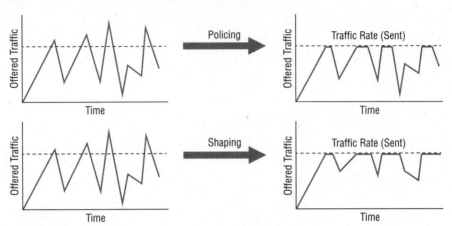

Policers and shapers identify traffic violations in a similar manner, but they differ in their response:

Policers   Since the policers make instant decision, you want to deploy them on the ingress if possible. This is because you want to drop traffic as soon as you receive it if it's going to be dropped anyway. Even so, you can still place them on an egress to control the amount of traffic per class. When traffic is exceeded, policers don't delay it, which means they do not introduce jitter or delay, they just check the traffic and can drop it or re-mark it. Just know that this means there's a higher drop probability, and it can cause a significant amount of TCP resends.

Shapers   Shapers are usually deployed between an enterprise network, on the egress side, and the service provider network to make sure you stay within the carrier's contract rate. If the traffic does exceed the rate, it will get policed by the provider and dropped. This allows the traffic to meet the SLA and means there will be fewer TCP resends than with policers. Be aware that shaping does introduce jitter and delay.

 Just remember that policers drop traffic and shapers delay it. Policers have significant TCP resends and shapers do not. Shapers introduce delay and jitter, but policers do not.

Policing

Policing is covered in the previous section.

Congestion Management

This section and the next section on congestion avoidance will cover congestion issues. If traffic exceeds network resources (always), the traffic gets queued, which is basically the temporary storage of backed-up packets. You perform queuing in order to avoid dropping packets. This isn't a bad thing. It's actually a good thing or all traffic would immediately be dropped if packets couldn't get processed immediately. However, traffic classes like VoIP would actually be better off just being immediately dropped unless you can somehow guarantee delay-free bandwidth for that traffic.

When congestion occurs, the congestion management tools are activated. There are two types, as shown in Figure 4.21.

FIGURE 4.21   Congestion management

Packets are assigned to various queues when the output interface is congested.

Let's take a closer look at congestion management:

Queuing (or buffering)   Buffering is the logic of ordering packets in output buffers. It is activated only when congestion occurs. When queues fill up, packets can be reordered so that the higher-priority packets can be sent out of the exit interface sooner than the lower-priority ones.

Scheduling   This is the process of deciding which packet should be sent out next and occurs whether or not there is congestion on the link.

Staying with scheduling for another minute, know that there are some schedule mechanisms that exist that you really need to be familiar with. We'll go over those, and then I'll head back over to a detailed look at queuing:

Strict priority scheduling   Low-priority queues are only serviced once the high-priority queues are empty. This is great if you are the one sending high-priority traffic, but it's possible that low-priority queues will never be processed. We call this traffic or queue starvation.

Round-robin scheduling   This is a rather fair technique because queues are serviced in a set sequence. You won't have starving queues here, but real-time traffic suffers greatly.

Weighted fair scheduling   By weighing the queues, the scheduling process will service some queues more often than others, which is an upgrade over round-robin. You won't have any starvation here either, but unlike with round-robin, you can give priority to real-time traffic. It does not, however, provide bandwidth guarantees.

Okay, let's run back over and finish queueing. Queuing typically is a layer 3 process, but some queueing can occur at layer 2 or even layer 1. Interestingly, if a layer 2 queue fills up, the data can be pushed into layer 3 queues, and when layer 1 (called the transmit ring or TX-ring queue), fills up, the data will be pushed to layer 2 and 3 queues. This is when QoS becomes active on the device. There are many different queuing mechanisms, with only two typically used today, but let's take a look at the legacy queuing methods first:

First in, first out (FIFO) A single queue with packets being processed in the exact order in which they arrived.

Priority queuing (PQ) This is not really a good queuing method because lower-priority queues are served only when the higher-priority queues are empty. There are only four queues, and low-priority traffic may never be sent.

Custom queuing (CQ) With up to 16 queues and round-robin scheduling, CQ prevents low-level queue starvation and provides traffic guarantees. But it doesn't provide strict priority for real-time traffic, so your VoIP traffic could end up being dropped.

Weighted fair queuing (WFQ) This was actually a pretty popular way of queuing for a long time because it divided up the bandwidth by the number of flows, which provided bandwidth for all applications. This was great for real-time traffic, but it doesn't offer any guarantees for a particular flow.

Now that you know about all the not-so-good queuing methods to use, let's take a look at the two newer queuing mechanisms that are recommended for today's rich-media networks, detailed in Figure 4.22.

FIGURE 4.22 Queuing mechanisms

The two new and improved queuing mechanisms you should now use in today's network are class-based weighted fair queuing and low latency queuing:

Class-based weighted fair queuing (CBWFQ) Provides fairness and bandwidth guarantees for all traffic, but it does not provide latency guarantees and is typically only used for data traffic management.

Low latency queuing (LLQ): LLQ is really the same thing as CBWFQ but with stricter priorities for real-time traffic. LLQ is great for both data and real-time traffic because it provides both latency and bandwidth guarantees.

In Figure 4.22, you can see the LLQ queuing mechanism, which is suitable for networks with real-time traffic. If you remove the low-latency queue (at the top), you're then left with CBWFQ, which is only used for data-traffic networks.

Tools for Congestion Avoidance

TCP changed our networking world when it introduced sliding windows as a flow-control mechanism in the mid-1990s. Flow control is a way for the receiving device to control the amount of traffic from a transmitting device.

If a problem occurred during a data transmission (always), the previous flow control methods used by TCP and other layer 4 protocols like SPX, which we used before sliding windows, would cut the transmission rate in half, and leave it there at the same rate, or lower, for the duration of the connection. This was certainly a point of contention with users!

TCP actually does cut transmission rates drastically if a flow control issue occurs, but it increases the transmission rate once the missing segments are resolved or the packets are finally processed. Because of this behavior, and although it was awesome at the time, this method can result in what we call tail drop. Tail drop is definitely suboptimal for today's networks because using it, we're not utilizing the bandwidth effectively.

Just to clarify, tail drop refers to the dropping of packets as they arrive when the queues on the receiving interface are full. This is a waste of precious bandwidth since TCP will just keep resending the data until it's happy again (meaning an ACK has been received). So now this brings up another new term, *TCP global synchronization*, where senders will reduce their transmission rate at the same time when packet loss occurs.

Congestion avoidance starts dropping packets before a queue fills, and it drops the packets by using traffic weights instead of just randomness. Cisco uses something called weighted random early detection (WRED), which is a queuing method that ensures that high-precedence traffic has lower loss rates than other traffic during congestion. This allows more important traffic, like VoIP, to be prioritized and dropped over what you'd consider less important traffic such as, for example, a connection to Facebook.

 Queuing algorithms manage the front of the queue and congestion mechanisms manage the back of the queue.

Figure 4.23 demonstrates how congestion avoidance works.

FIGURE 4.23   Congestion avoidance

If three traffic flows begin at different times, as shown in the example in Figure 4.23, and congestion occurs, using TCP could first cause tail drop, which drops the traffic as soon as it's received if the buffers are full. At that point TCP would start another traffic flow, synchronizing the TCP flows in waves, which would then leave much of the bandwidth unused.

Exam Essentials

Have a deep understanding of QoS.   You must understand QoS in detail, specifically marking; device trust; prioritization for voice, video, and data; shaping; policing; and congestion management.

Review Questions

You can find the answers in the Appendix.

1. Which command will display the CHAP authentication process as it occurs between two routers in the network?

    A. `show chap authentication`

    B. `show interface serial 0`

    C. `debug ppp authentication`

    D. `debug chap authentication`

2. Which of the following are true regarding the following command? (Choose two.)

    `R1(config-router)# neighbor 10.10.200.1 remote-as 6200`

    A. The local router R1 uses AS 6200.

    B. The remote router uses AS 6200.

    C. The local interface of R1 is 10.10.200.1.

    D. The neighbor IP address is 10.10.200.1.

    E. The neighbor's loopback interface is 10.10.200.1.

3. BGP uses which Transport layer protocol and port number?

    A. UDP/123

    B. TCP/123

    C. UDP/179

    D. TCP/179

    E. UDP/169

    F. TCP/169

4. Which command can you use to know the hold time on the two BGP peers?

    A. `show ip bgp`

    B. `show ip bgp summary`

    C. `show ip bgp all`

    D. `show ip bgp neighbor`

5. What does a next hop of 0.0.0.0 mean in the show ip bgp command output?

    ```
    Network           Next Hop         Metric LocPrf Weight Path
    *> 10.1.1.0/24      0.0.0.0               0         32768 ?
    *> 10.13.13.0/24    0.0.0.0               0         32768 ?
    ```

    A. The router does not know the next hop.

    B. The network is locally originated via the network command in BGP.

    C. It is not a valid network.

    D. The next hop is not reachable.

6. Which two of the following are GRE characteristics? (Choose two.)

   A. GRE encapsulation uses a protocol-type field in the GRE header to support the encapsulation of any OSI layer 3 protocol.

   B. GRE itself is stateful. It includes flow-control mechanisms by default.

   C. GRE includes strong security mechanisms to protect its payload.

   D. The GRE header, together with the tunneling IP header, creates at least 24 bytes of additional overhead for tunneled packets.

7. A GRE tunnel is flapping with the following error message:

   ```
   07:11:49: %LINEPROTO-5-UPDOWN:
             Line protocol on Interface Tunnel0, changed state to up
   07:11:55: %TUN-5-RECURDOWN:
             Tunnel0 temporarily disabled due to recursive routing
   07:11:59: %LINEPROTO-5-UPDOWN:
             Line protocol on Interface Tunnel0, changed state to down
   07:12:59: %LINEPROTO-5-UPDOWN:
   ```

   What could be the reason for the tunnel flapping?

   A. IP routing has not been enabled on the tunnel interface.

   B. There's an MTU issue on the tunnel interface.

   C. The router is trying to route to the tunnel destination address using the tunnel interface itself.

   D. An access list is blocking traffic on the tunnel interface.

8. Which of the following commands will not tell you if the GRE tunnel 0 is in up/up state?

   A. show ip interface brief

   B. show interface tunnel 0

   C. show ip interface tunnel 0

   D. show run interface tunnel 0

9. Which of the following PPP authentication protocols authenticates a device on the other end of a link with an encrypted password?

   A. MD5

   B. PAP

   C. CHAP

   D. DES

10. Which of the following encapsulates PPP frames in Ethernet frames and uses common PPP features like authentication, encryption, and compression?

   A. PPP

   B. PPPoA

   C. PPPoE

   D. Token Ring

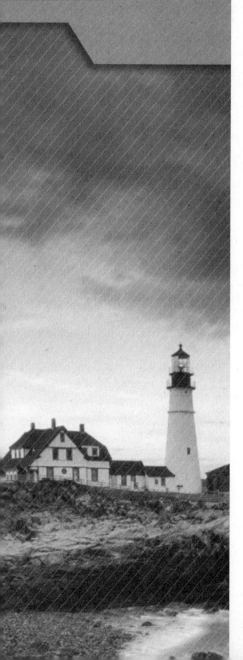

Chapter

5

Infrastructure Services

THE FOLLOWING CCNA ROUTING AND SWITCHING EXAM OBJECTIVES ARE COVERED IN THIS CHAPTER:

- ✓ Describe DNS lookup operation.

- ✓ Troubleshoot client connectivity issues involving DNS.

- ✓ Configure and verify DHCP on a router (excluding static reservations).

- ✓ Troubleshoot client- and router-based DHCP connectivity issues.

- ✓ Configure, verify, and troubleshoot basic HSRP.

- ✓ Configure, verify, and troubleshoot inside source NAT.

- ✓ Configure and verify NTP operating in a client/server mode.

In this chapter, I will discuss infrastructure services. These services include DNS, DHCP, HSRP, and NAT. I will cover the configuration, verification, and troubleshooting of these vital network services.

Describe DNS lookup operation

If you want to use a hostname instead of an IP address to connect to a remote device, the device that you're using to make the connection must be able to translate the hostname to an IP address.

There are two ways to resolve hostnames to IP addresses. The first is by building a host table on each router, and the second is to build a Domain Name System (DNS) server. The latter method is similar to creating a dynamic host table, assuming that you're dealing with dynamic DNS.

Building a Host Table

An important factor to remember is that although a host table provides name resolution, it does that only on the specific router that it was built upon. The command you use to build a host table on a router looks like this:

```
ip host host_name [tcp_port_number] ip_address
```

The default is TCP port number 23, but you can create a session using Telnet with a different TCP port number if you want. You can also assign up to eight IP addresses to a hostname.

Here's how I configured a host table on the SW-1 switch with two entries to resolve the names for the SW-2 and SW-3:

```
SW-1#config t
SW-1(config)#ip host SW-2 ?
  <0-65535>   Default telnet port number
  A.B.C.D     Host IP address
  additional  Append addresses

SW-1(config)#ip host SW-2 10.100.128.9
SW-1(config)#ip host SW-3 10.100.128.8
```

Notice that I can just keep adding IP addresses to reference a unique host, one after another. To view our newly built host table, I'll just use the show hosts command:

```
SW-1(config)#do sho hosts
Default domain is not set
Name/address lookup uses domain service
Name servers are 255.255.255.255


Codes: u - unknown, e - expired, * - OK, ? - revalidate
       t - temporary, p - permanent


Host                    Port  Flags      Age Type  Address(es)
SW-3                    None  (perm, OK)  0   IP    10.100.128.8
SW-2                    None  (perm, OK)  0   IP    10.100.128.9
```

In this output, you can see the two hostnames plus their associated IP addresses. The perm in the Flags column means that the entry has been manually configured. If it read temp, it would be an entry that was resolved by DNS.

 The show hosts command provides information on temporary DNS entries and permanent name-to-address mappings created using the ip host command.

To verify that the host table resolves names, try typing the hostnames at a router prompt. Remember that if you don't specify the command, the router will assume you want to telnet.

In the following example, I'll use the hostnames to telnet into the remote devices and press Ctrl+Shift+6 and then X to return to the main console of the SW-1 router:

```
SW-1#sw-3
Trying SW-3 (10.100.128.8)... Open

User Access Verification

Password:
SW-3> Ctrl+Shift+6
SW-1#
```

It worked—I successfully used entries in the host table to create a session to the SW-3 device by using the name to telnet into it. And just so you know, names in the host table are not case sensitive.

Notice that the entries in the following show sessions output now display the host-names and IP addresses instead of just the IP addresses:

```
SW-1#sh sessions
Conn Host                Address          Byte  Idle Conn Name
   1 SW-3                10.100.128.8      0    1    SW-3
*  2 SW-2                10.100.128.9      0    1    SW-2
SW-1#
```

If you want to remove a hostname from the table, all you need to do is use the no ip host command like this:

```
SW-1(config)#no ip host SW-3
```

The drawback to going with this host table method is that you must create a host table on each router in order to be able to resolve names. So clearly, if you have a whole bunch of routers and want to resolve names, using DNS is a much better option!

Using DNS to Resolve Names

If you have a lot of devices, you don't want to create a host table in each one of them unless you've also got a lot of time to waste. Since most of us don't, I highly recommend using a DNS server to resolve hostnames instead!

Anytime a Cisco device receives a command it doesn't understand, it will try to resolve it through DNS by default. Watch what happens when I type the special command todd at a Cisco router prompt:

```
SW-1#todd
Translating "todd"...domain server (255.255.255.255)
% Unknown command or computer name, or unable to find
  computer address
SW-1#
```

Because it doesn't know my name or the command I'm trying to type, it tries to resolve this through DNS. This is really annoying for two reasons: first, because it doesn't know my name <grin>, and second, because I need to hang out and wait for the name lookup to time out. You can get around this and prevent a time-consuming DNS lookup by using the no ip domain-lookup command on your router from global configuration mode.

So if you have a DNS server on your network, you'll need to add a few commands to make DNS name resolution work well for you:

- The first command is ip domain-lookup, which is turned on by default. It needs to be entered only if you previously turned it off with the no ip domain-lookup command. The command can be used without the hyphen as well with the syntax ip domain lookup.

- The second command is ip name-server. This sets the IP address of the DNS server. You can enter the IP addresses of up to six servers.

- The last command is ip domain-name. Although this command is optional, you really set it because it appends the domain name to the hostname you type in. Since DNS uses a fully qualified domain name (FQDN) system, you must have a second-level DNS name, in the form *domain.com*.

Here's an example of using these three commands:

```
SW-1#config t
SW-1(config)#ip domain-lookup
SW-1(config)#ip name-server ?
  A.B.C.D  Domain server IP address (maximum of 6)
SW-1(config)#ip name-server 4.4.4.4
SW-1(config)#ip domain-name lammle.com
SW-1(config)#^Z
```

Exam Essentials

Build a static host table on a router.   By using the global configuration command `ip host host_name [tcp_port_number] ip_address`, you can build a static host table on your router. You can apply multiple IP addresses against the same host entry.

Troubleshoot client connectivity issues involving DNS

After the DNS configurations have been set, you can test the DNS server by using a host-name to ping or telnet into a device like this:

```
SW-1#ping SW-3
Translating "SW-3"...domain server (4.4.4.4) [OK]
Type escape sequence to abort.
Sending 5, 100-byte ICMP Echos to 10.100.128.8, timeout is
  2 seconds:
!!!!!
Success rate is 100 percent (5/5), round-trip min/avg/max
  = 28/31/32 ms
```

Notice that the router uses the DNS server to resolve the name.

After a name is resolved using DNS, use the `show hosts` command to verify that the device cached this information in the host table. If I hadn't used the `ip domain-name lammle.com` command in the previous section, "Using DNS to Resolve Names" I would have needed to type in ping `sw-3.lammle.com`, which is kind of a hassle.

Exam Essentials

Verify the host table on a router.   You can verify the host table with the `show hosts` command.

Configure and verify DHCP on a router (excluding static reservations)

To configure a DHCP server for your hosts, you need the following information at minimum:

Network and mask for each LAN   Network ID, also called a scope. All addresses in a subnet can be leased to hosts by default.

Reserved/excluded addresses   Reserved addresses for printers, servers, routers, etc. These addresses will not be handed out to hosts. I usually reserve the first address of each subnet for the router, but you don't have to do this.

Default router   This is the router's address for each LAN.

DNS address   A list of DNS server addresses provided to hosts so they can resolve names.

Server

Here are your configuration steps:

1. Exclude the addresses you want to reserve. The reason you do this step first is because as soon as you set a network ID, the DHCP service will start responding to client requests.

2. Create your pool for each LAN using a unique name.

3. Choose the network ID and subnet mask for the DHCP pool that the server will use to provide addresses to hosts.

4. Add the address used for the default gateway of the subnet.

5. Provide the DNS server address(es).

6. If you don't want to use the default lease time of 24 hours, you need to set the lease time in days, hours, and minutes.

I'll configure the switch in Figure 5.1 to be the DHCP server for the Sales wireless LAN.

FIGURE 5.1   DHCP configuration example on a switch

Understand that this configuration could just have easily been placed on the router in Figure 5.1. Here's how we'll configure DHCP using the 192.168.10.0/24 network ID:

```
Switch(config)#ip dhcp excluded-address 192.168.10.1 192.168.10.10
Switch(config)#ip dhcp pool Sales_Wireless
Switch(dhcp-config)#network 192.168.10.0 255.255.255.0
Switch(dhcp-config)#default-router 192.168.10.1
Switch(dhcp-config)#dns-server 4.4.4.4
Switch(dhcp-config)#lease 3 12 15
```

First, you can see that I reserved 10 addresses in the range for the router, servers, and printers, etc. I then created the pool named Sales_Wireless, added the default gateway and DNS server, and set the lease to 3 days, 12 hours, and 15 minutes (which isn't really significant because I just set it that way for demonstration purposes). Pretty straightforward, right? The switch will now respond to DHCP client requests. But what happens if we need to provide an IP address from a DHCP server to a host that's not in our broadcast domain, or if we want to receive a DHCP address for a client from a remote server?

Relay

If you need to provide addresses from a DHCP server to hosts that aren't on the same LAN as the DHCP server, you can configure your router interface to relay or forward the DHCP client requests, as shown in Figure 5.2. If we don't provide this service, our router would receive the DHCP client broadcast, promptly discard it, and the remote host would never receive an address—unless we added a DHCP server on every broadcast domain! Let's take a look at how we would typically configure DHCP service in today's networks.

FIGURE 5.2   Configuring a DHCP relay

So we know that because the hosts off the router don't have access to a DHCP server, the router will simply drop their client request broadcast messages by default. To solve this problem, we can configure the Fa0/0 interface of the router to accept the DHCP client requests and forward them to the DHCP server like this:

```
Router#config t
Router(config)#interface fa0/0
Router(config-if)#ip helper-address 10.10.10.254
```

Now I know that was a pretty simple example, and there are definitely other ways to configure the relay, but rest assured that I've covered this objective for you. Also, I want you to know that ip helper-address forwards more than just DHCP client requests, so be sure to research this command before you implement it! Now that I've demonstrated how to create the DHCP service, let's take a minute to verify DHCP before moving on to NTP.

Client

The client configuration merely consists of configuring the router or switch as a DHCP client. This is done on a per-interface basis. On each interface, rather than configuring an IP address, execute the following command:

```
Router(config-if)#ip address dhcp
```

TFTP, DNS, and Gateway Options

Specifying a default gateway and a DNS server for DHCP clients was covered in the section "Server." To provide a TFTP server address of 192.168.2.9, execute the following command at the dhcp pool configuration prompt:

```
Router(config)#ip dhcp pool 50
Router(dhcp-config)#option 150 ip 192.168.2.9
```

Exam Essentials

Describe the functions of DHCP in the network.   Dynamic Host Configuration Protocol (DHCP) provides network configuration information (including IP addresses) to hosts, eliminating the need to perform the configurations manually.

Troubleshoot client- and router-based DHCP connectivity issues

Consider the following DHCP configuration:

```
Corp#config t
Corp(config)#ip dhcp excluded-address 192.168.10.1
```

```
Corp(config)#ip dhcp excluded-address 192.168.20.1
Corp(config)#ip dhcp pool SF_LAN
Corp(dhcp-config)#network 192.168.10.0 255.255.255.0
Corp(dhcp-config)#default-router 192.168.10.1
Corp(dhcp-config)#dns-server 4.4.4.4
Corp(dhcp-config)#exit
Corp(config)#ip dhcp pool LA_LAN
Corp(dhcp-config)#network 192.168.20.0 255.255.255.0
Corp(dhcp-config)#default-router 192.168.20.1
Corp(dhcp-config)#dns-server 4.4.4.4
Corp(dhcp-config)#exit
Corp(config)#exit
Corp#copy run start
Destination filename [startup-config]?
Building configuration...
```

Creating DHCP pools on a router is actually a simple process, and you would go about the configuration the same way on any router you wish to add a DHCP pool to. To designate a router as a DHCP server, you just create the pool name, add the network/subnet and the default gateway, and then exclude any addresses that you don't want handed out. You definitely want to make sure you've excluded the default gateway address, and you'd usually add a DNS server as well. I always add any exclusions first, and remember that you can conveniently exclude a range of addresses on a single line. Soon, I'll demonstrate verification commands, but first, we need to figure out why the Corp router can't assign IP addresses to remote networks by default!

Now I'm pretty sure I configured DHCP correctly, but I just have this nagging feeling I forgot something important. What could that be? Well, if some hosts are remote across a router, what would I need to do that would allow them to get an address from a DHCP server? If you concluded that I've got to configure the local router interfaces in those remote networks to forward the DHCP client requests to the server, you got it! For example if I had two routers (LA and SF) that I wanted to perform this forwarding, I would configure them with the IP address of the DHCP server (Corp).

Here's how we'd go about doing that:

```
LA#config t
LA(config)#int f0/0
LA(config-if)#ip helper-address 172.16.20.1
```

```
SF#config t
SF(config)#int f0/0
SF(config-if)#ip helper-address 172.16.10.1
```

Now to test my configuration of the DHCP server on the Corp router. I'm going to go to each host on the SF and LA routers and make them DHCP clients. By the way, I'm using an old router to represent "hosts," which just happens to work great for studying purposes. Here's how I did that:

```
SF_PC(config)#int e0
SF_PC(config-if)#ip address dhcp
SF_PC(config-if)#no shut
Interface Ethernet0 assigned DHCP address 192.168.10.8, mask 255.255.255.0
LA_PC(config)#int e0
LA_PC(config-if)#ip addr dhcp
LA_PC(config-if)#no shut
Interface Ethernet0 assigned DHCP address 192.168.20.4, mask 255.255.255.0
```

Nice! Don't you love it when things just work the first time? Sadly, this just isn't exactly a realistic expectation in the networking world, so we must be able to troubleshoot and verify our networks. Let's verify our DHCP server with a few show commands:

```
Corp#sh ip dhcp binding
Bindings from all pools not associated with VRF:
IP address          Client-ID/                Lease expiration        Type
                    Hardware address/
                    User name
192.168.10.8        0063.6973.636f.2d30.      Sept 16 2013 10:34 AM    Automatic
                    3035.302e.3062.6330.
                    2e30.3063.632d.4574.
                    30
192.168.20.4        0063.6973.636f.2d30.      Sept 16 2013 10:46 AM    Automatic
                    3030.322e.3137.3632.
                    2e64.3032.372d.4574.
                    30
```

We can see from earlier that our little DHCP server is working! Let's try another couple of commands:

```
Corp#sh ip dhcp pool SF_LAN
Pool SF_LAN :
 Utilization mark (high/low)    : 100 / 0
 Subnet size (first/next)       : 0 / 0
 Total addresses                : 254
 Leased addresses               : 3
 Pending event                  : none
 1 subnet is currently in the pool :
 Current index        IP address range                      Leased addresses
```

```
 192.168.10.9        192.168.10.1   - 192.168.10.254    3

Corp#sh ip dhcp conflict
IP address          Detection method  Detection time           VRF
```

The last command would tell us if we had two hosts with the same IP address, so it's good news because there are no conflicts reported! Two detection methods are used to confirm this:

- A ping from the DHCP server to make sure no other host responds before handing out an address

- A gratuitous ARP from a host that receives a DHCP address from the server

The DHCP client will send an ARP request with its new IP address, looking to see if anyone responds, and if so, it will report the conflict to the server.

Exam Essentials

Troubleshoot DHCP in the network.   Use the show ip dhcp pool, show ip dhcp binding, and show ip dhcp conflict commands to identify issues preventing proper operation of DHCP.

Configure, verify, and troubleshoot basic HSRP

HSRP is a Cisco proprietary protocol that can be run on most, but not all, of Cisco's router and multilayer switch models. It defines a standby group, and each standby group that you define includes the following routers:

- Active router
- Standby router
- Virtual router
- Any other routers that may be attached to the subnet

The problem with HSRP is that with it, only one router is active and two or more routers just sit there in standby mode and won't be used unless a failure occurs—not very cost effective or efficient! Figure 5.3 shows how only one router is used at a time in an HSRP group. The standby group will always have at least two routers participating in it. The primary players in the group are the one active router and one standby router that communicate to each other using multicast Hello messages. The Hello messages provide all of the required communication for the routers. The Hellos contain the information required to accomplish the election that determines the active and standby router positions. They also hold the key to the failover process. If the standby router stops receiving Hello packets from the active router, it then takes over the active router role, as shown in Figure 5.4.

FIGURE 5.3   HSRP active and standby routers

FIGURE 5.4   Example of HSRP active and standby routers swapping interfaces

Real World Scenario

Large Enterprise Network Outages with FHRPs

Years ago when HSRP was all the rage, and before VRRP and GLBP, enterprises used hundreds of HSRP groups. With the hello timer set to 3 seconds and a hold time of 10 seconds, these timers worked just fine and we had great redundancy with our core routers.

However, as we've seen in the last few years and certainly will see in the future, 10 seconds is now a lifetime! Some of my customers have been complaining with the failover time and loss of connectivity to their virtual server farm.

So lately I've been changing the timers to well below the defaults. Cisco had changed the timers so you could use sub-second times for failover. Because these are multicast packets, the overhead that is seen on a current high-speed network is almost nothing.

The hello timer is typically set to 200 msec and the hold time is 700 msec. The command is as follows:

```
(config-if)#Standby 1 timers msec 200 msec 700
```

This almost ensures that not even a single packet is lost when there is an outage.

Group Roles

Each of the routers in the standby group has a specific function and role to fulfill. The three main roles are as virtual router, active router, and standby router. Additional routers can also be included in the group.

Virtual router   As its name implies, the virtual router is not a physical entity. It really just defines the role that's held by one of the physical routers. The physical router that communicates as the virtual router is the current active router. The virtual router is nothing more than a separate IP address and MAC address to which packets are sent.

Active router   The active router is the physical router that receives data sent to the virtual router address and routes it onward to its various destinations. As I mentioned, this router accepts all the data sent to the MAC address of the virtual router in addition to the data that's been sent to its own physical MAC address. The active router processes the data that's being forwarded and will also answer any ARP requests destined for the virtual router's IP address.

Standby router   The standby router is the backup to the active router. Its job is to monitor the status of the HSRP group and quickly take over packet-forwarding responsibilities if the active router fails or loses communication. Both the active and standby routers transmit Hello messages to inform all other routers in the group of their role and status.

Other routers   An HSRP group can include additional routers, which are members of the group but don't take the primary roles of either active or standby states. These routers monitor the Hello messages sent by the active and standby routers to ensure that an active and standby router exists for the HSRP group that they belong to. They will forward data that's specifically addressed to their own IP addresses, but they will never forward data addressed to the virtual router unless elected to the active or standby state. These routers send "speak" messages based on the hello timer interval that informs other routers of their position in an election.

Interface Tracking

By now, you probably understand why having a virtual router on a LAN is a great idea. You also know why it's a very good thing that the active router can change dynamically, giving us much needed redundancy on our inside network. But what about the links to the upstream network or the Internet connection off of those HSRP-enabled routers? And how will the inside hosts know if an outside interface goes down or if they are sending packets to an active router that can't route to a remote network? Key questions, and HSRP does provide a solution for them; it's called interface tracking.

Figure 5.6 shows how HSRP-enabled routers can keep track of the interface status of the outside interfaces and how they can switch the inside active router as needed to keep the inside hosts from losing connectivity upstream.

FIGURE 5.6   Interface tracking setup

If the outside link of the active router goes down, the standby router will take over and become the active router. There is a default priority of 100 on routers configured with an HSRP interface, and if you raise this priority (we'll do this in a minute), it means your router has a higher priority to become the active router. The reason I am bringing this up now is because when a tracked interface goes down, it decrements the priority of the router on which the tracked interface went down.

Configuring and Verifying HSRP

Configuring and verifying the different HSRP can be pretty simple, especially regarding the Cisco objectives, but as with most technologies, you can quickly get into advanced configurations and territory with HSRP if you're not careful, so I'll show you exactly what you need to know.

The Cisco objectives don't cover much about the configuration of HSRP, but verification and troubleshooting is important, so I'll use a simple configuration on two routers here. Figure 5.7 shows the network I'll use to demonstrate HSRP.

FIGURE 5.7 HSRP configuration and verification

Gateway: 10.1.1.10

   This is a simple configuration for which you really need only one command:
standby *group* ip *virtual_ip*. After using this single mandatory command, I'll name the
group and set the interface on router HSRP1 so it wins the election and becomes the active
router by default.

```
HSRP1#config t
HSRP1(config)#int fa0/0
HSRP1(config-if)#standby ?
  <0-255>        group number
  authentication Authentication
  delay          HSRP initialisation delay
  ip             Enable HSRP and set the virtual IP address
  mac-address    Virtual MAC address
  name           Redundancy name string
  preempt        Overthrow lower priority Active routers
  priority       Priority level
  redirect       Configure sending of ICMP Redirect messages with an HSRP
                 virtual IP address as the gateway IP address
  timers         Hello and hold timers
  track          Priority tracking
  use-bia        HSRP uses interface's burned in address
  version        HSRP version
HSRP1(config-if)#standby 1 ip 10.1.1.10
HSRP1(config-if)#standby 1 name HSRP_Test
HSRP1(config-if)#standby 1 priority ?
  <0-255>  Priority value

HSRP1(config-if)#standby 1 priority 110
000047: %HSRP-5-STATECHANGE: FastEthernet0/0 Grp 1 state Speak -> Standby
000048: %HSRP-5-STATECHANGE: FastEthernet0/0 Grp 1 state Standby -> Active110
```

Priority

There are quite a few commands available to use in an advanced setting with the standby
command, but we'll stick with the simple commands that follow the Cisco objectives. First,
I numbered the group (1), which must be the same on all routers sharing HSRP duties; then
I added the virtual IP address shared by all routers in the HSRP group. Optionally, I named
the group and then set the priority of HSRP1 to 110, and I left HSRP2 to a default of 100.
The router with the highest priority will win the election to become the active router. Let's
configure the HSRP2 router now:

```
HSRP2#config t
HSRP2(config)#int fa0/0
HSRP2(config-if)#standby 1 ip 10.1.1.10
```

```
HSRP2(config-if)#standby 1 name HSRP_Test
*Jun 23 21:40:10.699:%HSRP-5-STATECHANGE:FastEthernet0/0 Grp 1 state
Speak -> Standby
```

I really only needed the first command—naming it was for administrative purposes only. Notice that the link came up and HSRP2 became the standby router because it had the lower priority of 100 (the default). Make a note that this priority comes into play only if both routers were to come up at the same time. This means that HSRP2 would be the active router, regardless of the priority, if it comes up first.

Let's take a look at the configurations with the show standby and show standby brief commands:

```
HSRP1(config-if)#do show standby
FastEthernet0/0 - Group 1
  State is Active
    2 state changes, last state change 00:03:40
  Virtual IP address is 10.1.1.10
  Active virtual MAC address is 0000.0c07.ac01
    Local virtual MAC address is 0000.0c07.ac01 (v1 default)
  Hello time 3 sec, hold time 10 sec
    Next hello sent in 1.076 secs
  Preemption disabled
  Active router is local
  Standby router is 10.1.1.2, priority 100 (expires in 7.448 sec)
  Priority 110 (configured 110)
  IP redundancy name is "HSRP_Test" (cfgd)


HSRP1(config-if)#do show standby brief
                     P indicates configured to preempt.
                     |
Interface  Grp Prio P State   Active          Standby         Virtual IP
Fa0/0       1   110   Active   local           10.1.1.2        10.1.1.10
```

Notice the group number in each output—it's a key troubleshooting spot! Each router must be configured in the same group or they won't work. Also, you can see the virtual MAC and configured virtual IP address, as well as the hello time of 3 seconds. The standby and virtual IP addresses are also displayed.

HSRP2's output tells us that it's in standby mode:

```
HSRP2(config-if)#do show standby brief
                     P indicates configured to preempt.
                     |
Interface  Grp Prio P State   Active          Standby         Virtual IP
Fa0/0       1   100   Standby 10.1.1.1        local           10.1.1.10
HRSP2(config-if)#
```

Notice so far that you have seen HSRP states of active and standby, but watch what happens when I disable Fa0/0:

```
HSRP1#config t
HSRP1(config)#interface Fa0/0
HSRP1(config-if)#shutdown
*Nov 20 10:06:52.369: %HSRP-5-STATECHANGE: Ethernet0/0 Grp 1 state Active -> Init
```

The HSRP went into Init state, meaning it's trying to initialize with a peer. The possible interface states for HSRP are shown in Table 5.1.

TABLE 5.1   HSRP states

State	Definition
Initial (INIT)	This is the state at the start. This state indicates that HSRP does not run. This state is entered through a configuration change or when an interface first becomes available.
Learn	The router has not determined the virtual IP address and has not yet seen an authenticated Hello message from the active router. In this state, the router still waits to hear from the active router.
Listen	The router knows the virtual IP address, but the router is neither the active router nor the standby router. It listens for Hello messages from those routers.
Speak	The router sends periodic Hello messages and actively participates in the election of the active and/or standby router. A router cannot enter speak state unless the router has the virtual IP address.
Standby	The router is a candidate to become the next active router and sends periodic Hello messages. With the exclusion of transient conditions, there is, at most, one router in the group in standby state.
Active	The router currently forwards packets that are sent to the group virtual MAC address. The router sends periodic Hello messages. With the exclusion of transient conditions, there must be, at most, one router in the active state in the group.

There is one other command that I want to cover. If you're studying and want to understand HSRP, you should learn to use this debug command and have your active and standby routers move. You'll really get to see what is going on:

```
HSRP2#debug standby
*Sep 15 00:07:32.344:HSRP:Fa0/0 Interface UP
```

```
*Sep 15 00:07:32.344:HSRP:Fa0/0 Initialize swsb, Intf state Up
*Sep 15 00:07:32.344:HSRP:Fa0/0 Starting minimum intf delay (1 secs)
*Sep 15 00:07:32.344:HSRP:Fa0/0 Grp 1 Set virtual MAC 0000.0c07.ac01
type: v1 default
*Sep 15 00:07:32.344:HSRP:Fa0/0 MAC hash entry 0000.0c07.ac01, Added
Fa0/0 Grp 1 to list
*Sep 15 00:07:32.348:HSRP:Fa0/0 Added 10.1.1.10 to hash table
*Sep 15 00:07:32.348:HSRP:Fa0/0 Grp 1 Has mac changed? cur 0000.0c07.ac01
new 0000.0c07.ac01
*Sep 15 00:07:32.348:HSRP:Fa0/0 Grp 1 Disabled -> Init
*Sep 15 00:07:32.348:HSRP:Fa0/0 Grp 1 Redundancy "hsrp-Fa0/0-1" state
Disabled -> Init
*Sep 15 00:07:32.348:HSRP:Fa0/0 IP Redundancy "hsrp-Fa0/0-1" added
*Sep 15 00:07:32.348:HSRP:Fa0/0 IP Redundancy "hsrp-Fa0/0-1" update,
Disabled -> Init
*Sep 15 00:07:33.352:HSRP:Fa0/0 Intf min delay expired
*Sep 15 00:07:39.936:HSRP:Fa0/0 Grp 1 MAC addr update Delete
from SMF  0000.0c07.ac01
*Sep 15 00:07:39.936:HSRP:Fa0/0 Grp 1 MAC addr update Delete
from SMF  0000.0c07.ac01
*Sep 15 00:07:39.940:HSRP:Fa0/0 ARP reload
```

HSRP Load Balancing

As you know, HSRP doesn't really perform true load balancing, but it can be configured to use more than one router at a time for use with different VLANs. This is different from the true load balancing that's possible with GLBP, which I'll demonstrate in a minute, but HSRP still performs a load-balancing act of sorts. Figure 5.8 shows how load balancing would look with HSRP.

How can you get two HSRP routers active at the same time? Well for the same subnet with this simple configuration, you can't, but if you trunk the links to each router, they'll run and be configured with a "router on a stick" (ROAS) configuration. This means that each router can be the default gateway for different VLANs, but you still can have only one active router per VLAN. Typically, in a more advanced setting you won't use HSRP for load balancing; you'll use GLBP, but you can do load-sharing with HSRP, and that is the topic of an objective, so we'll remember that, right? It comes in handy because it prevents situations where a single point of failure causes traffic interruptions. This HSRP feature improves network resilience by allowing for load-balancing and redundancy capabilities between subnets and VLANs.

FIGURE 5.8   HSRP load balancing per VLAN

Preemption

When preemption is set, it allows a router than has gone down to reassume the position of active router when it comes back online. It is set under the interface using the following command, where 1 is the group number.

```
Router(config-if)#standy 1 preempt
```

Version

HSRP comes in two versions, 1 and 2. If there is a version mismatch, both routers will become active and you'll again have duplicate IP address warnings.

In version 1, HSRP messages are sent to the multicast IP address 224.0.0.2 and UDP port 1985. HSRP version 2 uses the multicast IP address 224.0.0.102 and UDP port 1985. These IP addresses and ports need to be permitted in the inbound access lists. If the packets are blocked, the peers will not see each other and there will be no HSRP redundancy.

HSRP Troubleshooting

Besides HSRP verification, the troubleshooting of HSRP is the Cisco objective hotspot, so let's go through this.

Most of your HSRP misconfiguration issues can be solved by checking the output of the show standby command. In the output, you can see the active IP and the MAC address, the timers, the active router, and more, as shown earlier in the verification section.

There are several possible misconfigurations of HSRP, but these are what you need to pay attention to for your CCNA. Other than a version mismatch, you can run into these other issues:

Different HSRP virtual IP addresses configured on the peers   Console messages will notify you about this, of course, but if you configure it this way and the active router fails, the standby router takes over with a virtual IP address, which is different than the one used previously, and different than the one configured as the default-gateway address for end devices, so your hosts stop working, which defeats the purpose of a FHRP.

Different HSRP groups configured on the peers   This misconfiguration leads to both peers becoming active, and you'll start receiving duplicate IP address warnings.

Exam Essentials

Remember the HSRP virtual address.   The HSRP MAC address has only one variable piece in it. The first 24 bits still identify the vendor who manufactured the device (the organizationally unique identifier, or OUI). The next 16 bits in the address tell us that the MAC address is a well-known HSRP MAC address. Finally, the last 8 bits of the address are the hexadecimal representation of the HSRP group number.

Let me clarify all this with an example of what an HSRP MAC address would look like:

```
0000.0c07.ac0a
```

Configure, verify, and troubleshoot inside source NAT

Network Address Translation (NAT) is similar to Classless Inter-Domain Routing (CIDR) in that the original intention for NAT was to slow the depletion of available IP address space by allowing multiple private IP addresses to be represented by a much smaller number of public IP addresses.

Since then, it's been discovered that NAT is also a useful tool for network migrations and mergers, server load sharing, and creating "virtual servers." So in the following sections, I'm going to describe the basics of NAT functionality and the terminology common to NAT.

Because NAT really decreases the overwhelming amount of public IP addresses required in a networking environment, it comes in really handy when two companies that have duplicate internal addressing schemes merge. NAT is also a great tool to use when an organization changes its Internet service provider (ISP) but the networking manager needs to avoid the hassle of changing the internal address scheme.

Here's a list of situations when NAT can be especially helpful:

- When you need to connect to the Internet and your hosts don't have globally unique IP addresses

- When you've changed to a new ISP that requires you to renumber your network

- When you need to merge two intranets with duplicate addresses

Static

This type of NAT is designed to allow one-to-one mapping between local and global addresses. Keep in mind that the static version requires you to have one real Internet IP address for every host on your network.

Let's take a look at a simple example of a basic static NAT configuration:

```
ip nat inside source static 10.1.1.1 170.46.2.2
!
interface Ethernet0
 ip address 10.1.1.10 255.255.255.0
 ip nat inside
!
interface Serial0
 ip address 170.46.2.1 255.255.255.0
 ip nat outside
!
```

In the preceding router output, the ip nat inside source command identifies which IP addresses will be translated. In this configuration example, the ip nat inside source command configures a static translation between the inside local IP address 10.1.1.1 and the outside global IP address 170.46.2.2.

Scrolling farther down in the configuration, we find an ip nat command under each interface. The ip nat inside command identifies that interface as the inside interface. The ip nat outside command identifies that interface as the outside interface. When you look back at the ip nat inside source command, you can see that the command is referencing the inside interface as the source or starting point of the translation. You could also use the command like this: ip nat outside source. This option indicates that the interface you designated as the outside interface should become the source or starting point for the translation.

Pool

This type gives you the ability to map an unregistered IP address to a registered IP address from out of a pool of registered IP addresses. You don't have to statically configure your router to map each inside address to an individual outside address as you would using static NAT, but you do have to have enough real, bona fide IP addresses for everyone who's going to be sending packets to and receiving them from the Internet at the same time.

Basically, dynamic NAT really means we have a pool of addresses that we'll use to provide real IP addresses to a group of users on the inside. Because we don't use port numbers, we must have real IP addresses for every user who's trying to get outside the local network simultaneously.

Here is a sample output of a dynamic NAT configuration:

```
ip nat pool todd 170.168.2.3 170.168.2.254
    netmask 255.255.255.0
ip nat inside source list 1 pool todd
!
interface Ethernet0
 ip address 10.1.1.10 255.255.255.0
 ip nat inside
!
interface Serial0
 ip address 170.168.2.1 255.255.255.0
 ip nat outside
!
access-list 1 permit 10.1.1.0 0.0.0.255
!
```

The ip nat inside source list 1 pool todd command tells the router to translate IP addresses that match access-list 1 to an address found in the IP NAT pool named todd. Here the ACL isn't there to filter traffic for security reasons by permitting or denying traffic. In this case, it's there to select or designate what we often call interesting traffic. When interesting traffic has been matched with the access list, it's pulled into the NAT process to be translated. This is actually a common use for access lists, which aren't always just stuck with the dull job of just blocking traffic at an interface!

The command ip nat pool todd 170.168.2.3 170.168.2.254 netmask 255 .255.255.0 creates a pool of addresses that will be distributed to the specific hosts that require global addresses. When troubleshooting NAT for the Cisco objectives, always check this pool to confirm that there are enough addresses in it to provide translation for all the inside hosts. Last, check to make sure the pool names match exactly on both lines, remembering that they are case sensitive; if they don't, the pool won't work!

PAT

This is the most popular type of NAT configuration. Understand that overloading really is a form of dynamic NAT that maps multiple unregistered IP addresses to a single registered IP address (many-to-one) by using different source ports. Now, why is this so special? Well, because it's also known as *Port Address Translation (PAT)*, which is also commonly referred to as NAT Overload. Using PAT allows you to permit thousands of users to connect to the Internet using only one real global IP address—pretty slick, right? Seriously, NAT Overload is the real reason we haven't run out of valid IP addresses on the Internet. Really—I'm not joking!

This last example shows how to configure inside global address overloading. This is the typical form of NAT that we would use today. It's actually now rare to use static or dynamic NAT unless it is for something like statically mapping a server, for example.

Here is a sample output of a PAT configuration:

```
ip nat pool globalnet 170.168.2.1 170.168.2.1 netmask 255.255.255.0
ip nat inside source list 1 pool globalnet overload
!
interface Ethernet0/0
 ip address 10.1.1.10 255.255.255.0
 ip nat inside
!
interface Serial0/0
 ip address 170.168.2.1 255.255.255.0
 ip nat outside
!
access-list 1 permit 10.1.1.0 0.0.0.255
```

The nice thing about PAT is that these are the only differences between this configuration and the previous dynamic NAT configuration:

- Our pool of addresses has shrunk to only one IP address.
- We included the overload keyword at the end of our ip nat inside source command.

A really key factor to see in the example is that the one IP address that's in the pool for us to use is the IP address of the outside interface. This is perfect if you are configuring NAT Overload for yourself at home or for a small office that only has one IP address from your ISP. You could, however, use an additional address such as 170.168.2.2 if you had that address available to you as well, and doing that could prove very helpful in a very large implementation where you've got such an abundance of simultaneously active internal users that you need to have more than one overloaded IP address on the outside!

Simple Verification of NAT

As always, once you've chosen and configured the type of NAT you're going to run, which is typically PAT, you must be able to verify your configuration.

To see basic IP address translation information, use the following command:

```
Router#show ip nat translations
```

When looking at the IP NAT translations, you may see many translations from the same host to the corresponding host at the destination. Understand that this is typical when there are many connections to the same server.

You can also verify your NAT configuration via the debug ip nat command. This output will show the sending address, the translation, and the destination address on each debug line:

```
Router#debug ip nat
```

But wait—how do you clear your NAT entries from the translation table? Just use the clear ip nat translation command, and if you want to clear all entries from the NAT table, just use an asterisk (*) at the end of the command.

Testing and Troubleshooting NAT

Cisco's NAT gives you some serious power—and it does so without much effort, because the configurations are really pretty simple. But we all know nothing's perfect, so in case something goes wrong, you can figure out some of the more common culprits by running through this list of potential causes:

- Check the dynamic pools. Are they composed of the right scope of addresses?
- Check to see if any dynamic pools overlap.
- Check to see if the addresses used for static mapping and those in the dynamic pools overlap.
- Ensure that your access lists specify the correct addresses for translation.
- Make sure there aren't any addresses left out that need to be there, and ensure that none are included that shouldn't be.
- Check to make sure you've got both the inside and outside interfaces delimited properly.

A key thing to keep in mind is that one of the most common problems with a new NAT configuration often isn't specific to NAT at all—it usually involves a routing blooper. So, because you're changing a source or destination address in a packet, make sure your router still knows what to do with the new address after the translation!

The first command you should typically use is the show ip nat translations command:

```
Router#show ip nat trans
Pro    Inside global    Inside local    Outside local    Outside global
---    192.2.2.1        10.1.1.1        ---              ---
---    192.2.2.2        10.1.1.2        ---              ---
```

After checking out this output, can you tell me if the configuration on the router is static or dynamic NAT? The answer is yes, either static or dynamic NAT is configured because there's a one-to-one translation from the inside local to the inside global. Basically, by looking at the output, you can't tell if it's static or dynamic per se, but you absolutely can tell that you're not using PAT because there are no port numbers.

Let's take a look at another output:

```
Router#sh ip nat trans
Pro Inside global      Inside local       Outside local       Outside global
tcp 170.168.2.1:11003  10.1.1.1:11003     172.40.2.2:23       172.40.2.2:23
tcp 170.168.2.1:1067   10.1.1.1:1067      172.40.2.3:23       172.40.2.3:23
```

Okay, you can easily see that the previous output is using NAT Overload (PAT). The protocol in this output is TCP, and the inside global address is the same for both entries.

Supposedly the sky's the limit regarding the number of mappings the NAT table can hold. But this is reality, so things like memory and CPU, or even the boundaries set in place by the scope of available addresses or ports, can cause limitations on the actual number of entries. Consider that each NAT mapping devours about 160 bytes of memory. And sometimes the amount of entries must be limited for the sake of performance or because of policy restrictions, but this doesn't happen very often. In situations like these, just go to the `ip nat translation max-entries` command for help.

Another handy command for troubleshooting is `show ip nat statistics`. Deploying this gives you a summary of the NAT configuration, and it will count the number of active translation types too. Also counted are hits to an existing mapping as well any misses, with the latter causing an attempt to create a mapping. This command will also reveal expired translations. If you want to check into dynamic pools, their types, the total available addresses, how many addresses have been allocated and how many have failed, plus the number of translations that have occurred, just use the `pool` keyword.

Here is an example of the basic NAT debugging command:

```
Router#debug ip nat
NAT: s=10.1.1.1->192.168.2.1, d=172.16.2.2 [0]
NAT: s=172.16.2.2, d=192.168.2.1->10.1.1.1 [0]
NAT: s=10.1.1.1->192.168.2.1, d=172.16.2.2 [1]
NAT: s=10.1.1.1->192.168.2.1, d=172.16.2.2 [2]
NAT: s=10.1.1.1->192.168.2.1, d=172.16.2.2 [3]
NAT*: s=172.16.2.2, d=192.168.2.1->10.1.1.1 [1]
```

Notice the last line in the output and how the NAT at the beginning of the line has an asterisk (*). This means the packet was translated and fast-switched to the destination. What's fast-switched? Well in brief, fast-switching has gone by several aliases, such as cache-based switching and this nicely descriptive name, "route one switch many." The fast-switching process is used on Cisco routers to create a cache of layer 3 routing information to be accessed at layer 2 so packets can be forwarded quickly through a router without the routing table having to be parsed for every packet. As packets are packet switched (looked up in the routing table), this information is stored in the cache for later use if needed for faster routing processing.

Let's get back to verifying NAT. Did you know you can manually clear dynamic NAT entries from the NAT table? You can, and doing this can come in seriously handy if you need to get rid of a specific rotten entry without sitting around waiting for the timeout to expire! A manual clear is also really useful when you want to clear the whole NAT table to reconfigure a pool of addresses.

You also need to know that the Cisco IOS software just won't allow you to change or delete an address pool if any of that pool's addresses are mapped in the NAT table. The clear ip nat translations command clears entries—you can indicate a single entry via the global and local address and through TCP and UDP translations, including ports, or you can just type in an asterisk (*) to wipe out the entire table. But know that if you do that, only dynamic entries will be cleared because this command won't remove static entries.

Oh, and there's more—any outside device's packet destination address that happens to be responding to any inside device is known as the inside global (IG) address. This means that the initial mapping has to be held in the NAT table so that all packets arriving from a specific connection get translated consistently. Holding entries in the NAT table also cuts down on repeated translation operations happening each time the same inside machine sends packets to the same outside destinations on a regular basis.

Let me clarify: When an entry is placed into the NAT table the first time, a timer begins ticking and its duration is known as the translation timeout. Each time a packet for a given entry translates through the router, the timer gets reset. If the timer expires, the entry will be unceremoniously removed from the NAT table and the dynamically assigned address will then be returned to the pool. Cisco's default translation timeout is 86,400 seconds (24 hours), but you can change that with the ip nat translation timeout command.

Before we move on to actually using the commands I just talked about, let's go through a couple of NAT examples and see if you can figure out the best configuration to go with. To start, look at Figure 5.9 and ask yourself two things: Where would you implement NAT in this design? What type of NAT would you configure?

FIGURE 5.9   NAT example

In Figure 5.9, the NAT configuration would be placed on the Corporate router, and the configuration would be dynamic NAT with overload (PAT). In this next NAT example, what type of NAT is being used?

```
ip nat pool todd-nat 170.168.10.10 170.168.10.20 netmask 255.255.255.0
ip nat inside source list 1 pool todd-nat
```

The preceding command uses dynamic NAT without PAT. The pool in the command gives the answer away as dynamic, plus there's more than one address in the pool and there is no overload command at the end of our ip nat inside source command. This means we are not using PAT!

In the next NAT example, refer to Figure 5.10 and see if you can come up with the configuration needed.

FIGURE 5.10 Another NAT example

Console

Figure 5.10 shows a border router that needs to be configured with NAT and allow the use of six public IP addresses to the inside locals, 192.1.2.109 through 192.1.2.114. However, on the inside network, you have 62 hosts that use the private addresses of 192.168.10.65 through 192.168.10.126. What would your NAT configuration be on the border router?

Actually, two different answers would both work here, but the following would be my first choice based on the exam objectives:

```
ip nat pool Todd 192.1.2.109 192.1.2.109 netmask 255.255.255.248
access-list 1 permit 192.168.10.64 0.0.0.63
ip nat inside source list 1 pool Todd overload
```

The command ip nat pool Todd 192.1.2.109 192.1.2.109 netmask 255 .255.255.248 sets the pool name as Todd and creates a dynamic pool of only one address using NAT address 192.1.2.109. Instead of the netmask command, you can use the prefix-length 29 statement. Just in case you're wondering, you cannot do this on router interfaces as well!

The second answer would get you the exact same result of having only 192.1.2.109 as your inside global, but you can type this in and it will also work: `ip nat pool Todd 192 .1.2.109 192.1.2.114 netmask 255.255.255.248`. But this option really is a waste because the second through sixth addresses would only be used if there was a conflict with a TCP port number. You would use something like what I've shown in this example if you literally had about ten thousand hosts with one Internet connection! You would need it to help with the TCP-Reset issue when two hosts are trying to use the same source port number and get a negative acknowledgment (NAK). But in our example, we've only got up to 62 hosts connecting to the Internet at the same time, so having more than one inside global gets us nothing!

If you're fuzzy on the second line where the access list is set in the NAT configuration, this will become clearer when we cover access lists in Chapter 6, "Infrastructure Security." But this isn't difficult to grasp because it's easy to see in this access-list line that it's just the *network number* and *wildcard* used with that command. I always say, "Every question is a subnet question," and this one is no exception. The inside locals in this example were 192.168.10.65–126, which is a block of 64, or a 255.255.255.192 mask. As I've said in pretty much every chapter, you really need to be able to subnet quickly!

The command `ip nat inside source list 1 pool Todd overload` sets the dynamic pool to use PAT by using the `overload` command.

And be sure to add the `ip nat inside` and `ip nat outside` statements on the appropriate interfaces.

One more example, and then you are off to review questions.

The network in Figure 5.11 is already configured with IP addresses as shown in the figure, and there is only one configured host. However, you need to add 25 more hosts to the LAN. Now, all 26 hosts must be able to get to the Internet at the same time.

FIGURE 5.11 Last NAT example

By looking at the configured network, use only the following inside addresses to configure NAT on the Corp router to allow all hosts to reach the Internet:

- **Inside globals:** 198.18.41.129 through 198.18.41.134
- **Inside locals:** 192.168.76.65 through 192.168.76.94

This one is a bit more challenging because all we have to help us figure out the configuration is the inside globals and the inside locals. But even meagerly armed with these crumbs of information, plus the IP addresses of the router interfaces shown in the figure, we can still configure this correctly.

To do that, we must first determine what our block sizes are so we can get our subnet mask for our NAT pool. This will also equip us to configure the wildcard for the access list.

You should easily be able to see that the block size of the inside globals is 8 and the block size of the inside locals is 32. Know that it's critical not to stumble on this foundational information!

So we can configure NAT now that we have our block sizes:

```
ip nat pool Corp 198.18.41.129 198.18.41.134 netmask 255.255.255.248
ip nat inside source list 1 pool Corp overload
access-list 1 permit 192.168.76.64 0.0.0.31
```

Since we had a block of only 8 for our pool, we had to use the overload command to make sure all 26 hosts can get to the Internet at the same time.

There is one other simple way to configure NAT, and I use this command at my home office to connect to my ISP. One command line and it's done! Here it is:

```
ip nat inside source list 1 int s0/0/0 overload
```

I can't say enough how much I love efficiency, and being able to achieve something cool using one measly line always makes me happy! My one little powerfully elegant line essentially says, "Use my outside local as my inside global and overload it." Nice! Of course, I still had to create ACL 1 and add the inside and outside interface commands to the configuration, but this is a really nice, fast way to configure NAT if you don't have a pool of addresses to use.

Exam Essentials

Remember the three methods of NAT.   The three methods are static, dynamic, and overloading; the latter is also called PAT.

Understand static NAT.   This type of NAT is designed to allow one-to-one mapping between local and global addresses.

Understand dynamic NAT.   This version gives you the ability to map a range of unregistered IP addresses to a registered IP address from out of a pool of registered IP addresses.

Understand overloading.   Overloading really is a form of dynamic NAT that maps multiple unregistered IP addresses to a single registered IP address (many-to-one) by using different ports. It's also known as *PAT*.

Configure and verify NTP operating in a client/server mode

Network Time Protocol provides pretty much what it describes: time to all your network devices. To be more precise, NTP synchronizes clocks of computer systems over packet-switched, variable-latency data networks.

Typically you'll have an NTP server that connects through the Internet to an atomic clock. This time can then be synchronized through the network to keep all routers, switches, servers, etc. receiving the same time information.

Correct network time within the network is important:

- Correct time allows the tracking of events in the network in the correct order.

- Clock synchronization is critical for the correct interpretation of events within the syslog data.

- Clock synchronization is critical for digital certificates.

Making sure all your devices have the correct time is especially helpful for your routers and switches for looking at logs regarding security issues or other maintenance issues. Routers and switches issue log messages when different events take place—for example, when an interface goes down and then back up. As you already know, all messages generated by the IOS go only to the console port by default. However, those console messages can be directed to a syslog server.

A syslog server saves copies of console messages and can time-stamp them so you can view them at a later time. This is actually rather easy to do. Here would be your configuration on the SF router:

SF(config)#**service timestamps log datetime msec**

Even though I had the messages time-stamped with the command
service timestamps log datetime msec, this doesn't mean that we'll know the exact time if using default clock sources.

To make sure all devices are synchronized with the same time information, we'll configure our devices to receive the accurate time information from a centralized server, as shown here in the following command and in Figure 5.12:

SF(config)#**ntp server 172.16.10.1 version 4**

FIGURE 5.12   Synchronizing time information

Just use that one simple command on all your devices and each network device on your network will then have the same exact time and date information. You can then rest assured that your time stamps are accurate. You can also make your router or switch be an NTP server with the ntp master command.

To verify that our NTP client is receiving clocking information, we use the following commands:

SF#**sh ntp ?**
   associations NTP associations

```
   status          NTP status   status      VTP domain status

SF#sh ntp status
Clock is unsynchronized, stratum 16, no reference clock
nominal freq is 119.2092 Hz, actual freq is 119.2092 Hz, precision is 2**18
reference time is 00000000.00000000 (00:00:00.000 UTC Mon Jan 1 1900)
clock offset is 0.0000 msec, root delay is 0.00 msec
S1#sh ntp associations

address     ref clock     st  when  poll reach  delay  offset     disp
~172.16.10.1  0.0.0.0        16    -    64    0    0.0    0.00   16000.
 * master (synced), # master (unsynced), + selected, - candidate, ~ configured
```

You can see in the example that the NTP client in SF is not synchronized with the server by using the show ntp status command. The stratum value is a number from 1 to 15, and a lower stratum value indicates a higher NTP priority; 16 means there is no clocking received.

There are many other configurations of an NTP client that are available, such as authentication of NTP so a router or switch isn't fooled into changing the time of an attack, for example.

Exam Essentials

Understand how to configure NTP.   It's pretty simple to configure NTP, just like it was syslog, but we don't have to remember a bunch of options! It's just telling the syslog to mark the time and date and enable NTP:

```
SF(config)#service timestamps log datetime msec
SF(config)#ntp server 172.16.10.1 version 4
```

Review Questions

You can find the answers in the Appendix.

1. You need to configure all your routers and switches so they synchronize their clocks from one time source. What command will you type for each device?

    A. `clock synchronization ip_address`

    B. `ntp master ip_address`

    C. `sync ntp ip_address`

    D. `ntp server ip_address version number`

2. Which of the following are HSRP states? (Choose two.)

    A. INIT

    B. Active

    C. Established

    D. Idle

3. Which command configures an interface to enable HSRP with the virtual router IP address 10.1.1.10?

    A. `standby 1 ip 10.1.1.10`

    B. `ip hsrp 1 standby 10.1.1.10`

    C. `hsrp 1 ip 10.1.1.10`

    D. `standby 1 hsrp ip 10.1.1.10`

4. Which command displays the status of all HSRP groups on a Cisco router or layer 3 switch?

    A. `show ip hsrp`

    B. `show hsrp`

    C. `show standby hsrp`

    D. `show standby`

    E. `show hsrp groups`

5. Two routers are part of an HSRP standby group and there is no priority configured on the routers for the HSRP group. Which of the following statements is correct?

    A. Both routers will be in the active state.

    B. Both routers will be in the standby state.

    C. Both routers will be in the listen state.

    D. One router will be active, the other standby.

6. Which of the following statements is true about the HSRP version 1 Hello packet?

    A. HSRP Hello packets are sent to multicast address 224.0.0.5.

    B. HSRP RP Hello packets are sent to multicast address 224.0.0.2 with TCP port 1985.

    C. HSRP Hello packets are sent to multicast address 224.0.0.2 with UDP port 1985.

    D. HSRP Hello packets are sent to multicast address 224.0.0.10 with UDP port 1986.

7. Routers HSRP1 and HSRP2 are in HSRP group 1. HSRP1 is the active router with a priority of 120 and HSRP2 has the default priority. When HSRP1 reboots, HSRP2 will become the active router. Once HSRP1 comes back up, which of the following statements will be true? (Choose two.)

    A. HSRP1 will become the active router.

    B. HSRP2 will stay the active router.

    C. HSRP1 will become the active router if it is also configured to preempt.

    D. Both routers will go into speak state.

8. What is the multicast and port number used for HSRP version 2?

    A. 224.0.0.2, UDP port 1985

    B. 224.0.0.2, TCP port 1985

    C. 224.0.0.102, UDP port 1985

    D. 224.0.0.102, TCP port 1985

9. Which of the following are disadvantages of using NAT? (Choose three.)

    A. Translation introduces switching path delays.

    B. NAT conserves legally registered addresses.

    C. NAT causes loss of end-to-end IP traceability.

    D. NAT increases flexibility when connecting to the Internet.

    E. Certain applications will not function with NAT enabled.

    F. NAT reduces address overlap occurrence.

10. Which of the following are advantages of using NAT? (Choose three.)

    A. Translation introduces switching path delays.

    B. NAT conserves legally registered addresses.

    C. NAT causes loss of end-to-end IP traceability.

    D. NAT increases flexibility when connecting to the Internet.

    E. Certain applications will not function with NAT enabled.

    F. NAT remedies address overlap occurrence.

Chapter

6

Infrastructure Security

THE FOLLOWING CCNA ROUTING AND SWITCHING EXAM OBJECTIVES ARE COVERED IN THIS CHAPTER:

✓ Configure, verify, and troubleshoot port security.

✓ Describe common access layer threat mitigation techniques.

✓ Configure, verify, and troubleshoot IPv4 and IPv6 access list for traffic filtering.

✓ Verify ACLs using the APIC-EM Path Trace ACL Analysis tool.

✓ Configure, verify, and troubleshoot basic device hardening.

✓ Describe device security using AAA with TACACS+ and RADIUS.

In this chapter, I will discuss security issues. The topics will include port security and the common access layer attacks it can help prevent. It will also include the configuration verification and troubleshooting of access lists and the proper hardening of network devices. Finally, it will include a discussion of AAA systems including both TACACS+ and RAID.

Configure, verify, and troubleshoot port security

It's usually not a good thing to have your switches available for anyone to just plug into and play around with. I mean, we worry about wireless security, so why wouldn't we demand switch security just as much, if not more?

But just how do we actually prevent someone from simply plugging a host into one of our switch ports—or worse, adding a hub, switch, or access point into the Ethernet jack in their office? By default, MAC addresses will just dynamically appear in your MAC forward/filter database and you can stop them in their tracks by using port security!

Static

You can set a static MAC address in the MAC address table, but it's a ton of work. Just in case you want to do it, here's how it's done:

```
S3(config)#mac address-table ?
  aging-time    Set MAC address table entry maximum age
  learning      Enable MAC table learning feature
  move          Move keyword
  notification  Enable/Disable MAC Notification on the switch
  static        static keyword

S3(config)#mac address-table static aaaa.bbbb.cccc vlan 1 int fa0/7
S3(config)#do show mac address-table
          Mac Address Table
-------------------------------------------

Vlan    Mac Address      Type        Ports
----    -----------      --------    -----
```

```
  All    0100.0ccc.cccc    STATIC      CPU
[output cut]
    1    000e.83b2.e34b    DYNAMIC     Fa0/1
    1    0011.1191.556f    DYNAMIC     Fa0/1
    1    0011.3206.25cb    DYNAMIC     Fa0/1
    1    001a.4d55.2f7e    DYNAMIC     Fa0/1
    1    001b.d40a.0538    DYNAMIC     Fa0/1
    1    001c.575e.c891    DYNAMIC     Fa0/1
    1    aaaa.bbbb.0ccc    STATIC      Fa0/7
[output cut]
Total Mac Addresses for this criterion: 59
```

As shown in the Type column of the output, you can see that a static MAC address has now been assigned permanently to interface Fa0/7 and that it's also been assigned to VLAN 1 only.

Dynamic

When utilizing dynamic port security, you specify the total number of allowed MAC addresses and the switch will allow only that number simultaneously, without regard to what those MAC addresses are.

To enable dynamic port security, you simply enable port security on the port without specifying the allowed MAC address. The MAC will be learned and will be the only allowed address. The configuration is shown here:

```
SW1(config)#interface fa0/3
SW1(config-if)#switchport mode access
SW1(config-if)#switchport port-security
```

Sticky

Probably one of my favorite commands is the sticky command, and not just because it's got a cool name. It also makes very cool things happen! You can find this command under the mac-address command:

```
Switch(config-if)#switchport port-security mac-address sticky
Switch(config-if)#switchport port-security maximum 2
Switch(config-if)#switchport port-security violation shutdown
```

Basically, with the sticky command you can provide static MAC address security without having to type in absolutely everyone's MAC address on the network. I like things that save me time like that!

In the preceding example, the first two MAC addresses coming into the port "stick" to it as static addresses and will be placed in the running-config, but when a third address tried to connect, the port would shut down immediately.

The difference between dynamically learned MAC addresses configured by using the `switchport port-security` interface subcommand and sticky learned MAC addresses configured by using the `switchport port-security mac-address sticky` interface subcommand is that dynamically learned MAC addresses are not added to the running-config, whereas sticky learned MAC addresses are. Port security with sticky MAC addresses retains dynamically learned MAC addresses during a link-down condition.

Max MAC Addresses

If you want to set up a switch port to allow only one host per port and make sure the port will shut down if this rule is violated, use the following commands like this:

```
Switch(config-if)#switchport port-security maximum 1
Switch(config-if)#switchport port-security violation shutdown
```

These commands really are probably the most popular because they prevent random users from connecting to a specific switch or access point that's in their office. The port security default that's immediately set on a port when it's enabled is `maximum 1` and `violation shutdown`. This sounds okay, but the drawback to this is that it only allows a single MAC address to be used on the port, so if anyone, including you, tries to add another host on that segment, the switch port will immediately enter an error-disabled state and the port will turn amber. And when that happens, you have to manually go into the switch and re-enable the port by cycling it with a `shutdown` and then a `no shutdown` command.

Violation Actions

You can configure the device to take one of the following actions when a security violation occurs by using the `switchport port-security` command with the following parameters:

- `Protect`: The protect violation mode drops packets with unknown source addresses until you remove enough secure MAC addresses to drop below the maximum value.
- `Restrict`: The restrict violation mode also drops packets with unknown source addresses until you remove enough secure MAC addresses to drop below the maximum value. However, it also generates a log message, causes the security violation counter to increment, and sends an SNMP trap.
- `Shutdown`: Shutdown is the default violation mode. The shutdown violation mode puts the interface into an error-disabled state immediately. The entire port is shut down. Also, in this mode, the system generates a log message, sends an SNMP trap, and increments the violation counter. To make the interface usable, you must perform a shut/no shut on the interface.

Err-disable Recovery

When a port is error disabled, it is effectively shut down and no traffic is sent or received on that port. The port LED is set to the color orange, and when you issue the show interfaces command, the port status shows `err-disabled`. Here is an example of what an error-disabled port looks like from the command-line interface (CLI) of the switch:

```
switch#show interfaces gigabitethernet 3/1 status

Port    Name        Status      Vlan       Duplex Speed Type
Gi3/1               err-disabled 200        full    1000 1000BaseSX
```

To recover the disabled ports, use the following command. The first is for a max MAC address violation and the second is for a disallowed MAC address violation.

```
switch(Config)#errdisable recovery cause mac-limit
```

```
switch(Config)#errdisable recovery cause psecure-violation
```

Exam Essentials

Understand the reason for port security.   Port security restricts access to a switch based on MAC addresses.

Know the command to enable port security.   To enable port security on a port, you must first make sure the port is an access port with `switchport mode access` command and then use the `switchport port-security` command at the interface level. You can set the port security parameters before or after enabling port security.

Describe common access layer threat mitigation techniques

Since the access layer is both the point at which user devices connect to the network and the connection point between the network and client device, protecting it plays an important role in protecting other users, applications, and the network itself from attacks.

Some of the ways to protect the access layer (also shown in Figure 6.1) are covered in the following sections.

FIGURE 6.1   Mitigating threats at the access layer

802.1x

Identity-based networking is a concept that ties together several authentication, access control, and user policy components in order to provide users with the network services you want them to have.

In the past, for a user to connect to the Finance services, for example, a user had to be plugged into the Finance LAN or VLAN. However, with user mobility as one of the core requirements of modern networks, this is no longer practical, nor does it provide sufficient security.

Identity-based networking allows you to verify users when they connect to a switch port by authenticating them and placing them in the right VLAN based on their identity. Should any users fail to pass the authentication process, their access can be rejected, or they might be simply put in a guest VLAN. Figure 6.2 shows this process.

FIGURE 6.2   Identity-based networking

The IEEE 802.1x standard allows you to implement identity-based networking on wired and wireless hosts by using client/server access control. There are three roles:

Client   Also referred to as a supplicant, this software runs on a client that is 802.1x compliant.

Authenticator   Typically a switch, this controls physical access to the network and is a proxy between the client and the authentication server.

Authentication server (RADIUS)   This is a server that authenticates each client before making available any services.

DHCP Snooping

DHCP snooping is a layer 2 security feature that validates DHCP messages by acting like a firewall between untrusted hosts and trusted DHCP servers.

In order to stop rogue DHCP servers in the network, switch interfaces are configured as trusted or untrusted, where trusted interfaces allow all types of DHCP messages and untrusted interfaces allow only requests. Trusted interfaces are interfaces that connect to a DHCP server or are an uplink toward the DHCP server, as shown in Figure 6.3.

FIGURE 6.3   DHCP snooping and DAI

With DHCP snooping enabled, a switch also builds a DHCP snooping binding database, where each entry includes the MAC and IP address of the host as well as the DHCP lease time, binding type, VLAN, and interface. Dynamic ARP inspection also uses this DHCP snooping binding database.

Dynamic ARP Inspection (DAI)

DAI, used with DHCP snooping, tracks IP-to-MAC bindings from DHCP transactions to protect against ARP poisoning (which is an attacker trying to have your traffic be sent to him instead of to your valid destination). DHCP snooping is required in order to build the MAC-to-IP bindings for DAI validation.

Nondefault Native VLAN

You can change the trunk port native VLAN from VLAN 1, which many people do for security reasons. To change the native VLAN, use the following command:

```
S1(config)#int f0/15
S1(config-if)#switchport trunk native vlan ?
  <1-4094>  VLAN ID of the native VLAN when this port is in trunking mode

S1(config-if)#switchport trunk native vlan 4
1w6d: %CDP-4-NATIVE_VLAN_MISMATCH: Native VLAN mismatch discovered
on FastEthernet0/15 (4), with S3 FastEthernet0/1 (1)
```

So we've changed our native VLAN on our trunk link to 4, and by using the show running-config command, I can see the configuration under the trunk link:

```
S1#sh run int f0/15
Building configuration...
```

```
Current configuration : 202 bytes
!
interface FastEthernet0/15
 description 1st connection to S3
 switchport trunk encapsulation dot1q
 switchport trunk native vlan 4
 switchport trunk allowed vlan 4,6,12,15
 switchport mode trunk
end
```

Oops—wait a minute! You didn't think it would be this easy and would just start working, did you? Of course not! Here's the rub: If all switches don't have the same native VLAN configured on the given trunk links, then we'll start to receive this error, which happened immediately after I entered the command:

```
1w6d: %CDP-4-NATIVE_VLAN_MISMATCH: Native VLAN mismatch discovered
on FastEthernet0/15 (4), with S3 FastEthernet0/1 (1).
```

Actually, this is a good, noncryptic error, so either we can go to the other end of our trunk link(s) and change the native VLAN or we set the native VLAN back to the default to fix it. Here's how we'd do that:

```
S1(config-if)#no switchport trunk native vlan
1w6d: %SPANTREE-2-UNBLOCK_CONSIST_PORT: Unblocking FastEthernet0/15
on VLAN0004. Port consistency restored.
```

Now our trunk link is using the default VLAN 1 as the native VLAN. Just remember that all switches on a given trunk must use the same native VLAN or you'll have some serious management problems. These issues won't affect user data, just management traffic between switches. Now, let's mix it up by connecting a router into our switched network and configure inter-VLAN communication.

Exam Essentials

Understand how to mitigate threats at the access layer. You can mitigate threats at the access layer by using port security, changing the native VLAN id, DHCP snooping, dynamic ARP inspection, and identity-based networking.

Configure, verify, and troubleshoot IPv4 and IPv6 access list for traffic filtering

An *access list* is essentially a list of conditions that categorize packets, and they really come in handy when you need to exercise control over network traffic. An ACL would be your tool of choice for decision making in these situations.

One of the most common and easiest-to-understand uses of access lists is to filter unwanted packets when implementing security policies. For example, you can set them up to make very specific decisions about regulating traffic patterns so that they'll allow only certain hosts to access web resources on the Internet while restricting others. With the right combination of access lists, network managers arm themselves with the power to enforce nearly any security policy they can invent.

Creating access lists is really a lot like programming a series of if-then statements—if a given condition is met, then a given action is taken. If the specific condition isn't met, nothing happens and the next statement is evaluated. Access-list statements are basically packet filters that packets are compared against, categorized by, and acted upon accordingly. Once the lists are built, they can be applied to either inbound or outbound traffic on any interface. Applying an access list causes the router to analyze every packet crossing that interface in the specified direction and take the appropriate action.

There are three important rules that a packet follows when it's being compared with an access list:

- The packet is always compared with each line of the access list in sequential order—it will always start with the first line of the access list, move on to line 2, then line 3, and so on.

- The packet is compared with lines of the access list only until a match is made. Once it matches the condition on a line of the access list, the packet is acted upon and no further comparisons take place.

- There is an implicit "deny" at the end of each access list—this means that if a packet doesn't match the condition on any of the lines in the access list, the packet will be discarded.

Each of these rules has some powerful implications when you're filtering IP packets with access lists, so keep in mind that creating effective access lists definitely takes some practice.

There are several types of access lists: standard, extended, and named.

Standard

Standard IP access lists filter network traffic by examining the source IP address in a packet. You create a *standard IP access list* by using the access-list numbers 1–99 or numbers in the expanded range of 1300–1999 because the type of ACL is generally differentiated using a number. Based on the number used when the access list is created, the router knows which type of syntax to expect as the list is entered. By using numbers 1–99 or 1300–1999, you're telling the router that you want to create a standard IP access list, so the router will expect syntax specifying only the source IP address in the test lines.

The following output displays a good example of the many access-list number ranges that you can use to filter traffic on your network. The IOS version delimits the protocols you can specify access for:

```
Corp(config)#access-list ?
```

```
  <1-99>        IP standard access list
  <100-199>     IP extended access list
  <1000-1099>   IPX SAP access list
```

```
<1100-1199>        Extended 48-bit MAC address access list
<1200-1299>        IPX summary address access list
<1300-1999>        IP standard access list (expanded range)
<200-299>          Protocol type-code access list
<2000-2699>        IP extended access list (expanded range)
<2700-2799>        MPLS access list
<300-399>          DECnet access list
<700-799>          48-bit MAC address access list
<800-899>          IPX standard access list
<900-999>          IPX extended access list
dynamic-extended   Extend the dynamic ACL absolute timer
rate-limit         Simple rate-limit specific access list
```

Wow—there certainly are lot of old protocols listed in that output! IPX and DECnet would no longer be used in any of today's networks. Let's take a look at the syntax used when creating a standard IP access list:

```
Corp(config)#access-list 10 ?
  deny     Specify packets to reject
  permit   Specify packets to forward
  remark   Access list entry comment
```

As I said, by using the access-list numbers 1–99 or 1300–1999, you're telling the router that you want to create a standard IP access list, which means you can only filter on source IP address.

Once you've chosen the access-list number, you need to decide whether you're creating a permit or deny statement. I'm going to create a deny statement now:

```
Corp(config)#access-list 10 deny ?
  Hostname or A.B.C.D  Address to match
  any                  Any source host
  host                 A single host address
```

The next step is more detailed because there are three options available in it:

1. The first option is the any parameter, which is used to permit or deny any source host or network.

2. The second choice is to use an IP address to specify either a single host or a range of them.

3. The last option is to use the host command to specify a specific host only.

The any command is pretty obvious—any source address matches the statement, so every packet compared against this line will match. The host command is relatively simple too, as you can see here:

```
Corp(config)#access-list 10 deny host ?
  Hostname or A.B.C.D  Host address
Corp(config)#access-list 10 deny host 172.16.30.2
```

This tells the list to deny any packets from host 172.16.30.2. The default parameter is host. In other words, if you type **access-list 10 deny 172.16.30.2**, the router assumes you mean host 172.16.30.2 and that's exactly how it will show in your running-config.

But there's another way to specify either a particular host or a range of hosts, and it's known as wildcard masking. In fact, to specify any range of hosts, you must use wildcard masking in the access list.

So exactly what is wildcard masking? Coming up, I'm going to show you using a standard access list example.

Wildcard Masking

Wildcards are used with access lists to specify an individual host, a network, or a specific range of a network or networks. The block sizes you learned about earlier used to specify a range of addresses are key to understanding wildcards.

Let me pause here for a quick review of block sizes before we go any further. I'm sure you remember that the different block sizes available are 64, 32, 16, 8, and 4. When you need to specify a range of addresses, you choose the next-largest block size for your needs. So if you need to specify 34 networks, you need a block size of 64. If you want to specify 18 hosts, you need a block size of 32. If you specify only 2 networks, then go with a block size of 4.

Wildcards are used with the host or network address to tell the router a range of available addresses to filter. To specify a host, the address would look like this:

```
172.16.30.5 0.0.0.0
```

The four zeros represent each octet of the address. Whenever a zero is present, it indicates that the octet in the address must match the corresponding reference octet exactly. To specify that an octet can be any value, use the value 255. Here's an example of how a /24 subnet is specified with a wildcard mask:

```
172.16.30.0 0.0.0.255
```

This tells the router to match up the first three octets exactly, but the fourth octet can be any value.

Okay—that was the easy part. But what if you want to specify only a small range of subnets? This is where block sizes come in. You have to specify the range of values in a block size, so you can't choose to specify 20 networks. You can only specify the exact amount that the block size value allows. This means that the range would have to be either 16 or 32, but not 20.

Let's say that you want to block access to the part of the network that ranges from 172.16.8.0 through 172.16.15.0. To do that, you would go with a block size of 8, your network number would be 172.16.8.0, and the wildcard would be 0.0.7.255. The 7.255 equals the value the router will use to determine the block size. So together, the network number and the wildcard tell the router to begin at 172.16.8.0 and go up a block size of eight addresses to network 172.16.15.0.

This really is easier than it looks! I could certainly go through the binary math for you, but no one needs that kind of pain because all you have to do is remember that the wildcard is always one number less than the block size. So, in our example, the wildcard would be 7 since our block size is 8. If you used a block size of 16, the wildcard would be 15. Easy, right?

Just to make you've got this, we'll go through some examples that will definitely help you nail it down. The following example tells the router to match the first three octets exactly but that the fourth octet can be anything:

```
Corp(config)#access-list 10 deny 172.16.10.0 0.0.0.255
```

The next example tells the router to match the first two octets and that the last two octets can be any value:

```
Corp(config)#access-list 10 deny 172.16.0.0 0.0.255.255
```

Now, try to figure out this next line:

```
Corp(config)#access-list 10 deny 172.16.16.0 0.0.3.255
```

This configuration tells the router to start at network 172.16.16.0 and use a block size of 4. The range would then be 172.16.16.0 through 172.16.19.255, and by the way, the Cisco objectives seem to really like this one!

Let's keep practicing. What about this next one?

```
Corp(config)#access-list 10 deny 172.16.16.0 0.0.7.255
```

This example reveals an access list starting at 172.16.16.0 going up a block size of 8 to 172.16.23.255.

Let's keep at it... What do you think the range of this one is?

```
Corp(config)#access-list 10 deny 172.16.32.0 0.0.15.255
```

This one begins at network 172.16.32.0 and goes up a block size of 16 to 172.16.47.255. You're almost done practicing! After a couple more, we'll configure some real ACLs.

```
Corp(config)#access-list 10 deny 172.16.64.0 0.0.63.255
```

This example starts at network 172.16.64.0 and goes up a block size of 64 to 172.16.127.255.

What about this last example?

```
Corp(config)#access-list 10 deny 192.168.160.0 0.0.31.255
```

This one shows us that it begins at network 192.168.160.0 and goes up a block size of 32 to 192.168.191.255.

Here are two more things to keep in mind when working with block sizes and wildcards:

Each block size must start at 0 or a multiple of the block size. For example, you can't say that you want a block size of 8 and then start at 12. You must use 0–7, 8–15, 16–23, etc. For a block size of 32, the ranges are 0–31, 32–63, 64–95, etc.

The command any is the same thing as writing out the wildcard 0.0.0.0 255.255.255.255.

Wildcard masking is a crucial skill to master when creating IP access lists, and it's used identically when creating standard and extended IP access lists.

Standard Access List Example

In this section, you'll learn how to use a standard access list to stop specific users from gaining access to the finance department LAN.

In Figure 6.4, a router has three LAN connections and one WAN connection to the Internet. Users on the Sales LAN should not have access to the Finance LAN, but they should be able to access the Internet and the marketing department files. The Marketing LAN needs to access the Finance LAN for application services.

FIGURE 6.4   IP access list example with three LANs and a WAN connection

We can see that the following standard IP access list is configured on the router:

```
Lab_A#config t
Lab_A(config)#access-list 10 deny 172.16.40.0 0.0.0.255
Lab_A(config)#access-list 10 permit any
```

It's very important to remember that the any command is the same thing as saying the following using wildcard masking:

```
Lab_A(config)#access-list 10 permit 0.0.0.0 255.255.255.255
```

Since the wildcard mask says that none of the octets are to be evaluated, every address matches the test condition, so this is functionally doing the same as using the any keyword.

At this point, the access list is configured to deny source addresses from the Sales LAN to the Finance LAN and to allow everyone else. But remember, no action will be taken until the access list is applied on an interface in a specific direction!

But where should this access list be placed? If you place it as an incoming access list on Fa0/0, you might as well shut down the FastEthernet interface because all of the Sales LAN devices will be denied access to all networks attached to the router. The best place to apply this access list is on the Fa0/1 interface as an outbound list:

```
Lab_A(config)#int fa0/1
Lab_A(config-if)#ip access-group 10 out
```

Doing this completely stops traffic from 172.16.40.0 from getting out FastEthernet0/1. It has no effect on the hosts from the Sales LAN accessing the Marketing LAN and the Internet because traffic to those destinations doesn't go through interface Fa0/1. Any packet trying to exit out Fa0/1 will have to go through the access list first. If there was an inbound list placed on Fa0/0, then any packet trying to enter interface Fa0/0 would have to go through the access list before being routed to an exit interface.

Now, let's take a look at another standard access list example. Figure 6.5 shows an internetwork of two routers with four LANs.

FIGURE 6.5 IP standard access list example 2

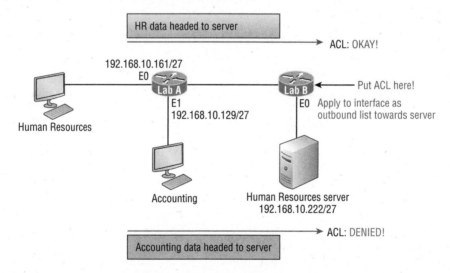

Now we're going to stop the Accounting users from accessing the Human Resources server attached to the Lab_B router but allow all other users access to that LAN using a standard ACL. What kind of standard access list would we need to create and where would we place it to achieve our goals?

The real answer is that we should use an extended access list and place it closest to the source! But this question specifies using a standard access list, and as a rule, standard ACLs are placed closest to the destination. In this example, Ethernet 0 is the outbound interface on the Lab_B router and here's the access list that should be placed on it:

```
Lab_B#config t
Lab_B(config)#access-list 10 deny 192.168.10.128 0.0.0.31
```

```
Lab_B(config)#access-list 10 permit any
Lab_B(config)#interface Ethernet 0
Lab_B(config-if)#ip access-group 10 out
```

Keep in mind that to be able to answer this question correctly, you really need to understand subnetting, wildcard masks, and how to configure and implement ACLs. The Accounting subnet is the 192.168.10.128/27, which is a 255.255.255.224, with a block size of 32 in the fourth octet.

With all this in mind and before we move on to restricting Telnet access on a router, let's take a look at one more standard access list example. This one is going to require some thought. In Figure 6.6, you have a router with four LAN connections and one WAN connection to the Internet.

FIGURE 6.6   IP standard access list example 3

Okay—you need to write an access list that will stop access from each of the four LANs shown in the diagram to the Internet. Each of the LANs reveals a single host's IP address, which you need to use to determine the subnet and wildcards of each LAN to configure the access list.

Here is an example of what your answer should look like, beginning with the network on E0 and working through to E3:

```
Router(config)#access-list 1 deny 172.16.128.0 0.0.31.255
Router(config)#access-list 1 deny 172.16.48.0 0.0.15.255
Router(config)#access-list 1 deny 172.16.192.0 0.0.63.255
Router(config)#access-list 1 deny 172.16.88.0 0.0.7.255
Router(config)#access-list 1 permit any
Router(config)#interface serial 0
Router(config-if)#ip access-group 1 out
```

Sure, you could have done this with one line:

```
Router(config)#access-list 1 deny 172.16.0.0 0.0.255.255
```

But what fun is that?

And remember the reasons for creating this list. If you actually applied this ACL on the router, you'd effectively shut down access to the Internet, so why even have an Internet connection? I included this exercise so you can practice how to use block sizes with access lists, which is vital for succeeding when you take the Cisco exam!

Extended

Let's go back to the standard IP access list example where you had to block all access from the Sales LAN to the finance department and add a new requirement. You now must allow Sales to gain access to a certain server on the Finance LAN but not to other network services for security reasons. What's the solution? Applying a standard IP access list won't allow users to get to one network service but not another because a standard ACL won't allow you to make decisions based on both source and destination addresses. It makes decisions based only on source address, so we need another way to achieve our new goal—but what is it?

Using an *extended access list* will save the day because extended ACLs allow us to specify source and destination addresses as well as the protocol and port number that identify the upper-layer protocol or application. An extended ACL is just what we need to effectively allow users access to a physical LAN while denying them access to specific hosts—even specific services on those hosts!

We're going to take a look at the commands we have in our arsenal, but first, you need to know that you must use the extended access-list range from 100 to 199. The 2000–2699 range is also available for extended IP access lists.

After choosing a number in the extended range, you need to decide what type of list entry to make. For this example, I'm going with a deny list entry:

```
Corp(config)#access-list 110 ?
  deny      Specify packets to reject
  dynamic   Specify a DYNAMIC list of PERMITs or DENYs
  permit    Specify packets to forward
  remark    Access list entry comment
```

And once you've settled on the type of ACL, you then need to select a protocol field entry:

```
Corp(config)#access-list 110 deny ?
  <0-255>   An IP protocol number
  ahp       Authentication Header Protocol
  eigrp     Cisco's EIGRP routing protocol
```

```
esp       Encapsulation Security Payload
gre       Cisco's GRE tunneling
icmp      Internet Control Message Protocol
igmp      Internet Gateway Message Protocol
ip        Any Internet Protocol
ipinip    IP in IP tunneling
nos       KA9Q NOS compatible IP over IP tunneling
ospf      OSPF routing protocol
pcp       Payload Compression Protocol
pim       Protocol Independent Multicast
tcp       Transmission Control Protocol
udp       User Datagram Protocol
```

 NOTE If you want to filter by Application layer protocol, you have to choose the appropriate layer 4 transport protocol after the permit or deny statement. For example, to filter Telnet or FTP, choose TCP since both Telnet and FTP use TCP at the Transport layer. Selecting IP wouldn't allow you to specify a particular application protocol later and only filter based on source and destination addresses.

So now, let's filter an Application layer protocol that uses TCP by selecting TCP as the protocol and indicating the specific destination TCP port at the end of the line. Next, we'll be prompted for the source IP address of the host or network and we'll choose the any command to allow any source address:

```
Corp(config)#access-list 110 deny tcp ?
  A.B.C.D  Source address
  any      Any source host
  host     A single source host
```

After we've selected the source address, we can then choose the specific destination address:

```
Corp(config)#access-list 110 deny tcp any ?
  A.B.C.D  Destination address
  any      Any destination host
  eq       Match only packets on a given port number
  gt       Match only packets with a greater port number
  host     A single destination host
  lt       Match only packets with a lower port number
  neq      Match only packets not on a given port number
  range    Match only packets in the range of port numbers
```

In this output, you can see that any source IP address that has a destination IP address of 172.16.30.2 has been denied:

```
Corp(config)#access-list 110 deny tcp any host 172.16.30.2 ?
  ack          Match on the ACK bit
  dscp         Match packets with given dscp value
  eq           Match only packets on a given port number
  established  Match established connections
  fin          Match on the FIN bit
  fragments    Check non-initial fragments
  gt           Match only packets with a greater port number
  log          Log matches against this entry
  log-input    Log matches against this entry, including input interface
  lt           Match only packets with a lower port number
  neq          Match only packets not on a given port number
  precedence   Match packets with given precedence value
  psh          Match on the PSH bit
  range        Match only packets in the range of port numbers
  rst          Match on the RST bit
  syn          Match on the SYN bit
  time-range   Specify a time-range
  tos          Match packets with given TOS value
  urg          Match on the URG bit
  <cr>
```

And once we have the destination host addresses in place, we just need to specify the type of service to deny using the equal to command, entered as eq. The following help screen reveals the options available now. You can choose a port number or use the application name:

```
Corp(config)#access-list 110 deny tcp any host 172.16.30.2 eq ?
  <0-65535>  Port number
  bgp        Border Gateway Protocol (179)
  chargen    Character generator (19)
  cmd        Remote commands (rcmd, 514)
  daytime    Daytime (13)
  discard    Discard (9)
  domain     Domain Name Service (53)
  drip       Dynamic Routing Information Protocol (3949)
  echo       Echo (7)
  exec       Exec (rsh, 512)
```

```
finger        Finger (79)
ftp           File Transfer Protocol (21)
ftp-data      FTP data connections (20)
gopher        Gopher (70)
hostname      NIC hostname server (101)
ident         Ident Protocol (113)
irc           Internet Relay Chat (194)
klogin        Kerberos login (543)
kshell        Kerberos shell (544)
login         Login (rlogin, 513)
lpd           Printer service (515)
nntp          Network News Transport Protocol (119)
pim-auto-rp   PIM Auto-RP (496)
pop2          Post Office Protocol v2 (109)
pop3          Post Office Protocol v3 (110)
smtp          Simple Mail Transport Protocol (25)
sunrpc        Sun Remote Procedure Call (111)
syslog        Syslog (514)
tacacs        TAC Access Control System (49)
talk          Talk (517)
telnet        Telnet (23)
time          Time (37)
uucp          Unix-to-Unix Copy Program (540)
whois         Nicname (43)
www           World Wide Web (HTTP, 80)
```

Now let's block Telnet (port 23) to host 172.16.30.2 only. If the users want to use FTP, fine—that's allowed. The log command is used to log messages every time the access list entry is hit. This can be an extremely cool way to monitor inappropriate access attempts, but be careful because in a large network, this command can overload your console's screen with messages!

Here's our result:

```
Corp(config)#access-list 110 deny tcp any host 172.16.30.2 eq 23 log
```

This line says to deny any source host trying to telnet to destination host 172.16.30.2. Keep in mind that the next line is an implicit deny by default. If you apply this access list to an interface, you might as well just shut the interface down because by default, there's an implicit deny all at the end of every access list. So we've got to follow up the access list with the following command:

```
Corp(config)#access-list 110 permit ip any any
```

The IP in this line is important because it will permit the IP stack. If TCP was used instead of IP in this line, then UDP, etc. would all be denied. Remember, that 0.0.0.0 255.255.255.255 is the same command as any, so the command could also look like this:

```
Corp(config)#access-list 110 permit ip 0.0.0.0 255.255.255.255
0.0.0.0 255.255.255.255
```

But if you did this, when you looked at the running-config, the commands would be replaced with the any any. I like efficiency so I'll just use the any command because it requires less typing.

As always, once our access list is created, we must apply it to an interface with the same command used for the IP standard list:

```
Corp(config-if)#ip access-group 110 in
```

Or this:

```
Corp(config-if)#ip access-group 110 out
```

Next, we'll check out some examples of how to use an extended access list.

Extended Access List Example 1

For our first scenario, we'll use Figure 6.7. What do we need to do to deny access to a host at 172.16.50.5 on the finance department LAN for both Telnet and FTP services? All other services on this and all other hosts are acceptable for the sales and marketing departments to access.

FIGURE 6.7   Extended ACL example 1

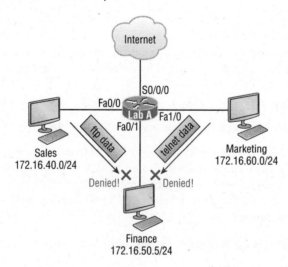

Here's the ACL we must create:

```
Lab_A#config t
Lab_A(config)#access-list 110 deny tcp any host 172.16.50.5 eq 21
Lab_A(config)#access-list 110 deny tcp any host 172.16.50.5 eq 23
Lab_A(config)#access-list 110 permit ip any any
```

The access-list 110 tells the router we're creating an extended IP ACL. The tcp is the protocol field in the Network layer header. If the list doesn't say tcp here, you cannot filter by TCP port numbers 21 and 23 as shown in the example. Remember that these values indicate FTP and Telnet, which both use TCP for connection-oriented services. The any command is the source, which means any source IP address, and the host is the destination IP address. This ACL says that all IP traffic will be permitted from any host except FTP and Telnet to host 172.16.50.5 from any source.

 Remember that instead of the host 172.16.50.5 command when we created the extended access list, we could have entered 172.16.50.5 0.0.0.0. There would be no difference in the result other than the router would change the command to host 172.16.50.5 in the running-config.

After the list is created, it must be applied to the FastEthernet 0/1 interface outbound because we want to block all traffic from getting to host 172.16.50.5 and performing FTP and Telnet. If this list was created to block access only from the Sales LAN to host 172.16.50.5, then we'd have put this list closer to the source, or on FastEthernet 0/0. In that situation, we'd apply the list to inbound traffic. This highlights the fact that you really need to analyze each situation carefully before creating and applying ACLs!

Now let's go ahead and apply the list to interface Fa0/1 to block all outside FTP and Telnet access to the host 172.16.50.5:

```
Lab_A(config)#int fa0/1
Lab_A(config-if)#ip access-group 110 out
```

Extended Access List Example 2

We're going to use Figure 6.6 again, which has four LANs and a serial connection. We need to prevent Telnet access to the networks attached to the E1 and E2 interfaces.

The configuration on the router would look something like this, although the answer can vary:

```
Router(config)#access-list 110 deny tcp any 172.16.48.0 0.0.15.255
eq 23
Router(config)#access-list 110 deny tcp any 172.16.192.0 0.0.63.255
eq 23
Router(config)#access-list 110 permit ip any any
Router(config)#interface Ethernet 1
```

```
Router(config-if)#ip access-group 110 out
Router(config-if)#interface Ethernet 2
Router(config-if)#ip access-group 110 out
```

Here are the key factors to understand from this list:

- First, you need to verify that the number range is correct for the type of access list you are creating. In this example, it's extended, so the range must be 100–199.

- Second, you must verify that the protocol field matches the upper-layer process or application, which in this case is TCP port 23 (Telnet).

The protocol parameter must be TCP since Telnet uses TCP. If it were TFTP instead, then the protocol parameter would have to be UDP because TFTP uses UDP at the Transport layer

- Third, verify that the destination port number matches the application you're filtering for. In this case, port 23 matches Telnet, which is correct, but know that you can also type **telnet** at the end of the line instead of 23.

- Finally, the test statement permit ip any any is important to have there at the end of the list because it means to enable all packets other than Telnet packets destined for the LANs connected to Ethernet 1 and Ethernet 2.

Extended Access List Example 3

I want to guide you through one more extended ACL example before we move on to named ACLs. Figure 6.8 displays the network we're going to use for this last scenario.

FIGURE 6.8   Extended ACL example 3

In this example, we're going to allow HTTP access to the Finance server from source Host B *only*. All other traffic will also be permitted. We need to be able to configure this in only three test statements, and then we'll need to add the interface configuration.

Let's take what we've learned and knock this one out:

```
Lab_A#config t
Lab_A(config)#access-list 110 permit tcp host 192.168.177.2
host 172.22.89.26 eq 80
Lab_A(config)#access-list 110 deny tcp any host 172.22.89.26 eq 80
Lab_A(config)#access-list 110 permit ip any any
```

This is really pretty simple! First we need to permit Host B HTTP access to the Finance server. But since all other traffic must be allowed, we must detail who cannot HTTP to the Finance server, so the second test statement is there to deny anyone else from using HTTP on the Finance server. Finally, now that Host B can HTTP to the Finance server and everyone else can't, we'll permit all other traffic with our third test statement.

Not so bad—this just takes a little thought! But wait—we're not done yet because we still need to apply this to an interface. Since extended access lists are typically applied closest to the source, we should simply place this inbound on F0/0, right? Well, this is one time we're not going to follow the rules. Our challenge required us to allow only HTTP traffic to the Finance server from Host B. If we apply the ACL inbound on Fa0/0, then the branch office would be able to access the Finance server and perform HTTP. So in this example, we need to place the ACL closest to the destination:

```
Lab_A(config)#interface fastethernet 0/1
Lab_A(config-if)#ip access-group 110 out
```

Named

Named access lists are just another way to create standard and extended access lists. In medium to large enterprises, managing ACLs can become a real hassle over time! A handy way to make things easier is to copy the access list to a text editor, edit the list, then paste the new list back into the router, which works pretty well if it weren't for the "pack rat" mentality. It's really common to think things like, "What if I find a problem with the new list and need to back out of the change?" This and other factors cause people to hoard unapplied ACLs, and over time, they can seriously build up on a router, leading to more questions, like, "What were these ACLs for? Are they important? Do I need them?" All good questions, and named access lists are the answer to this problem!

And of course, this kind of thing can also apply to access lists that are up and running. Let's say you come into an existing network and are looking at access lists on a router. Suppose you find an access list 177, which happens to be an extended access list that's a whopping 93 lines long. This leads to more of the same bunch of questions and can even lead to needless existential despair! Instead, wouldn't it be a whole lot easier to identify an access list with a name like "FinanceLAN" rather than one mysteriously dubbed "177"?

To our collective relief, named access lists allow us to use names for creating and applying either standard or extended access lists. There's really nothing new or different about these ACLs aside from being readily identifiable in a way that makes sense to humans, but there are some subtle changes to the syntax. So let's re-create the standard access list we created earlier for our test network in Figure 6.8 using a named access list:

```
Lab_A#config t
Lab_A(config)# ip access-list ?
  extended    Extended Access List
  log-update  Control access list log updates
  logging     Control access list logging
  resequence  Resequence Access List
  standard    Standard Access List
```

Notice that I started by typing **ip access-list**, not **access-list**. Doing this allows me to enter a named access list. Next, I'll need to specify it as a standard access list:

```
Lab_A(config)#ip access-list standard ?
  <1-99>       Standard IP access-list number
  <1300-1999>  Standard IP access-list number (expanded range)
  WORD         Access-list name


Lab_A(config)#ip access-list standard BlockSales
Lab_A(config-std-nacl)#
```

I've specified a standard access list, then added the name, BlockSales. I definitely could've used a number for a standard access list, but instead, I chose to use a nice, clear, descriptive name. And notice that after entering the name, I hit Enter and the router prompt changed. This confirms that I'm now in named access list configuration mode and that I'm entering the named access list:

```
Lab_A(config-std-nacl)#?
Standard Access List configuration commands:
  default  Set a command to its defaults
  deny     Specify packets to reject
  exit     Exit from access-list configuration mode
  no       Negate a command or set its defaults
  permit   Specify packets to forward

Lab_A(config-std-nacl)#deny 172.16.40.0 0.0.0.255
Lab_A(config-std-nacl)#permit any
Lab_A(config-std-nacl)#exit
```

```
Lab_A(config)#^Z
Lab_A#
```

So I've entered the access list and then exited configuration mode. Next, I'll take a look at the running configuration to verify that the access list is indeed in the router:

```
Lab_A#sh running-config | begin ip access
ip access-list standard BlockSales
 deny    172.16.40.0 0.0.0.255
 permit any
!
```

And there it is: The BlockSales access list has truly been created and is in the running-config of the router. Next, I'll need to apply the access list to the correct interface:

```
Lab_A#config t
Lab_A(config)#int fa0/1
Lab_A(config-if)#ip access-group BlockSales out
```

Clear skies! At this point, we've re-created the work done earlier using a named access list. But let's take our IP extended example, shown in Figure 6.8, and redo that list using a named ACL instead as well.

Same business requirements: Allow HTTP access to the Finance server from source Host B only. All other traffic is permitted.

```
Lab_A#config t
Lab_A(config)#ip access-list extended 110
Lab_A(config-ext-nacl)#permit tcp host 192.168.177.2 host 172.22.89.26 eq 80
Lab_A(config-ext-nacl)#deny tcp any host 172.22.89.26 eq 80
Lab_A(config-ext-nacl)#permit ip any any
Lab_A(config-ext-nacl)#int fa0/1
Lab_A(config-if)#ip access-group 110 out
```

Okay—true—I named the extended list with a number, but sometimes it's okay to do that! I'm guessing that named ACLs don't seem all that exciting or different to you, do they? Maybe not in this configuration, except that I don't need to start every line with `access-list 110`, which is nice. But where named ACLs really shine is that they allow us to insert, delete, or edit a single line.

Monitoring Access Lists

It's always good to be able to verify a router's configuration. Table 6.1 lists the commands that we can use to achieve that.

TABLE 6.1   Commands used to verify access-list configuration

Command	Effect
show access-list	Displays all access lists and their parameters configured on the router. Also shows statistics about how many times the line either permitted or denied a packet. This command does not show you which interface the list is applied on.
show access-list 110	Reveals only the parameters for access list 110. Again, this command will not reveal the specific interface the list is set on.
show ip access-list	Shows only the IP access lists configured on the router
show ip interface	Displays which interfaces have access lists set on them
show running-config	Shows the access lists and the specific interfaces that have ACLs applied on them

We've already used the show running-config command to verify that a named access list was in the router, so now let's take a look at the output from some of the other commands.

The show access-list command will list all ACLs on the router, whether they're applied to an interface or not:

```
Lab_A#show access-list
Standard IP access list 10
    10 deny    172.16.40.0, wildcard bits 0.0.0.255
    20 permit any
Standard IP access list BlockSales
    10 deny    172.16.40.0, wildcard bits 0.0.0.255
    20 permit any
Extended IP access list 110
    10 deny tcp any host 172.16.30.5 eq ftp
    20 deny tcp any host 172.16.30.5 eq telnet
    30 permit ip any any
    40 permit tcp host 192.168.177.2 host 172.22.89.26 eq www
    50 deny tcp any host 172.22.89.26 eq www
Lab_A#
```

First, notice that access list 10 as well as both of our named access lists appear on this list—remember, my extended named ACL was named 110! Second, notice that even though I entered actual numbers for TCP ports in access list 110, the show command gives us the protocol names rather than TCP ports for serious clarity.

But wait! The best part is those numbers on the left side: 10, 20, 30, etc. Those are called sequence numbers, and they allow us to edit our named ACL. Here's an example where I added a line into the named extended ACL 110:

```
Lab_A (config)#ip access-list extended 110
Lab_A (config-ext-nacl)#21 deny udp any host 172.16.30.5 eq 69
Lab_A#show access-list
[output cut]
Extended IP access list 110
    10 deny tcp any host 172.16.30.5 eq ftp
    20 deny tcp any host 172.16.30.5 eq telnet
    21 deny udp any host 172.16.30.5 eq tftp
    30 permit ip any any
    40 permit tcp host 192.168.177.2 host 172.22.89.26 eq www
    50 deny tcp any host 172.22.89.26 eq www
```

You can see that I added line 21. I could have deleted a line or edited an existing line as well—very nice!

Here's the output of the show ip interface command:

```
Lab_A#show ip interface fa0/1
FastEthernet0/1 is up, line protocol is up
  Internet address is 172.16.30.1/24
  Broadcast address is 255.255.255.255
  Address determined by non-volatile memory
  MTU is 1500 bytes
  Helper address is not set
  Directed broadcast forwarding is disabled
  Outgoing access list is 110
  Inbound access list is not set
  Proxy ARP is enabled
  Security level is default
  Split horizon is enabled
[output cut]
```

Be sure to notice the bold line indicating that the outgoing list on this interface is 110, yet the inbound access list isn't set. What happened to BlockSales? I had configured that outbound on Fa0/1! That's true, I did, but I configured my extended named ACL 110 and applied it to Fa0/1 as well. You can't have two lists on the same interface, in the same direction, so what happened here is that my last configuration overwrote the BlockSales configuration.

And as I've already mentioned, you can use the show running-config command to see any and all access lists.

IPv6 Extended Access Lists

First, understand that you can only create named extended IPv6 ACLs, so you don't need to specify standard or extended in your named list, and although you won't see any sequence numbers, you can still somewhat edit a named IPv6 ACL, meaning you can delete a single line but there is no way to insert a line other than at the end of the ACL.

In addition, there's an implicit deny ip any any at the bottom of every IPv4 access list. However, IPv6 access lists actually have *three* implied statements at the bottom:

- permit icmp any any nd-na
- permit icmp any any nd-ns
- deny ipv6 any any

The two permit statements are required for neighbor discovery, which is an important protocol in IPv6 because it's the replacement for ARP.

Using Figure 6.9 network layout and IPv6 addresses, let's create an IPv6 extended named ACL that blocks Telnet to Server1 with an IPv6 address of 2001:db8:3c4d:1:a14c:8c33:2d1:be3d from PC1 with a destination IPv6 address of 2001:db8:3c4d:3:2ef:1823:8938. Since it's an IPv6 extended named ACL (always), we'll place it closest to the source address if possible.

FIGURE 6.9   IPv6 Extended ACL example

Step 1: Test that you can telnet to the remote host:

```
R1#telnet 2001:db8:3c4d:1:a14c:8c33:2d1:be3d
Trying 2001:db8:3c4d:1:a14c:8c33:2d1:be3d... Open

Server1>
```

Okay, great, but that was way too much effort! Let's create an entry into the hosts table of R1 so I don't have to type an IPv6 address when trying to access that host:

```
R1(config)#ipv6 host Server1 2001:db8:3c4d:1:a14c:8c33:2d1:be3d
R1(config)#do sh host
[output cut]

Host Port Flags Age Type Address(es)
Server1 None (perm, OK) 0 IPV6 2001:DB8:3C4D:1:A14C:8C33:2D1:BE3D
```

Now I can just type this from now on (the name is case sensitive):

```
R1#telnet Server1
Trying 2001:DB8:3C4D:1:A14C:8C33:2D1:BE3D... Open

Server1>
```

Or better yet, just the name (telnet is the default):

```
R1#Server1
Trying 2001:DB8:3C4D:1:A14C:8C33:2D1:BE3D... Open

Server1>exit
```

Also, ping using the name:

```
R1#ping Server1
Type escape sequence to abort.
Sending 5, 100-byte ICMP Echos to 2001:DB8:3C4D:1:A14C:8C33:2D1:BE3D,
timeout is 2 seconds:
!!!!!
Success rate is 100 percent (5/5), round-trip min/avg/max = 0/0/1 ms
```

Step 2: Create an ACL on R2 that stops telnet to the remote host Server1 (2001:db8:3c4d:1:a14c:8c33:2d1:be3d). The name is absolutely case sensitive when applying to an interface:

```
R2(config)#ipv6 access-list Block_Telnet
R2(config-ipv6-acl)#
```

Step 3: Once you have created the named list, add your test parameters:

```
R2(config-ipv6-acl)#deny tcp host 2001:DB8:3C4D:2:21A:6DFF:FE37:A44F
host 2001:DB8:3C4D:1:A14C:8C33:2D1:BE3D eq telnet
R2(config-ipv6-acl)#permit ipv6 any any
```

Step 4: Configure your ACP on your router interface.

Since we're adding this to the R2 router in Figure 6.9, add it to interface FastEthernet 0/1, stopping traffic closest to the source, and use the command ipv6 traffic-filter:

```
R2(config)#int fa0/1
R2(config-if)#ipv6 traffic-filter Block_Telnet out
```

Step 5: Test your access list by telnetting from Server1 on the R1 router:

```
R1#Server1
Trying 2001:DB8:3C4D:1:A14C:8C33:2D1:BE3D ...Open


Server1>
```

Hmm... and I tried really hard not to make a typo! Let's take a look:

```
R2#sh access-lists
IPv6 access list Block_Telnet
    deny tcp host 2001:DB8:3C4D:2:21A:6DFF:FE37:A44F host
2001:DB8:3C4D:1:A14C:8C33:2D1:BE3D eq telnet (96 match(es))
    permit ipv6 any any (181 match(es))
```

By verifying the IPv6 addresses with the interfaces of the routers, this list looks correct. It's important to verify your addresses with a show ipv6 interface brief command. Let's take a look:

```
R1#sh ipv6 int brief
FastEthernet0/0 [up/up]
    FE80::2E0:B0FF:FED2:B701
    2001:DB8:3C4D:3:21A:6DFF:FE37:A44E
FastEthernet0/1 [up/up]
    FE80::2E0:B0FF:FED2:B702
    2001:DB8:3C4D:2:21A:6DFF:FE37:A44F
```

Since R1 Fa0/1 is my source address, we can see that this address is correct in my ACL. Let's take a look at the destination device:

```
Server1#sh ipv6 int br
    FastEthernet0/0 [up/up]
    FE80::260:70FF:FED8:DD01
    2001:DB8:3C4D:1:A14C:8C33:2D1:BE3D
```

Yup, this one is correct too! My IPv6 ACL is correct, so now we need to check our interface.

Step 6: Fix and/or edit your access list and/or interfaces:

```
R2#show running-config
[output cut]
```

```
!
interface FastEthernet0/0
     no ip address
     duplex auto
     speed auto
     ipv6 address 2001:DB8:3C4D:1:21A:6DFF:FE37:A443/64
     ipv6 rip 1 enable
!
interface FastEthernet0/1
     no ip address
     ipv6 traffic-filter Block_Telnet out
     duplex auto
     speed auto
     ipv6 address 2001:DB8:3C4D:2:21A:6DFF:FE64:9B3/64
     ipv6 rip 1 enable
!
```

Unlike with IPv4, where we can use the show ip interface command to see if an ACL is set, we can only use the show running-config command to verify if an IPv6 ACL is set on an interface. In the preceding output, we can see that I certainly did set the ACL to the interface Fa0/1. However, I configured it to out instead of in on the interface. Let's fix that:

R2#config t
R2(config)#**int fa0/1**
R2(config-if)#**no ipv6 traffic-filter Block_Telnet out**
R2(config-if)#**ipv6 traffic-filter Block_Telnet in**

Step 7: Retest your ACL:

R1#Server1

```
Trying 2001:DB8:3C4D:1:A14C:8C33:2D1:BE3D ...%
Connection timed out; remote host not responding
R1#
```

Looks good! Although I don't recommend using this method to block telnet to a router, it was a great way to test our IPv6 ACLs.

Exam Essentials

Remember the standard and extended IP access-list number ranges.   The number ranges you can use to configure a standard IP access list are 1–99 and 1300–1999. The number ranges for an extended IP access list are 100–199 and 2000–2699.

Understand the term implicit *deny*.   At the end of every access list is an implicit *deny*. What this means is that if a packet does not match any of the lines in the access list, it will be discarded. Also, if you have nothing but deny statements in your list, the list will not permit any packets.

Understand the standard IP access-list configuration command.   To configure a standard IP access list, use the access-list numbers 1–99 or 1300–1999 in global configuration mode. Choose permit or deny, then choose the source IP address you want to filter on using one of the three techniques covered in this discussion of access lists.

Understand the extended IP access-list configuration command.   To configure an extended IP access list, use the access-list numbers 100–199 or 2000–2699 in global configuration mode. Choose permit or deny, the Network layer protocol field, the source IP address you want to filter on, the destination address you want to filter on, and finally, the Transport layer port number if TCP or UDP has been specified as the protocol.

Remember the command to verify an access list on a router interface.   To see whether an access list is set on an interface and in which direction it is filtering, use the show ip interface command. This command will not show you the contents of the access list, merely which access lists are applied on the interface.

Remember the command to verify the access-list configuration.   To see the configured access lists on your router, use the show access-list command. This command will not show you which interfaces have an access list set.

Verify ACLs using the APIC-EM Path Trace ACL Analysis tool

Cisco Application Policy Infrastructure Controller Enterprise Module (APIC-EM) is a Cisco SDN controller, which uses open APIs for policy-based management and security through a single controller, abstracting the network and making network services simpler. APIC-EM provides centralized automation of policy-based application profiles, and the APIC-EM northbound interface is the only API that you'll need to control your network programmatically. Through this programmability, automated network control helps IT to respond quickly to new business opportunities. The APIC-EM also includes support for greenfield (new installations) and brownfield (current or old installations) deployments, which allows you to implement programmability and automation with the infrastructure that you already have.

APIC-EM is pretty cool, easy to use (although that's up for debate), and automates the tasks that network engineers have been doing for well over 20 years. At first glance this seems like it will replace our current jobs, and in some circumstances, people resistant to change will certainly be replaced. But you don't have to be one of them if you start planning now. Figure 6.10 demonstrates exactly where the APCI-EM controller sits in the SDN stack.

FIGURE 6.10   Where APIC-EM fits in the SDN stack

Cisco APIC-EM's northbound interface is only an API, but southbound interfaces are implemented with something called a service abstraction layer (SAL), which talks to the network elements via SNMP and CLI. Using the SNMP and the CLI allows APIC-EM to work with legacy Cisco products, and soon APIC-EM will be able to use NETCONF too. The network devices can be either physical or virtual, including Nexus data center switches, ASA firewalls, ASR routers, or even third-party load balancers. The managed devices must be specific to ACI; in other words, a special NX-OS or ASR IOS version is required to add the southbound APIs required to communicate with the APIC controller.

The APIC-EM API is REST based, which as you know allows you to discover and control your network using HTTP by using the GET, POST, PUT, and DELETE options along with JSON (JavaScript Object Notation) and XML (eXtensible Markup Language) syntax.

In Figure 6.11 are some important features of Cisco APIC-EM that are covered in the CCNA objectives.

FIGURE 6.11   APIC-Enterprise Module screen

On the left of the screen you can see the Discovery button. This provides the network information database, which scans the network and provides the inventory, including all network devices; the network devices are also shown on the Device Inventory page.

There's also a network topology visualization, which reveals the physical topology discovered, as shown in the layout on Figure 6.11. This auto-discovers and maps network devices to a physical topology with detailed device-level data, including the discovered hosts. And take note of that IWAN button. It provides the provisioning of IWAN network profiles with simple business policies. Plus there is a Path Trace button, which I will talk about next.

But wait... Before I move on to the path trace functionality of APIC-EM, let me go over a few more promising features with you. In the APIC-EM is the Zero-Touch Deployment feature, which finds a new device via the controller scanner and automatically configures it. You can track user identities and endpoints by exchanging the information with the Cisco Identity Service Engine (Cisco ISE) via the Identity Manager. You can also quickly set and enforce QoS priority policies with the QoS deployment and change management feature and accelerate ACL management by querying and analyzing ACLs on each network device. This means you can quickly identify ACL misconfiguration using the ACL analysis! And last but not least, using the Policy Manager, the controller translates a business policy into a network-device-level policy. The Policy Manager can enforce the policy for a specific user at various times of the day, across wired and wireless networks.

Now let's take a look at the very vital path tracing feature of APIC-EM.

Using APIC-EM for Path Tracing

An important objective in this intelligent networks section is the path tracing ability in the APIC-EM. Matter of fact, I've mostly been using the APIC-EM for just this feature in order to help me troubleshoot my virtual networks, and it does it very well. And it looks cool too!

Pushing toward staying tight to the CCNA objectives here, you really want to know that you can use the path trace service of APIC-EM for ACL analysis. Doing this allows you to examine the path that a specific type of packet travels as it makes its way across the network from a source to a destination node, and it can use IP and TCP/UDP ports when diagnosing an application issue. If there is an ACL on an interface that blocks a certain application, you'll see this in a GUI output. I cannot tell you how extremely helpful this is in the day-to-day administration of your networks!

The result of a path trace will be a GUI representation of the path that a packet takes across all the devices and links between the source and destination, and you can choose to provide the output of a reverse path as well. Although I could easily do this same work manually, it would certainly be a whole lot more time consuming if I did! APIC-EM's Path Trace app actually does the work for you with just a few clicks at the user interface.

Once you fill in the fields for the source, destination, and optionally, the application, the path trace is initiated. You'll then see the path between hosts, plus the list of each device along the path, illustrated in Figure 6.12.

FIGURE 6.12   APIC-Enterprise Module path trace sample

Okay, here you can see the complete path taken from host A to host B. I chose to view the reverse path as well. In this particular case, we weren't being blocked by an ACL, but if a packet actually was being blocked for a certain application, we'd see the exact interface where the application was blocked and why. Here is more detail on how my trace occurred.

First, the APIC-EM Discovery finds the network topology. At this point I can now choose the source and destination address of a packet and, alternately, port numbers and the application that can be used. The MAC address table, IP routing tables, and so on are used by the APIC-EM to find the path of the packet through the network. Finally, the GUI will show you the path, complete with device and interface information.

Last point: The APIC-EM is free, and most of the applications off the NBI are built in and included, but there are some solution applications that need a license. So if you have a VM with at least 64 gigs of RAM, you're set!

Exam Essentials

Understand APIC-EM and the path trace.   Read through Verify ACLs using the APIC-EM Path Trace ACL Analysis tool section, which cover the CCNA objectives fully.

Configure, verify, and troubleshoot basic device hardening

Hardening a device is the process of ensuring the device is secured from attack. There are a number of steps that should be taken as standard operating procedure to lock down infrastructure devices. In the following sections, we'll discuss the most important of these.

Local Authentication

There are five passwords you'll need to secure your Cisco routers: console, auxiliary, telnet (VTY), enable password, and enable secret. The enable secret and enable password are the ones used to set the password for securing privileged mode. Once the enable commands are set, users will be prompted for a password. The other three are used to configure a password when user mode is accessed through the console port, through the auxiliary port, or via Telnet.

Let's take a look at each of these now.

Enable Passwords

You set the enable passwords from global configuration mode like this:

```
Todd(config)#enable ?
 last-resort Define enable action if no TACACS servers
             respond
 password    Assign the privileged level password
 secret      Assign the privileged level secret
 use-tacacs  Use TACACS to check enable passwords
```

The following list describes the enable password parameters:

last-resort   This allows you to still enter the device if you set up authentication through a TACACS server and it's not available. It won't be used if the TACACS server is working.

password   This sets the enable password on older, pre-10.3 systems and isn't ever used if an enable secret is set.

secret   The newer, encrypted password that overrides the enable password if it has been set

use-tacacs   This tells the router or switch to authenticate through a TACACS server. It comes in really handy when you have lots of routers because changing the password on a multitude of them can be insanely tedious. It's much easier to simply go through the TACACS server and change the password only once!

Here's an example that shows how to set the enable passwords:

```
Todd(config)#enable secret todd
Todd(config)#enable password todd
The enable password you have chosen is the same as your
  enable secret. This is not recommended. Re-enter the
  enable password.
```

If you try to set the enable secret and enable passwords the same, the device will give you a polite warning to change the second password. Make a note to yourself that if there aren't any old legacy routers involved, you don't even bother to use the enable password!

User-mode passwords are assigned via the `line` command like this:

```
Todd(config)#line ?
  <0-16>   First Line number
  console  Primary terminal line
  vty      Virtual terminal
```

And these two lines are especially important for the exam objectives:

console Sets a console user-mode password

vty Sets a Telnet password on the device. If this password isn't set, then by default, Telnet can't be used.

To configure user-mode passwords, choose the line you want and configure it using the `login` command to make the switch prompt for authentication. Let's focus in on the configuration of individual lines now.

Console Password

We set the console password with the `line console 0` command, but look at what happened when I tried to type **line console ?** from the `(config-line)#` prompt—I received an error! Here's the example:

```
Todd(config-line)#line console ?
% Unrecognized command
Todd(config-line)#exit
Todd(config)#line console ?
  <0-0>   First Line number
Todd(config)#line console 0
Todd(config-line)#password console
Todd(config-line)#login
```

You can still type **line console 0** and that will be accepted, but the help screens just don't work from that prompt. Type **exit** to go back one level, and you'll find that your help screens now work. This is a "feature." Really.

Because there's only one console port, I can only choose line console 0. You can set all your line passwords to the same password, but doing this isn't exactly a brilliant security move!

And it's also important to remember to apply the `login` command or the console port won't prompt for authentication. The way Cisco has this process set up means you can't set the `login` command before a password is set on a line because if you set it but don't then set a password, that line won't be usable. You'll actually get prompted for a password that doesn't exist, so Cisco's method isn't just a hassle; it makes sense and is a feature after all!

 Definitely remember that although Cisco has this "password feature" on its routers starting with IOS 12.2 and above, it's not included in older IOSs.

Okay, there are a few other important commands you need to know regarding the console port.

For one, the exec-timeout 0 0 command sets the time-out for the console EXEC session to zero, ensuring that it never times out. The default time-out is 10 minutes.

> If you're feeling mischievous, try this on people at work: Set the exec-timeout command to 0 1. This will make the console time out in 1 second, and to fix it, you have to continually press the down arrow key while changing the time-out time with your free hand!

Logging synchronous is such a cool command that it should be a default, but it's not. It's great because it's the antidote for those annoying console messages that disrupt the input you're trying to type. The messages will still pop up, but at least you get returned to your device prompt without your input being interrupted! This makes your input messages oh-so-much easier to read!

Here's an example of how to configure both commands:

```
Todd(config-line)#line con 0
Todd(config-line)#exec-timeout ?
  <0-35791>  Timeout in minutes
Todd(config-line)#exec-timeout 0 ?
  <0-2147483>  Timeout in seconds
  <cr>
Todd(config-line)#exec-timeout 0 0
Todd(config-line)#logging synchronous
```

> You can set the console to go from never timing out (0 0) to timing out in 35,791 minutes and 2,147,483 seconds. Remember that the default is 10 minutes.

Telnet Password

To set the user-mode password for Telnet access into the router or switch, use the line vty command. IOS switches typically have 16 lines, but routers running the Enterprise edition have considerably more. The best way to find out how many lines you have is to use that handy question mark like this:

```
Todd(config-line)#line vty 0 ?
% Unrecognized command
Todd(config-line)#exit
Todd(config)#line vty 0 ?
  <1-15>  Last Line number
  <cr>
```

```
Todd(config)#line vty 0 15
Todd(config-line)#password telnet
Todd(config-line)#login
```

This output clearly shows that you cannot get help from your (config-line)# prompt. You must go back to global config mode in order to use the question mark (?).

So what will happen if you try to telnet into a device that doesn't have a VTY password set? You'll receive an error saying the connection has been refused because the password isn't set. So, if you telnet into a switch and receive a message like this one that I got from Switch B:

```
Todd#telnet SwitchB
Trying SwitchB (10.0.0.1)...Open

Password required, but none set
[Connection to SwitchB closed by foreign host]
Todd#
```

it means the switch doesn't have the VTY password set. But you can still get around this and tell the switch to allow Telnet connections without a password by using the no login command:

```
SwitchB(config-line)#line vty 0 15
SwitchB(config-line)#no login
```

WARNING   I definitely do not recommend using the no login command to allow Telnet connections without a password, unless you're in a testing or classroom environment. In a production network, always set your VTY password!

After your IOS devices are configured with an IP address, you can use the Telnet program to configure and check your routers instead of having to use a console cable. You can use the Telnet program by typing **telnet** from any command prompt (DOS or Cisco).

Auxiliary Password

To configure the auxiliary password on a router, go into global configuration mode and type **line aux ?**. And by the way, you won't find these ports on a switch. This output shows that you only get a choice of 0–0, which is because there's only one port:

```
Todd#config t
Todd(config)#line aux ?
  <0-0>  First Line number
Todd(config)#line aux 0
Todd(config-line)#login
```

```
% Login disabled on line 1, until 'password' is set
Todd(config-line)#password aux
Todd(config-line)#login
```

Secure Password

Because only the enable secret password is encrypted by default, you'll need to manually configure the user-mode and enable passwords for encryption.

Notice that you can see all the passwords except the enable secret when performing a show running-config on a switch:

```
Todd#sh running-config
Building configuration...

Current configuration : 1020 bytes
!
! Last configuration change at 00:03:11 UTC Mon Mar 1 1993
!
version 15.0
no service pad
service timestamps debug datetime msec
service timestamps log datetime msec
no service password-encryption
!
hostname Todd
!
enable secret 4 ykw.3/tgsOuy9.6qmgG/EeYOYgBvfX4v.S8UNA9Rddg
enable password todd
!
[output cut]
!
line con 0
 password console
 login
line vty 0 4
 password telnet
 login
line vty 5 15
 password telnet
 login
!
end
```

To manually encrypt your passwords, use the service password-encryption command. Here's how:

```
Todd#config t
Todd(config)#service password-encryption
Todd(config)#exit
Todd#show run
Building configuration...
!
!
enable secret 4 ykw.3/tgsOuy9.6qmgG/EeYOYgBvfX4v.S8UNA9Rddg
enable password 7 1506040800
!
[output cut]
!
!
line con 0
 password 7 050809013243420C
 login
line vty 0 4
 password 7 06120A2D424B1D
 login
line vty 5 15
 password 7 06120A2D424B1D
 login
!
end
Todd#config t
Todd(config)#no service password-encryption
Todd(config)#^Z
Todd#
```

Nicely done—the passwords will now be encrypted. All you need to do is encrypt the passwords, perform a show run, then turn off the command if you want. This output clearly shows us that the enable password and the line passwords are all encrypted.

I want to stress some points about password encryption. I said, if you set your passwords and then turn on the service password-encryption command, you have to perform a show running-config before you turn off the encryption service or your passwords won't be encrypted. You don't have to turn off the encryption service at all—you'd only do that if your switch is running low on processes. And if you turn on the service before you set your passwords, then you don't even have to view them to have them encrypted.

Access to Device

Access to a device can be controlled at any line (console, terminal, or aux) with the use of access lists applied to the line as shown in the section "Local Authentication." In the following sections, we'll take a look at another method of securing access using SSH.

Source Address

Controlling access by IP address is done though the implementation of access lists as described in the section "Local Authentication."

Telnet/SSH

I strongly recommend using Secure Shell (SSH) instead of Telnet because it creates a more secure session. The Telnet application uses an unencrypted data stream, but SSH uses encryption keys to send data so your username and password aren't sent in the clear, vulnerable to anyone lurking around!

Here are the steps for setting up SSH:

1. Set your hostname:

    ```
    Router(config)#hostname Todd
    ```

2. Set the domain name—both the hostname and domain name are required for the encryption keys to be generated:

    ```
    Todd(config)#ip domain-name Lammle.com
    ```

3. Set the username to allow SSH client access:

    ```
    Todd(config)#username Todd password Lammle
    ```

4. Generate the encryption keys for securing the session:

    ```
    Todd(config)#crypto key generate rsa
    The name for the keys will be: Todd.Lammle.com
    Choose the size of the key modulus in the range of 360 to
    4096 for your General Purpose Keys. Choosing a key modulus
    Greater than 512 may take a few minutes.

    How many bits in the modulus [512]: 1024
    % Generating 1024 bit RSA keys, keys will be non-exportable...
    [OK] (elapsed time was 6 seconds)

    Todd(config)#
    1d14h: %SSH-5-ENABLED: SSH 1.99 has been enabled*June 24
    19:25:30.035: %SSH-5-ENABLED: SSH 1.99 has been enabled
    ```

5. Enable SSH version 2 on the device—not mandatory, but strongly suggested:

    ```
    Todd(config)#ip ssh version 2
    ```

6. Connect to the VTY lines of the switch or router:

    `Todd(config)#`**`line vty 0 15`**

7. Configure your access protocols:

    ```
    Todd(config-line)#transport input ?
      all      All protocols
      none     No protocols
      ssh      TCP/IP SSH protocol
      telnet   TCP/IP Telnet protocol
    ```

    Beware of this next line, and make sure you never use it in production because it's a horrendous security risk:

    `Todd(config-line)#`**`transport input all`**

    I recommend using the next line to secure your VTY lines with SSH:

    ```
    Todd(config-line)#transport input ssh ?
      telnet   TCP/IP Telnet protocol
      <cr>
    ```

I actually do use Telnet once in a while when a situation arises that specifically calls for it. It just doesn't happen very often. But if you want to go with Telnet, here's how you do that:

`Todd(config-line)#`**`transport input ssh telnet`**

Know that if you don't use the keyword `telnet` at the end of the command string, then only SSH will work on the device. You can go with either, just so long as you understand that SSH is way more secure than Telnet.

Login Banner

A very good reason for having a *banner* is to give any and all who dare attempt to telnet or sneak into your internetwork a little security notice. And they're very cool because you can create and customize them so that they'll greet anyone who shows up on the router with exactly the information you want them to have!

Here are the three types of banners you need to be sure you're familiar with:

- Exec process creation banner
- Login banner
- Message of the day banner

And you can see them all illustrated in the following code:

```
Todd(config)#banner ?
  LINE         c banner-text c, where 'c' is a delimiting character
  exec         Set EXEC process creation banner
  incoming     Set incoming terminal line banner
```

```
login            Set login banner
motd             Set Message of the Day banner
prompt-timeout   Set Message for login authentication timeout
slip-ppp         Set Message for SLIP/PPP
```

Message of the day (MOTD) banners are the most widely used banners because they give a message to anyone connecting to the router via Telnet or an auxiliary port or even through a console port as seen here:

```
Todd(config)#banner motd ?
LINE c banner-text c, where 'c' is a delimiting character
Todd(config)#banner motd #
Enter TEXT message. End with the character '#'.
$ Acme.com network, then you must disconnect immediately.
#
Todd(config)#^Z (Press the control key + z keys to return to privileged mode)
Todd#exit

con0 is now available

Press RETURN to get started.
If you are not authorized to be in Acme.com network, then you
must disconnect immediately.
Todd#
```

This MOTD banner essentially tells anyone connecting to the device to get lost if they're not on the guest list. The part to focus upon here is the delimiting character, which is what informs the router the message is done. Clearly, you can use any character you want for it except for the delimiting character in the message itself. Once the message is complete, press Enter, then the delimiting character, and then press Enter again. Everything will still work if you don't follow this routine unless you have more than one banner. If that's the case, make sure you do follow it or your banners will all be combined into one message and put on a single line!

You can set a banner on one line like this:

```
Todd(config)#banner motd x Unauthorized access prohibited! x
```

Let's take a minute to go into more detail about the other two types of banners I mentioned:

Exec banner   You can configure a line-activation (exec) banner to be displayed when EXEC processes such as a line activation or an incoming connection to a VTY line have been created. Simply initiating a user exec session through a console port will activate the exec banner.

Login banner   You can configure a login banner for display on all connected terminals. It will show up after the MOTD banner but before the login prompts. This login banner can't be disabled on a per-line basis, so to globally disable it you've got to delete it with the no banner login command.

Here's what a login banner output looks like:

```
!
banner login ^C
------------------------------------------------------------------
Cisco Router and Security Device Manager (SDM) is installed on this device.
This feature requires the one-time use of the username "cisco"
with the password "cisco". The default username and password
have a privilege level of 15.
Please change these publicly known initial credentials using
SDM or the IOS CLI.
Here are the Cisco IOS commands.
username <myuser>  privilege 15 secret 0 <mypassword>
no username cisco
Replace <myuser> and <mypassword> with the username and
password you want to use.
For more information about SDM please follow the instructions
in the QUICK START GUIDE for your router or go to http://www.cisco.com/go/sdm
------------------------------------------------------------------
^C
!
```

The previous login banner should look pretty familiar to anyone who's ever logged into an ISR router because it's the banner Cisco has in the default configuration for its ISR routers.

Exam Essentials

Differentiate the enable password and enable secret password.   Both of these passwords are used to gain access into privileged mode. However, the enable secret password is newer and is always encrypted by default. Also, if you set the enable password and then set the enable secret, only the enable secret will be used.

Describe the configuration and use of banners.   Banners provide information to users accessing the device and can be displayed at various login prompts. They are configured with the banner command and a keyword describing the specific type of banner.

Set the enable secret on a router.   To set the enable secret, you use the global config command enable secret. Do not use enable secret password *password* or you will set your password to *password password*. Here is an example:

```
enable
config t
enable secret todd
```

Set the console password on a router.   To set the console password, use the following sequence:

```
enable
config t
line console 0
password todd
login
```

Set the Telnet password on a router.   To set the Telnet password, the sequence is as follows:

```
enable
config t
line vty 0 4
password todd
login
```

Describe the advantages of using Secure Shell and list its requirements.   Secure Shell (SSH) uses encrypted keys to send data so that usernames and passwords are not sent in the clear. It requires that a hostname and domain name be configured and that encryption keys be generated.

Describe device security using AAA with TACACS+ and RADIUS

Of course we only want authorized IT folks to have administrative access to our network devices such as routers and switches, and in a small to medium-sized network, just using local authentication is sufficient.

However, if you have hundreds of devices, managing administrative connectivity would be nearly impossible since you'd have to configure local authentication on each device by hand, and if you changed just one password, it can take hours to update your network.

Since maintaining the local database for each network device for the size of the network is usually not feasible, you can use an external authentication, authorization, and accounting (AAA) server that will manage all user and administrative access needs for an entire network. The two most popular options for external AAA are RADIUS and TACACS+, both covered next.

RADIUS

Remote Authentication Dial-In User Service, or *RADIUS*, was developed by the Internet Engineering Task Force—the IETF—and is basically a security system that works to guard the network against unauthorized access. RADIUS, which uses only UDP, is an open standard implemented by most major vendors, and it's one of the most popular types of security servers around because it combines authentication and authorization services into a single process. So after users are authenticated, they are then authorized for network services.

RADIUS implements a client/server architecture, where the typical client is a router, switch, or AP and the typical server is a Windows or Unix device that's running RADIUS software.

The authentication process has three distinct stages:

1. The user is prompted for a username and password.

2. The username and encrypted password are sent over the network to the RADIUS server.

3. The RADIUS server replies with one of the following:

Response	Meaning
Accept	The user has been successfully authenticated.
Reject	The username and password are not valid.
Challenge	The RADIUS server requests additional information.
Change Password	The user should select a new password.

It's important to remember that RADIUS encrypts only the password in the access-request packet from the client to the server. The remainder of the packet is unencrypted.

Configuring RADIUS

To configure a RADIUS server for console and VTY access, first you need to enable AAA services in order to configure all the AAA commands. Configure the aaa new-model command in the global configuration mode.

```
Router(config)# aaa new-model
```

The aaa new-model command immediately applies local authentication to all lines and interfaces (except line con 0). So, to avoid being locked out of the router or switch, you should define a local username and password before starting the AAA configuration.

Now, configure a local user.

```
Router(config)#username Todd password Lammle
```

Creating this user is super important because you can then use this same locally created user if the external authentication server fails! If you don't create this and you can't get to the server, you're going to end up doing a password recovery.

Next, configure a RADIUS server using any name and the RADIUS key that is configured on the server.

```
Router(config)#radius server SecureLogin
Router(config-radius-server)#address ipv4 10.10.10.254
```

```
Router(config-radius-server)#key MyRadiusPassword
```

Now, add your newly created RADIUS server to an AAA group of any name.

```
Router(config)#aaa group server radius MyRadiusGroup
Router(config-sg-radius)#server name SecureLogin
```

Last, configure this newly created group to be used for AAA login authentication. If the RADIUS server fails, the fallback to local authentication should be set.

```
Router(config)# aaa authentication login default group MyRadiusGroup local
```

TACACS+

Terminal Access Controller Access Control System (TACACS+) is also a security server that's Cisco proprietary and uses TCP. It's really similar in many ways to RADIUS; however, it does all that RADIUS does and more, including multiprotocol support.

TACACS+ was developed by Cisco Systems, so it's specifically designed to interact with Cisco's AAA services. If you're using TACACS+, you have the entire menu of AAA features available to you—and it handles each security aspect separately, unlike RADIUS:

- Authentication includes messaging support in addition to login and password functions.
- Authorization enables explicit control over user capabilities.
- Accounting supplies detailed information about user activities.

Configuring TACACS+

This is pretty much identical to the RADIUS configuration.

To configure a TACACS+ server for console and VTY access, first you need to enable AAA services in order to configure all the AAA commands. Configure the aaa new-model command in the global configuration mode (if it isn't already enabled).

```
Router(config)# aaa new-model
```

Now, configure a local user if you haven't already.

```
Router(config)#username Todd password Lammle
```

Next, configure a TACACS+ server using any name and the key that is configured on the server.

```
Router(config)#radius server SecureLoginTACACS+
Router(config-radius-server)#address ipv4 10.10.10.254
Router(config-radius-server)#key MyTACACS+Password
```

Now, add your newly created TACACS+ server to a AAA group of any name.

```
Router(config)#aaa group server radius MyTACACS+Group
Router(config-sg-radius)#server name SecureLoginTACACS+
```

Last configure this newly created group to be used for AAA login authentication. If the TACACS+ server fails, the fallback to local authentication should be set.

```
Router(config)# aaa authentication login default group MyTACACS+Group local
```

Exam Essentials

Understand TACACS+ and RADIUS.   TACACS+ is Cisco proprietary, uses TCP, and can separate services. RADIUS is an open standard, uses UDP, and cannot separate services.

Review Questions

You can find the answers in the Appendix.

1. Which of the following commands will enable AAA on a router?
   A. `aaa enable`
   B. `enable aaa`
   C. `new-model aaa`
   D. `aaa new-model`

2. Which of the following will mitigate access layer threats? (Choose two.)
   A. Port security
   B. Access lists
   C. Dynamic ARP inspection
   D. AAA

3. Which of the following is not true about DHCP snooping?
   A. DHCP snooping validates DHCP messages received from untrusted sources and filters out invalid messages.
   B. DHCP snooping builds and maintains the DHCP snooping binding database, which contains information about untrusted hosts with leased IP addresses.
   C. DHCP snooping rate-limits DHCP traffic from trusted and untrusted sources.
   D. DHCP snooping is a layer 2 security feature that acts like a firewall between hosts.

4. Which of the following are true about TACACS+? (Choose two.)
   A. TACACS+ is a Cisco proprietary security mechanism.
   B. TACACS+ uses UDP.
   C. TACACS+ combines authentication and authorization services as a single process— after users are authenticated, they are also authorized.
   D. TACACS+ offers multiprotocol support.

5. Which of the following is not true about RADIUS?
   A. RADIUS is an open standard protocol.
   B. RADIUS separates AAA services.
   C. RADIUS uses UDP.
   D. RADIUS encrypts only the password in the access-request packet from the client to the server. The remainder of the packet is unencrypted.

6. Which of the following statements is false when a packet is being compared to an access list?

A. It's always compared with each line of the access list in sequential order.

B. Once the packet matches the condition on a line of the access list, the packet is acted upon and no further comparisons take place.

C. There is an implicit "deny" at the end of each access list.

D. Until all lines have been analyzed, the comparison is not over.

7. You need to create an access list that will prevent hosts in the network range of 192.168.160.0 to 192.168.191.0. Which of the following lists will you use?

A. `access-list 10 deny 192.168.160.0 255.255.224.0`

B. `access-list 10 deny 192.168.160.0 0.0.191.255`

C. `access-list 10 deny 192.168.160.0 0.0.31.255`

D. `access-list 10 deny 192.168.0.0 0.0.31.255`

8. You have created a named access list called BlockSales. Which of the following is a valid command for applying this to packets trying to enter interface Fa0/0 of your router?

A. `(config)#ip access-group 110 in`

B. `(config-if)#ip access-group 110 in`

C. `(config-if)#ip access-group Blocksales in`

D. `(config-if)#BlockSales ip access-list in`

9. Which access list statement will permit all HTTP sessions to network 192.168.144.0/24 containing web servers?

A. `access-list 110 permit tcp 192.168.144.0 0.0.0.255 any eq 80`

B. `access-list 110 permit tcp any 192.168.144.0 0.0.0.255 eq 80`

C. `access-list 110 permit tcp 192.168.144.0 0.0.0.255 192.168.144.0 0.0.0.255 any eq 80`

D. `access-list 110 permit udp any 192.168.144.0 eq 80`

10. Which of the following access lists will allow only HTTP traffic into network 196.15.7.0?

A. `access-list 100 permit tcp any 196.15.7.0 0.0.0.255 eq www`

B. `access-list 10 deny tcp any 196.15.7.0 eq www`

C. `access-list 100 permit 196.15.7.0 0.0.0.255 eq www`

D. `access-list 110 permit ip any 196.15.7.0 0.0.0.255`

E. `access-list 110 permit www 196.15.7.0 0.0.0.255`

Chapter

7

Infrastructure Management

THE FOLLOWING CCNA ROUTING AND SWITCHING EXAM OBJECTIVES ARE COVERED IN THIS CHAPTER:

- ✓ Configure and verify device-monitoring protocols.

- ✓ Troubleshoot network connectivity issues using ICMP echo-based IP SLA.

- ✓ Configure and verify device management.

- ✓ Configure and verify initial device configuration.

- ✓ Perform device maintenance.

- ✓ Use Cisco IOS tools to troubleshoot and resolve problems.

- ✓ Describe network programmability in enterprise network architecture.

In this chapter, I will discuss managing the devices that comprise your network infrastructure. The topics will include device maintenance and the monitoring of devices. We'll also describe the tools used to troubleshoot and resolve issues and I will close the chapter with a discussion of network programmability.

Configure and verify device-monitoring protocols

Although *Simple Network Management Protocol (SNMP)* certainly isn't the oldest protocol ever, it's still pretty old, considering it was created way back in 1988 (RFC 1065)!

SNMP is an Application layer protocol that provides a message format for agents on a variety of devices to communicate with network management stations (NMSs)—for example, Cisco Prime or HP Openview. These agents send messages to the NMS station, which then either reads or writes information in the database that's stored on the NMS and called a management information base (MIB).

The NMS periodically queries or polls the SNMP agent on a device to gather and analyze statistics via GET messages. End devices running SNMP agents would send an SNMP trap to the NMS if a problem occurs. This is demonstrated in Figure 7.1.

FIGURE 7.1 SNMP GET and TRAP messages

Admins can also use SNMP to provide some configurations to agents as well, called SET messages. In addition to polling to obtain statistics, SNMP can be used for analyzing information and compiling the results in a report or even a graph. Thresholds can be used to trigger a notification process when exceeded. Graphing tools are used to monitor the CPU statistics of Cisco devices like a core router. The CPU should be monitored continuously and the NMS can graph the statistics. Notification will be sent when any threshold you've set has been exceeded.

SNMP has three versions, with version 1 being rarely, if ever, implemented today. Here's a summary of these three versions.

SNMPv1

SNMPv1 supports plain-text authentication with community strings and uses only UDP.

SNMPv2c

SNMPv2 supports plain-text authentication with community strings with no encryption but provides GET BULK, which is a way to gather many types of information at once and minimize the number of GET requests. It offers a more detailed error message reporting method called INFORM, but it's not more secure than v1. It uses UDP even though it can be configured to use TCP.

SNMPv3

SNMPv3 supports strong authentication with MD5 or SHA, providing confidentiality (encryption) and data integrity of messages via DES or DES-256 encryption between agents and managers. GET BULK is a supported feature of SNMPv3, and this version also uses TCP.

Management Information Base (MIB)

With so many kinds of devices and so much data that can be accessed, there needed to be a standard way to organize this plethora of data, so MIB to the rescue! A *management information base (MIB)* is a collection of information that's organized hierarchically and can be accessed by protocols like SNMP. RFCs define some common public variables, but most organizations define their own private branches along with basic SNMP standards. Organizational IDs (OIDs) are laid out as a tree with different levels assigned by different organizations, with top-level MIB OIDs belonging to various standards organizations.

Vendors assign private branches in their own products. Let's take a look at Cisco's OIDs, which are described in words or numbers to locate a particular variable in the tree, as shown in Figure 7.2.

FIGURE 7.2   Cisco's MIB OIDs

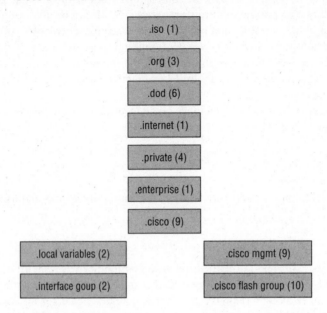

Luckily, you don't need to memorize the OIDs in Figure 7.2 for the Cisco exams!

To obtain information from the MIB on the SNMP agent, you can use several different operations:

- **GET:** This operation is used to get information from the MIB to an SNMP agent.

- **SET:** This operation is used to get information to the MIB from an SNMP manager.

- **WALK:** This operation is used to list information from successive MIB objects within a specified MIB.

- **TRAP:** This operation is used by the SNMP agent to send a triggered piece of information to the SNMP manager.

- **INFORM:** This operation is the same as a trap, but it adds an acknowledgment that a trap does not provide.

Configuring SNMP

Configuring SNMP is a pretty straightforward process for which you only need a few commands. These five steps are all you need to run through to configure a Cisco device for SNMP access:

1. Configure where the traps are to be sent.

2. Enable SNMP read-write access to the router.

3. Configure SNMP contact information.

4. Configure SNMP location.

5. Configure an ACL to restrict SNMP access to the NMS hosts.

The only required configuration is the IP address of the NMS station (Step 1 above) and the community string (Step 2 above) because the other three are optional. The community string acts as a password or authentication string. Here's an example of a typical SNMP router configuration:

```
Router(config)#snmp-server host 1.2.3.4
Router(config)#snmp-server community ?
  WORD  SNMP community string

Router(config)#snmp-server community Todd ?
  <1-99>       Std IP accesslist allowing access with this community string
  <1300-1999> Expanded IP accesslist allowing access with this community
               string
  WORD        Access-list name
  ipv6        Specify IPv6 Named Access-List
  ro          Read-only access with this community string
  rw          Read-write access with this community string
  view        Restrict this community to a named MIB view
  <cr>

Router(config)#snmp-server community Todd rw
Router(config)#snmp-server location Boulder
Router(config)#snmp-server contact Todd Lammle
Router(config)#ip access-list standard Protect_NMS_Station
Router(config-std-nacl)#permit host 192.168.10.254
```

Entering the `snmp-server` command enables SNMPv1 on the Cisco device.

You can enter the ACL directly in the SNMP configuration to provide security, using either a number or a name. Here is an example:

```
Router(config)#snmp-server community Todd Protect_NMS_Station rw
```

Notice that even though there's a boatload of configuration options under SNMP, you only really need to work with a few of them to configure a basic SNMP trap setup on a router. First, I set the IP address of the NMS station where the router will send the traps; then I chose the community name of Todd with RW access (read-write), which means the NMS will be able to retrieve and modify MIB objects from the router. Location and contact information comes in really handy for troubleshooting the configuration. Make sure you understand that the ACL protects the NMS from access, not the devices with the agents!

Let's define the SNMP read and write options.

Read-only   Gives authorized management stations read access to all objects in the MIB except the community strings and doesn't allow write access

Read-write   Gives authorized management stations read and write access to all objects in the MIB but doesn't allow access to the community strings

Syslog

Reading system messages from a switch's or router's internal buffer is the most popular and efficient method of seeing what's going on with your network at a particular time. But the best way is to log messages to a *syslog* server, which stores messages from you and can even time-stamp and sequence them for you, and it's easy to set up and configure!

Syslog allows you to display, sort, and even search messages, all of which makes it a really great troubleshooting tool. The search feature is especially powerful because you can use keywords and even severity levels. Plus, the server can email admins based on the severity level of the message.

Network devices can be configured to generate a syslog message and forward it to various destinations. These four examples are popular ways to gather messages from Cisco devices:

- Logging buffer (on by default)
- Console line (on by default)
- Terminal lines (using the `terminal monitor` command)
- Syslog server

As you already know, all system messages and debug output generated by the IOS go out only the console port by default and are also logged in buffers in RAM. And you also know that Cisco routers aren't exactly shy about sending messages! To send message to the VTY lines, use the `terminal monitor` command. We'll also add a small configuration needed for syslog, which I'll show you soon in the configuration section.

So by default, we'd see something like this on our console line:

```
*Oct 21 17:33:50.565:%LINK-5-CHANGED:Interface FastEthernet0/0, changed
state to administratively down
*Oct 21 17:33:51.565:%LINEPROTO-5-UPDOWN:Line protocol on
Interface FastEthernet0/0, changed state to down
```

And the Cisco router would send a general version of the message to the syslog server that would be formatted into something like this:

```
Seq no:timestamp: %facility-severity-MNEMONIC:description
```

The system message format can be broken down in this way:

Seq no   This stamp logs messages with a sequence number, but not by default. If you want this output, you've got to configure it.

timestamp   Data and time of the message or event, which again will show up only if configured

facility   The facility to which the message refers

severity   A single-digit code from 0 to 7 that indicates the severity of the message

MNEMONIC   Text string that uniquely describes the message

description   Text string containing detailed information about the event being reported

The severity levels, from the most severe level to the least severe, are explained in Table 7.1. Informational is the default and will result in all messages being sent to the buffers and console.

TABLE 7.1   Severity levels

Severity Level	Explanation
Emergency (severity 0)	System is unusable.
Alert (severity 1)	Immediate action is needed.
Critical (severity 2)	Critical condition
Error (severity 3)	Error condition
Warning (severity 4)	Warning condition
Notification (severity 5)	Normal but significant condition
Informational (severity 6)	Normal information message
Debugging (severity 7)	Debugging message

 If you are studying for your Cisco exam, you need to memorize Table 7.1.

Understand that only emergency-level messages will be displayed if you've configured severity level 0. But if, for example, you opt for level 4 instead, level 0 through 4 will be displayed, giving you emergency, alert, critical, error, and warning messages too. Level 7 is the highest-level security option and displays everything, but be warned that going with it could have a serious impact on the performance of your device. So always use debugging commands carefully, with an eye on the messages you really need to meet your specific business requirements!

Configuring and Verifying Syslog

As I said, Cisco devices send all log messages of the severity level you've chosen to the console. They'll also go to the buffer, and both happen by default. Because of this, it's good to know that you can disable and enable these features with the following commands:

```
Router(config)#logging ?
  Hostname or A.B.C.D  IP address of the logging host
  buffered             Set buffered logging parameters
  buginf               Enable buginf logging for debugging
  cns-events           Set CNS Event logging level
  console              Set console logging parameters
  count                Count every log message and timestamp last occurrence
  esm                  Set ESM filter restrictions
  exception            Limit size of exception flush output
  facility             Facility parameter for syslog messages
  filter               Specify logging filter
  history              Configure syslog history table
  host                 Set syslog server IP address and parameters
  monitor              Set terminal line (monitor) logging parameters
  on                   Enable logging to all enabled destinations
  origin-id            Add origin ID to syslog messages
  queue-limit          Set logger message queue size
  rate-limit           Set messages per second limit
  reload               Set reload logging level
  server-arp           Enable sending ARP requests for syslog servers when
                       first configured
  source-interface     Specify interface for source address in logging
                       transactions
  trap                 Set syslog server logging level
  userinfo             Enable logging of user info on privileged mode enabling

Router(config)#logging console
Router(config)#logging buffered
```

Wow—as you can see in this output, there are plenty of options you can use with the logging command! The preceding configuration enabled the console and buffer to receive all log message of all severities, and don't forget that this is the default setting for all Cisco IOS devices. If you want to disable the defaults, use the following commands:

```
Router(config)#no logging console
Router(config)#no logging buffered
```

I like leaving the console and buffer commands on in order to receive the logging info, but that's up to you. You can see the buffers with the show logging command here:

```
Router#sh logging
Syslog logging: enabled (11 messages dropped, 1 messages rate-limited,
                0 flushes, 0 overruns, xml disabled, filtering disabled)
    Console logging: level debugging, 29 messages logged, xml disabled,
                filtering disabled
    Monitor logging: level debugging, 0 messages logged, xml disabled,
                filtering disabled
    Buffer logging: level debugging, 1 messages logged, xml disabled,
                filtering disabled
    Logging Exception size (4096 bytes)
    Count and timestamp logging messages: disabled
No active filter modules.

    Trap logging: level informational, 33 message lines logged

Log Buffer (4096 bytes):
*Jun 21 23:09:37.822: %SYS-5-CONFIG_I: Configured from console by console
Router#
```

The default trap (message from device to NMS) level is debugging, but you can change this too. And now that you've seen the system message format on a Cisco device, I want to show you how you can also control the format of your messages via sequence numbers and time stamps, which aren't enabled by default. We'll begin with a basic, simple example of how to configure a device to send messages to a syslog server, demonstrated in Figure 7.3.

FIGURE 7.3   Messages sent to a syslog server

Syslog server

I want to look at the console messages
of the SF router from last night.

A syslog server saves copies of console messages and can time-stamp them for viewing at a later time. This is actually pretty easy to configure, and here's how doing that would look on the SF router:

```
SF(config)#logging 172.16.10.1
SF(config)#logging informational
```

This is awesome—now all the console messages will be stored in one location to be viewed at your convenience! I typically use the logging host *ip_address* command, but logging *ip_address* without the host keyword gets the same result.

We can limit the amount of messages sent to the syslog server, based on severity, with the following command:

```
SF(config)#logging trap ?
  <0-7>          Logging severity level
  alerts         Immediate action needed        (severity=1)
  critical       Critical conditions            (severity=2)
  debugging      Debugging messages             (severity=7)
  emergencies    System is unusable             (severity=0)
  errors         Error conditions               (severity=3)
  informational  Informational messages         (severity=6)
  notifications  Normal but significant conditions (severity=5)
  warnings       Warning conditions             (severity=4)
  <cr>
SF(config)#logging trap informational
```

Notice that we can use either the number or the actual severity level name—and they are in alphabetical order, not severity order, which makes it even harder to memorize the order! (Thanks, Cisco!) Since I went with severity level 6 (Informational), I'll receive messages for levels 0 through 6. These are referred to as local levels as well, such as, for example, local6—no difference.

Now let's configure the router to use sequence numbers:

```
SF(config)#no service timestamps
SF(config)#service sequence-numbers
SF(config)#^Z
000038: %SYS-5-CONFIG_I: Configured from console by console
```

When you exit configuration mode, the router will send a message like the one shown in the preceding code lines. Without the time stamps enabled, we'll no longer see a time and date, but we will see a sequence number.

So we now have the following:

- **Sequence number:** 000038
- **Facility:** %SYS
- **Severity level:** 5
- **MNEMONIC:** CONFIG_I
- **Description:** Configured from console by console

I want to stress that of all of these, the severity level is what you need to pay attention to the most for the Cisco exams as well as for a means to control the amount of messages sent to the syslog server.

Exam Essentials

Remember the differences between SNMPv2 and SNMPv3.   SNMPv2 uses UDP but can use TCP; however, v2 still sends data to the NMS station in clear text, exactly like SNMPv1, plus SNMPv2 implemented GETBULK and INFORM messages. SNMPv3 uses TCP and authenticates users, plus it can use ACLs in the SNMP strings to protect the NMS station from unauthorized use.

Troubleshoot network connectivity issues using ICMP echo-based IP SLA

I want to mention one thing that can help you troubleshoot your IP network, and this is using IP Service-Level Agreements (SLAs), which will allow us to use IP SLA ICMP echo to test far-end devices instead of pinging manually.

There are several reasons to use the IP SLA measurements:

- Edge-to-edge network availability monitoring
    - For example, packet loss statistics
- Network performance monitoring and network performance visibility
    - For example, network latency and response time
- Troubleshooting basic network operation
    - For example, end-to-end network connectivity

Here are the steps to configure IP SLA:

Step 1: Enable an IP SLA operation, which enters the IP SLA configuration mode. Choose any number from 1 to 2.1 billion as an operation number.

```
R1(config)#ip sla 1
```

Step 2: Configure the IP SLA ICMP Echo test and destination.

```
R1(config-ip-sla)#icmp?
icmp-echo   icmp-jitter
```

```
R1(config-ip-sla)#icmp-echo ?
  Hostname or X:X:X:X::X
  Hostname or A.B.C.D  Destination IPv6/IP address or hostname
```

```
R1(config-ip-sla)#icmp-echo 172.16.20.254
```

Step 3: Set the test frequency.

```
R1(config-ip-sla-echo)#frequency ?
```

```
  <1-604800>  Frequency in seconds (default 60)
```

R1(config-ip-sla-echo)#**frequency 10**

Step 4: Schedule your IP SLA test.

```
R1(config-ip-sla-echo)#exit
R1(config)#ip sla schedule ?
  <1-2147483647>  Entry number

R1(config)#ip sla schedule 1 life ?
  <0-2147483647>  Life seconds (default 3600)
  forever         continue running forever

R1(config)#ip sla schedule 1 life forever start-time ?
  after     Start after a certain amount of time from now
  hh:mm     Start time (hh:mm)
  hh:mm:ss  Start time (hh:mm:ss)
  now       Start now
  pending   Start pending

R1(config)#ip sla schedule 1 life forever start-time now
```

Step 5: Verify IP SLA operation.
Use the following commands:

```
Show ip sla configuration
Show ip sla statistics
```

R1 should have an ICMP Echo test configured to the remote server address and the test should run every 10 seconds and be scheduled to run forever.

```
R1#show ip sla configuration
IP SLAs Infrastructure Engine-II
Entry number: 1
Owner:
Tag:
Type of operation to perform: icmp-echo
Target address/Source address: 172.16.20.254/0.0.0.0
Type Of Service parameter: 0x0
Request size (ARR data portion): 28
Operation timeout (milliseconds): 5000
Verify data: No
Vrf Name:
```

```
Schedule:
   Operation frequency (seconds): 10  (not considered if randomly scheduled)
   Next Scheduled Start Time: Start Time already passed
   Group Scheduled : FALSE
   Randomly Scheduled : FALSE
   Life (seconds): Forever
   Entry Ageout (seconds): never
   Recurring (Starting Everyday): FALSE
   Status of entry (SNMP RowStatus): Active
[output cut]

R1#sh ip sla statistics
IPSLAs Latest Operation Statistics

IPSLA operation id: 1
Type of operation: icmp-echo
        Latest RTT: 1 milliseconds
Latest operation start time: *15:27:51.365 UTC Mon Jun 6 2016
Latest operation return code: OK
Number of successes: 38
Number of failures: 0
Operation time to live: Forever
```

The IP SLA 1 test on R1 has been successfully performed 38 times and the test never failed.

Exam Essentials

Describe the steps to configure IP SLA.   The steps in order are as follows:

   Step 1: Enable an IP SLA operation.

   Step 2: Configure the IP SLA ICMP Echo test and destination.

   Step 3: Set the test frequency.

   Step 4: Schedule your IP SLA test.

   Step 5: Verify IP SLA operation.

Configure and verify device management

There are a number of settings that are commonly configured on a device to aid in the management of the device. In this section, we'll talk about some of these settings and we'll also discuss other tools that help you to manage the routers and switches in your network.

Backup and Restore Device Configuration

Any changes that you make to the configuration are stored in the running-config file. And if you don't enter a copy run start command after you make a change to running-config, that change will totally disappear if the device reboots or gets powered down. As always, backups are good, so you'll want to make another backup of the configuration information just in case the router or switch completely dies on you. Even if your machine is healthy and happy, it's good to have a backup for reference and documentation reasons!

Next, I'll cover how to copy the configuration of a router to a TFTP server as well as how to restore that configuration.

Backing Up the Cisco Configuration

To copy the configuration from an IOS device to a TFTP server, you can use either the copy running-config tftp or the copy startup-config tftp command. Either one will back up the router configuration that's currently running in DRAM or one that's stored in NVRAM.

Verifying the Current Configuration

To verify the configuration in DRAM, use the show running-config command (sh run for short) like this:

```
Router#show running-config
Building configuration...

Current configuration : 855 bytes
!
version 15.0
```

The current configuration information indicates that the router is running version 15.0 of the IOS.

Verifying the Stored Configuration

Next, you should check the configuration stored in NVRAM. To see this, use the show startup-config command (sh start for short) like this:

```
Router#sh start
Using 855 out of 524288 bytes
!
! Last configuration change at 04:49:14 UTC Fri Mar 5 1993
!
version 15.0
```

The first line shows you how much room your backup configuration is taking up. Here, we can see that NVRAM is about 524 KB and that only 855 bytes of it are being used. But memory is easier to reveal via the show version command when you're using an ISR router.

If you're not sure that the files are the same and the running-config file is what you want to go with, then use the `copy running-config startup-config` command. This will help you ensure that both files are in fact the same. I'll guide you through this in the next section.

Copying the Current Configuration to NVRAM

By copying running-config to NVRAM as a backup, as shown in the following output, you ensure that your running-config will always be reloaded if the router gets rebooted. Starting in the 12.0 IOS, you'll be prompted for the filename you want to use:

```
Router#copy running-config startup-config
Destination filename [startup-config]?[enter]
Building configuration...
[OK]
```

The reason the filename prompt appears is that there are now so many options you can use when using the copy command—check it out:

```
Router#copy running-config ?
  flash:          Copy to flash: file system
  ftp:            Copy to ftp: file system
  http:           Copy to http: file system
  https:          Copy to https: file system
  null:           Copy to null: file system
  nvram:          Copy to nvram: file system
  rcp:            Copy to rcp: file system
  running-config  Update (merge with) current system configuration
  scp:            Copy to scp: file system
  startup-config  Copy to startup configuration
  syslog:         Copy to syslog: file system
  system:         Copy to system: file system
  tftp:           Copy to tftp: file system
  tmpsys:         Copy to tmpsys: file system
```

Copying the Configuration to a TFTP Server

Once the file is copied to NVRAM, you can make a second backup to a TFTP server by using the `copy running-config tftp` command, or `copy run tftp` for short. I'm going to set the hostname to Todd before I run this command:

```
Todd#copy running-config tftp
Address or name of remote host []? 10.10.10.254
Destination filename [todd-confg]?
!!
776 bytes copied in 0.800 secs (970 bytes/sec)
```

If you have a hostname already configured, the command will automatically use the hostname plus the extension -confg as the name of the file.

Restoring the Cisco Configuration

What do you do if you've changed your running-config file and want to restore the configuration to the version in the startup-config file? The easiest way to get this done is to use the copy startup-config running-config command, or copy start run for short, but this will work only if you copied running-config into NVRAM before you made any changes! Of course, a reload of the device will work too!

If you did copy the configuration to a TFTP server as a second backup, you can restore the configuration using the copy tftp running-config command (copy tftp run for short), or the copy tftp startup-config command (copy tftp start for short), as shown in the following output. Just so you know, the old command we used to use for this is config net:

```
Todd#copy tftp running-config
Address or name of remote host []?10.10.10.254
Source filename []?todd-confg
Destination filename[running-config]?[enter]
Accessing tftp://10.10.10.254/todd-confg...
Loading todd-confg from 10.10.10.254 (via FastEthernet0/0):
!!
[OK - 776 bytes]
776 bytes copied in 9.212 secs (84 bytes/sec)
Todd#
*Mar  7 17:53:34.071: %SYS-5-CONFIG_I: Configured from
    tftp://10.10.10.254/todd-confg by console
```

Okay, here we can see that the configuration file is an ASCII text file, meaning that before you copy the configuration stored on a TFTP server back to a router, you can make changes to the file with any text editor.

> Remember that when you copy or merge a configuration from a TFTP server to a freshly erased and rebooted router's RAM, the interfaces are shut down by default and you must manually enable each interface with the no shutdown command.

Erasing the Configuration

To delete the startup-config file on a Cisco router or switch, use the command erase startup-config, like this:

```
Todd#erase startup-config
Erasing the nvram filesystem will remove all configuration files!
    Continue? [confirm][enter]
[OK]
Erase of nvram: complete
```

```
*Mar  7 17:56:20.407: %SYS-7-NV_BLOCK_INIT: Initialized the geometry of nvram
Todd#reload
System configuration has been modified. Save? [yes/no]:n
Proceed with reload? [confirm][enter]
 *Mar  7 17:56:31.059: %SYS-5-RELOAD: Reload requested by console.
    Reload Reason: Reload Command.
```

This command deletes the contents of NVRAM on the switch and router. If you type **reload** while in privileged mode and say no to saving changes, the switch or router will reload and come up into setup mode.

Using Cisco Discovery Protocol or LLDP for Device Discovery

Cisco Discovery Protocol (CDP) is a proprietary protocol designed by Cisco to help administrators collect information about locally attached devices. Armed with CDP, you can gather hardware and protocol information about neighbor devices, which is crucial information to have when troubleshooting and documenting the network. Another dynamic discovery protocol is Link Layer Discovery Protocol (LLDP), but instead of being proprietary like CDP, it is vendor independent.

Let's start by exploring the CDP timer and CDP commands we'll need to verify our network.

Getting CDP Timers and Holdtime Information

The show cdp command (sh cdp for short) gives you information about two CDP global parameters that can be configured on Cisco devices:

- *CDP timer* delimits how often CDP packets are transmitted out all active interfaces.
- *CDP holdtime* delimits the amount of time that the device will hold packets received from neighbor devices.

Both Cisco routers and switches use the same parameters. Check out Figure 7.4 to see how CDP works within a switched network that I set up for my switching labs in this book.

FIGURE 7.4   Cisco Discovery Protocol

The output on my 3560 SW-3 looks like this:

```
SW-3#sh cdp
Global CDP information:
        Sending CDP packets every 60 seconds
        Sending a holdtime value of 180 seconds
        Sending CDPv2 advertisements is enabled
```

This output tells us that the default transmits every 60 seconds and will hold packets from a neighbor in the CDP table for 180 seconds. I can use the global commands cdp holdtime and cdp timer to configure the CDP holdtime and timer on a router if necessary like this:

```
SW-3(config)#cdp ?
  advertise-v2  CDP sends version-2 advertisements
  holdtime      Specify the holdtime (in sec) to be sent in packets
  run           Enable CDP
  timer         Specify the rate at which CDP packets are sent (in sec)
  tlv           Enable exchange of specific tlv information

SW-3(config)#cdp holdtime ?
  <10-255>  Length of time  (in sec) that receiver must keep this packet

SW-3(config)#cdp timer ?
  <5-254>  Rate at which CDP packets are sent (in  sec)
```

You can turn off CDP completely with the no cdp run command from global configuration mode of a router and enable it with the cdp run command:

```
SW-3(config)#no cdp run
SW-3(config)#cdp run
```

To turn CDP off or on for an interface, use the no cdp enable and cdp enable commands.

Gathering Neighbor Information

The show cdp neighbors command (sh cdp nei for short) delivers information about directly connected devices. It's important to remember that CDP packets aren't passed through a Cisco switch and that you only see what's directly attached. So this means that if your router is connected to a switch, you won't see any of the Cisco devices connected to that switch!

The following output shows the show cdp neighbors command I used on my SW-3:

```
SW-3#sh cdp neighbors
Capability Codes: R - Router, T - Trans Bridge, B - Source Route Bridge
                  S - Switch, H - Host, I - IGMP, r - Repeater, P - Phone,
                  D - Remote, C - CVTA, M - Two-port Mac Relay Device ID
```

```
Local   Intrfce    Holdtme   Capability   Platform   Port ID
SW-1    Fas 0/1    170          S I        WS-C3560-  Fas 0/15
SW-1    Fas 0/2    170          S I        WS-C3560-  Fas 0/16
SW-2    Fas 0/5    162          S I        WS-C3560-  Fas 0/5
SW-2    Fas 0/6    162          S I        WS-C3560-  Fas 0/6
```

Okay—we can see that I'm directly connected with a console cable to the SW-3 switch and also that SW-3 is directly connected to two other switches. However, do we really need the figure to draw out our network? We don't! CDP allows me to see who my directly connected neighbors are and gather information about them. From the SW-3 switch, we can see that there are two connections to SW-1 and two connections to SW-2. SW-3 connects to SW-1 with ports Fas 0/1 and Fas 0/2, and we have connections to SW-2 with local interfaces Fas 0/5 and Fas 0/6. Both the SW-1 and SW-2 switches are 3650 switches, and SW-1 is using ports Fas 0/15 and Fas 0/16 to connect to SW-3. SW-2 is using ports Fas 0/5 and Fas 0/6.

To sum this up, the device ID shows the configured hostname of the connected device, that the local interface is our interface, and that the port ID is the remote devices' directly connected interface. Remember that all you get to view are directly connected devices!

Table 7.2 summarizes the information displayed by the show cdp neighbors command for each device.

TABLE 7.2   Output of the **show cdp neighbors** command

Field	Description
Device ID	The hostname of the device directly connected
Local Interface	The port or interface on which you are receiving the CDP packet
Holdtime	The remaining amount of time the router will hold the information before discarding it if no more CDP packets are received
Capability	The capability of the neighbor—the router, switch, or repeater. The capability codes are listed at the top of the command output.
Platform	The type of Cisco device directly connected. In the previous output, the SW-3 shows it's directly connected to two 3560 switches.
Port ID	The neighbor device's port or interface on which the CDP packets are multicast

It's imperative that you can look at the output of a show cdp neighbors command and decipher the information gained about the neighbor device's capability, whether it's a router or switch, the model number (platform), your port connecting to that device (local interface), and the port of the neighbor connecting to you (port ID).

Another command that will deliver the goods on neighbor information is the
show cdp neighbors detail command (show cdp nei de for short). This command can be
run on both routers and switches, and it displays detailed information about each device connected to the device you're running the command on. Check out the router output in Listing 7.1.

Listing 7.1: Showing CDP neighbors

```
SW-3#sh cdp neighbors detail
-------------------------
Device ID: SW-1
Entry address(es):
  IP address: 10.100.128.10
Platform: cisco WS-C3560-24TS,  Capabilities: Switch IGMP
Interface: FastEthernet0/1,  Port ID (outgoing port): FastEthernet0/15
Holdtime : 137 sec

Version :
Cisco IOS Software, C3560 Software (C3560-IPSERVICESK9-M),
Version 12.2(55)SE7, RELEASE SOFTWARE (fc1)
Technical Support: http://www.cisco.com/techsupport
Copyright (c) 1986-2013 by Cisco Systems, Inc.
Compiled Mon 28-Jan-13 10:10 by prod_rel_team

advertisement version: 2
Protocol Hello:  OUI=0x00000C, Protocol ID=0x0112;
payload len=27, value=00000000FFFFFFFF010221FF000000000000001C575EC880Fc00f000
VTP Management Domain: 'NULL'
Native VLAN: 1
Duplex: full
Power Available TLV:

    Power request id: 0, Power management id: 1,
Power available: 0, Power management level: -1
Management address(es):
  IP address: 10.100.128.10
-------------------------


[ouput cut]


-------------------------
Device ID: SW-2
Entry address(es):
  IP address: 10.100.128.9
```

```
Platform: cisco WS-C3560-8PC,  Capabilities: Switch IGMP
Interface: FastEthernet0/5,  Port ID (outgoing port): FastEthernet0/5
Holdtime : 129 sec

Version :
Cisco IOS Software, C3560 Software (C3560-IPBASE-M),
Version 12.2(35)SE5, RELEASE SOFTWARE (fc1)
Copyright (c) 1986-2007 by Cisco Systems, Inc.
Compiled Thu 19-Jul-07 18:15 by nachen

advertisement version: 2
Protocol Hello:  OUI=0x00000C, Protocol ID=0x0112;
payload len=27, value=00000000FFFFFFFF010221FF000000000000B41489D91880Fc00f000
VTP Management Domain: 'NULL'
Native VLAN: 1
Duplex: full
Power Available TLV:

   Power request id: 0, Power management id: 1,
Power available: 0, Power management level: -1
Management address(es):
  IP address: 10.100.128.9
[output cut]
```

So what's revealed here? First, we've been given the hostname and IP address of all directly connected devices. And in addition to the same information displayed by the show cdp neighbors command (see Table 7.2), the show cdp neighbors detail command tells us about the IOS version and IP address of the neighbor device—that's quite a bit!

The show cdp entry * command displays the same information as the show cdp neighbors detail command. There isn't any difference between these commands.

 Real World Scenario

CDP Can Save Lives!

Karen has just been hired as a senior network consultant at a large hospital in Dallas, Texas, so she's expected to be able to take care of any problem that rears its ugly head. As if that weren't enough pressure, she also has to worry about the horrid possibility that people won't receive correct health care solutions—even the correct medications—if the network goes down. Talk about a potential life-or-death situation!

But Karen is confident and begins her job optimistically. Of course, it's not long before the network reveals that it has a few problems. Unfazed, she asks one of the junior administrators for a network map so she can troubleshoot the network. This person tells her that the old senior administrator, who she replaced, had them with him and now no one can find them. The sky begins to darken!

Doctors are calling every couple of minutes because they can't get the necessary information they need to take care of their patients. What should she do?

It's CDP to the rescue! And it's a gift that this hospital happens to be running Cisco routers and switches exclusively, because CDP is enabled by default on all Cisco devices. Karen is also in luck because the disgruntled former administrator didn't turn off CDP on any devices before he left!

So all Karen has to do now is to use the show cdp neighbors detail command to find all the information she needs about each device to help draw out the hospital network, bringing it back up to speed so the personnel who rely upon it can get on to the important business of saving lives!

The only snag for you nailing this in your own network is if you don't know the passwords of all those devices. Your only hope then is to somehow find out the access passwords or to perform password recovery on them.

So, use CDP—you never know when you may end up saving someone's life.

By the way, this is a true story!

Documenting a Network Topology Using CDP

With that moving real-life scenario in mind, I'm now going to show you how to document a sample network by using CDP. You'll learn to determine the appropriate router types, interface types, and IP addresses of various interfaces using only CDP commands and the show running-config command. And you can only console into the Lab_A router to document the network. You'll have to assign any remote routers the next IP address in each range. We'll use a different figure for this example—Figure 7.5— to help us to complete the necessary documentation.

FIGURE 7.5   Documenting a network topology using CDP

   In this output, you can see that you have a router with four interfaces: two FastEthernet and two serial. First, determine the IP addresses of each interface by using the show running-config command like this:

```
Lab_A#sh running-config
Building configuration...

Current configuration : 960 bytes
!
version 12.2
service timestamps debug uptime
service timestamps log uptime
no service password-encryption
!
hostname Lab_A
!
ip subnet-zero
!
!
interface FastEthernet0/0
 ip address 192.168.21.1 255.255.255.0
 duplex auto
!
interface FastEthernet0/1
 ip address 192.168.18.1 255.255.255.0
 duplex auto
!
interface Serial0/0
ip address 192.168.23.1 255.255.255.0
!
interface Serial0/1
ip address 192.168.28.1 255.255.255.0
!
ip classless
!
line con 0
line aux 0
line vty 0 4
!
end
```

With this step completed, you can now write down the IP addresses of the Lab_A router's four interfaces. Next, you must determine the type of device on the other end of each of these interfaces. It's easy—just use the show cdp neighbors command:

```
Lab_A#sh cdp neighbors
Capability Codes: R - Router, T - Trans Bridge, B - Source Route Bridge
S - Switch, H - Host, I - IGMP, r - Repeater
Device ID    Local Intrfce    Holdtme    Capability Platform   Port ID
Lab_B        Fas 0/0          178        R          2501       E0
Lab_C        Fas 0/1          137        R          2621       Fa0/0
Lab_D        Ser 0/0          178        R          2514       S1
Lab_E        Ser 0/1          137        R          2620       S0/1
```

Wow—looks like we're connected to some old routers! But it's not our job to judge. Our mission is to draw out our network, so it's good that we've got some nice information to meet the challenge with now. By using both the show running-config and show cdp neighbors commands, we know about all the IP addresses of the Lab_A router, the types of routers connected to each of the Lab_A router's links, and all the interfaces of the remote routers.

Now that we're equipped with all the information gathered via show running-config and show cdp neighbors, we can accurately create the topology in Figure 7.6.

FIGURE 7.6 Network topology documented

If we needed to, we could've also used the show cdp neighbors detail command to view the neighbor's IP addresses. But since we know the IP addresses of each link on the Lab_A router, we already know what the next available IP address is going to be.

Link Layer Discovery Protocol (LLDP)

Before moving on from CDP, I want to tell you about a nonproprietary discovery protocol that provides pretty much the same information as CDP but works in multi-vendor networks.

The IEEE created a new standardized discovery protocol called 802.1AB for Station and Media Access Control Connectivity Discovery. We'll just call it *Link Layer Discovery Protocol (LLDP)*.

LLDP defines basic discovery capabilities, but it was also enhanced to specifically address the voice application, and this version is called LLDP-MED (Media Endpoint Discovery). It's good to remember that LLDP and LLDP-MED are not compatible.

LLDP has the following configuration guidelines and limitations:

- LLDP must be enabled on the device before you can enable or disable it on any interface.

- LLDP is supported only on physical interfaces.

- LLDP can discover up to one device per port.

- LLDP can discover Linux servers.

You can turn off LLDP completely with the no lldp run command from global configuration mode of a device and enable it with the lldp run command, which enables it on all interfaces as well.

```
SW-3(config)#no lldp run
SW-3(config)#lldp run
```

To turn LLDP off or on for an interface, use the lldp transmit and lldp receive commands.

```
SW-3(config-if)#no lldp transmit
SW-3(config-if)#no lldp receive

SW-3(config-if)#lldp transmit
SW-3(config-if)#lldp receive
```

Licensing

IOS licensing is now done quite differently than it was with previous versions of the IOS. Actually, there was no licensing before the new 15.0 IOS code, just your word and honor, and we can only guess based on how all products are downloaded on the Internet daily how well that has worked out for Cisco!

Starting with the IOS 15.0 code, things are much different—almost too different. I can imagine that Cisco will come back toward the middle on its licensing issues, so that the administration and management won't be as detailed as it is with the new 15.0 code license, but you can be the judge of that after reading this section.

A new ISR router is pre-installed with the software images and licenses that you ordered, and so as long as you ordered and paid for everything you need, you're set! If not, you can just install another license, which can be a tad tedious at first—enough so that installing a license was made an objective on the Cisco exam! Of course, it can be done, but it definitely requires some effort. As is typical with Cisco, if you spend enough money on their products, they tend to make it easier on you and your administration, and the licensing for the newest IOS is no exception, as you'll soon see.

On a positive note, Cisco provides evaluation licenses for most software packages and features that are supported on the hardware you purchased, and it's always nice to be able to try it out before you buy. Once the temporary license expires after 60 days, you need to acquire a permanent license in order to continue to use the extended features that aren't available in your current version. This method of licensing allows you to enable a router to use different parts of the IOS. So, what happens after 60 days? Well, nothing—back to the honor system for now. This is now called *Right-To-Use (RTU) licensing*, and it probably won't always be available via your honor, but for now it is.

But that's not the best part of the new licensing features. Prior to the 15.0 code release, there were eight different software feature sets for each hardware router type. With the IOS 15.0 code, the packaging is now called a *universal image*, meaning all feature sets are available in one file with all features packed neatly inside. So instead of the pre-15.0 IOS file packages of one image per feature set, Cisco now just builds one universal image that includes all of them in the file. Even so, we still need a different universal image per router model or series, just not a different image for each feature set as we did with previous IOS versions.

To use the features in the IOS software, you must unlock them using the software activation process. Since all features available are inside the universal image already, you can just unlock the features you need as you need them, and of course pay for these features when you determine that they meet your business requirements. All routers come with something called the IP Base licensing, which is the prerequisite for installing all other features.

There are three different technology packages available for purchase that can be installed as additional feature packs on top of the prerequisite IP Base (default), which provides entry-level IOS functionality. These are as follows:

Data: MPLS, ATM, and multiprotocol support

Unified Communications: VoIP and IP telephony

Security: Cisco IOS Firewall, IPS, IPsec, 3DES, and VPN

For example, if you need MPLS and IPsec, you'll need the default IP Base, Data, and Security premium packages unlocked on your router.

To obtain the license, you'll need the unique device identifier (UDI), which has two components: the product ID (PID) and the serial number of the router. The show license UDI command provides this information in an output as shown:

```
Router#sh license udi
Device#   PID                 SN                UDI
----------------------------------------------------------------
*0        CISCO2901/K9        FTX1641Y07J       CISCO2901/K9:FTX1641Y07J
```

After the time has expired for your 60-day evaluation period, you can either obtain the license file from the Cisco License Manager (CLM), which is an automated process, or use the manual process through the Cisco Product License Registration portal. Typically only larger companies will use the CLM because you'd need to install software on a server, which then keeps track of all your licenses for you. If you have just a few licenses that you use, you can opt for the manual web browser process found on the Cisco Product License Registration portal and then just add in a few CLI commands. After that, you just basically keep track of putting all the different license features together for each device you manage. Although this sounds like a lot of work, you don't need to perform these steps often. But clearly, going with the CLM makes a lot of sense if you have bunches of licenses to manage because it will put together all the little pieces of licensing for each router in one easy process.

When you purchase the software package with the features that you want to install, you need to permanently activate the software package using your UDI and the *product authorization key (PAK)* that you received with your purchase. This is essentially your receipt acknowledging that you purchased the license. You then need to connect the license with a particular router by combining the PAK and the UDI, which you do online at the Cisco Product License Registration portal (www.cisco.com/go/license). If you haven't already registered the license on a different router, and it is valid, Cisco will then email you your permanent license, or you can download it from your account.

But wait! You're still not done. You now need to activate the license on the router. Whew... maybe it's worthwhile to install the CLM on a server after all! Staying with the manual method, you need to make the new license file available to the router either via a USB port on the router or through a TFTP server. Once it's available to the router, you'll use the license install command from privileged mode.

Assuming that you copied the file into flash memory, the command would look like something like this:

```
Router#license install ?
  archive:  Install from archive: file system
  flash:    Install from flash: file system
  ftp:      Install from ftp: file system
  http:     Install from http: file system
  https:    Install from https: file system
  null:     Install from null: file system
  nvram:    Install from nvram: file system
  rcp:      Install from rcp: file system
  scp:      Install from scp: file system
  syslog:   Install from syslog: file system
  system:   Install from system: file system
  tftp:     Install from tftp: file system
  tmpsys:   Install from tmpsys: file system
  xmodem:   Install from xmodem: file system
  ymodem:   Install from ymodem: file system
Router#license install flash:FTX1628838P_201302111432454180.lic
Installing licenses from "flash::FTX1628838P_201302111432454180.lic"
```

```
Installing...Feature:datak9...Successful:Supported
1/1 licenses were successfully installed
0/1 licenses were existing licenses
0/1 licenses were failed to install
April 12 2:31:19.786: %LICENSE-6-INSTALL: Feature datak9 1.0 was
installed in this device. UDI=CISCO2901/K9:FTX1628838P;
StoreIndex=1:Primary License Storage

April 12 2:31:20.078: %IOS_LICENSE_IMAGE_APPLICATION-6-LICENSE_LEVEL:
Module name =c2800 Next reboot level = datak9 and License = datak9
```

You need to reboot to have the new license take effect. Now that you have your license installed and running, how do you use Right-To-Use licensing to check out new features on your router? Let's look into that now.

Right-To-Use Licenses (Evaluation Licenses)

Originally called evaluation licenses, Right-To-Use (RTU) licenses are what you need when you want to update your IOS to load a new feature but either don't want to wait to get the license or just want to test if this feature will truly meet your business requirements. This makes sense because if Cisco made it complicated to load and check out a feature, they could potentially miss out on a sale! Of course if the feature does work for you, they'll want you to buy a permanent license, but again, this is on the honor system at the time of this writing.

Cisco's license model allows you to install the feature you want without a PAK. The Right-To-Use license works for 60 days before you would need to install your permanent license. To enable the Right-To-Use license, you would use the license boot module command. The following demonstrates starting the Right-To-Use license on my 2900 series router, enabling the security module named securityk9:

```
Router(config)#license boot module c2900 technology-package securityk9
PLEASE READ THE FOLLOWING TERMS CAREFULLY. INSTALLING THE LICENSE
OR LICENSE KEY PROVIDED FOR ANY CISCO PRODUCT FEATURE OR USING
SUCHPRODUCT FEATURE CONSTITUTES YOUR FULL ACCEPTANCE OF THE
FOLLOWING TERMS. YOU MUST NOT PROCEED FURTHER IF YOU ARE NOT WILLING
TO BE BOUND BY ALL THE TERMS SET FORTH HEREIN.
[output cut]
Activation of the software command line interface will be evidence of
your acceptance of this agreement.

ACCEPT? [yes/no]: yes

% use 'write' command to make license boot config take effect on next boot
Feb 12 01:35:45.060: %IOS_LICENSE_IMAGE_APPLICATION-6-LICENSE_LEVEL:
```

```
Module name =c2900 Next reboot level = securityk9 and License = securityk9

Feb 12 01:35:45.524: %LICENSE-6-EULA_ACCEPTED: EULA for feature
securityk9 1.0 has been accepted. UDI=CISCO2901/K9:FTX1628838P;
StoreIndex=0:Built-In License Storage
```

Once the router is reloaded, you can use the security feature set. And it is really nice that you don't need to reload the router again if you choose to install a permanent license for this feature. The show license command shows the licenses installed on the router:

```
Router#show license
Index 1 Feature: ipbasek9
      Period left: Life time
      License Type: Permanent
      License State: Active, In Use
      License Count: Non-Counted
      License Priority: Medium
Index 2 Feature: securityk9
      Period left: 8 weeks  2 days
      Period Used: 0  minute  0  second
      License Type: EvalRightToUse
      License State: Active, In Use
      License Count: Non-Counted
      License Priority: None
Index 3 Feature: uck9
      Period left: Life time
      License Type: Permanent
      License State: Active, In Use
      License Count: Non-Counted
      License Priority: Medium
Index 4 Feature: datak9
      Period left: Not Activated
      Period Used: 0  minute  0  second
      License Type: EvalRightToUse
      License State: Not in Use, EULA not accepted
      License Count: Non-Counted
      License Priority: None
Index 5 Feature: gatekeeper
 [output cut]
```

You can see in the preceding output that the ipbasek9 is permanent and the securityk9 has a license type of EvalRightToUse. The show license feature command provides the same information as show license, but it's summarized into one line as shown in the next output:

```
Router#sh license feature
```

Feature name	Enforcement	Evaluation	Subscription	Enabled	RightToUse
ipbasek9	no	no	no	yes	no
securityk9	yes	yes	no	no	yes
uck9	yes	yes	no	yes	yes
datak9	yes	yes	no	no	yes
gatekeeper	yes	yes	no	no	yes
SSL_VPN	yes	yes	no	no	yes
ios-ips-update	yes	yes	yes	no	yes
SNASw	yes	yes	no	no	yes
hseck9	yes	no	no	no	no
cme-srst	yes	yes	no	yes	yes
WAAS_Express	yes	yes	no	no	yes
UCVideo	yes	yes	no	no	yes

The show version command also shows the license information at the end of the command output:

```
Router#show version
[output cut]
License Info:

License UDI:

--------------------------------------------------
Device#    PID                 SN
--------------------------------------------------
*0         CISCO2901/K9        FTX1641Y07J

Technology Package License Information for Module:'c2900'

-----------------------------------------------------------------
Technology    Technology-package        Technology-package
              Current     Type          Next reboot
-----------------------------------------------------------------
ipbase        ipbasek9    Permanent     ipbasek9
security      None        None          None
uc            uck9        Permanent     uck9
data          None        None          None

Configuration register is 0x2102
```

The `show version` command shows if the license was activated. Don't forget, you'll need to reload the router to have the license features take effect if the license evaluation is not already active.

Backing Up and Uninstalling the License

It would be a shame to lose your license if it has been stored in flash and your flash files become corrupted. So always back up your IOS license!

If your license has been saved in a location other than flash, you can easily back it up to flash memory via the `license save` command:

```
Router#license save flash:Todd_License.lic
```

The previous command will save your current license to flash. You can restore your license with the `license install` command I demonstrated earlier.

There are two steps to uninstalling the license on a router. First, to uninstall the license you need to disable the technology package, using the `no license boot module` command with the keyword `disable` at the end of the command line:

```
Router#license boot module c2900 technology-package securityk9 disable
```

The second step is to clear the license. To achieve this from the router, use the `license clear` command and then remove the license with the `no license boot module` command:

```
Router#license clear securityk9
Router#config t
Router(config)#no license boot module c2900 technology-package securityk9 disable
Router(config)#exit
Router#reload
```

After you run through the preceding commands, the license will be removed from your router.

Here's a summary of the license commands I used in this chapter. These are important commands to have down, and you really need to understand these to meet the Cisco objectives:

- `show license` determines the licenses that are active on your system. It also displays a group of lines for each feature in the currently running IOS image along with several status variables related to software activation and licensing, both licensed and unlicensed features.

- `show license feature` allows you to view the technology package licenses and feature licenses that are supported on your router along with several status variables related to software activation and licensing. This includes both licensed and unlicensed features.

- `show license udi` displays the unique device identifier (UDI) of the router, which comprises the product ID (PID) and serial number of the router.

- `show version` displays various pieces of information about the current IOS version, including the licensing details at the end of the command's output.
- `license install url` installs a license key file into a router.
- `license boot module` installs a Right-To-Use license feature on a router.

 To help you organize a large amount of licenses, search on www.cisco.com for the Cisco Smart Software Manager. This web page enables you to manage all your licenses from one centralized website. With Cisco Smart Software Manager, you organize and view your licenses in groups that are called *virtual accounts*, which are collections of licenses and product instances.

Logging

Network devices can be configured to generate a syslog message and forward it to various destinations. These four examples are popular ways to gather messages from Cisco devices:

- Logging buffer (on by default)
- Console line (on by default)
- Terminal lines (using the `terminal monitor` command)
- Syslog server

Logging is covered in the section, "Configuring and Verifying Syslog" earlier in this chapter.

Timezone

To set the time zone for display purposes, use the `clock timezone` global configuration command. To set the time to Coordinated Universal Time (UTC), use the no form of this command.

```
clock timezone zone hours-offset [minutes-offset]

no clock timezone
```

Loopback

Loopback interfaces are logical interfaces. The advantage of these interfaces is that unlike physical interfaces, they never go down. If you want to use a loopback interface as a diagnostic port, you can create a loopback interface as so:

```
Todd(config)#interface loopback ?
<0-2147483647> Loopback interface number
Todd(config)#interface loopback 0
```

```
*May 19 03:06:42.697: %LINEPROTO-5-UPDOWN: Line prot
changed state to ups
Todd(config-if)#ip address 20.20.20.1 255.255.255.0
```

Now I can use this port for diagnostics, and even as my source port of my ping or traceroute, as so:

```
Todd#ping
Protocol [ip]:
Target IP address: 10.1.1.1
Repeat count [5]:
Datagram size [100]:
Timeout in seconds [2]:
Extended commands [n]: y
Source address or interface: 20.20.20.1
Type of service [0]:
Set DF bit in IP header? [no]:
Validate reply data? [no]:
Data pattern [0xABCD]:
Loose, Strict, Record, Timestamp, Verbose[none]:
Sweep range of sizes [n]:
Type escape sequence to abort.
Sending 5, 100-byte ICMP Echos to 10.1.1.1, timeout is 2 seconds:
Packet sent with a source address of 20.20.20.1
```

These logical interfaces are great for diagnostics and for using them in our home labs where we don't have any real interfaces to play with, but we'll also use them in our OSPF configurations.

Exam Essentials

Describe the value of CDP and LLDP. Cisco Discovery Protocol can be used to help you document as well as troubleshoot your network. LLDP is a nonproprietary protocol that can provide the same information as CDP.

List the information provided by the output of the show cdp neighbors **command.** The show cdp neighbors command provides the following information: device ID, local interface, holdtime, capability, platform, and port ID (remote interface).

Back up an IOS image. By using the privileged-mode command copy flash tftp, you can back up a file from flash memory to a TFTP (network) server.

Restore or upgrade an IOS image. By using the privileged-mode command copy tftp flash, you can restore or upgrade a file from a TFTP (network) server to flash memory.

Describe best practices to prepare to back up an IOS image to a network server.   Make sure that you can access the network server, ensure that the network server has adequate space for the code image, and verify the file naming and path requirement.

Remember how to install a permanent and Right-To-Use license.   To install a permanent license on a router, use the `install license url` command. To install an evaluation feature, use the `license boot module` command.

Remember the verification commands used for licensing in the new ISR G2 routers.   The `show license` command determines the licenses that are active on your system. The `show license feature` command allows you to view the technology package licenses and feature licenses that are supported on your router. The `show license udi` command displays the unique device identifier (UDI) of the router, which comprises the product ID (PID) and serial number of the router, and the `show version` command displays information about the current IOS version, including the licensing details at the end of the command's output.

Configure and verify initial device configuration

We connect to a Cisco device to configure it, verify its configuration, and check statistics, and although there are different approaches to this, the first place you would usually connect to is the console port. The *console port* is usually an RJ45, 8-pin modular connection located at the back of the device, and there may or may not be a password set on it by default.

You can also connect to a Cisco device through an *auxiliary port*, which is really the same thing as a console port, so it follows that you can use it as one. The main difference with an auxiliary port is that it also allows you to configure modem commands so that a modem can be connected to the router. This is a cool feature because it lets you dial up a remote router and attach to the auxiliary port if the router is down and you need to configure it remotely, *out-of-band*. One of the differences between Cisco routers and switches is that switches do not have an auxiliary port.

The third way to connect to a Cisco device is *in-band*, through the program *Telnet* or *Secure Shell (SSH)*. In-band means configuring the device via the network, the opposite of *out-of-band*.

Bringing Up a Device

When you first bring up a Cisco IOS device, it will run a power-on self-test—a POST. Upon passing that, the machine will look for and then load the Cisco IOS from flash memory if an IOS file is present, then expand it into RAM. As you probably know, flash memory is electronically erasable programmable read-only memory—an EEPROM. The next step is for the IOS to locate and load a valid configuration known as the startup-config that will be stored in *nonvolatile RAM (NVRAM)*.

Once the IOS is loaded and up and running, the startup-config will be copied from NVRAM into RAM and from then on it's referred to as the running-config.

But if a valid startup-config isn't found in NVRAM, your switch will enter setup mode, giving you a step-by-step dialog to help configure some basic parameters on it.

You can also enter setup mode at any time from the command line by typing the command **setup** from privileged mode, which I'll get to in a minute. Setup mode only covers some basic commands and generally isn't really all that helpful. Here's an example:

```
Would you like to enter the initial configuration dialog? [yes/no]: y

At any point you may enter a question mark '?' for help.
Use ctrl-c to abort configuration dialog at any prompt.
Default settings are in square brackets '[]'.

Basic management setup configures only enough connectivity
for management of the system, extended setup will ask you
to configure each interface on the system

Would you like to enter basic management setup? [yes/no]: y
Configuring global parameters:

  Enter host name [Switch]: Ctrl+C
Configuration aborted, no changes made.
```

  You can exit setup mode at any time by pressing Ctrl+C.

I highly recommend going through setup mode once, then never again because you should always use the CLI instead!

Command-Line Interface (CLI)

I sometimes refer to the CLI as "cash line interface" because the ability to create advanced configurations on Cisco routers and switches using the CLI will earn you some decent cash!

Entering the CLI

After the interface status messages appear and you press Enter, the Switch> prompt will pop up. This is called *user exec mode,* or user mode for short, and although it's mostly used to view statistics, it is also a stepping stone along the way to logging in to *privileged exec mode,* called privileged mode for short.

You can view and change the configuration of a Cisco router only while in privileged mode, and you enter it via the enable command like this:

```
Switch>enable
Switch#
```

The Switch# prompt signals you're in privileged mode where you can both view and change the switch configuration. You can go back from privileged mode into user mode by using the disable command:

```
Switch#disable
Switch>
```

You can type **logout** from either mode to exit the console:

```
Switch>logout

Switch con0 is now available
Press RETURN to get started.
```

Next, I'll show how to perform some basic administrative configurations.

Overview of Router Modes

To configure from a CLI, you can make global changes to the router by typing **configure terminal** or just **config t**. This will get you into global configuration mode where you can make changes to the running-config. Commands run from global configuration mode are predictably referred to as global commands, and they are typically set only once and affect the entire router.

Type **config** from the privileged-mode prompt and then press Enter to opt for the default of terminal like this:

```
Switch#config
Configuring from terminal, memory, or network [terminal]? [press enter]
Enter configuration commands, one per line.  End with CNTL/Z.
Switch(config)#
```

At this point, you make changes that affect the router as a whole (globally), hence the term *global configuration mode*. For instance, to change the running-config—the current configuration running in dynamic RAM (DRAM)—use the configure terminal command, as I just demonstrated.

CLI Prompts

Let's explore the different prompts you'll encounter when configuring a switch or router now, because knowing them well will really help you orient yourself and recognize exactly where you are at any given time while in configuration mode. I'm going to demonstrate some of the prompts used on a Cisco switch and cover the various terms used along the way. Make sure you're very familiar with them, and always check your prompts before making any changes to a router's configuration!

We're not going to venture into every last obscure command prompt you could potentially come across in the configuration mode world because that would get us deep into territory that's beyond the scope of this book. Instead, I'm going to focus on the prompts you absolutely must know to pass the exam plus the very handy and seriously vital ones you'll need and use the most in real-life networking—the cream of the crop.

Interfaces

To make changes to an interface, you use the interface command from global configuration mode:

```
Switch(config)#interface ?
  Async              Async interface
  BVI                Bridge-Group Virtual Interface
  CTunnel            CTunnel interface
  Dialer             Dialer interface
  FastEthernet       FastEthernet IEEE 802.3
  Filter             Filter interface
  Filtergroup        Filter Group interface
  GigabitEthernet    GigabitEthernet IEEE 802.3z
  Group-Async        Async Group interface
  Lex                Lex interface
  Loopback           Loopback interface
  Null               Null interface
  Port-channel       Ethernet Channel of interfaces
  Portgroup          Portgroup interface
  Pos-channel        POS Channel of interfaces
  Tunnel             Tunnel interface
  Vif                PGM Multicast Host interface
  Virtual-Template   Virtual Template interface
  Virtual-TokenRing  Virtual TokenRing
  Vlan               Catalyst Vlans
  fcpa               Fiber Channel
  range              interface range command
Switch(config)#interface fastEthernet 0/1
Switch(config-if)#
```

Did you notice that the prompt changed to Switch(config-if)#? This tells you that you're in *interface configuration mode*. And wouldn't it be nice if the prompt also gave you an indication of what interface you were configuring? Well, at least for now we'll have to live without the prompt information, because it doesn't. But it should already be clear to you that you really need to pay attention when configuring an IOS device!

Line Commands

To configure user-mode passwords, use the line command. The prompt then becomes Switch(config-line)#:

```
Switch(config)#line ?
  <0-16>    First Line number
  console   Primary terminal line
  vty       Virtual terminal
Switch(config)#line console 0
Switch(config-line)#
```

The line console 0 command is a global command, and sometimes you'll also hear people refer to global commands as major commands. In this example, any command typed from the (config-line) prompt is known as a subcommand.

Access List Configurations

To configure a standard named access list, you'll need to get to the prompt Switch(config-std-nacl)#:

```
Switch#config t
Switch(config)#ip access-list standard Todd
Switch(config-std-nacl)#
```

What you see here is a typical basic standard ACL prompt. There are various ways to configure access lists, and the prompts are only slightly different from this particular example.

Routing Protocol Configurations

I need to point out that we don't use routing or router protocols on 2960 switches, but we can and will use them on my 3560 switches. Here is an example of configuring routing on a layer 3 switch:

```
Switch(config)#router rip
IP routing not enabled
Switch(config)#ip routing
Switch(config)#router rip
Switch(config-router)#
```

Router and Switch Interfaces

Interface configuration is arguably the most important router configuration because without interfaces, a router is a pretty useless object. Furthermore, interface configurations must be totally precise to enable communication with other devices. Network layer addresses, media type, bandwidth, and other administrator commands are all used to configure an interface.

On a layer 2 switch, interface configurations typically involve a lot less work than router interface configuration. Check out the output from the powerful verification command show ip interface brief, which reveals all the interfaces on my 3560 switch:

```
Todd#sh ip interface brief
Interface            IP-Address       OK? Method Status        Protocol
Vlan1                192.168.255.8    YES DHCP   up                  up
FastEthernet0/1      unassigned       YES unset  up                  up
FastEthernet0/2      unassigned       YES unset  up                  up
FastEthernet0/3      unassigned       YES unset  down              down
FastEthernet0/4      unassigned       YES unset  down              down
FastEthernet0/5      unassigned       YES unset  up                  up
FastEthernet0/6      unassigned       YES unset  up                  up
FastEthernet0/7      unassigned       YES unset  down              down
FastEthernet0/8      unassigned       YES unset  down              down
GigabitEthernet0/1   unassigned       YES unset  down              down
```

The previous output shows the default routed port found on all Cisco switches (VLAN 1), plus eight switch FastEthernet interface ports, with one port being a Gigabit Ethernet port used for uplinks to other switches.

Different routers use different methods to choose the interfaces used on them. For instance, the following command shows one of my 2800 ISR Cisco routers with two FastEthernet interfaces along with two serial WAN interfaces:

```
Router>sh ip int brief
Interface       IP-Address     OK? Method Status               Protocol
FastEthernet0/0 192.168.255.11 YES DHCP   up                        up
FastEthernet0/1 unassigned     YES unset  administratively down   down
Serial0/0/0     unassigned     YES unset  administratively down   down
Serial0/1/0     unassigned     YES unset  administratively down   down
Router>
```

Previously, we always used the interface *type number* sequence to configure an interface, but the newer routers come with an actual physical slot and include a port number on the module plugged into it. So on a modular router, the configuration would be interface *type slot/port*, as demonstrated here:

```
Todd#config t
Todd(config)#interface GigabitEthernet 0/1
Todd(config-if)#
```

You can see that we are now at the Gigabit Ethernet slot 0, port 1 prompt, and from here we can make configuration changes to the interface. Make note of the fact that you can't just type **int gigabitethernet 0**. No shortcuts on the slot/port—you've got to type the slot/port variables in the command: **type slot/port** or, for example, **int gigabitethernet 0/1** (or just **int g0/1**).

Once in interface configuration mode, we can configure various options. Keep in mind that speed and duplex are the two factors to be concerned with for the LAN:

```
Todd#config t
Todd(config)#interface GigabitEthernet 0/1
Todd(config-if)#speed 1000
Todd(config-if)#duplex full
```

So what's happened here? Well basically, this has shut off the autodetect mechanism on the port, forcing it to only run gigabit speeds at full-duplex. For the ISR series router, it's basically the same, but you get even more options! The LAN interfaces are the same, but the rest of the modules are different—they use three numbers instead of two. The three numbers used here can represent slot/subslot/port, but this depends on the card used in the ISR router. For the objectives, you just need to remember this: The first 0 is the router itself. You then choose the slot and then the port. Here's an example of a serial interface on my 2811:

```
Todd(config)#interface serial ?
  <0-2>  Serial interface number
Todd(config)#interface serial 0/0/?
  <0-1>  Serial interface number
Todd(config)#interface serial 0/0/0
Todd(config-if)#
```

This might look a little dicey to you, but I promise it's really not that hard! It helps to remember that you should always view the output of the show ip interface brief command or a show running-config output first so you know the exact interfaces you have to deal with. Here's one of my 2811's output that has even more serial interfaces installed:

```
Todd(config-if)#do show run
Building configuration...
[output cut]
!
interface FastEthernet0/0
 no ip address
 shutdown
 duplex auto
 speed auto
!
interface FastEthernet0/1
 no ip address
 shutdown
```

```
   duplex auto
   speed auto
 !
interface Serial0/0/0
   no ip address
   shutdown
   no fair-queue
 !
interface Serial0/0/1
   no ip address
   shutdown
 !
interface Serial0/1/0
   no ip address
   shutdown
 !
interface Serial0/2/0
   no ip address
   shutdown
   clock rate 2000000
 !
   [output cut]
```

For the sake of brevity, I didn't include my complete running-config, but I've displayed all you really need. You can see the two built-in FastEthernet interfaces, the two serial interfaces in slot 0 (0/0/0 and 0/0/1), the serial interface in slot 1 (0/1/0), and the serial interface in slot 2 (0/2/0). And once you see the interfaces like this, it makes it a lot easier to understand how the modules are inserted into the router.

Just understand that if you type **interface e0** on an old 2500 series router, **interface fastethernet 0/0** on a modular router (such as the 2800 series router), or **interface serial 0/1/0** on an ISR router, all you're actually doing is choosing an interface to configure. Essentially, they're all configured the same way after that.

Let's delve deeper into our router interface discussion by exploring how to bring up the interface and set an IP address on it next.

Bringing Up an Interface

You can disable an interface with the interface command shutdown and enable it with the no shutdown command. Just to remind you, all switch ports are enabled by default and all router ports are disabled by default, so we're going to talk more about router ports than switch ports in the next few sections.

If an interface is shut down, it'll display as administratively down when you use the show interfaces command (sh int for short):

```
Router#sh int f0/0
FastEthernet0/1 is administratively down, line protocol is down
[output cut]
```

Another way to check an interface's status is via the show running-config command. You can bring up the router interface with the no shutdown command (no shut for short):

```
Router(config)#int f0/0
Router(config-if)#no shutdown
*August 21 13:45:08.455: %LINK-3-UPDOWN: Interface FastEthernet0/0,
    changed state to up
Router(config-if)#do show int f0/0
FastEthernet0/0 is up, line protocol is up
[output cut]
```

Configuring an IP Address on an Interface

Even though you don't have to use IP on your routers, it's usually what everyone uses. To configure IP addresses on an interface, use the ip address command from interface configuration mode and remember that you do not set an IP address on a layer 2 switch port!

```
Todd(config)#int f0/1
Todd(config-if)#ip address 172.16.10.2 255.255.255.0
```

Also, don't forget to enable the interface with the no shutdown command. Remember to look at the command show interface int output to see if the interface is administratively shut down or not. Show ip int brief and show running-config will also give you this information.

> The ip address *address mask* command starts the IP processing on the router interface. Again, you do not configure an IP address on a layer 2 switch interface!

Okay—now if you want to add a second subnet address to an interface, you have to use the secondary parameter. If you type another IP address and press Enter, it will replace the existing primary IP address and mask. This is definitely one of the Cisco IOS's coolest features!

So let's try it. To add a secondary IP address, just use the secondary parameter:

```
Todd(config-if)#ip address 172.16.20.2 255.255.255.0 ?
  secondary  Make this IP address a secondary address
  <cr>
```

```
Todd(config-if)#ip address 172.16.20.2 255.255.255.0 secondary
Todd(config-if)#do sh run
Building configuration...
[output cut]

interface FastEthernet0/1
 ip address 172.16.20.2 255.255.255.0 secondary
 ip address 172.16.10.2 255.255.255.0
 duplex auto
 speed auto
!
```

But I've got to stop here to tell you that I really wouldn't recommend having multiple IP addresses on an interface because it's really inefficient. I showed you how anyway just in case you someday find yourself dealing with an MIS manager who's in love with really bad network design and makes you administer it! And who knows? Maybe someone will ask you about it someday and you'll get to seem really smart because you know this.

Exam Essentials

Describe the use of setup mode.   Setup mode is automatically started if a router boots and no startup-config is in NVRAM. You can also bring up setup mode by typing setup from privileged mode. Setup provides a minimum amount of configuration in an easy format for someone who does not understand how to configure a Cisco router from the command line.

Differentiate user, privileged, and global configuration modes, both visually and from a command capabilities perspective.   User mode, indicated by the routername> prompt, provides a command-line interface with very few available commands by default. User mode does not allow the configuration to be viewed or changed. Privileged mode, indicated by the routername# prompt, allows a user to both view and change the configuration of a router. You can enter privileged mode by typing the command **enable** and entering the enable password or enable secret password, if set. Global configuration mode, indicated by the *routername*(config)# prompt, allows configuration changes to be made that apply to the entire router (as opposed to a configuration change that might affect only one interface, for example).

Recognize additional prompts available in other modes and describe their use.   Additional modes are reached via the global configuration prompt, *routername*(config)#, and their prompts include interface mode, router(config-if)#, for making interface settings; line configuration mode, router(config-line)#, used to set passwords and make other settings to various connection methods; and routing protocol modes for various routing protocols, router(config-router)#, used to enable and configure routing protocols.

Describe the process of preparing an interface for use.   To use an interface, you must configure it with an IP address and subnet mask in the same subnet of the hosts that will be connecting to the switch that is connected to that interface. It also must be enabled with the no shutdown command. A serial interface that is connected back to back with another router serial interface must also be configured with a clock rate on the DCE end of the serial cable.

Perform device maintenance

There will be activities that will be recurring that maintain the devices. In the following sections, we'll talk about what some of these processes and procedures are.

Cisco IOS Upgrades and Recovery (SCP, FTP, TFTP, and MD5 Verify)

What happens if you need to restore the Cisco IOS to flash memory to replace an original file that has been damaged or if you want to upgrade the IOS? You can download the file from a TFTP server to flash memory by using the copy tftp flash command. This command requires the IP address of the TFTP host and the name of the file you want to download.

However, since IOSs can be very large today, we may want to use something other than TFTP, which is unreliable and can only transfer smaller files. Check this out:

```
Corp#copy ?
/erase Erase destination file system.
/error Allow to copy error file.
/noverify Don't verify image signature before reload.
/verify Verify image signature before reload.
archive: Copy from archive: file system
cns: Copy from cns: file system
flash: Copy from flash: file system
ftp: Copy from ftp: file system
http: Copy from http: file system
https: Copy from https: file system
null: Copy from null: file system
nvram: Copy from nvram: file system
rcp: Copy from rcp: file system
running-config Copy from current system configuration
scp: Copy from scp: file system
startup-config Copy from startup configuration
```

```
system: Copy from system: file system
tar: Copy from tar: file system
tftp: Copy from tftp: file system
tmpsys: Copy from tmpsys: file system
xmodem: Copy from xmodem: file system
ymodem: Copy from ymodem: file system
```

You can see from the output above that we have many options, and for the larger file we'll use FTP or SCP to copy our IOS into or from routers and switches, and we can even perform an MD5 verification with the /verify at the end of a command.

I'll just use TFTP for our examples because it's easiest. But before you begin, make sure the file you want to place in flash memory is in the default TFTP directory on your host. When you issue the command, TFTP won't ask you where the file is, so if the file you want to use isn't in the default directory of the TFTP host, this just won't work.

```
Router# copy tftp flash
Address or name of remote host []? 1.1.1.2
Source filename []? c2800nm-advsecurityk9-mz.151-4.M6.bin
Destination filename [c2800nm-advsecurityk9-mz.151-4.M6.bin]? [enter]
%Warning: There is a file already existing with this name
Do you want to over write? [confirm] [enter]
Accessing tftp://1.1.1.2/ c2800nm-advsecurityk9-mz.151-4.M6.bin...
Loading c2800nm-advsecurityk9-mz.151-4.M6.bin from 1.1.1.2 (via
FastEthernet0/0): !!!!!!!!!!!!!!!!!!!!!!!!!!!!!!!!!!!!!!!!!!!!!!!!!!!!!!!!!!!!!!
[OK - 21710744 bytes]
45395968 bytes copied in 82.880 secs (261954 bytes/sec)
Router#
```

In the preceding example, I copied the same file into flash memory, so it asked me if I wanted to overwrite it. Remember that we are "playing" with files in flash memory. If I had just corrupted my file by overwriting it, I won't know for sure until I reboot the router. Be careful with this command! If the file is corrupted, you'll need to do an IOS-restore from ROM monitor mode.

If you are loading a new file and you don't have enough room in flash memory to store both the new and existing copies, the router will ask to erase the contents of flash memory before writing the new file into flash memory, and if you are able to copy the IOS without erasing the old version, then make sure you remember to use the boot system flash: ios-file command.

 A Cisco router can become a TFTP server host for a router system image that's run in flash memory. The global configuration command is tftp-server flash:ios-file.

There is one other way you can restore the IOS on a router, but it takes a while. You can use what is called the Xmodem protocol to actually upload an IOS file into flash memory through the console port. You'd use the Xmodem through the console port procedure if you had no network connectivity to the router or switch.

Password Recovery and Configuration Register

All Cisco routers have a 16-bit software register that's written into NVRAM. By default, the *configuration register* is set to load the Cisco IOS from *flash memory* and to look for and load the startup-config file from NVRAM. In the following sections, I am going to discuss the configuration register settings and how to use these settings to provide password recovery on your routers.

Understanding the Configuration Register Bits

The 16 bits (2 bytes) of the configuration register are read from 15 to 0, from left to right. The default configuration setting on Cisco routers is 0x2102. This means that bits 13, 8, and 1 are on, as shown in Table 7.3. Notice that each set of 4 bits (called a nibble) is read in binary with a value of 8, 4, 2, 1.

TABLE 7.3   The configuration register bit numbers

Configuration Register		2					1			0			2	
Bit number	15	14	13	12	11	10 9	8	7	6	5	4	3	2	1	0
Binary	0	0	1	0	0	0 0	1	0	0	0	0	0	0	1	0

Add the prefix *0x* to the configuration register address. The *0x* means that the digits that follow are in hexadecimal.

Table 7.4 lists the software configuration bit meanings. Notice that bit 6 can be used to ignore the NVRAM contents. This bit is used for password recovery—something I'll go over with you soon in the section "Recovering Passwords."

Remember that in hex, the scheme is 0–9 and A–F (A = 10, B = 11, C = 12, D = 13, E = 14, and F = 15). This means that a 210F setting for the configuration register is actually 210(15), or 1111 in binary.

TABLE 7.4   Software configuration meanings

Bit	Hex	Description
0–3	0x0000–0x000F	Boot field (see Table 7.5)
6	0x0040	Ignore NVRAM contents.
7	0x0080	OEM bit enabled
8	0x101	Break disabled
10	0x0400	IP broadcast with all zeros
5, 11–12	0x0800–0x1000	Console line speed
13	0x2000	Boot default ROM software if network boot fails
14	0x4000	IP broadcasts do not have net numbers.
15	0x8000	Enable diagnostic messages and ignore NVRAM contents.

The boot field, which consists of bits 0–3 in the configuration register (the last 4 bits), controls the router boot sequence and locates the Cisco IOS. Table 7.5 describes the boot field bits.

TABLE 7.5   The boot field (configuration register bits 00–03)

Boot Field	Meaning	Use
00	ROM monitor mode	To boot to ROM monitor mode, set the configuration register to 2100. You must manually boot the router with the b command. The router will show the rommon> prompt.
01	Boot image from ROM	To boot the mini-IOS image stored in ROM, set the configuration register to 2101. The router will show the Router(boot)> prompt. The mini-IOS is not available in all routers and is also referred to as RXBOOT.
02–F	Specifies a default boot filename	Any value from 2102 through 210F tells the router to use the boot commands specified in NVRAM.

Checking the Current Configuration Register Value

You can see the current value of the configuration register by using the show version command (sh version or show ver for short), as demonstrated here:

```
Router>sh version
Cisco IOS Software, 2800 Software (C2800NM-ADVSECURITYK9-M),
Version 15.1(4)M6, RELEASE SOFTWARE (fc2)
[output cut]
Configuration register is 0x2102
```

The last information given from this command is the value of the configuration register. In this example, the value is 0x2102—the default setting. The configuration register setting of 0x2102 tells the router to look in NVRAM for the boot sequence.

Notice that the show version command also provides the IOS version, and in the preceding example, it shows the IOS version as 15.1(4)M6.

The show version command will display system hardware configuration information, the software version, and the names of the boot images on a router.

To change the configuration register, use the config-register command from global configuration mode.

```
Router(config)#config-register 0x2142
Router(config)#do sh ver
[output cut]
Configuration register is 0x2102 (will be 0x2142 at next reload)
```

It's important that you are careful when you set the configuration register!

If you save your configuration and reload the router and it comes up in setup mode, the configuration register setting is probably incorrect.

Boot System Commands

Did you know that you can configure your router to boot another IOS if the flash is corrupted? Well, you can. You can boot all of your routers from a TFTP server, but it's old school, and people just don't do it anymore; it's just for backup in case of failure.

There are some boot commands you can play with that will help you manage the way your router boots the Cisco IOS—but please remember, we're talking about the router's IOS here, *not* the router's configuration!

```
Router>en
Router#config t
```

```
Enter configuration commands, one per line.  End with CNTL/Z.
Router(config)#boot ?
  bootstrap  Bootstrap image file
  config     Configuration file
  host       Router-specific config file
  network    Network-wide config file
  system     System image file
```

The boot command truly gives you a wealth of options, but first, I'll show you the typical settings that Cisco recommends. So let's get started—the boot system command will allow you to tell the router which system IOS file to boot from flash memory. Remember that the router, by default, boots the first system IOS file found in flash. You can change that with the following commands, as shown in the output:

```
Router(config)#boot system ?
  WORD   TFTP filename or URL
  flash  Boot from flash memory
  ftp    Boot from a server via ftp
  mop    Boot from a Decnet MOP server
  rcp    Boot from a server via rcp
  rom    Boot from rom
  tftp   Boot from a tftp server
Router(config)#boot system flash c2800nm-advsecurityk9-mz.151-4.M6.bin
```

Notice I could boot from FLASH, FTP, ROM, TFTP, or other useless options. The command I used configures the router to boot the IOS listed in it. This is a helpful command for when you load a new IOS into flash and want to test it, or even when you want to totally change which IOS is loading by default.

The next command is considered a fallback routine, but as I said, you can make it a permanent way to have your routers boot from a TFTP host. Personally, I wouldn't necessarily recommend doing this (single point of failure); I'm just showing you that it's possible:

```
Router(config)#boot system tftp ?
  WORD   System image filename
Router(config)#boot system tftp c2800nm-advsecurityk9-mz.151-4.M6.bin?
  Hostname or A.B.C.D  Address from which to download the file
  <cr>
Router(config)#boot system tftp c2800nm-advsecurityk9-mz.151-4.M6.bin 1.1.1.2
Router(config)#
```

As your last recommended fallback option—the one to go to if the IOS in flash doesn't load and the TFTP host does not produce the IOS—load the mini-IOS from ROM like this:

```
Router(config)#boot system rom
Router(config)#do show run | include boot system
```

```
boot system flash c2800nm-advsecurityk9-mz.151-4.M6.bin
boot system tftp c2800nm-advsecurityk9-mz.151-4.M6.bin 1.1.1.2
boot system rom
Router(config)#
```

If the preceding configuration is set, the router will try to boot from the TFTP server if flash fails, and if the TFTP boot fails, the mini-IOS will load after six unsuccessful attempts of trying to locate the TFTP server.

In the next section, I'll show you how to load the router into ROM monitor mode so you can perform password recovery.

Recovering Passwords

If you're locked out of a router because you forgot the password, you can change the configuration register to help you get back on your feet. As I said earlier, bit 6 in the configuration register is used to tell the router whether to use the contents of NVRAM to load a router configuration.

The default configuration register value is 0x2102, meaning that bit 6 is off. With the default setting, the router will look for and load a router configuration stored in NVRAM (startup-config). To recover a password, you need to turn on bit 6. Doing this will tell the router to ignore the NVRAM contents. The configuration register value to turn on bit 6 is 0x2142.

Here are the main steps to password recovery:

1. Boot the router and interrupt the boot sequence by performing a break, which will take the router into ROM monitor mode.

2. Change the configuration register to turn on bit 6 (with the value 0x2142).

3. Reload the router.

4. Say "no" to entering setup mode, then enter privileged mode.

5. Copy the startup-config file to running-config, and don't forget to verify that your interfaces are re-enabled.

6. Change the password.

7. Reset the configuration register to the default value.

8. Save the router configuration.

9. Reload the router (optional).

I'm going to cover these steps in more detail in the following sections. I'll also show you the commands to restore access to ISR series routers.

You can enter ROM monitor mode by pressing Ctrl+Break or Ctrl+Shift+6, then b, during router bootup. But if the IOS is corrupt or missing, if there's no network connectivity available to find a TFTP host, or if the mini-IOS from ROM doesn't load (meaning the default router fallback failed), the router will enter ROM monitor mode by default.

Interrupting the Router Boot Sequence

Your first step is to boot the router and perform a break. This is usually done by pressing the Ctrl+Break key combination when using HyperTerminal (personally, I use SecureCRT or PuTTY) while the router first reboots.

```
System Bootstrap, Version 15.1(4)M6, RELEASE SOFTWARE (fc2)
Copyright (c) 1999 by cisco Systems, Inc.
TAC:Home:SW:IOS:Specials for info
PC = 0xfff0a530, Vector = 0x500, SP = 0x680127b0
C2800 platform with 32768 Kbytes of main memory
PC = 0xfff0a530, Vector = 0x500, SP = 0x80004374
monitor: command "boot" aborted due to user interrupt
rommon 1 >
```

Notice the line `monitor: command "boot" aborted due to user interrupt`. At this point, you will be at the `rommon 1>` prompt, which is called the ROM monitor mode.

Changing the Configuration Register

As I explained earlier, you can change the configuration register from within the IOS by using the `config-register` command. To turn on bit 6, use the configuration register value 0x2142.

 NOTE Remember that if you change the configuration register to 0x2142, the startup-config will be bypassed and the router will load into setup mode.

To change the bit value on a Cisco ISR series router, you just enter the following command at the `rommon 1>` prompt:

```
rommon 1 >confreg 0x2142
You must reset or power cycle for new config to take effect
rommon 2 >reset
```

Reloading the Router and Entering Privileged Mode

At this point, you need to reset the router like this:

- From the ISR series router, type **I** (for initialize) or **reset**.

- From an older series router, type **I**.

The router will reload and ask if you want to use setup mode (because no startup-config is used). Answer no to entering setup mode, press Enter to go into user mode, and then type **enable** to go into privileged mode.

Viewing and Changing the Configuration

Now you're past the point where you would need to enter the user-mode and privileged-mode passwords in a router. Copy the startup-config file to the running-config file:

```
copy startup-config running-config
```

Or use the shortcut:

```
copy start run
```

The configuration is now running in *random access memory (RAM)*, and you're in privileged mode, meaning that you can now view and change the configuration. But you can't view the enable secret setting for the password since it is encrypted. To change the password, do this:

```
config t
enable secret todd
```

Resetting the Configuration Register and Reloading the Router

After you're finished changing passwords, set the configuration register back to the default value with the config-register command:

```
config t
config-register 0x2102
```

It's important to remember to enable your interfaces after copying the configuration from NVRAM to RAM.

Finally, save the new configuration with a copy running-config startup-config and use reload to reload the router.

 If you save your configuration and reload the router and it comes up in setup mode, the configuration register setting is probably incorrect.

To sum this up, we now have Cisco's suggested IOS backup routine configured on our router: flash, TFTP host, ROM.

File System Management

Cisco has created a file system called Cisco IFS that allows you to work with files and directories just as you would from a Windows DOS prompt. The commands you use are dir, copy, more, delete, erase or format, cd and pwd, and mkdir and rmdir.

Working with IFS gives you the ability to view all files, even those on remote servers. And you definitely want to find out if an image on one of your remote servers is valid before you copy it, right? You also need to know how big it is—size matters here! It's also a really good idea to take a look at the remote server's configuration and make sure it's all good before loading that file on your router.

It's very cool that IFS makes the file system user interface universal—it's not platform specific anymore. You now get to use the same syntax for all your commands on all of your routers, no matter the platform!

Sound too good to be true? Well, it kind of is because you'll find out that support for all commands on each file system and platform just isn't there. But it's really no big deal since various file systems differ in the actions they perform; the commands that aren't relevant to a particular file system are the very ones that aren't supported on that file system. Be assured that any file system or platform will fully support all the commands you need to manage it.

Another cool IFS feature is that it cuts down on all those obligatory prompts for a lot of the commands. If you want to enter a command, all you have to do is type all the necessary info straight into the command line—no more jumping through hoops of prompts! So, if you want to copy a file to an FTP server, all you'd do is first indicate where the desired source file is on your router, pinpoint where the destination file is to be on the FTP server, determine the username and password you're going to use when you want to connect to that server, and type it all in on one line—sleek! And for those of you resistant to change, you can still have the router prompt you for all the information it needs and enjoy entering a more elegantly minimized version of the command than you did before.

But even in spite of all this, your router might still prompt you—even if you did everything right in your command line. It comes down to how you've got the `file prompt` command configured and which command you're trying to use. But no worries—if that happens, the default value will be entered right there in the command, and all you have to do is hit Enter to verify the correct values.

IFS also lets you explore various directories and inventory files in any directory you want. Plus, you can make subdirectories in flash memory or on a card, but you only get to do that if you're working on one of the more recent platforms.

And get this—the new file system interface uses URLs to determine the whereabouts of a file. So just as they pinpoint places on the web, URLs now indicate where files are on your Cisco router, or even on a remote file server! You just type URLs right into your commands to identify where the file or directory is. It's really that easy—to copy a file from one place to another, you simply enter the copy *source-url destination-url* command—sweet! IFS URLs are a tad different than what you're used to though, and there's an array of formats to use that vary depending on where, exactly, the file is that you're after.

We're going to use Cisco IFS commands pretty much the same way that we used the copy command in the section "Cisco IOS Upgrades and Recovery (SCP, FTP, TFTP, and MD5 Verify)" earlier:

- For backing up the IOS
- For upgrading the IOS
- For viewing text files

Okay—with all that down, let's take a look at the common IFS commands available to us for managing the IOS. I'll get into configuration files soon, but for now I'm going to get you started with going over the basics used to manage the new Cisco IOS.

dir Same as with Windows, this command lets you view files in a directory. Type **dir**, hit Enter, and by default you get the contents of the `flash:/` directory output.

copy   This is one popular command, often used to upgrade, restore, or back up an IOS. But as I said, when you use it, it's really important to focus on the details—what you're copying, where it's coming from, and where it's going to land.

more   Same as with Unix, this will take a text file and let you look at it on a card. You can use it to check out your configuration file or your backup configuration file.

show file   This command will give you the skinny on a specified file or file system, but it's kind of obscure because people don't use it a lot.

delete   Three guesses—yep, it deletes stuff. But with some types of routers, not as well as you'd think. That's because even though it whacks the file, it doesn't always free up the space it was using. To actually get the space back, you have to use something called the squeeze command too.

erase/format   Use these with care—make sure that when you're copying files, you say no to the dialog that asks you if you want to erase the file system! The type of memory you're using determines if you can nix the flash drive or not.

cd/pwd   Same as with Unix and DOS, cd is the command you use to change directories. Use the pwd command to print (show) the working directory.

mkdir/rmdir   Use these commands on certain routers and switches to create and delete directories—the mkdir command for creation and the rmdir command for deletion. Use the cd and pwd commands to change into these directories.

Exam Essentials

Understand configuration register commands and settings.   The 0x2102 setting is the default on all Cisco routers and tells the router to look in NVRAM for the boot sequence. 0x2101 tells the router to boot from ROM, and 0x2142 tells the router not to load the startup-config in NVRAM to provide password recovery.

Perform password recovery.   The steps in the password recovery process are interrupt the router boot sequence, change the configuration register, reload the router and enter privileged mode, copy the startup-config file to running-config and verify that your interfaces are re-enabled, change/set the password, save the new configuration, reset the configuration register, and reload the router.

Restore or upgrade an IOS image.   By using the privileged-mode command copy tftp flash, you can restore or upgrade a file from a TFTP (network) server to flash memory.

Describe best practices to prepare to back up an IOS image to a network server.   Make sure that you can access the network server, ensure that the network server has adequate space for the code image, and verify the file naming and path requirement.

Understand and use Cisco IFS file system management commands.   The commands to use are dir, copy, more, delete, erase or format, cd and pwd, and mkdir and rmdir, as well as system:running-config and nvram:startup-config.

Use Cisco IOS tools to troubleshoot and resolve problems

To assist with the process of maintaining the network, you have a number of IOS tools at your disposal to assist you in troubleshooting and resolving issues. In the following sections I'll add some detail to the use of some tools I have already mentioned and introduce some additional tools that are available to you.

Ping and Traceroute with Extended Option

You can use the ping and traceroute commands to test connectivity to remote devices, and both of them can be used with many protocols, not just IP. But don't forget that the show ip route command is a great troubleshooting command for verifying your routing table and the show interfaces command will reveal the status of each interface to you.

Using the *ping* Command

So far, you've seen lots of examples of pinging devices to test IP connectivity and name resolution using the DNS server. To see all the different protocols that you can use with the *Ping* program, type **ping ?**:

```
SW-1#ping ?
  WORD  Ping destination address or hostname
  clns  CLNS echo
  ip    IP echo
  ipv6  IPv6 echo
  tag   Tag encapsulated IP echo
  <cr>
```

The ping output displays the minimum, average, and maximum times it takes for a ping packet to find a specified system and return. Here's an example:

```
SW-1#ping SW-3
Translating "SW-3"...domain server (4.4.4.4) [OK]
Type escape sequence to abort.
Sending 5, 100-byte ICMP Echos to 10.100.128.8, timeout is
  2 seconds:
!!!!!
Success rate is 100 percent (5/5), round-trip min/avg/max
  = 28/31/32 ms
```

This output tells us that the DNS server was used to resolve the name and the device was pinged in a minimum of 28 ms (milliseconds), an average of 31 ms, and up to 32 ms. This network has some latency!

> The ping command can be used in user and privileged mode but not configuration mode!

Using the *traceroute* Command

Traceroute—the traceroute command, or trace for short—shows the path a packet takes to get to a remote device. It uses time to live (TTL), time-outs, and ICMP error messages to outline the path a packet takes through an internetwork to arrive at a remote host.

The trace command, which you can deploy from either user mode or privileged mode, allows you to figure out which router in the path to an unreachable network host should be examined more closely as the probable cause of your network's failure.

To see the protocols that you can use with the traceroute command, type **traceroute ?**:

```
SW-1#traceroute ?
  WORD      Trace route to destination address or hostname
  appletalk AppleTalk Trace
  clns      ISO CLNS Trace
  ip        IP Trace
  ipv6      IPv6 Trace
  ipx       IPX Trace
  mac       Trace Layer2 path between 2 endpoints
  oldvines  Vines Trace (Cisco)
  vines     Vines Trace (Banyan)
  <cr>
```

The traceroute command shows the hop or hops that a packet traverses on its way to a remote device.

> Do not get confused! You can't use the tracert command; that's a Windows command. For a router, use the traceroute command!

Here's an example of using tracert on a Windows prompt—notice that the command is tracert, not traceroute:

```
C:\>tracert www.whitehouse.gov

Tracing route to a1289.g.akamai.net [69.8.201.107]
```

```
over a maximum of 30 hops:

   1      *          *           *       Request timed out.
   2     53 ms     61 ms       53 ms    hlrn-dsl-gw15-207.hlrn.qwest.net
[207.225.112.207]
   3     53 ms     55 ms       54 ms    hlrn-agw1.inet.qwest.net [71.217.188.113]
   4     54 ms     53 ms       54 ms    hlr-core-01.inet.qwest.net [205.171.253.97]
   5     54 ms     53 ms       54 ms    apa-cntr-01.inet.qwest.net [205.171.253.26]
   6     54 ms     53 ms       53 ms    63.150.160.34
   7     54 ms     54 ms       53 ms    www.whitehouse.gov [69.8.201.107]

Trace complete.
```

Terminal Monitor

One of the locations to which the logging system can direct system messages is the terminal monitor. When you're connected to the device remotely, system messages will not appear on the screen as they normally do unless you have directed the messages to the terminal. Setting the system to do so is covered in the section "Syslog" earlier in this chapter.

Log Events

Cisco devices send all log messages of the severity level you've chosen to the console. They'll also go to the buffer, and both happen by default. Events stored in the log can be extremely helpful in troubleshooting an issue. A detailed coverage of logging is in the section "Syslog" earlier in this chapter.

Local SPAN

A traffic sniffer can be a valuable tool for monitoring and troubleshooting your network. However, since the inception of switches into our networks more than 20 years ago, troubleshooting has become more difficult since we can't just plug an analyzer into a switch port and be able to read all the network traffic. Before we had switches, we used hubs, and when a hub receives a digital signal on one port, the hub sends out a copy of that digital signal on all ports except on the port where the hub received the signal. This allows a traffic sniffer that is connected to a hub port to receive all traffic in the network.

Modern local networks are essentially switched networks. After a switch boots, it starts to build up a layer 2 forwarding table based on the source MAC addresses of the different packets that the switch receives. After the switch builds this forwarding table, it then forwards traffic that is destined for a MAC address directly to the exit port. By default, this prevents a traffic sniffer that is connected to another port from receiving the unicast traffic. The SPAN feature was therefore introduced on switches to help solve this problem.

The SPAN feature allows you to analyze network traffic passing through the port by sending a copy of the traffic to another port on the switch that has been connected to a network analyzer or other monitoring device. SPAN copies the traffic that the device receives and/or sends on source ports to a destination port for analysis.

For example, if you would like to analyze the traffic flowing from PC1 to PC2 shown in Figure 7.7, you need to specify a source port of where you want to capture the data. You can either configure the interface Fa0/1 to capture the ingress traffic or the interface Fa0/3 to capture the egress traffic—your choice! Second, specify the destination port interface where the sniffer is connected and will capture the data, in this example Fa0/2. The traffic flowing from PC1 to PC2 will then be copied to that interface, and you will be able to analyze it with a traffic sniffer.

FIGURE 7.7   Using SPAN for troubleshooting

The following steps will configure SPAN on S1:

Step 1: Associate a SPAN session number with the source port of what you want to monitor:

```
S1(config)#monitor session 1 source interface f0/1
```

Step 2: Associate a SPAN session number with the destination interface:

```
S1(config)#monitor session 1 dest interface f0/2
```

Step 3: Verify that the SPAN session has been configured correctly:

```
S1(config)#do sh monitor
Session 1
---------
Type                : Local Session
Source Ports        :
    Both            : Fa0/1
Destination Ports   : Fa0/2
    Encapsulation   : Native
          Ingress   : Disabled
```

Now connect up your network analyzer into port F0/2 and enjoy!

Exam Essentials

Describe the function of the `ping` command.   Packet Internet Groper (`ping`) uses ICMP echo requests and ICMP echo replies to verify an active IP address on a network.

Ping a valid host ID from the correct prompt.   You can ping an IP address from a router's user mode or privileged mode but not from configuration mode, unless you use the do command. You must ping a valid address, such as 1.1.1.1.

Describe network programmability in enterprise network architecture

Right now, in our current, traditional networks, our router and switch ports are the only devices that are not virtualized. So this is what we're really trying to do here—virtualize our physical ports.

First, understand that our current routers and switches run an operating system, such as Cisco IOS, that provides network functionality. This has worked well for us for 25 years or so, but it is way too cumbersome now to configure, implement, and troubleshoot these autonomous devices in today's large, complicated networks. Before you even get started, you have to understand the business requirements and then push that out to all the devices. This can take weeks or even months since each device is configured, maintained, and monitored separately.

Before we can talk about the new way to network our ports, you need to understand how our current networks forward data, which happens via these two planes:

Data plane   This plane, also referred to as the forwarding plane, is physically responsible for forwarding frames of packets from its ingress to egress interfaces using protocols managed in the control plane. Here, data is received, the destination interface is looked up, and the forwarding of frames and packets happens, so the data plane relies completely on the control plane to provide solid information.

Control plane   This plane is responsible for managing and controlling any forwarding table that the data plane uses. For example, routing protocols such as OSPF, EIGRP, RIP, and BGP as well as IPv4 ARP, IPv6 NDP, switch MAC address learning, and STP are all managed by the control plane.

Now that you understand that there are two planes used to forward traffic in our current or legacy network, let's take a look at the future of networking.

Function of a Controller

If you have worked on any enterprise Wi-Fi installations in the last decade, you would have designed your physical network and then configured a type of network controller that managed all the wireless APs in the network. It's hard to imagine that anyone would install a wireless network today without some type of controller in an enterprise network, where the access points (APs) receive their directions from the controller on how to manage the wireless frames and the APs have no operating system or brains to make many decisions on their own.

The same is now true for our physical router and switch ports, and it's precisely this centralized management of network frames and packets that Software Defined Networking (SDN) provides to us.

Separation of Control Plane and Data Plane

SDN removes the control plane intelligence from the network devices by having a central controller manage the network instead of having a full operating system (Cisco IOS, for example) on the devices. In turn, the controller manages the network by separating the control and data (forwarding) planes, which automates configuration and the remediation of all devices.

So instead of the network devices each having individual control planes, we now have a centralized control plane, which consolidates all network operations in the SDN controller. APIs allow for applications to control and configure the network without human intervention. The APIs are another type of configuration interface just like the CLI, SNMP, or GUI interfaces, which facilitate machine-to-machine operations.

The SDN architecture slightly differs from the architecture of traditional networks by adding a third layer, the application plane, as described here and shown in Figure 7.8:

Data (or forwarding) plane   Contains network elements, meaning any physical or virtual device that deals with data traffic.

Control plane   Usually a software solution, the SDN controllers reside here to provide centralized control of the router and switches that populate the data plane, removing the control plane from individual devices.

Application plane   This new layer contains the applications that communicate their network requirements toward the controller using APIs.

FIGURE 7.8   The SDN architecture

SDN is pretty cool because your applications tell the network what to do based on business needs instead of you having to do it. Then the controller uses the APIs to pass instructions on to your routers, switches, or other network gear. So instead of taking weeks or months to push out a business requirement, the solution now only takes minutes.

Northbound and Southbound APIs

There are two sets of APIs that SDN uses and they are very different. As you already know, the SDN controller uses APIs to communicate with both the application and data planes. Communication with the data plane is defined with southbound interfaces, while services are offered to the application plane using the northbound interface. Let's take a deeper look at this oh-so-vital CCNA objective.

Southbound APIs

Logical southbound interface (SBIs) APIs (or device-to-control-plane interfaces) are used for communication between the controllers and network devices. They allow the two devices to communicate so that the controller can program the data plane forwarding tables of your routers and switches. SBIs are pictured in Figure 7.9.

FIGURE 7.9   Southbound interfaces

Since all the network drawings had the network gear below the controller, the APIs that talked to the devices became known as southbound, meaning, "out the southbound interface of the controller." And don't forget that with SDN, the term *interface* is no longer referring to a physical interface!

Unlike northbound APIs, southbound APIs have many standards, and you absolutely must know them well for the objectives. Let's talk about them now:

OpenFlow   Describes an industry-standard API, which the ONF (opennetworking.org) defines. It configures white label switches, meaning that they are nonproprietary, and as a result defines the flow path through the network. All the configuration is done through NETCONF.

NETCONF   Although not all devices support NETCONF yet, what this provides is a network management protocol standardized by the IETF. Using RPC, you can install, manipulate, and delete the configuration of network devices using XML.

> NETCONF is a protocol that allows you to modify the configuration of a networking device, but if you want to modify the device's forwarding table, then the OpenFlow protocol is the way to go.

onePK   A Cisco proprietary SBI that allows you to inspect or modify the network element configuration without hardware upgrades. This makes life easier for developers by providing software development kits for Java, C, and Python.

OpFlex   The name of the southbound API in the Cisco ACI world is OpFlex, an open-standard, distributed control system. Understand that OpenFlow first sends detailed and complex instructions to the control plane of the network elements in order to implement a new application policy—something called an imperative SDN model. On the other hand, OpFlex uses a declarative SDN model because the controller, which Cisco calls the APIC, sends a more abstract, "summary policy" to the network elements. The summary policy makes the controller believe that the network elements will implement the required changes using their own control planes, since the devices will use a partially centralized control plane.

Northbound APIs

To communicate from the SDN controller and the applications running over the network, you'll use northbound interfaces (NBIs), pictured in Figure 7.10.

FIGURE 7.10   Northbound interfaces

By setting up a framework that allows the application to demand the network setup with the configuration that it needs, the NBIs allow your applications to manage and control the network. This is priceless for saving time because you no longer need to adjust and tweak your network to get a service or application running correctly.

The NBI applications include a wide variety of automated network services, from network virtualization and dynamic virtual network provisioning to more granular firewall monitoring, user identity management, and access policy control. This allows for cloud orchestration applications that tie together, for server provisioning, storage, and networking that enables a complete rollout of new cloud services in minutes instead of weeks!

Sadly, at this writing there is no single northbound interface that you can use for communication between the controller and all applications. So instead, you use various and sundry northbound APIs, with each one working only with a specific set of applications.

Most of the time, applications used by NBIs will be on the same system as the APIC controller, so the APIs don't need to send messages over the network since both programs run on the same system. However, if they don't reside on the same system, REST (Representational State Transfer) comes into play; it uses HTTP messages to transfer data over the API for applications that sit on different hosts.

Exam Essentials

Understand SDN.   Understand how a controller works, and especially the control and data planes as well as the northbound and southbound APIs.

Review Questions

You can find the answers in the Appendix.

1. How can you efficiently restrict the read-only function of a requesting SNMP management station based on the IP address?

   A. Place an ACL on the logical control plane.

   B. Place an ACL on the line when configuring the RO community string.

   C. Place an ACL on the VTY line.

   D. Place an ACL on all router interfaces.

2. A switch is configured with the `snmp-server community Cisco RO` command running SNMPv2c. An NMS is trying to communicate to this router via SNMP, so what can be performed by the NMS? (Choose two.)

   A. The NMS can only graph obtained results.

   B. The NMS can graph obtained results and change the hostname of the router.

   C. The NMS can only change the hostname of the router.

   D. The NMS can use GETBULK and return many results.

3. Which is true regarding SNMP? (Choose two.)

   A. SNMPv2c offers more security than SNMPv1.

   B. SNMPv3 uses TCP and introduced the GETBULK operation.

   C. SNMPv2c introduced the INFORM operation.

   D. SNMPv3 provides the best security of the three versions.

4. Which of the following is a standards-based protocol that provides dynamic network discovery?

   A. DHCP

   B. LLDP

   C. DDNS

   D. SSTP

   E. CDP

5. You are troubleshooting a connectivity problem in your corporate network and want to isolate the problem. You suspect that a router on the route to an unreachable network is at fault. What IOS user exec command should you issue?

   A. `Router>ping`

   B. `Router>trace`

   C. `Router>show ip route`

   D. `Router>show interface`

   E. `Router>show cdp neighbors`

6. You copy a configuration from a network host to a router's RAM. The configuration looks correct, yet it is not working at all. What could the problem be?

   A. You copied the wrong configuration into RAM.

   B. You copied the configuration into flash memory instead.

   C. The copy did not override the no shutdown command in running-config.

   D. You copied the configuration into NVRAM.

7. At which of the following prompts can you rename the router?

   A. router>

   B. router#

   C. router(config)#

   D. router(config-if)#

8. The corporate office sends you a new router to connect, but upon connecting the console cable, you see that there is already a configuration on the router. What should be done before a new configuration is entered in the router?

   A. RAM should be erased and the router restarted.

   B. Flash should be erased and the router restarted.

   C. NVRAM should be erased and the router restarted.

   D. The new configuration should be entered and saved.

9. What command can you use to determine the IP address of a directly connected neighbor?

   A. show cdp

   B. show cdp neighbors

   C. show cdp neighbors detail

   D. show neighbor detail

10. According to the output, what interface does SW-2 use to connect to SW-3?

    SW-3#**sh cdp neighbors**
    Capability Codes: R - Router, T - Trans Bridge, B - Source Route BridgeS -
    Switch, H - Host, I - IGMP, r - Repeater, P - Phone, D - Remote, C - CVTA,
    M - Two-port Mac Relay Device ID

Local Intrfce		Holdtme	Capability	Platform	Port ID
SW-1	Fas 0/1	170	S I	WS-C3560-	Fas 0/15
SW-1	Fas 0/2	170	S I	WS-C3560-	Fas 0/16
SW-2	Fas 0/5	162	S I	WS-C3560-	Fas 0/2

    A. Fas 0/1

    B. Fas 0/16

    C. Fas 0/2

    D. Fas 0/5

Appendix

Answers to Review Questions

Chapter 1: Network Fundamentals

1. A. Fiber-optic cables are the only ones that have a core surrounded by a material called cladding.

2. A. The device shown is a hub and hubs place all ports in the same broadcast domain and the same collision domain.

3. B. Secure Shell (SSH) protocol sets up a secure session that's similar to Telnet over a standard TCP/IP connection and is employed for doing things like logging into systems, running programs on remote systems, and moving files from one system to another.

4. B. The connection between the two switches requires a crossover and the connection from the hosts to the switches requires a straight-through.

5. B. The all-hub network at the bottom is one collision domain; the bridge network on top equals three collision domains. Add in the switch network of five collision domains—one for each switch port—and you get a total of nine.

6. C. Between a host and switch a straight through cable is required.

7. B. There are two octets in the network portion of a Class B address.

8. C. The IEEE Ethernet Data Link layer has two sublayers, the Media Access Control (MAC) layer and the Logical Link Control (LLC) layer.

9. C. Wireless AP's are very popular today and will be going away about the same time that rock n' roll does. The idea behind these devices (which are layer 2 bridge devices) is to connect wireless products to the wired Ethernet network. The wireless AP will create a single collision domain and is typically its own dedicated broadcast domain as well.

10. A. Hubs operate on the Physical Layer as they have no intelligence and send all traffic in all directions.

Chapter 2: LAN Switching Technologies

1. A. Layer 2 switches and bridges are faster than routers because they don't take up time looking at the Network Layer header information. They do make use of the Data Link layer information.

2. show mac address table. This is output generated by the show mac address table command.

3. B. Since the MAC address is not present in the table, it will send the frame out of all ports in the same VLAN with the exception of the port on which it was received.

4. Address learning, forward/filter decisions, and loop avoidance. The three functions are address learning, forward/filter decisions, and loop avoidance.

5. A, D. In the output shown, you can see that the port is in Secure-shutdown mode and the light for the port would be amber. To enable the port again, you'd need to do the following:

```
S3(config-if)#shutdown
S3(config-if)#no shutdown
```

6. D. The organizationally unique identifier (OUI) is assigned by the IEEE to an organization composed of 24 bits, or 3 bytes, which in turn assigns a globally administered address also comprising 24 bits, or 3 bytes, that's supposedly unique to each and every adapter it manufactures.

7. A. Backoff on an Ethernet network is the retransmission delay that's enforced when a collision occurs. When that happens, a host will only resume transmission after the forced time delay has expired. Keep in mind that after the backoff has elapsed, all stations have equal priority to transmit data.

8. B. FCS is a field at the end of the frame that's used to store the cyclic redundancy check (CRC) answer. The CRC is a mathematical algorithm that's based on the data in the frame and run when each frame is built. When a receiving host receives the frame and runs the CRC, the answer should be the same. If not, the frame is discarded, assuming errors have occurred.

9. A, E. Physical addresses or MAC addresses are used to identify devices at layer 2. MAC addresses are only used to communicate on the same network. To communicate on different networks, we have to use layer 3 addresses (IP addresses).

10. D. Here's a list of ways VLANs simplify network management:

- Network adds, moves, and changes are achieved with ease by just configuring a port into the appropriate VLAN.
- A group of users that need an unusually high level of security can be put into its own VLAN so that users outside of the VLAN can't communicate with them.
- As a logical grouping of users by function, VLANs can be considered independent from their physical or geographic locations.
- VLANs greatly enhance network security if implemented correctly.
- VLANs increase the number of broadcast domains while decreasing their size.

Chapter 3: Routing Technologies

1. `show ip route`. The `ip route` command is used to display the routing table of a router.

2. B. In the new 15 IOS code, Cisco defines a different route called a local route. Each has a /32 prefix defining a route just for the one address, which is the router's interface.

3. A, B. Although option D almost seems right, it is not; the mask option is the mask used on the remote network, not the source network. Since there is no number at the end of the static route, it is using the default administrative distance of 1.

4. C, F. The switches are not used as either a default gateway or other destination. Switches have nothing to do with routing. It is very important to remember that the destination MAC address will always be the router's interface. The destination address of a frame, from HostA, will be the MAC address of the Fa0/0 interface of RouterA. The destination address of a packet will be the IP address of the network interface card (NIC) of the HTTPS server. The destination port number in the segment header will have a value of 443 (HTTPS).

5. B. This mapping was learned dynamically, which means it was learned through ARP.

6. B. Hybrid protocols use aspects of both distance vector and link state—for example, EIGRP. Be advised, however, that Cisco typically just calls EIGRP an advanced distance-vector routing protocol. Do not be misled by the way the question is worded.

7. A. Since the destination MAC address is different at each hop, it must keep changing. The IP address, which is used for the routing process, does not.

8. no shutdown. Yes, you have to do a no shutdown on the VLAN interface.

9. B. The encapsulation command specifying the VLAN for the subinterface must be present under both subinterfaces.

10. A. With a multilayer switch, enable IP routing and create one logical interface for each VLAN using the interface vlan *number* command and you're now doing inter-VLAN routing on the backplane of the switch!

Chapter 4: WAN Technologies

1. C. The command debug ppp authentication will show you the authentication process that PPP uses across point-to-point connections.

2. B, D. Since BGP does not automatically discover neighbors like other routing protocols do, you have to explicitly configure them using the neighbor *peer-ip-address* remote-as *peer-as-number* command.

3. D. BGP uses TCP as the transport mechanism, which provides reliable connection-oriented delivery. BGP uses TCP port 179. Two routers that are using BGP form a TCP connection with one another. These two BGP routers are called "peer routers," or "neighbors."

4. D. The show ip bgp neighbor command is used to see the hold time on two BGP peers.

5. B. The 0.0.0.0 in the next hop field output of the show ip bgp command means that the network was locally entered on the router with the network command into BGP.

6. A, D. GRE tunnels have the following characteristics: GRE uses a protocol-type field in the GRE header so any layer 3 protocol can be used through the tunnel. GRE is stateless and has no flow control. GRE offers no security. GRE creates additional overhead for tunneled packets—at least 24 bytes.

7. C. If you receive this flapping message when you configure your GRE tunnel, this means that you used your tunnel interface address instead of the tunnel destination address.

8. D. The show running-config interface tunnel 0 command will show you the configuration of the interface, not the status of the tunnel.

9. C. PPP uses PAP and CHAP as authentication protocols. PAP is clear text; CHAP uses an MD5 hash.

10. C. PPPoE encapsulates PPP frames in Ethernet frames and uses common PPP features like authentication, encryption, and compression. PPPoA is used for ATM.

Chapter 5: Infrastructure Services

1. D. To enable a device to be an NTP client, use the ntp server *IP_address* version *number* command at global configuration mode. That's all there is to it! Assuming your NTP server is working of course.

2. A, B. A router interface can be in many states with HSRP; the states are shown in Table 5.1.

3. A. Only option A has the correct sequence to enable HSRP on an interface.

4. D. This is a question that I used in a lot of job interviews with prospects. The show standby command is your friend when dealing with HSRP.

5. D. There is nothing wrong with leaving the priorities at the defaults of 100. The first router up will be the active router.

6. C. In version 1, HSRP messages are sent to the multicast IP address 224.0.0.2 and UDP port 1985. HSRP version 2 uses the multicast IP address 224.0.0.102 and UDP port 1985.

7. B, C. If HSRP1 is configured to preempt, then it will become active because of the higher priority; if not, HSRP2 will stay the active router.

8. C. In version 1, HSRP messages are sent to the multicast IP address 224.0.0.2 and UDP port 1985. HSRP version 2 uses the multicast IP address 224.0.0.102 and UDP port 1985.

9. A, C, E. NAT is not perfect and can cause some issues in some networks, but most networks work just fine. NAT can cause delays and troubleshooting problems, and some applications just won't work.

10. B, D, F. NAT is not perfect, but there are some advantages. It conserves global addresses, which allow us to add millions of hosts to the Internet without "real" IP addresses. This provides flexibility in our corporate networks. NAT can also allow you to use the same subnet more than once in the same network without overlapping networks.

Chapter 6: Infrastructure Security

1. D. To enable the AAA commands on a router or switch, use the global configuration command aaa new-model.

2. A, C. To mitigate access layer threats, use port security, DHCP snooping, dynamic ARP inspection, and identity-based networking.

3. D. DHCP snooping validates DHCP messages, builds and maintains the DHCP snooping binding database, and rate-limits DHCP traffic for trusted and untrusted sources.

4. A, D. TACACS+ uses TCP, is Cisco proprietary, and offers multiprotocol support as well as separated AAA services.

5. B. Unlike with TACACS+, separating AAA services is not an option when configuring RADIUS.

6. D. It's compared with lines of the access list only until a match is made. Once the packet matches the condition on a line of the access list, the packet is acted upon and no further comparisons take place.

7. C. The range of 192.168.160.0 to 192.168.191.0 is a block size of 32. The network address is 192.168.160.0 and the mask would be 255.255.224.0, which for an access list must be a wildcard format of 0.0.31.255. The 31 is used for a block size of 32. The wildcard is always one less than the block size.

8. C. Using a named access list just replaces the number used when applying the list to the router's interface. `ip access-group Blocksales in` is correct.

9. B. The list must specify TCP as the Transport layer protocol and use a correct wildcard mask (in this case 0.0.0.255), and it must specify the destination port (80). It also should specify any as the set of computers allowed to have this access.

10. A. The first thing to check in a question like this is the access-list number. Right away, you can see that the second option is wrong because it is using a standard IP access-list number. The second thing to check is the protocol. If you are filtering by an upper-layer protocol, then you must be using either UDP or TCP; this eliminates the fourth option. The third and last options have the wrong syntax.

Chapter 7: Infrastructure Management

1. B. You can enter the ACL directly in the SNMP configuration to provide security, using either a number or a name. Here is an example:

```
Router(config)#snmp-server community Todd Protect_NMS_Station ro
```

2. A, D. With a read-only community string, no changes can be made to the router. However, SNMPv2c can use GETBULK to create and return multiple requests at once.

3. C, D. SNMPv2c introduced the GETBULK and INFORM SNMP messages but didn't have any different security than SNMPv1. SNMPv3 uses TCP and provides encryption and authentication.

4. B. The IEEE created a new standardized discovery protocol called 802.1AB for Station and Media Access Control Connectivity Discovery. We'll just call it Link Layer Discovery Protocol (LLDP).

5. B. The command `traceroute` (`trace` for short), which can be issued from user mode or privileged mode, is used to find the path a packet takes through an internetwork and will also show you where the packet stops because of an error on a router.

6. C. Since the configuration looks correct, you probably didn't screw up the copy job. However, when you perform a copy from a network host to a router, the interfaces are automatically shut down and need to be manually enabled with the `no shutdown` command.

7. C. This will get you into global configuration mode where you can make changes to the running-config. Commands run from global configuration mode are predictably referred to as global commands, and they are typically set only once and affect the entire router.

8. C. Before you start to configure the router, you should erase the NVRAM with the `erase startup-config` command and then reload the router using the `reload` command.

9. C. This command can be run on both routers and switches and it displays detailed information about each device connected to the device you're running the command on, including the IP address.

10. C. The Port ID column describes the interfaces on the remote device end of the connection.

Index

Note to the Reader: Throughout this index **boldfaced** page numbers indicate primary discussions of a topic. *Italicized* page numbers indicate illustrations.

Q

R

Comprehensive Online Learning Environment

Register on Sybex.com to gain access to the comprehensive online interactive learning environment and test bank to help you study for your CCNA Routing and Switching exams.

The online test bank includes the following:

- **Practice Exams** to test your knowledge of the material
- **Digital Flashcards** to reinforce your learning and provide last-minute test prep before the exam
- **Searchable Glossary** to define the key terms you'll need to know for the exam

Go to http://www.wiley.com/go/sybextestprep to register and gain access to this comprehensive study tool package.

30% off On-Demand IT Video Training from ITProTV

ITProTV and Sybex have partnered to provide 30% off a Premium annual or monthly membership. ITProTV provides a unique, custom learning environment for IT professionals and students alike, looking to validate their skills through vendor certifications. On-demand courses provide over 1,000 hours of video training with new courses being added every month, while labs and practice exams provide additional hands-on experience. For more information on this offer and to start your membership today, visit http://itpro.tv/sybex30/.

SYBEX®
A Wiley Brand